THE HISTORY

OF THE

"CAST-IRON SIXTH"

THE
"CAST-IRON SIXTH"

A HISTORY OF THE SIXTH BATTALION LONDON REGIMENT
(The City of London Rifles)

BY

Capt. E. G. Godfrey, M.C.

PUBLISHED BY F. S. STAPLETON
FOR THE OLD COMRADES' ASSOCIATION, THE CITY OF LONDON RIFLES
17, SUMNER STREET, LONDON, S.E.1
1938

Col. W. F. MILDREN, C.B., C.M.G., D.S.O.
(Later Brigadier-General Commanding 141st Brigade.)

Frontispiece

A FOREWORD

BY

BRIGADIER-GENERAL W. F. MILDREN, C.B., C.M.G., D.S.O., T.D.

I HAVE often remarked at functions of the Old Comrades' Association which I have attended, that during the War the 6th London Regt. always managed, somehow or other, to put up a good " show." What it did was never very spectacular perhaps, and its name did not appear in the headlines of the newspapers; but it did what it was told to do, and it carried on, often in face of great difficulties. There were times when it had to perform hard and unpleasant tasks, but it did them, and when it failed, I think it can be said that few battalions could have succeeded.

This book is a record of the work and devotion of the officers and other ranks belonging to the three battalions which composed the 6th London Regt.

The 6th London Regt. has a very strong Old Comrades' Association, and that is what one would expect. They are putting up a good show just as they used to do. They have retained the spirit of comradeship that they found in the War, and it is a good thing that Old Comrades should maintain that friendship, and keep alive the memories of the War, and the recollection of the sacrifices made in it.

I hope this History will help them to do that, and will be a constant reminder to the officers, non-commissioned officers, and men who served in the 6th London Regt. of those who were with them during a stirring time.

W. F. M.

PREFACE

This history concerns the 6th Battalion, London Regiment, the City of London Rifles. It is not a history of the Volunteer and Territorial movements or of the Great War; but because the City of London Rifles played important parts in them they are included in the narrative. Indeed, because most of those now living who served in its ranks were war-time soldiers, and because during the War the *Sixth* grew to the size of having two battalions on active service and a reserve battalion, most of the book is devoted to the years 1914-1919.

One or other of these two service battalions was employed in most of the principal battles on the British Western Front, and this coincidence has fortunately made it possible when describing the actions in which they were engaged to tell something of the War, chapter by chapter, as a continuous narrative. In each chapter, moreover, emphasis has been placed on some particular aspect of military training, or operations, such as communication between front and rear, transport difficulties, individual exploits, and so on; whilst to facilitate reading, at the head of each page appears the number of the battalion being discussed (1st/6th, 2nd/6th, Res./6th) and the date concerned; and in the margins appear the names of the places occupied. In the text, the terms *Sixth*, *First*, and *Second* have been used to represent the battalion, and the two service battalions into which it grew.

For materials to go upon, I have had the benefit (apart from the Official History of the War and the standard textbooks on the subject) of the War Diaries of the two service battalions, and of innumerable documents, placed at my disposal by those who served in them, including diaries, letters, and personal accounts, from which many quotations have been included in the text. Thus, although I have planned and written this history and must take sole responsibility for its many imperfections, it is true to say that it is the work of many pens. A list of acknowledgements to those for whose help I am especially indebted appears elsewhere, but mention must be made here of some of those to whom the thanks of the Old Comrades' Association are particularly due. As Honorary Secretary of the Association, Mr. F. S. Stapleton has throughout given constant encouragement and most valuable advice, and has himself personally seen the book through the Press, and the care he has taken is equalled only by that of Mr. S. A. Alexander, who has been responsible for the actual production of it. A special measure of appreciation must be extended to Mr. R. G. Emery, without whose help it would have been impossible to complete the work. Not only has he been indefatigable in the collection of material and photographs, but has himself contributed much to the History, as well as providing some delightful woodcuts. Captain H. L. Gilks, M.C., has kindly read the proofs for Press.

Finally, it has to be recorded that without the kindness of Brig.-Gen. W. F. Mildren, C.B., C.M.G., D.S.O., T.D., who has done so much already for the Association, this book would probably never have been published.

London, 1938 E. G. G.

1. COL. GEORGE CRUIKSHANK, 1859–1869. 2. COL. R. GREENE, V.D., 1897–1902.
3. COL. R. W. SMITH, V.D., 1902–1912. 4. LT.-COL. G. D. M. MOORE, 1913–1914.
5. A SERGEANT (COL.-SGT. H. GREEN) SHOWING THE HEAD-DRESS WORN IN 1914.

Plate 1

1

3

2

1. COL.-SGT. L. W. MANLEY IN 1897, SHOWING THE CHANGE OF HEADDRESS FROM THE SHAKO TO THE HELMET. 2. WARRANT OFFICERS AND SERGEANTS OF THE 2ND LONDON VOLUNTEER BATTALION, CITY OF LONDON RIFLES, IN 1902. 3. AN INSPECTION ON THE HORSE GUARDS PARADE, SHOWING THE FULL-DRESS UNIFORM FROM 1908 ONWARDS.

Plate 2

CITY OF LONDON RIFLES OLD COMRADES' ASSOCIATION

Chairman, Officers and Committee

Chairman:
Mr. A. F. Papworth

Deputy Chairman:
Mr. A. W. Johnson

Hon. Sec., F. S. Stapleton

Hon. Treas., Capt. F. W. Short

Hon. Assist. Sec., G. R. Doubleday

Hon. Assist. Treas., P. L. V. Raybaud

C. Buckland
W. M. Cohen
S. S. Dinmore
R. Drage
R. D. Ellis
B. Gambey

J. Hobday
H. J. Kemp
Capt. W. Merrett
H. G. Millard
T. Percivall
F. Ryland
J. Sharp

C. Snow
R. Stenner
F. Stiles
J. Sullivan
J. A. Webb
S. Williams

ACKNOWLEDGEMENTS.

Grateful acknowledgements are made to all those who in one way or another have contributed to the pages of this book, and especially to:

Col. W. W. Hughes, Col. M. J. Macdonald, "A. E. S.," and Mr. R. G. Emery, for extensive contributions to various chapters; to W. Beggis, A. J. Cowherd, F. G. Kent, L. W. Mynott, R. H. Saunders, and F. Stillwell, for the loan of private and other documents; to J. Allen, C. Bitton, Major W. S. Borthwick, Col. A. T. Cannon, F. J. Cook, Capt. S. W. F. Crofts, Major E. Clay, A. T. M. Cresswell, G. R. Doubleday, R. D. Ellis, A. C. Gross, W. J. Hamer, H. M. Hodges, Capt. I. H. W. Idris, J. Lumsden, J. W. Manley, R. C. M. McLeish, Capt. A. Morrow, H. Palowkar, T. W. Percivall, R. Stenner, Capt. F. H. H. Thomas, Maj. J. Thomson, F. Thorndyke, Col. F. Gordon Tucker, C. A. Weir, A. Yelf, for contributions of various kinds; to Col. R. M. Barrington-Ward, Col. C. B. Benson, Capt. W. H. Brasher, M. H. Davies, C. Hooton, Capt. H. L. Gilks, Maj. H. D. Myer, J. Sharp, Maj. John Venning, C. C. Withers, for collaboration on various matters; to Col. W. J. Newton and R. G. Emery for drawings included in the text; to Capt. R. L. Godfrey, Welsh Regiment, for copying the War Diaries, and E. M. Idale for secretarial work; and to the following members of the advisory panel whose names are not mentioned above or as members of the Committee:
S. Alexander, A. L. Cownley, Capt. S. T. Cooke, Capt. E. Phillips, C. U. Sutton.

LIST OF MAPS

CONTENTS

DIVISIONAL AND BRIGADE COMMANDERS

under whom the Battalions served on

THE WESTERN FRONT, 1915-19

DIVISIONAL COMMANDERS.

47TH DIVISION.

1915-1916.
Lt.-Gen. Sir Charles St. Leger Barter, K.C.B., K.C.M.G., C.V.O.

1916-1918.
Lt.-Gen. Sir Geo. Gorringe, K.C.B., K.C.M.G., D.S.O.

58TH DIVISION.

1917.
Major-Gen. Sir H. D. Fanshawe, K.C.B., K.C.M.G.

1917-1918.
Major-Gen. A. B. E. Cator, D.S.O.

1918.
Major-Gen. N. M. Smyth, V.C., K.C.B.

1918-1919.
Major-Gen. F. W. Ramsay, C.M.G., D.S.O.

BRIGADE COMMANDERS.

140TH BRIGADE.

1915-1916.
Brig.-Gen. G. L. Cuthbert, C.B., C.M.G.

1916-1917.
Brig.-Gen. The Viscount Hampden, K.C.B., C.M.G.

1917-1918.
Brig.-Gen. H. B. P. L. Kennedy, C.M.G., D.S.O.

174TH BRIGADE.

1917-1918.
Brig.-Gen. C. G. Higgins, C.M.G., D.S.O.

1918-1919.
Brig.-Gen. A. Maxwell, C.B., C.M.G., D.S.O. and Bar.

BATTLE HONOURS

South Africa, 1900-1902. Festubert, 1915. Loos. Flers-Courcelette. Le Transloy. Messines, 1917. Ypres, 1917. Menin Road. Polygon Wood. Passchendaele. Cambrai, 1917. St. Quentin. Avre. Amiens. Albert, 1918. Bapaume, 1918. Hindenburg Line. Epehy. Pursuit to Mons. France and Flanders, 1915-1918.

HONOURS

The list of recipients of decorations given below has been compiled from official and unofficial sources and may not be complete or exact in every particular. It includes the names of those belonging to other units who fought with one or other of the two service battalions of the *Sixth*. Against each name is given the decoration awarded, the year in which it was earned, and the rank held by the recipient at the time.

Honorary Colonel—1888-1914.
Field-Marshal Earl Roberts, V.C., K.G., K.P., O.M., V.D.

Honorary Colonel—1919-1936.
Brig.-Gen. W. F. Mildren, C.B., C.M.G., D.S.O., T.D.

DISTINGUISHED SERVICE ORDER AND BAR
Benson, Lt.-Col. C. B.—1917-1919—Second Battalion.

DISTINGUISHED SERVICE ORDER
Foord, Col. A. G.—1917—Second Battalion.
Hughes, Major E. W.—1918—First Battalion.
Hughes, Lt.-Col. W. W.—1918—First Battalion, att. 17th Battalion.
Mildren, Lt.-Col. W. F.—1917—First Battalion.
Neely, Lt.-Col. G. H.—1918—First Battalion, att. 18th Battalion.
Whitehead, Lt.-Col. W. J.—1917—First Battalion, att. 8th Battalion.

ORDER OF THE BRITISH EMPIRE
Cannon, Col. A. T.
Thomas, Capt. F. H. H.
Wilkinson, Rev. A. E.

MILITARY CROSS AND ONE BAR
Anderson, Capt. D. W., 1917-1918.
Neely, Capt., Major, G. H., 1917-1918.
Sampson, Sec.-Lt., Capt., A. C., 1917-1918.

MILITARY CROSS
Bailey, Sec.-Lt. F. F., 1919.
Booth, Sec.-Lt. T. J., 1918.
Brooke, Capt. T. W., 1916.
Browne, Major H. M., 1917.
Buller, Major M. L., 1917.
Burt Smith, Sec.-Lt. B., 1916.
Cooke, Capt. S. T., 1918.
Crofts, Capt. S. W. F., 1917.
De Muth, Capt. O. (R.A.M.C.), 1917.
Eve, Capt. H. V., 1917.
Farrington, Sec.-Lt. C. H., 1917.
Geraty, Capt. L. (R.A.M.C.), 1917.
Gilks, Capt. H. L., 1917.
Godfrey, Capt. E. G., 1917.
Hart, Lt. H. V., 1917.
Hill, Capt. F., 1917.
Hughes, Capt. E. W., 1916.
Hughes, Capt. W. W., 1916.
Idris, Capt. I. H. W., 1918.
Johnston, Capt. H. A. L., 1918.
Jones, C.S.Maj., 1916.
Kidson, Capt. N. S., 1917.
Leapman, Sec.-Lt. L. C., 1918.
Macdonald, Capt. M. J., 1916.
Maxted, Sec.-Lt. C. B., 1917.
Maynard, Major J. E., 1918.
Nightingale, Sec.-Lt. H. G. C., 1918.
Ordish, Capt. H. T., 1917.
Phillips, R.S.Maj. F. E., 1918.
Plunkett, Sec.-Lt. H. J., 1918.
Scott, Lieut. A. E., 1918.
Smith, Lieut. A. E. S., 1918.
Smith, Lt. L. J., 1917.
Smithers, Sec.-Lt., 1917.
Spencer, Sec-Lt. J. W., 1917.
Stancourt, Sec.-Lt. G. H. R., 1918.

Military Cross—(*continued*).

Thorndyke, C.S.Maj. F., 1917.
Venning, Maj. J., 1917.
Wilkinson, Rev. A. E., 1916.
Willcocks, Lt. G. H., 1917.
Worrall, Capt. E. E., 1917.

FRENCH CROIX DE GUERRE (with palms)

Mildren, W. F., Brig.-Gen., 1918.

MEMBER OF THE BRITISH EMPIRE

Clay, Major E.

DISTINGUISHED CONDUCT MEDAL

Allen, J. C. O., L.-Cpl., 1916.
Allen, J., Sgt., 1917.
Bailey, F. F., C.S.Maj., 1916.
Bailey, W. J., L.-Cpl., 1917.
Baker, B., Sgt., 1918.
Barnes, R., Col.-Sgt., 1900.
Burke, F. J., Rfm., 1915.
Butler, A., Cpl., 1916.
Challoner, F. G., Rfm., 1915.
Cox, J. A., C.S.Maj., 1916.
Cuss, F. S., Rfm., 1916.
Death, E., Rfm., 1916.
Dudley, J., Cpl., 1917.
Gold, Cpl., 1918.
Gordon, L., L.-Cpl., 1915.
Hassack, W., Cpl., 1916.
Hill, F., Capt., 1915.
Hollis, F., Sgt., 1916.
Hyneman, H. L., Rfm., 1916.
Jackson, H. L., L.-Cpl., 1916.
Palowkar, H., C.S.Maj., 1917.
Redding, E. J., L.-Cpl., 1916.
Roberts, F., Sgt., 1917.
Thorndyke, F., C.S.Maj., 1917.
Webb, J. A., Sgt., 1918.
Wilson, G. W., Sgt., 1918.
Wyman, A. E., L.-Cpl., 1916.
Yelf, A., C.S.Maj., 1915.

MILITARY MEDAL AND ONE BAR

Candler, J. E., L.-Cpl., 1916, 1917.
Ellis, E. E., Sgt., 1917-1917.
Mills, J. F., L.-Cpl., 1916, 1916.
Church, W. C., Sgt., 1916, 1916.
Vinall, H. F., Rfm., 1917-1918.

MILITARY MEDAL

Ablin, J. G., Cpl., 1916.
Addicott, E., Rfm., 1916.
Apsden, R., L.-Cpl., 1916.
Atkinson, F., L.-Cpl., 1917.
Baker, E., Cpl., 1916.
Baker, F. L., Rfm., 1917.
Barnett, T., Rfm., 1917.
Baxter, A., L.-Cpl., 1916.
Bentley, J., Rfm., 1917.
Bitton, B., Sgt., 1916.
Blumire, W., Rfm., 1917.
Bond, L. E., Rfm., 1916.
Brett, C. J., Rfm., 1917.
Brown, C. J., Sgt., 1917.
Bruin, F., Sgt., 1917.
Buckles, G., L.-Cpl., 1917.
Buffin, T., Rfm., 1916.
Bullock, F., Rfm., 1916.
Bunkell, W., Sgt., 1917.
Burgess, E. M., Rfm., 1917.
Burville, E. C., Rfm., 1917.
Busby, L. J., Cpl., 1917.
Butcher, J., Rfm., 1917.
Caddick, J. H., L.-Cpl., 1917.
Capon, E., Rfm., 1916.
Chamberlain, V.N., Rfm., 1917.
Chilman, T. J., Cpl., 1918.
Church, A., Rfm., 1917.
Clark, C. V., Rfm., 1917.
Cohen, E., Rfm., 1917.
Coleman, G. C., Cpl., 1917.
Collier, J. A., Rfm., 1916.
Collingwood, G., Rfm., 1917.
Collyer, L. W., L.-Cpl., 1917.
Cook, F. J., Sgt., 1916.
Cook, G., Rfm., 1917.

Military Medal—(*continued*).

Copping, A. M., Sec.-Lt., 1916.
Crews, H. S., L.-Cpl., 1916.
Dock, J. J., L.-Cpl., 1917.
Dove, J. A., Rfm., 1917.
Everard, J. W., Rfm., 1917.
Freeman, H. E., L.-Cpl., 1916.
Freemont, L., Rfm., 1917.
Fudge, P. J., Rfm., 1917.
Garrod, W. G., Sgt., 1917.
Giles, W. B. F., Cpl., 1917.
Giles, W. G., L.-Cpl., 1918.
Gilson, R., Rfm., 1918.
Girling, H. W., Cpl., 1917.
Gold, A., Rfm., 1917.
Goode, J. E., Sgt., 1917.
Gray, W. H., L.-Cpl., 1917.
Green, H. R., Sgt., 1916.
Greenslade, W. W., Cpl., 1917.
Greenland F. W., Rfm., 1917.
Gullick, C. J., L.-Cpl., 1917.
Grundy, W., C.Q.M.Sgt., 1917.
Haacke, E. C., L.-Cpl., 1916.
Hall, F., Sgt., 1916.
Hall, F. G., Sgt., 1916.
Harris, D., Rfm., 1917.
Harris, W. H., Rfm., 1917.
Hart, A. G., Sgt., 1917.
Hart, S., L.-Cpl., 1916.
Harvey, C. E., Rfm., 1918.
Hawkins, T. H., Sgt., 1917.
Houghton, H., Sgt., 1916.
Hulland, R. P., Sgt., 1916.
Hunt, M. R., Rfm., 1917.
Huson, A., L.-Cpl., 1916.
Iveson, A. E., Rfm., 1917.
Jeffrey, W., Cpl., 1917.
Jewiss, A., L.-Cpl., 1918.
Johnson, F., Rfm., 1916.
Johnson, W., Rfm., 1917.
Kimber, E. H., Rfm., 1917.
Lamborn, C., L.-Cpl., 1917.
Leader, E. C., Rfm., 1917.
Leslie, R., Rfm., 1916.
Lothian, R., Rfm., 1917.
Lumsden, J., Rfm., 1917.
McGreggor, J. H., Rfm., 1917.
Maggs, W. E., Sgt., 1917.
Males, W. H., Rfm., 1916.
Marchant, W., Rfm., 1917.
Marritt, F. C., Cpl., 1917.
Mason, E., Rfm., 1917.
May, C., Sgt. (in England), 1916.
Millett, F., Rfm., 1916.
Mills, J. F., L.-Cpl., 1917.
Moore, S., Rfm., 1916.
Morris, A., L.-Cpl., 1917.
Morris, W. D., Rfm., 1916.
Murphy, A., Rfm., 1916.
Oliver, J., Rfm., 1917.
Parnall, C. H., L.-Cpl., 1917.
Pearson, B., Rfm., 1917.
Pennell, C. H., Cpl., 1917.
Porter, D., Rfm., 1917.
Redford, S., Rfm., 1917.
Reynolds, E. S., Sgt., 1917.
Richards, B. J., Cpl., 1916.
Rook, F., Rfm., 1917.
Rose, J., Cpl., 1917.
Rose, W. T., L.-Cpl., 1917.
Ruffell, S. G., Rfm., 1917.
Rush, C. M., C.S.Maj., 1916.
Scott, H. E., Rfm., 1917.
Searle, C., Sgt., 1917.
Shaw, W., Rfm., 1916.
Skitter, W. A., Rfm., 1917.
Snow, H. B., L.-Cpl., 1917.
Sparks, G., Rfm., 1917.
Sparling, T. W., Rfm., 1917.
Stevens, H., L.-Cpl., 1917.
Stoner, H., L.-Cpl., 1917.
Swan, Sgt., 1917.
Swanson, A., Cpl., 1917.
Taylor, A. L., Rfm., 1916.
Templar, E., C.S.Maj., 1918.
Thomas, E., Rfm., 1916.
Thompson, H. P., Rfm., 1917.
Thompson, J. F., Sgt., 1916.
Thornbury, W., L.-Cpl., 1917.
Thorndyke, F., C.S.Maj., 1917.
Thorne, T. C., L.-Cpl., 1916.
Thornett, C., Sgt., 1917.
Thorpe-Tracey, R. T. C., L.-Cpl., 1916.
Toothill, W. T., Rfm., 1917.
Townshend, H. T., L.-Cpl., 1917.
Tully, J., L.-Cpl., 1917.

Military Medal—(*continued*).

Wade, H., Sgt., 1917.
Warren, A., Cpl., 1916.
Weir, C. H., Cpl., 1917.
Wheeler, A. J., Sgt., 1916.
Williams, J. Rfm., 1916.
Wingate, E. J., Sgt., 1917.
Worboys, W., Sgt., 1917.
Worrall, W. E., Sgt., 1917.
Yelland, F., Sgt., 1917.

MERITORIOUS SERVICE MEDAL

Buckland, C., Sgt., 1918.
Davies, M. H., C.Q.M.Sgt., 1919.
Dorling, A., Cpl., 1919.
Emery, R. G., Driver, 1918.
Johnson, A. W., C.Q.M.Sgt., 1917.
Percivall, T., R.Q.M.Sgt., 1918.
Price, C., Sgt., 1919.
Solman, Sgt., 1919.
Stenner, R., C.S.Maj., 1918.
Ward, T. J., C.S.Maj., 1918.

ALBERT MEDAL

Williams, S., L.-Cpl., 1916.

FRENCH CROIX DE GUERRE

Ellis, E., Sgt., 1918.
Hill, F., Capt., 1915.
Graysmark, J. T., C.S.Maj., 1917.
Morris, E., C.S.Maj., 1917.
Yelf., A., C.S.Maj., 1915.

MEDAILLE MILITAIRE

Knight, F. C., C.Q.M.Sgt., 1917.
Savill, B., Sgt., 1918.
Jupp, W. H., Sgt., 1917.

BELGIAN CROIX DE GUERRE

Houghton, H., Sgt., 1918.
Wade, H., Sgt., 1918.

RUSSIAN ORDER OF ST. STANISLAUS

Stenner, R., C.S.Maj., 1918.

VOLUNTEER DECORATION

Cantlon, L. M., Col., 1895.
Collinson, F. G., Col., 1900.
Green, R. G., Lt.-Col., 1895.
Simpson, T. W., Lt.-Col., 1907.
Smith, R. W., Col., 1902.

TERRITORIAL DECORATION

Boothby, R. C., Lt.-Col.
Borthwick, W. S., Major.
Cannon, A. T., Col.
Hughes, E. W., Col.
Macdonald, M. J., Col.
Mildren, W. F., Brig.-Gen.
Short, S. E., Major.
Thomas, F. H. H., Capt.
Wilkinson, A. E., Rev.

OFFICERS:

Mentioned in Dispatches	36
Mention (Lieut. A. Morrow)	1
Mentioned in War Office Communiqué	5

W.O.s, N.C.O.s and MEN:

Mentioned in Dispatches	21
Mention (C.S.Maj. G. Montier)	1
Mentioned in War Office Communiqué	3

Chapter I

THE BIRTH OF A BATTALION

Nearly a thousand years have passed since Britain was last invaded. Thanks to her geographical position, to the wisdom of her rulers, and to the sturdy qualities of her people, Britain has remained immune when other nations less favourably placed have been overrun by hostile armies. None the less, the people of the Islands have never quite forgotten the miseries and degradation of foreign domination: and whenever there has been a threat to her existence, they have at once responded to the call to arms. When the Spaniards prepared their Armada, when Napoleon concentrated his armies at Boulogne, and when Europe blazed up in 1914, the thought uppermost in men's minds was: Is it invasion?

Volunteer Movement

The formation of the Volunteer Movement in 1859 was due almost entirely to the suspicion and fear engendered by the increase in the size of the French fleet. The Crimean War was over, the Indian Mutiny finally suppressed; but Europe was in a turmoil. War was being waged in Italy (then in revolution), between Austria and France; and in that year of strife and uncertainty the battalion that later was to become the City of London Rifles was born.

Col. Cruikshank

The Volunteer Movement attracted all classes, and eminent men were not slow in coming forward to make their contribution to it. Among them was the celebrated artist Cruikshank, and to him belongs the honour of raising the battalion and becoming its first commanding officer. Upon formation, the unit bore the name of the 24th Battalion of the Surrey Regiment. It had headquarters in Newington Causeway, and was organised on an eight-company basis. General Havelock was its Honorary Colonel.

The battalion did not, however, retain its original name for long. The story goes that because of a movement on foot to attach it to the 7th Battalion of the same regiment, Col. Cruikshank, being determined to keep it intact and as an independent unit, made overtures to Lord Salisbury, then Lord-Lieutenant of the County of Middlesex, with a view to its transference to the Middlesex Regiment.* The offer was accepted, and in 1862, four years after

*Cruikshank was born in 1792, and as a young man served as a private in the Loyal North British Volunteers. He was, therefore, sixty-seven years old when he took command. Prof. William Bates, his biographer, has the following incident to record: "He joined the Havelock, or 48th Middlesex Rifle Corps—all, by-the-by, total abstainers—of which he became Lieutenant-Colonel. This post he continued to hold in spite of the expressed opinion of his officers that he was, from his great age, incompetent for the duties of the position. A memorial on the subject was sent to the Lord-Lieutenant, and by him forwarded to the War Office. The result was an order, in 1869, to cashier every one of the fourteen officers who had signed the document. The regiment was left with three or four officers only—an octogenarian commander, and the rest mere lads. His own resignation followed." This helps to explain the reason for the amalgamation.

its formation, and the battalion was renamed the 48th Battalion, the Middlesex Regiment. The story goes that during these negotiations one stipulation was made ; the new unit was to be recruited definitely as a temperance battalion, and this distinguishing word was engraved upon the metal clasp of the soldier's belt. The uniform of the new unit was of " rifle " green with scarlet facings, and the headdress, at first, a shako with cock's feathers to the front.

The conditions of service, if not severe, were sufficiently exacting to ensure that only those willing to make real sacrifices for it should join the battalion. A member had to pay an annual subscription for the honour of belonging to it, and had to buy his own uniform. Indeed, at first, he had to provide his own arms. Ammunition for musketry training was supplied by the Government, but owing to the variety of firearms in use, and the difficulty of supplying ammunition suitable for all the different makes in use, this policy was abandoned, and the old Snider breech-loader (converted from the Enfield muzzle-loader) officially issued.

Early Training

Training took place in the evenings and during week-ends, favourite places for drill and "sham-fights" being Hampstead Heath and Wimbledon Common. The only " annual " training the battalion received was during Easter at Chatham and Portsmouth. This was due to the fact that no funds were available to pay for the expenses incurred in going " under canvas " during the summer. No pay was given, and no allowances were admissible other than a small bounty of £1 granted annually *to the battalion* in respect of each enlisted man. Occasionally funds were sufficiently strong to warrant the holding of a summer camp, and one of the earliest, if not the first, was held at Cannock Chase, in Staffordshire.

Probably the first ceremonial event in which the battalion participated took place at Dover in 1864, when a review of Volunteer units was made by the Duke of Cambridge. So severe was the weather that the troops piled arms and were dismissed and thus, when the duke arrived with his staff, the parade presented a rather unusual spectacle. The *assembly* was hurriedly blown, and when all were reported present the review commenced. One interesting fact is worth recording in connection with it: the battalion was formed up for the review immediately in front of another Volunteer unit, the 2nd Battalion of the City of London Volunteer Regiment. This unit had been raised in 1859 by Messrs. Eyre and Spottiswood, the well-known printers, who enlisted in it most of their employees. Its first commander was Major G. A. Spot, who was succeeded in 1866 by a regular officer of the Indian Army, Lt.-Col. F. R. Aikman, V.C. In 1872, the two units were amalgamated, the combined battalion being given the name of the 2nd Bn., City of London

Maj. Spot Col. Aikman

Regiment (Volunteers) with the subsidiary title of the 10th Bn., King's Royal Rifle Corps. The uniform of the 48th Bn., Middlesex Regiment was retained, save that a rifle-busby was substituted for the shako, and headquarters were established at Cooks Court, Carey Street. Lt.-Col. C. B. Vickers, then commanding the 48th Bn., Middlesex Regiment, became the amalgamated unit's first commanding officer.

Col. Vickers

As may be supposed, there was a fine muster for the Easter camp of the year of amalgamation—no less than ten strong companies formed up for review on the Brighton Downs. Indeed, for many years training at Eastertide continued as the most important event of the year, and in the '70's, Fort Elson, Brockhurst, Widley, Nelson, and Winchester were visited; but in 1879 a week's training at Rushmore, Aldershot, took place in the summer. Besides "camp," there were three other important annual events: the "City March" by all London units, including artillery and engineers, from the Embankment to Hyde Park, where drill was performed; the "Brigade Drill," also in Hyde Park, when the 1st (London Rifle Brigade), 2nd (City of London Rifles), 3rd (later the Shiny Seventh), and the 24th Middlesex (Post Office Rifles), comprising the brigade, performed the usual drill movements; and thirdly, the "Annual Inspection," usually at the Horse Guards.

Annual Events

Outstanding events worth recording during this period were the review of the Volunteers by Queen Victoria, and the lining of the route on both sides of Cockspur Street upon the return (1883) of the troops from Egypt. This task now frequently fell to the Volunteers, and the battalion was used to it. One of the earliest occasions when it had been so employed was on the arrival of the Danish Princess, Alexandra, prior to her engagement to the late King Edward VII. As the old 48th Middlesex, the battalion had then lined the route between Hyde Park Corner and Marble Arch.

In 1887 the "memorial" stone to the present headquarters* was laid, and the building being completed in the following year, was opened by the Duke of Cambridge. The City Companies contributed to the building fund, but much of the money had been raised by holding an assault-at-arms in the old Royal Aquarium.

Two summer camps were held, one of which (1899) is memorable for the night operations conducted by the late General Sir Redvers Buller, in which the whole of the troops in the Aldershot Command took part. A marked feature of these last ten years of the century was the number of occasions upon which the battalion managed to do their training for a week or a fortnight in the summer, instead of over the Easter holidays.

---

*57a Farringdon Road.

For many years, the battalion, organised upon a nine-company basis, had been overstrength, an additional company having been formed. Detailed particulars are not out of place, even in a brief historical sketch, and it is as well to record the names of the principal officers and warrant officers of the time (1895.)

Honorary Colonel:	FIELD-MARSHALL LORD ROBERTS, V.C., G.C.B., G.C.S.I., G.C.I.E.
Commanding Officer:	COLONEL L. M. CANTLON, V.D.
Majors:	HON. LT.-COL. R. G. GREEN, V.D., and HON. LT.-COL. H. E. RODWELL
Adjutant:	CAPT. H. C. HOWARD, K.R.R.
A Company:	CAPT. and HON. MAJOR R. W. SMITH; LIEUT. HUMMEL; LIEUT. R. BAKER; COL.-SGT. R. COX
B Company:	CAPT. C. E. EARLE; SEC.-LT. E. T. LOCKETT; COL.-SGT. HORE
C Company:	CAPT. W. J. Y. WARREN; COL.-SGT. FORT
D Company:	SEC.-LT. B. F. HUNTSMAN; COL.-SGT. SAUNDERS
E Company:	CAPT. F. ROSS-THOMSON; COL.-SGT. PUNTER
F Company:	CAPT. A. G. SPOTTISWOOD; COL.-SGT. RANDLE
G Company:	SEC.-LT. G. E. HILLMAN; COL.-SGT. HODGSON
H Company:	SEC.-LT. G. C. MILLETT; COL.-SGT. A. NEWMAN
K Company:	CAPT. D. W. WESTMACOTT; COL.-SGT. J. SCAMMELL
Ambulance Section:	SURGEON-LIEUT. S. M. COPEMAN, M.D., SURGEON-LIEUT. W. A. BOND, M.D.; SGT. BELSTON
Volunteer Staff:	O.R.SGT. MANLEY; STAFF SGTS. ABBOTT and ALLEN
Signal Section:	SGT. HANCOCK

BUGLE-MAJOR STREVENS. BANDMASTER H. T. WELCH

Organisation

For administrative and many other purposes the battalion was divided into halves, each commanded by a major—the right-half battalion comprising Companies A to E inclusive, and the left-half battalion Companies F to K, inclusive. During the year in question, no less than thirty-eight warrant officers, N.C.O.'s, and privates (the term "rifleman" was not then in use), qualified as marksmen, Sgt. W. Hare winning the War Office badge for the highest aggregate score in the annual musketry course.

Col. Cantlon
Col. Green

Colonel Cantlon, who had commanded the unit since 1880, and to whom was largely due its development, efficiency, and prestige, retired in 1897, and Major and Hon. Colonel R. G. Green, V.D., took his place.

The same year (1897) saw Queen Victoria's Jubileé, with the attendant ceremonies in June, the battalion lining the route in the Mall. Later in the year, Queen Victoria made a tour of South London, when the unit was called upon to perform a similar service. Annual training, as was now the custom, took place in August and lasted a week. The site of the camp, pitched on Cove Common, Aldershot, is worth recording, for in that area, once occupied for a week's intensive training, now stands what was never dreamed of by those attending camp—an aerodrome. In the summer of the same year, King Edward VII, then Prince of Wales, reviewed the Volunteers upon the Horse Guards Ground.

The following year saw the opening of the Blackwall Tunnel by His Royal Highness, at which the battalion assisted by lining the route. In that year the annual camp was held for one week at Bourley Common, Aldershot, and was notable for the introduction of the " Rifle " helmet and the " Slade-Wallace " leather equipment—the forerunner of that at present in use. By now payment of a shilling a day had been introduced to supplement the rations officially supplied; but still the one dress only was recognised, that of " rifle " green with scarlet-and-green facings, which had to suffice for all occasions. Great was the joy, in consequence, when in the following year (1899) blue serge trousers and jackets were issued as " service dress." But blessings in the Army are seldom unmixed, and when the new clothing was worn for the first time, during annual training of that year, many discovered with dismay that the blue dye was not fast. After strenuous field operations, when perspiration had been free and plentiful, the colour would leave its almost indelible marks upon the skin, and the battalion would resemble an army of Ancient Britons covered in woad.

Pay when training

Chapter 2

THE WAR IN SOUTH AFRICA

The fact that the Volunteers were now being equipped, however inadequately, was due to the clouding of the international horizon. During the 18th and 19th centuries, Great Britain had looked upon Germany's rise to power with both admiration and respect, culminating in wonder at the sight of her rapid and easy victory over France (1871). Although hitherto not regarded as a menace, before the end of the century a very real change in England's attitude to Germany was apparent. Articles in the Press and utterances by prominent men drew attention to her ever-increasing strength, and the possibility of an invasion by Germany came to be envisaged. A telegram of congratulation sent by the Kaiser to Kruger, the President of the Boer Republic of Transvaal, on the failure of the notorious Jameson raid (January 3rd, 1896), lent colour to the suggestion that Germany had designs on Britain. The Volunteer Force, it will be remembered, had its origin in the fear of attack by France; now, the threat was from a different quarter, but it was met in the same manner, by entrusting the defence of the Islands to the Volunteers. Great as would be their responsibility of assisting the Regular Army in this task, it would be infinitely greater were the latter to be sent on active service abroad. Britain's imperial policy had already necessitated the "Regulars" being sent to the uttermost ends of the earth, and if, as many expected, war should break out in South Africa, and Germany take advantage of the Regular Army's absence, the task of defending their country would fall largely on the shoulders of the Volunteers.

Jameson raid

The fundamental cause of the South African War was that large numbers of British people had entered the Transvaal, following the discovery of immense quantities of gold. In time, they outnumbered the Boer population, and, moreover, clamoured for equal rights to vote with the Boers in the selection of the Boer Parliament. This the Boers would not grant, arguing that to give the British settlers the vote would mean, owing to their preponderance in numbers, nothing less than handing over the Republic to Britain.

War broke out in 1899 (October) and the Orange Free State elected to join the Boers in the struggle. At 2 a.m. one day early in that month, an emergency parade of the battalion was ordered, and the drill-hall was filled to overflowing. Volunteers were called for to join a force, then in process of formation, termed the City Imperial Volunteers, to be made up of detachments of specially selected men from units of the London Volunteer battalions.

C.I.V's.

Many more than required offered their services, and after a rigorous medical inspection, the following thirty-six were selected: Col.-Sgt. Moore; Sgts. Biller, Seabrook, Holladay, Kennedy, Blaber, Cook, Pole; Cpls. A. Lee, G. Lee, Haag; Ptes. Hayes, Stock, Mustoe, Carter, Newland, Strachan, Wright, Rayal, Costin, Edwards, Flewer, Kiernan, Shepherd, Barrett, Failes, Guest, Hanlon, Bewsey, Hammond, Snow, Clarke, Slight, Summerling, Phillips, Dight.

The first contingent sailed from Southampton on January 13th, 1900, in two troopers, arriving at Cape Town early in the following month. Within a very few days of landing, the C.I.V. were moved up to the front and received their baptism of fire during the capture of Jacobsdaal (February 16th). Later, on March 6th, they were again in action at Britstown, suffering many casualties. When the Boer general, Cronje, surrendered at the end of February, the C.I.V. had the distinction of being detailed to act as his bodyguard.

Lord Roberts

Lord Roberts (who some years earlier had honoured the battalion by consenting to become its Honorary Colonel) and Lord Kitchener, landed in South Africa in January, 1900, and quickly perceiving the situation, called for more troops. As a consequence, volunteers were again enrolled, this time to form a Special Service Company (No. 1) of the King's Royal Rifle Corps, which comprised detachments from the West Middlesex, the Queen Victoria's, the Queen's Westminster, and the 2nd London Volunteer Battalions.

K.R.R.C.

The medical examination was on this occasion as exacting as previously, and of the many who offered themselves, Capt. Warren and the following twenty-five 'other-ranks' were selected: Sgt. McNally; Cpl. Whitney; Ptes. Boyd, Clowes, R. Donahue, Jones, Maidman, Neil, Pope, Percivall, V. Pye, Willocks, Davies, A. J. Costin, C. W. Costin, Cash, Bussey, C. F. Clowes, Williams, Parsons, Musselbrook, Merritt, Lyus, Hodges, and Gambie.

The No. 1 Special Service Company K.R.R.C., after a period of training at Gosport, sailed from Southampton in the middle of March (1900) on the s.s. Tagus, and had a pleasant voyage, during which they were inoculated against enteric fever. On arrival at Cape Town the troops disembarked and re-embarked upon the s.s. Nile, which took them to Durban, where, in consequence of the shallowness of water, they were landed from the transport by surface craft, being loaded into the small vessels by baskets lowered from the trooper.

From Durban the Company was transported by rail to Pietermaritzburg, where they stayed the night, proceeding the following day, again by rail, to

Modder Spruit, there to join the 2nd Battalion K.R.R.C., which formed a unit of General Buller's Natal Field Force.

At Modder Spruit, the detachment suffered the greatest of all losses, the death of its commander, Capt. Warren, who died towards the end of April, after severe attacks of dysentery. Capt. Warren had been, at home, the officer in charge of the school-of-arms, and such was his personality and popularity that upon his volunteering for service overseas, those attending his classes to a man clamoured to go with him. His untimely death robbed the detachment of an excellent officer and a born leader.

Laing's Neck

The Special Company remained with the 2nd Battalion K.R.R.C., having its baptism of fire when in action at the Battle of Laing's Neck, until that unit was transferred to India about the middle of July. It was then attached to the 3rd Battalion K.R.R.C., where in the neighbourhood of Heidelburg, it was mainly engaged in outpost duty. In October, 1900, the Special Company was moved to Ladysmith, where it was organised into parties to man the block-houses, which, thanks to Lord Kitchener's resource and energy, were being rapidly constructed as an effective barrier against the Boer raids. Defences at Sunday's River, Elands Laagte, Modder Spruit, and the Colenso Railway Bridge over the Tugela River were among the many points held by the Company.

Ladysmith

The detachment returned to England in 1901, less strong in numbers than upon its departure, fifteen months before. Besides Capt. Warren, Pte. J. Williams had died, and some had been invalided home broken in health.

The first detachment, which had joined the City Imperial Volunteers, and which had borne its share of the campaign with courage and fortitude, returned earlier to England (1900) none, fortunately, having died or been killed. The reception received by the returning soldiers at the hands of the Londoners (October 29th) almost beggars description. The route, needless to say, was lined with troops, the battalion itself doing this duty in Cheapside, but such was the size and excitement of the crowds, that the troops soon found themselves of little use in keeping the road clear. Greater and greater grew the press, until eventually there was nothing at places but a narrow path between banks of cheering people, through which the returning troops had to pass, sometimes in single file. It was dusk, too, before the march was over, and this added to the difficulty of keeping the crowds in place.

The official reception took place at the Mansion House, and with it, generally, closed a chapter of military history, the importance of which was not fully realised until some fourteen years later. When mobilised in 1914, the Territorial Force contained many who had seen service in South Africa, and to

EARL ROBERTS OF KANDAHAR, V.C., K.P., G.C.B., G.C.S.I., G.C.I.E.
For many years Hon. Colonel of City of London Rifles.
Born at Cawnpore, India, 1832—Died in France, November 14th, 1914.

Plate 3

Above: SOME OF THE MEMBERS OF THE BATTALION WHO SERVED IN SOUTH AFRICA WITH THE C.I.V.'S.

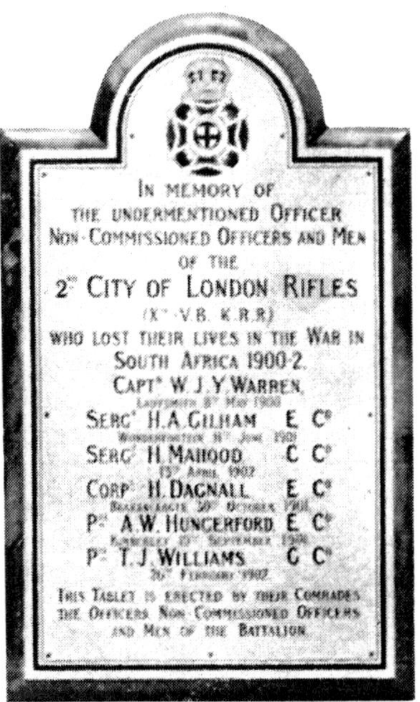

Right: THE MEMORIAL TO THOSE WHO DIED IN THE SOUTH AFRICAN WAR.

A K.R.R.C. CADET BAYONET-FIGHTING TEAM (ALL OF WHOM SERVED WITH THE SIXTH IN FRANCE)

BORDON, 1910.

CAMBERLEY, 1911.

Plate 5

1

2

3

1. THE BATTALION BAND, 1909.
2. MARCHING OUT OF CAMP AT LULWORTH, 1912.
3. CAMP HILL CAMP, CROWBOROUGH, 1914.

Plate 6

Sgt. SUTTON.

Sgt. VANDERKAMP.

Sgt. ROBINSON.

Sgt. GIRLING, M.M.

Sgt. F. PEEBLES.

Sgt. PITE.

C.Q.M.Sgt. COHEN.

R.Q.M.Sgt. PARRISH.

Sgt. LAMONT.

C.SMaj. CASTLEMAN.

R.S.Maj. HADLEY.

"MILES STONE."—For many years the Regimental Mascot. He was a member of the famous "Stone" breed owned by Lord Charles Beresford.

Sgt. PENNELL, M.M.

C.S.Maj. TEMPLAR, M.M.

Sgt. SEARLE, M.M.

Sgt. COLE.

Sgt. GUNTER.

Sgt. CUMMINGS.

R.Q.M.Sgt. KENT.

Cpl. FULLER.

Sgt. G. WICKS.

Plate 7

this factor must largely be attributed the smoothness with which the Territorial Force was then mobilised and so soon took the field.

The detachments furnished by the battalion to the two units referred to, by no means comprised all who left its ranks for service in South Africa. Many joined Regular units, and some went to the length of enlisting in the South African Police Force. Among the former must be mentioned Sgt. Gillham, who joined the Imperial Yeomanry, and was killed at Woonderfontein in June, 1901. His and other names are inscribed upon the memorial of brass and Brazilian onyx erected upon the north wall inside the battalion's headquarters, where, surrounded by the names of those who fell in the Great War, it testifies to an equal spirit of self-sacrifice.

* * * * *

Whilst these detachments had been overseas, the battalion at home exerted itself to the utmost in securing efficiency. The year 1900 saw it at full strength doing fifteen days annual training upon the gun-wharf of Sheerness, where it co-operated with the Navy in defensive tactics, including the embarking and disembarking of troops. The gift of two machine-guns, with limbers, from friends, filled a real want, and a strong machine-gun section was formed under Lieut. Schwersee, the sergeant-instructor being Sgt. H. Beer. Attention, too, was being given to co-operation with other units; thus, in the following year the battalion found itself, during annual training at Shorncliffe, a part of the 23rd Field Army Corps, which comprised, among other units, the 1st Volunteer Battalion Royal Fusiliers, 16th Volunteer Battalion Middlesex Regiment (then the London Irish Rifles), and 16th Volunteer Battalion London Regiment (then the Queen's Westminsters). So successful was this camp that another was held in the following year (1902) at the same place, and with the same organisation obtaining. The Coronation of King Edward VII, on August 4th, took place whilst the battalion was under canvas, and was appropriately marked with a " feu de joie " and other important, if less official, celebrations. A detachment was sent to London for the occasion, lined the route, and, in consequence, three Coronation medals were subsequently awarded to the unit, and were presented, for excellent reasons, to three of the keenest members of the battalion —Lieut. Harrild, Col.-Sgt. R. Doggrell, and Pte. Walters, the last having the distinction of being the oldest rifleman then serving. The Great Queen who had reigned for nearly sixty-four years had died in 1901, and on the occasion of the royal funeral a detachment from the battalion had lined part of the route of the procession, occupying positions near the Marble Arch. Thus the

Machine-gun Section formed

B

battalion had assisted at the ceremonies connected with the death of one monarch and the accession of another.

Col. Walter Smith

In 1902 Colonel Green retired, to be succeeded in command by Major and Hon. Colonel R. Walter Smith, V.D., who continued the policy of his predecessor of building up a strong school-of-arms. These annual displays provided a source of entertainment such as is to-day rarely witnessed, for apart from the usual exhibitions of bayonet-drill and physical training, there were items in the programme, such as fencing (foils), cavalry and infantry sword exercises, and a demonstration of various sword feats. During this year a tug-of-war team from the school-of-arms, weighing 110 stones, pulled against a team provided by the 1st Cadet Battalion K.R.R.C., at the Guildhall, the prizes being presented (March 15th) by Lady Trotter, whose husband, Major Trotter, K.C.V.O., took a keen and personal interest in the Volunteers. The annual training of the following year took place at Shorncliffe, and in 1904 and 1905, at Sway, in the New Forest.

Esher Committee

Since the South African War, statesmen had been regarding the Volunteer Force with growing interest, particularly since so many had followed their "Regular" comrades on active service, and the War Office, in 1905, saw fit to clothe the Force in khaki. The whole problem of defence, and the military resources of the country were, in fact, engaging the attention of the government. Briefly, the land forces at their disposal were the Regular Army, the Militia, the Yeomanry, and the Volunteers; and as a result of the Esher Committee's recommendation in 1904, a General Staff at the War Office had been created. As to detailed organisation, and well-thought-out plans of co-operation between the various branches of the Service, there were virtually none. What the country needed was a man of vision, free from military traditions, who could envisage the whole problem of mutual support, and who could mould the existing institutions, so that in time of war, there would be machinery for immediate action, and a plan for systematic development.

Territorial Force

Lord Haldane, subtle and philosophic, to whom was entrusted the War Office in 1906, was such a man, and to him the country owes a debt of gratitude impossible to repay. To Lord Haldane's orderly mind, the loose and ill-defined organisation of Regulars, Militia, Yeomanry, and Volunteers, was so distasteful that he lost no time in reorganisation, and working through the newly created General Staff, wrought changes of immense importance in the Regular Army, and brought into being, in 1908, the Territorial and Reserve Forces, adopting for them the regular formations of divisions and brigades. In this way an Expeditionary Force of the Regular Army, of one Cavalry and six Infantry Divisions (over 150,000 men) was brought into being, and troops for defensive purposes, to be called upon in the event of the Regular Army's being sent abroad, were placed upon a systematised basis. It is enough to say that upon the declaration of war in 1914, this organisation was tested to the limit, and answered all calls made upon it, and the Regular Army was in its allotted position twelve days after the breach with Germany.

As regards the Yeomanry and Volunteers, now organised to form a Territorial Force of fourteen mounted brigades and an equal number of Infantry Divisions, with Artillery and Engineers, the rearrangement was such as to make little difference to individual units. What changes there were consisted mainly in alterations in nomenclature, the grouping of units, the appointment of Regular general officers to command divisions, and the establishment of County Territorial Associations.

In conformity with the general plan, the number of the battalion (2nd London Volunteer Battalion) was altered, and known henceforth as the 6th Battalion of the London Regiment (T.F.), but the name "City of London Rifles" remained as before. Other changes were few. The battalion continued to be organised upon an eight-company basis, with its internal organisation of right- and left-half battalion. Colonel R. Walter Smith, V.D., continued as its Commanding Officer, and companies were furnished by such well-known firms as Gamages (C Coy.), The South Metropolitan Gas Co. (D Coy.), Harmsworth (E Coy.), Associated Newspapers (F Coy.), and Spottiswoode (G Coy.).

6th Bn. London Regt.

Chapter 3

MOBILISATION

Shortly after midnight of the 4-5th August, 1914, the Foreign Office made the following announcement:

" Owing to the summary rejection by the German Government of the request made by His Majesty's Government for assurances that the neutrality of Belgium will be respected, His Majesty's Ambassador at Berlin has received his passports, and His Majesty's Government have declared to the German Government that a State of War exists between Great Britain and Germany as from 11 p.m. on the 4th August."

The fatal hour had struck. For years Field-Marshal Lord Roberts, Honorary Colonel of the battalion, had been warning the country daily, almost hourly, of the approaching catastrophe.

Since the Haldane reorganisation of the Army and the creation of the Territorial Force, the battalion had voluntarily undergone what might be described as an intensive training, and that year (1908) saw a general influx of recruits, and the formation of the " Daily Mail " Company. Training now was as if war was imminent. The annual camps at Ludgershall, in 1908, and at Perham Down, in 1909, both being for fifteen days, are noteworthy for the strenuous work done. The following year was well commenced with a Whitsun manœuvre consisting of a route-march at Barnet (Herts), where the battalion spent part of the night billeted in the Militia Barracks, and the other part on parade as a consequence of a midnight alarm. That year, during annual training at Borden, a field operation, embracing an outpost scheme, was planned, in which other units co-operated. Two years later, at Lulworth Cove, the battalion was again co-operating with the regular forces, on this occasion the Royal Navy supporting an attack from the sea.

Ludgershall

Perham Down

Lulworth Cove

" The war is bound to come!" Few believed that it might be to-morrow; yet the signs were unmistakable. So definite was the War Office view that mobilisation schemes were ordered to be prepared even by Territorial units, and early in 1913 the main details of that drawn up for the battalion were made known, and each serving officer was instructed in the duties which would fall to him in the event of an order to mobilise being given.

The mobilisation of the Regular Army took place some days before the declaration of war, and the permanent staff attached to the battalion received their mobilisation orders on July 27th, which, however, did not require them to rejoin their units. The general feeling was that it might yet be possible to avoid war, and consequently, preparations for the forthcoming annual training, this year to be held at Cowgate, Eastbourne, proceeded as if no untoward incidents were occurring. **Eastbourne**

Thus, Sunday, August 2nd, 1914, saw the battalion at about 2 p.m., marching into camp. On arrival companies were dismissed. For an hour the usual activities of a unit taking over canvas continued, whilst in the marquee, set aside as an Orderly-room, the clerks were arranging a temporary office. An orderly from Brigade Headquarters arrived bearing a telegram. The Regimental Sergeant-Major opened it, read its contents, and immediately ordered, in a voice heard over two-thirds of the camp, the battalion to fall in. The Commanding Officer, Colonel Moore, to whom the telegram was immediately passed, had the "alarm" sounded. For the City of London Rifles the War had commenced. Within two hours the battalion was marching back to Eastbourne Station, thence to return to London. The train journey lasted for hours, and the excitement of it was increased by the innumerable rumours which an obliging civil population generously supplied. Every bridge and tunnel, it was said, was mined; many titled people had been arrested as spies, assassinations had been frequent, and actions at sea, in which the entire British Navy had been sunk, was already an admitted fact. **Col. Moore**

On reaching headquarters late that evening, orders were issued that all ranks should proceed to their homes and await written orders to mobilise—twenty N.C.O.'s and riflemen, however, being retained as runners. **London**

The drill-hall at this time was being reconstructed. The present wing, housing the Officers' Mess, Sergeants' Mess, and Men's Canteen did not then exist, and where the billiards-room now overlooks the Hall, was nothing but floored rafters, upon which were kept military stores of various kinds. At 7 p.m. on the following day (Monday, August 3rd, Bank Holiday), a telephone message from Brigade Headquarters informed the battalion that the order to mobilise was being sent, and on this, the official forms were immediately dispatched by post to all serving members, the officers being summoned by telegram.

As may well be supposed, many, after their night's rest, had returned to Farringdon Road in anticipation of receiving their mobilisation orders, and in an incredibly short space of time a full battalion was reported present. But the drill-hall was never built as sleeping quarters for 700 riflemen, and consequently, it became necessary to commandeer the neighbouring Hugh Middleton Schools as barracks, A Company (Lieut. E. W. Hughes)* remaining at headquarters. Within a day or so, the unit was recruited to its full strength of 1,031 N.C.O.'s and men, about 200 of them being provided by a remarkably fine contingent from the K.R.R.C. Cadets, who, under Capt. Booth, enlisted in a body.

K.R.R.C. Cadets

The object of the creation of the Territorial Force had been to provide the country with a means of land defence in the event of the Regular Army's being sent abroad, and on no serving member, officer or man, was foreign service obligatory; and although the position was clear, there were yet many who were eager to place themselves completely at the disposal of the Government. To the younger soldiers, the War which had just commenced was regarded as offering opportunities of great adventure; and if, as to many seemed certain, it would be over in six months, no time was to be lost in an endeavour to see active service. Within a week, therefore, the War Office, finely sensing the temper of the new force, issued orders that Territorial units would be accepted for Imperial Service, provided ninety per cent of their members volunteered for it. This percentage, the *Sixth* easily obtained, and thus the battalion became available for service overseas. It remained in London, however, until the middle of the month, when orders were received for it to proceed by route-march to Bisley. On the first day, by a short march, it reached, and was billeted in schools and similar buildings bordering Wimbledon Common, where web-equipment was issued; the second night was spent at Weybridge in similar accommodation; and by the third, Bisley was reached.

Bisley

Here, a large canvas concentration camp, fenced with barbed wire, had been hurriedly established, and here the time was spent in refitting, and in training in field operations, and here, also, all were vaccinated, some of whom were immediately transferred by the medical officers to hospitals in London, whence they rejoined the unit some weeks later.

About the middle of September a move from Bisley to Crowborough commenced, the first day's march taking the battalion as far as Merrow (Surrey), where the inhabitants surpassed themselves in the matter of hospitality, by providing what must be described as a regular feast. The battalion had marched its way from London to this old-world village, and the highways and byways of Surrey had awakened to the unusual tramp, tramp, tramp of feet, such as had never before been known.

Merrow

As one describes it: "Workers of all departments of industry swung along to the tunes of the band, and when that music ceased, mouth-organ

*Later, Colonel E. W. Hughes, D.S.O., M.C.

players led the troops singing the latest songs of the day: " Tipperary," " When the Midnight Choo-Choo leaves for Alabam," a marching-song introduced by the cadets, called, " Dan, Dan," and the regimental theme song:

> " When the war is over we're going to live in clover,
> When the war is over we're going to have a fair,
> Come to-morrow night, and you'll be sure to see a fight,
> There'll be razors aflyin' in the air."

Following this verse, the whole battalion along the line of route, would harmonise the chorus:

> " There's someone in the house with Dinah,
> Someone in the house, I know ;
> There's someone in the house with Dinah,
> Playing on the ol' banjo !"

The vaccination at Bisley had been a wretched business; it quickly made a number of men (round about eighty) extremely ill. First the parts affected became inflamed, and later, a kind of fever attacked them. On leaving Merrow, the worst cases began to fall-out by the roadside, unable to carry their arms and equipment. Those unable to go farther were collected together and taken by train to Jarvis Brook, Lieut. Craven, Sgt. C. Watts, and Cpl. S. Short* being in charge. During that and the following night, the men were quartered in a large corrugated-iron straw shed on Sir Lindsay Hogg's estate. Sir Lindsay Hogg and his entire household did everything possible to alleviate the men's sufferings, by supplying fomentations, dressings, and food. Later, billets were found for them, in which they had to manage as best they could until well enough to rejoin the battalion at Crowborough. Some of the men, anxious about their condition, returned to their homes, knowing that there they would get proper treatment, although this course necessitated their taking " French leave."

Meanwhile, the battalion continued its journey, marching on the second day from Merrow to Reigate, via Effingham Towers, and on the third day to East Grinstead, during which His Late Majesty, King George V, took the salute as units of the brigade went past in column of route. The brigade remained in East Grinstead for a few days before occupying a camp but recently laid out at the top of the hill to the south of Crowborough. No words

Reigate
East Grinstead
Crowborough

*Later, Major S. Short, T.D.

could adequately describe its state of incompleteness. It was without water, the pipe-line being still under construction, and it had no sanitary arrangements. Canvas was short, and no provision had been made for personal ablutions, a shortcoming hastily overcome by a bath improvised by sinking a tarpaulin sheet into the ground, but its situation, in the vicinity of the transport lines, caused it to be less frequented than might otherwise have been the case. Further, blankets were short, and it was not until the "Weekly Dispatch" had drawn attention to this deficiency that a good night's sleep was possible.

Crowborough Colonel Moore had a reputation for seeing the humorous side of things, and his many "asides" were much enjoyed, and added to his popularity. Known throughout the battalion as "Nutty," the Commanding Officer's character was a curious mixture of sternness and easy familiarity which won for him both respect and affection. He could joke or strike a comic attitude without losing dignity, but woe betide anyone who took advantage of him on that score. No pen-picture can convey an adequate impression of his complex nature, although the number of stories told about him is legion, and the following brief account of some night operations contains some grim humour which, in a sense, was typical of him.

"One night at Crowborough the battalion had to attack an imaginary enemy advancing from Fairwarp. The eight company-scouts had to advance in extended order ahead of the battalion. The night was dirty and black with fog and rain, and consequently, contact with them was lost. A sudden halt occurred, when 'Nutty' fell knee-deep into a muddy swamp. The news quickly spread, and the irritated troops following him gave vent to their pleasure with cackles and howls of laughter. Realising the meaning of this hilarity, 'Nutty' continued to wade through the slush, and ordered the whole battalion to follow him; the atmosphere of merriment changed immediately."

The stay at Crowborough lasted until November 4th, during which the training consisted mostly of field and night operations, with many hours of trench digging. Sometimes the units in the brigade would co-operate to provide training in mutual support and the maintenance of communications; and as an outcome of it, an indefinable affection as keen as its corresponding rivalry, grew up between the four battalions. Great was the regret, therefore, when the brigade was broken up, the 5th Battalion (London Rifle Brigade) going to France, and the 6th and 8th Battalions, on November 4th, joining *Watford* the 2nd London Division, then stationed at St. Albans, Hatfield, and Watford, the battalion itself finding billets in the last.

Most of the time at Watford was devoted to musketry and field operations, a night alarm in the early hours of December 26th being specially memorable. The festivities of the previous day and a "silver thaw" added to the excitement of the moment, and proved as much as many could stand. Apart from these festivities, Christmas Day itself had been made memorable by the gift of a pipe from the City Territorial Association to every man in the battalion. Colonel Moore was a bitter opponent of cigarette smoking, and the gift was in keeping with his views. *Watford*

The physical fitness of the British Army has always been a proud boast, and Capt. Bate, R.A.M.C., nicknamed "Bokank," the medical officer, maintained that tradition in the unit. He had "needled" everyone at Bisley, nursed them at Crowborough, and saw all in the nude at Watford, supervising an initiation which all had to undergo before being declared fit for foreign service. The ceremony consisted of saying "Ah" a dozen times, bending down, and coughing; and if as a result of it all one complained of headache, the treatment would be "Medicine and Duty," and Sgt. Collins would give the unfortunate sufferer a No. 9 pill.

In January, 1915, the battalion was reorganised into four double companies, A Company being commanded by Capt. W. F. Mildren,* B Company by Capt. R. C. Boothby,† C Company by Capt. E. L. Phillips, and D Company by Capt. M. A. F. Cotton. At this time Captain Seagrim, Indian Army, was posted to the battalion and appointed Adjutant. A further change, and one, at the time, naturally regretted by all ranks, was the retirement of Colonel Moore, who since 1912 had commanded the battalion, and been largely responsible for the high state of efficiency reached. His place was taken in the following month by Lt.-Col. Simpson, V.D., an officer who had seen considerable service in the West Riding Regiment. *Col. Simpson*

The stay at Watford will ever be remembered, for it was here that lasting friendships were formed both with comrades and with those on whom officers and men were billeted. It was from here, too, that the battalion marched to St. Albans to attend a memorial service to Field-Marshal Earl Roberts, who, on a visit to his beloved Indian troops, but recently arrived in France, was stricken down, an early casualty in a war for so long predicted by him. It was at Watford that the buglers were equipped with Bersaglieri horns; it was at Watford that the battalion was trained, examined, and equipped for its coming ordeal; and it was from Watford at midnight, on March 16th, 1915, that it started the long journey that held honour for all.

---

*Later, Brig.-Gen. W. F. Mildren, C.B., C.M.G., D.S.O., T.D.
†Later, Colonel R. C. Boothby, T.D.

Chapter 4

ON ACTIVE SERVICE

Early, the following morning (March 17th) the train arrived at Southampton. The battalion detrained, and for twelve hours it waited upon the quayside to embark. At 7 p.m. the order was given

S.S. *Marguerite*

to board the s.s. Marguerite, and at the same time the rolling-stock of the battalion was loaded on to the transport ship, s.s. Blackwell, the strictest silence being maintained. A vigilant Navy had swept the seas, but the menace of the enemy submarine was ever present. No word was spoken, no light was shown. Save for the gentle lapping of the waters against the vessel's sides, the stillness was complete. The solemnity of the occasion was lost on no one. The hour of departure had come. The realisation of men's dependence on the Absolute was intensified. Then, from a corner of the vessel voices could be heard, scarcely audible, singing in unison. In a moment the tune had been caught, and in another, a thousand voices were singing reverently:

"Eternal Father, strong to save,
Whose arm hath bound the restless wave,
Who bidd'st the mighty ocean deep,
Its own appointed limits keep;
O hear us when we cry to Thee,
For those in peril on the sea."

The s.s. Marguerite was now slowly moving from the harbour. The hymn finished, and was followed by another:

"O God our help in ages past,
Our hope——"

Out of the darkness loomed another vessel. It bore no sailing lights, but amidships, well illuminated, was exhibited a great red cross. A hospital ship was bringing the remnants of other battalions home again.

Many had professed to recognise the troopship which now bore them, as none other than an old cross-channel steamer, which had been taken off that service some years previously on account of unseaworthiness. The passage was fortunately uneventful, and Le Havre was reached by dawn on the 18th, the battalion moving to Camp No. 6 on disembarkation. Here the night was spent in bitter cold, with no coverings save that which a greatcoat could *Le Havre*

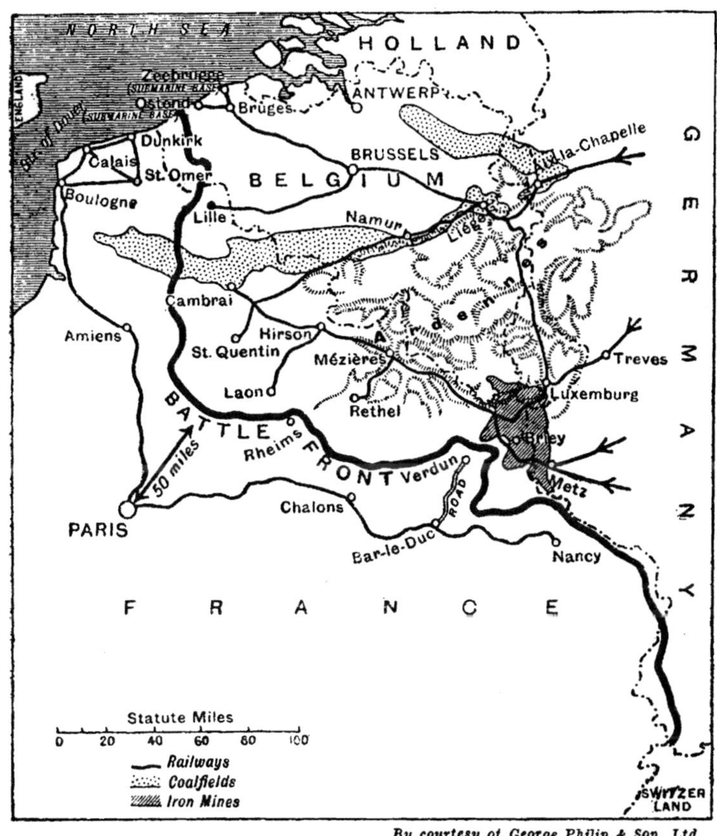

By courtesy of George Philip & Son, Ltd

MAP I.—THE ALLIED FRONT FROM THE SEA TO SWITZERLAND AT THE BEGINNING OF 1915.

provide, and despite the initial novelty of everything, all felt miserable. For months past officers, men, and horses had lived in relative luxury, and this sleeping in tents, on rain-soaked ground, high on a hill-top (afterwards known as the " Pimple ") was anything but comfortable. An advance-party of six, under Sgt. " Jock " Cannon, had indeed left England three days before the battalion, so as to have everything ready for it on its arrival at Le Havre, but true to army tradition, on landing, Sgt. Cannon could get no orders or information as to the battalion's precise destination, and so nothing could be done but wait until it arrived. The party rejoined it the following day.

Le Havre

The morning came at last, and in due course the battalion was ready to move off to the railhead and there entrain and be conveyed to " somewhere near the front." The trucks were marked " 40 hommes ou 8 chevaux en longue," and when both animals and men were aboard the train steamed slowly out of Le Havre, and after a hundred stops, eventually reached Berguette.

All along the line, little French children would either be cadging for " bisqueet " or " booly-beef," or else trying to sell " shockolar " and " orarnge," and most of them expressed themselves forcibly. " Ingleesh soldar no bloody bon!" was frequently heard, and some threw stones at the trucks as they continued their monotonous journey. On and on went the train at a speed which seemed rarely to exceed four miles an hour, and there was nothing for its occupants to do but listen to the incessant rattle of the eight wheels passing over the joints in the rails of the track: Bomp, bomp ; bomp, bomp. Bomp, bomp ; bomp, bomp. Evidently, most of the troops noticed this monotonous rhythm, for in time all were whistling " O weel may the keel row " to the beat of the wheels.

Occasionally the train would pass a peculiarly dressed peasant, in forage-hat, blue overalls, patched, and feet in sabots. Someone would shout something ; the Frenchman would call back, and the majority of the occupants of the train would cheer. The Frenchman would then shout something that sounded like, " Boocoo maird." No one knew what that meant, but it seemed friendly enough, and the response would be another cheer. The pretty French girls so often talked about had yet to be seen, and their complete absence led to the belief that they were being purposely kept hidden from British eyes. Elderly women with anything but graceful lines were abundant. Indeed, most of the work, whether on the land or in the towns, seemed to be done by them: bakers, butchers, milkmen, fishmongers, and postmen, were women, and they went about their jobs in a thoroughly " workmanlike " manner, filling the places of their men-folk who had been called to the colours.

Berguette

The train journey from Le Havre to Berguette, which was reached sufficiently early on March 20th for the sunrise to be witnessed, lasted twenty hours, and was but the first of many similar experiences of rail travel in France.

At Berguette, a nine-miles march along a poplar-lined, cobbled road to billets in Raimbert, a small mining town, awaited the battalion, where on the next day, Sunday, a church parade was held, the service being conducted by the officer commanding, in the absence of a padre. Next day, the battalion was inspected by Field-Marshal Sir John French, Commander-in-Chief of the British Expeditionary Force, who for months had been asking the War Office to send him Territorial units. This inspection well satisfied him as the battalion's bearing and efficiency, and apparently, as a consequence, events began to move in rapid succession. *Raimbert*

* * * * *

On Wednesday, March 24th, the battalion left Raimbert for Béthune, about nine miles away, and arrived there at dusk. The march over cobbled roads was anything but pleasant, and troops and horses were very tired by the end of it. The battalion was billeted in the orphanage, but the transport lines were in six inches of mud on a slope nearby, the officers' horses being quartered, some in a yard, and some in the box-stables of a neighbouring chateau, in which were also the officers' mounts of the 2nd Bn., Staffordshire Regiment, and the 1st Bn., King's Royal Rifle Corps. At first the grooms found the Regular Army grooms much on their dignity, but they were very good fellows, and soon ready to teach the Territorials all they knew. As one described it: "Any one of them knew more about a quick and smart turn-out than all our Cockney amateur 'ostlers put together. Our accent amused them, and theirs amused us. In a few days they made old soldiers of us, taught us how to make wisps and pull and make swish tails for each of our horses; they cured the cracks and sore heels from which our horses had suffered from the heel-pegs at Le Havre. It was in this stable that Lieut. Neely saw the C.O.'s turn-out of the 1st K.R.R.C.'s (2nd Division). He liked the effect of the Martingale, and before we moved on, Lloyd, the saddler, had plaited a very smart one for "Nigger," a long-standing cause of amusement to the members of the transport." *Bethune*

The following day, A Company proceeded into the front line trenches for a period of instruction under the South Staffordshire Regiment, and on the next, the remaining three companies were inspected by the G.O.C., 2nd Inf. Bde., Brig.-Gen. Fanshawe,* at Annequin, a village lying on the Béthune—La Bassée road, who, in a few brief words, gave those paraded much good advice. From then until the following Thursday the remaining companies went forward for instruction in the front line system, being attached in rotation *Annequin*

*Later, Maj.-General, commanding the 58th Division.

to the 1st Bn., K.R.R.C., whose position in the line was on the extreme right of the British Army. The companies not actually holding the position were engaged upon repairing communication trenches.

The War had opened in 1914 with an attack by Germany through Belgium, with the object of striking at Paris, and as a counter-stroke, an advance by France through her former province of Alsace. Although seriously delayed by the Belgian Army, the German movement had been successful, and by the end of August was rapidly approaching the French capital. On September 6th the Battle of the Marne commenced, resulting in an almost immediate retirement of the German Armies operating against Paris, and led, in the beginning of October, to that series of operations which have come to be known as the " Race to the Sea."

The object of the British and the French was to form a junction with the Belgian Army and thus present a united front covering the coalfields of Béthune and Lens. By Christmas, 1914, therefore, a more or less continuous system of trenches had been thrown up by the opposing armies, whose pickets had consolidated their positions, and whose outpost systems had become highly organised.

In this northward movement, the Germans had seized La Bassée, and the high ground to the north and south of it, and the British took Béthune, a town lying eight miles to the west. Each was chosen as a defensive position, for between them lay a belt of marshy ground, not unlike the fen land of Norfolk. Once some respite had been gained, the British had pushed forward their outpost line, in spite of the low-lying nature of the ground, until it stood

Cuinchy

but three miles from La Bassée, in front of Cuinchy, Givenchy, and Festubert. It was in the trench system opposite Cuinchy that the four companies of the battalion had undergone their instruction, and it was the communication trenches leading to it upon which they had now been at work for a week, when not in the line. By April 1st, therefore, the battalion had received an introduction, not only to methods of siege warfare, involving the use of improvised hand-grenades, mining, sniping, and the repair of trenches, but had learnt a good deal of the nature of the ground they were about to hold alone.

On A Company this duty first devolved, the tour lasting for twenty-four hours, and terminating at 3 p.m. on April 2nd. During it, Sgt. W. Morris was killed and eight other ranks wounded. Thus it was on a Good Friday that the first of the regiment's one thousand dead made the supreme sacrifice. The first sight of severely wounded men is always unnerving, and those near Sgt. Morris and his wounded comrades were very much upset. It was Major Mildren who bound up his wounds and comforted him, and quietly to those around, said: "You will see worse than this before long." B Company relieved A Company that afternoon, and just before dawn the following morning, a British mine was sprung beneath the German front line. Elaborate precautions had been taken to avoid the noise made by the sappers being heard in the enemy trenches, and when the mine was fired the surprise was complete. A hostile barrage was put down immediately, and during the bombardment the Second-in-Command of the battalion, Major E. A. Myer, who was in the trenches at the time, was struck by shrapnel and killed. Major Myer had served in the battalion since 1898, and his keenness, marked efficiency, and personality, had made him deservedly popular with all, and his untimely death robbed the battalion of a gallant officer, and caused profound grief, which gave place gradually to a determination to live up to that example of self-sacrifice he had continuously set.

Cuinchy

In due course all four companies, A, B, C, and D, had held the line at the "Brickfields" alone, and the battalion was withdrawn to Raimbert, where it remained for ten days, practising attacks against entrenched positions, and digging lines of trenches by day and night. Following the short stay at Raimbert, it returned to Béthune, and ultimately entered the line at Givenchy, on April 19th, as a unit, relieving the 1st Bn., K.R.R.C., and having on its immediate right the King's Liverpool Regiment. Here, the battalion had unpleasant experiences. Two German mines were fired, apparently doing more damage to their own lines than to ours, but a regular stream of well-placed minenwerfer shells continually made breaches in the breastworks. To make matters worse, a dead cow lay just beyond one of the saps in no-man's-land, and putrefying, it stank. The Germans shot steadily at it, making matters far worse, and nightly parties had to visit the beast and throw chloride of lime upon it, to overcome the stench. Unpleasant as were these visits, the battalion's bards profited by them, and soon a new song, "Poor Old Cow," was heard upon the march.

By now an introduction to modern warfare had been given to all units in the division, thus enabling it to play its part as a self-contained unit. On April 23rd, the battalion was relieved by the 7th Bn., London Regt., and after a stay of nine days in billets at Lapugnoy and of one in Gorre, again entered the line (May 4th) itself to relieve another unit of the division, the 17th Bn., whose sector lay facing Festubert. At Lapugnoy, the battalion had its first experience of being billeted in French houses, and many enjoyed real hospitality, including clean sheets and blankets. One house, occupied by some men of the "Shiny Seventh" caught fire and was burnt to the ground, despite the efforts made to put it out.

Lapugnoy
Festubert

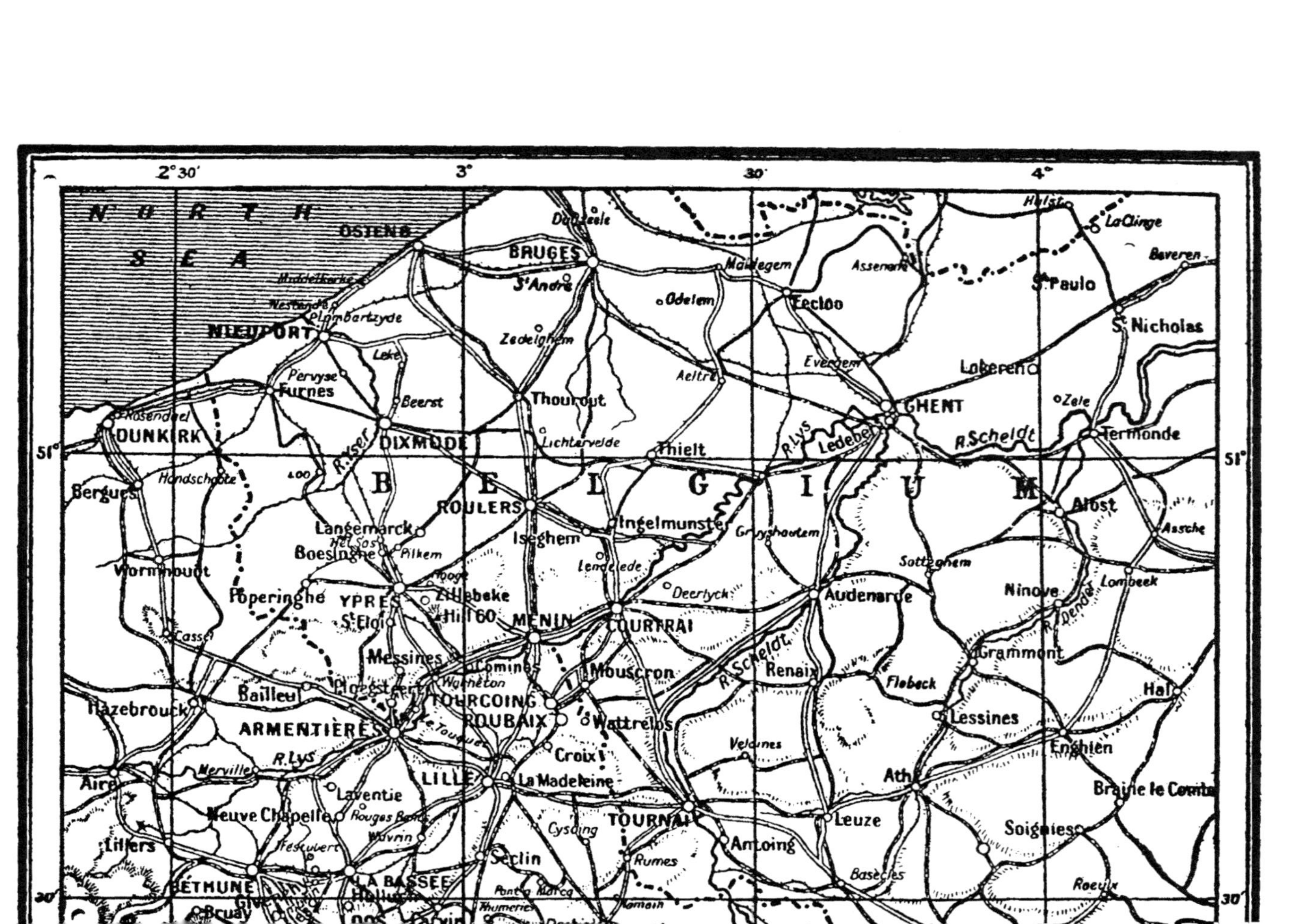

2°30′
3°
30′
4°
51°
30′
NORTH SEA
BELGIUM
OSTEND
BRUGES
St André
Odelem
Maldegem
Eecloo
Assenede
St Paulo
La Clinge
Helst
Baveren
St Nicholas
Lokeren
Zele
GHENT
Termonde
R. Scheldt
R. Lys
Ledeberg
Evergem
Aeltre
Middelkerke
Nieuport
Lombartzyde
Zedelghem
Thourout
Lichtervelde
Thielt
Pervyse
Furnes
Leke
Beerst
DIXMUDE
R. Yser
DUNKIRK
Rosendael
Hondschoote
Bergues
ROULERS
Langemarck
Het Sas
Boesinghe
Pilkem
Iseghem
Ingelmunster
Gruyshautem
Lendelede
Deerlyck
Wormhoudt
Poperinghe
YPRES
Zillebeke
Hooge
Hill 60
St Eloi
MENIN
COURTRAI
Audenarde
Sottegem
Ninove
Lombeek
Alost
Assche
R. Dender
Grammont
Cassel
Messines
Comines
Warneton
Mouscron
Renaix
Flobeck
Lessines
Hal
Hazebrouck
Bailleul
Ploegsteert
TOURCOING
ROUBAIX
Wattrelos
ARMENTIÈRES
Le Touquet
Croix
Velaines
Enghien
Aire
Merville
R. Lys
Laventie
LILLE
La Madeleine
Ath
Braine le Comte
Neuve Chapelle
Rouges Bancs
Wavrin
Cysoing
TOURNAI
Leuze
Soignies
Lillers
Festubert
Seclin
Antoing
Rumes
BÉTHUNE
LA BASSÉE
Basècles
Roeulx
Pont à Marcq
Bruay

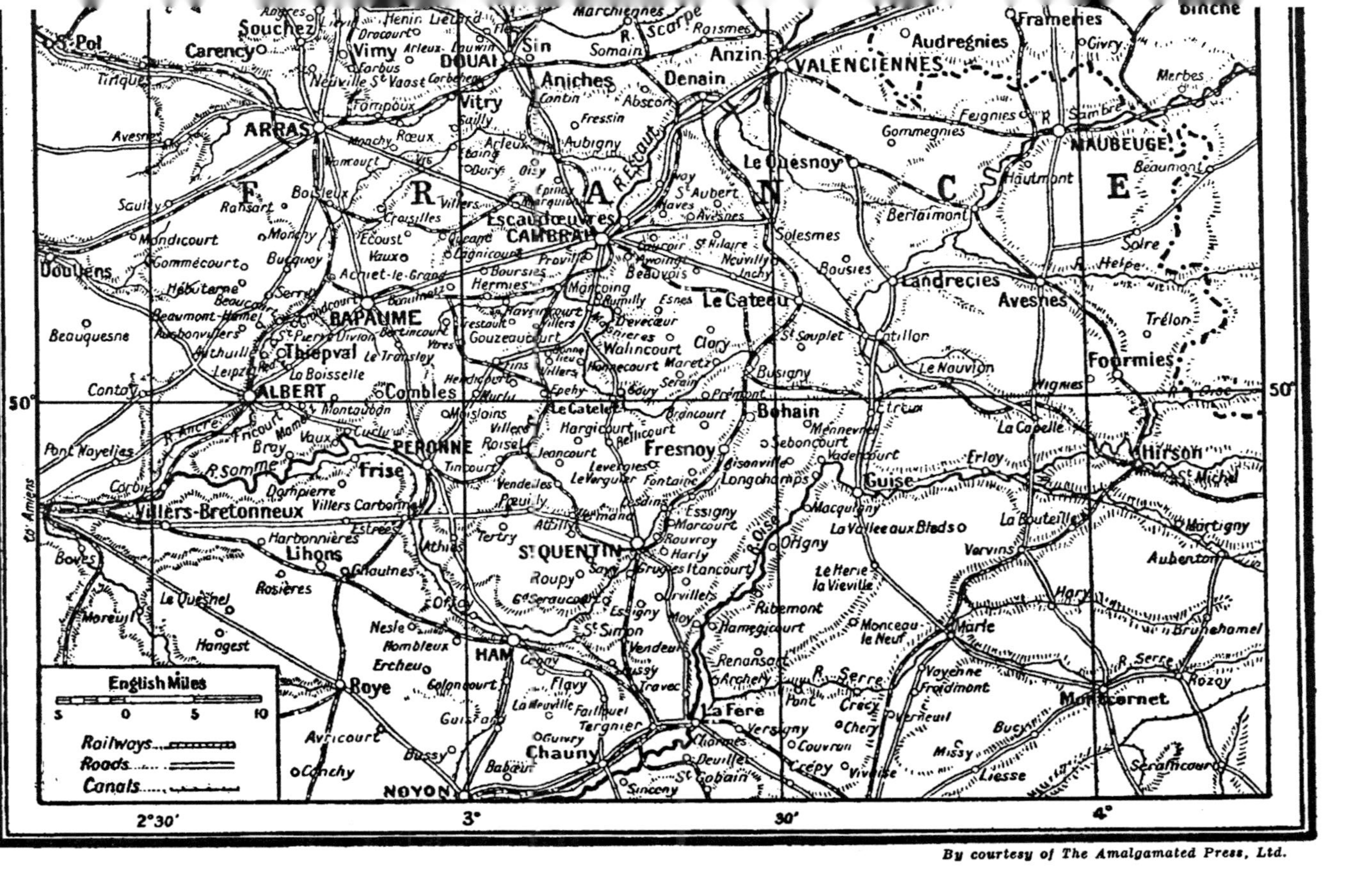

By courtesy of The Amalgamated Press, Ltd.

MAP 2.—AREA OF THE MAIN OPERATIONS OF THE BRITISH ARMIES IN FRANCE, 1914—1919.

C

On May 8th began the artillery preparation for the French attack on the Lorette and Vimy Ridges, lying but a few miles to the south of La Bassée, which was to cost the French Army nearly 200,000 casualties. As support for this major operation, an attack against the entrenched position to the north of Festubert had been decided upon, but the assault by the troops of the First Army on May 9th met with little success. It caused, however, the conflagration to extend southwards. Thereupon the *Sixth* was detailed to act as supports to the 8th Battalion, occupying a position east of Gorre and Annequin.

Festubert

No further action was required of it that day, however, and on the following, it returned to billets at the Tuning Fork in Gorre, and on the 10th moved to Annequin. Here it was subjected to bombing from the air, and partly to avoid casualties, the battalion moved two days later back to Gorre, two companies occupying bivouacs in a wood behind a chateau.

Gorre
Annequin

The action of the British divisions was, of course, subsidiary to the main French assault, but they were called to attack repeatedly to pin the enemy to his defensive positions. In the offensive the major rôle was being played by Regular troops and the Canadians, for as yet Territorials were considered as being hardly fitted for such responsibility. But an attack on Sunday, 16th, by the 7th Division and Canadians, both of which suffered heavy casualties, necessitated the employment of the 47th Division in the battle. On this day the battalion took up positions in the "intermediate" line of trenches, where they remained for four days supplying working parties day and night, mainly for the purpose of building breastworks, near the shell-swept Willow road, to form a defensive flank. Many casualties amongst all ranks occurred during this strenuous and hazardous work, and in a sense all were glad when orders came for the battalion to relieve the 15th Battalion in the front line. The relief was complete by midnight on the 20th, and the *Sixth* was holding the line.

Willow Road

* * * * *

When studying any battle, attention is apt to be concentrated upon those actually engaged in attack or defence, whereas often by far the more strenuous endeavours have to be made by those not actually serving in the front line. Cooks, stores personnel, and transport, often thought of as miles from the scene of action, were, in fact, frequently called upon to perform duties and to run risks as great as any in the line; and often, indeed, their exertions far surpassed any that the companies were called upon to perform. It was a point of honour with them that at all costs rations should be delivered to their comrades in the line, and if men, horses, and limbers were blown sky-high, then others must be sent up at once ; and, if as a result of heavy shelling roads became impassable for limbers, then pack animals must be led to their destination ; and if even they could not pass, then food, stores, and ammunition must be man-handled to battalion headquarters. During the Battle of Festubert, for example, while the battalion was in the front line, conditions were so bad that Q.M.Sgt. Johnson had to deliver A Company's rations by means of a wheelbarrow. The following, written by a member of the Transport Section, gives some idea of the work performed and the difficulties encountered : *Festubert*

" Many wondered if it was worse in the line than on the road to headquarters. Some of the ' Old timers ' in Béthune had said it was worse on the roads a mile behind the line than it was at the Breastworks. The Q.M. stores and the horse-lines were at Gorre, and one night, on the return journey, the rain just teemed down. Above the din and crashing of the 18-pounders, could be heard thunder, and the flashes of lightning seemed to light the whole of the convoy.

" Crash ! A shell had burst about twenty yards away—horses were getting out of hand, and mules backed the limber into a ditch. What a night ! And what a mix-up ! Nobody could see anybody, and yet no damage was done. They were all shouting at the animals to get a move on.

" Batteries of artillery and transports were moving along the rain-sodden, cobbled roads ; Canadians and Scottish regiments were straggling along in batches of platoons, or had halted by the roadside, most of them arranging their ground-sheets around their shoulders to resemble a cape. Roars of artillery began to succeed each other faster and faster. Thunder and lightning —what a combination !—the great bombardment becoming more and more intense. In the continuous chain of flashes, the limbers ahead could be seen. The horses were covered with white lather, through sheer fear of the terrible rendings all around. Everything becomes a jumble, and general confusion prevails. Limber-poles could be seen almost perpendicular; horses getting over the traces, and breetchings slipping over their hindquarters. The rear half of a limber in front had skewed into the ditch, waist-deep with mud, by the side of the road.

" This was the night of hell prior to the great Battle of Festubert. On, on, ankle-deep in slime and mud, and, after another half-hour's trundling through this heavy going, the transport arrived, half-drowned, at battalion headquarters. Shrapnel was bursting overhead ; machine-gun and rifle fire too near to be comfortable ; the consistent ping, ping of stray bullets passing all around.

" Many had volunteered to act as spare men with the rations and ammunition limbers that night. Some went forward from battalion headquarters to find a fatigue-party. After half an hour's wading through mud and slush, some of our ' boys ' were found escorting prisoners through some breastworks.

" A little way ahead the combined crashing of ' coalboxes ' and the splitting tornado created by the overhead shrapnel, the mournful whizzing and whistling through the air as the fragments sought their final resting place. Ping, ping, ping, ping! Some of the Jerries were firing much too high. Pop-pop-pop-pop-pop-pop-pop!—sometimes a little quicker than others—tss-tss-tss-tss, so the bullets would finally gasp, as they buried themselves in the earth around. Crash! A portion of the breastworks sagged! And so on. Through all this, men would duck and dodge, a muck-sweat creeping over everyone. The men in the companies didn't seem to mind much about things, but there was a persistent cry of ' stretcher-bearers.' At length a party from the foremost breastworks arrived and unloaded the ammunition limbers.

" Later, when back in the transport lines at Gorre, one could cast his mind over the events of the night, and determine that from that time on, the claims of the men in the line should always come first."

* * * * *

Festubert

As has been seen, the *Sixth* had taken over a sector of the front line on the 20th. Here the battalion remained for ten days, taking an active if stationary part in the battle. A heavy bombardment directed against the breastworks commenced as soon as the battalion reached its positions, and continued almost without interruption from the 21st to the 25th. Breastworks were demolished by high-explosive shells, and shrapnel was poured over the levelled parapets. Quite clearly, such activity presaged some hostile action. It came on the 23rd, after the Canadian Division on the right had attacked the " Orchard " opposite Givenchy, capturing the trench system in the neighbourhood. Evidently the Germans were aware of the assault that was to be delivered, for they were prepared, and resisted strenuously, and counter-attacked in the afternoon. The German assault was delivered across the front held by the *Sixth*, and the attackers presented excellent targets at about 500 yards range. So effective was the infantry fire that the enemy was forced to retire, on two occasions waving white flags.

The battle went on for two more days, with the Canadians consolidating their positions at Givenchy, and the 47th Division holding the left flank, with the 8th Battalion fighting with bomb and bullet on the left of the *Sixth*, to drive the enemy from positions from which they could enfilade the newly-gained territory. In this task some of the bombers from the *Sixth* assisted, and for the part the whole battalion played, General Alderton, commanding the Canadian Division, gave generous thanks. It should be recorded, however, that the 8th Battalion subsequently had some hard things to say about the *Sixth*, whose musketry may or may not have caused casualties in their ranks. *Festubert*

One final assault at Givenchy was made on the 25th, by the 142nd (3rd London) Infantry Brigade, and although all objectives were taken, the ground could not be held on account of the deadly enfilade fire directed at it, against which the infantry, without artillery support, was well-nigh helpless.

Individual acts of heroism during the battle were numerous, and one scarcely deserves mention more than another; and how is it possible to praise too highly those who, at times of greatest stress, never forgot their humour—men like Cpl. Martin, whose funny stories on one occasion restored moral to very weary Canadians?

Yet some should be recorded here. What, for example, could be more inspiring than the act performed by Cpl. Sharp, of the Signal Section? Communication between Battalion and Company Headquarters broke down, and two signallers sent out to repair the wires did not return. Thereupon, Cpl. Sharp himself went to investigate and soon came upon the bodies of his two comrades, evidently killed by shell-fire before they had commenced their task. There was no time to be lost. Casting around he met two Canadian signallers, and with Rfm. Burke, of the *Sixth*, carried wire from a small dump in a garden behind a demolished house to the place where the wires had been cut. Then working quickly but calmly under heavy fire, he repaired the breaks. Then he sent Rfm. Burke to report to Battalion Headquarters that communication had been re-established; and it was typical of him that he should say nothing when subsequently an award to Rfm. Burke—doubtless well-deserved—seemed to suggest that his own act had gone unnoticed.

"L.-Cpl. Gordon, of the stretcher-bearers, worked for four days and four nights under heavy fire attending the wounded, and also gave the Canadians a helping hand with their wounded and killed, until he himself was badly hit in the face, but still his determined pluck would not allow him to leave off until ordered to do so by an officer," writes a comrade. L.-Cpl. Gordon was awarded the D.C.M. There is no greater inspiration than the knowledge that in adversity succour is at hand.

The casualties at the Battle of Festubert were heavy, the wounded being far more than anticipated, and the scenes immediately behind the line were almost indescribable, and even the following pen-picture gives but an inadequate glimpse of the sufferings endured:

" The long trail of the wounded from the advance dressing station were filing along to the hospital at Béthune. Arm cases were walking—leg cases, if possible, were dragging themselves and staggering along. Stretcher cases were being rushed by in ambulances following each other at intervals of about 300 yards—one long stream of broken humanity.

" An officer of the battalion went to the hospital at Béthune to see if any of our men were there.

" The ' walking-wounded ' sat about in their crude, more crimson-than-white, bandages. To move with any element of freedom was a matter of impossibility. The rapidly gathering wounded displayed the terrible hardships the troops were undergoing at the breastworks—they just sat and lounged about with drawn, yellow faces,* covered with a week's beard.

" Groaning, moaning, mixed with occasional whimpering, and shoulders shaking to pathetic sobbing; some sitting in a dazed, vacant state; others, who had yet to feel the intense pain of their crushed limbs, chatting and smoking. To inquiries of ' How are things going at the front?' most of the answers were: ' Hell! The whole place wiped out.'

" An R.A.M.C. corporal would occasionally break out with:

" ' Where have you got it?'

" ' Arm.'

" ' Over there!'

" ' You a leg case?'

" ' Yes.'

" ' In there!'

" A burly, businesslike-looking sergeant would bustle in shouting: ' All arm and leg cases who have received attention and labels, outside, please!', and improvised ambulances, in the form of lorries, would afterwards carry these cases a few more kilometres down the road to the advanced clearing hospital at Lillers.

" Some of the wounds were dreadful. There were smashed jaw-bones, eyes shot away, and mouths battered to pulp. Here and there would be seen a leg minus a foot, or an arm minus the hand. A little to the right a massive guardsman with an arm hanging by about two inches of flesh. A medley of

*Although spared the later horrors of gas, the fumes from the German " lyddite " shells affected many men, and caused a number of casualties. A gas-alarm was given in the front-line, and the battalion was issued with a gauze pad, like a brassard, to tie across the mouth, but some used their " balaclava " helmets to keep the fumes out of their lungs.

gashes in heads, sides, backs, thighs, stomachs, and buttocks. Crushed feet, hands, arms, and legs. Huddled forms with twitching faces and trembling limbs, as if paralysed—the results of shell-shock. Many were dying, others were dead, and these were hurriedly carried to the rear of the building to await burial."*

* * * * *

The Battle of Festubert was over. The battalion had been spared the fate of those whose gallant conduct on the 24th had cost them so dearly, but it had suffered severely. It had rendered incalculable service, at first, by keeping lines of communication open and, later, by holding the line against counter-attacks, and it had learned lessons of inestimable value, fully appreciated when called upon shortly to pass through an even greater ordeal.

FIRST BATTALION COMPANY COMMANDERS AND WARRANT OFFICERS AT

THE BATTLE OF FESTUBERT—MAY, 1915

	Officer Commanding: Colonel Simpson, V.D. R.S.Maj. Clay	Second-in-Command: Major Mildren	Adjutant: Capt. W. W. Hughes R.Q.M.Sgt. Percival
A Co.	Capt. Booth (killed)	C.S.Maj. Yelf	C.Q.M.Sgt. Johnson
B Co.	Major Boothby (wounded)	C.S.Maj. Bailey	C.Q.M.Sgt. Kent
C Co.	Capt. Phillips (wounded)	C.S.Maj. Cannon	C.Q.M.Sgt. Diggins
D Co.	Capt. Cotton (killed)	C.S.Maj. Stenner	C.Q.M.Sgt. Sharpe (wounded)

Quartermaster: Lieut. Thomas

Machine-Guns: Capt. E. W. Hughes; Lieut. Lowy; Sgt. Cox; Cpl. Brennan; Cpl. Dennett

Signallers: Sgt. Houghton; Sgt. Montgomery; Cpl. Sharp

Stretcher-Bearers: Capt. Bate; Sgt. Collins; Sgt. Owers

Transport: Lieut. Neely; Sgt. Gibbons

Cooks: Sgt. Britten; Cpl. Fleming

*R. G. Emery.

Chapter 5

THE FORMATION OF THE SECOND BATTALION

A nation, when it embarks upon a war, must have two considerations of equal value prominently in mind; first, the effective employment of its military forces, and secondly, the maintenance of those forces as efficient fighting units. Of the two, perhaps, the second presents the greater problem.

When the Great War broke out in 1914, the transportation of the "Contemptible Little Army" to the Continent and its subsequent employment with the French Army was regarded as no mean achievement, but it soon became apparent that the country's more difficult task would be the maintenance of that army in the field. Two facts of prime importance immediately manifested themselves; the expenditure of ammunition reached alarming totals, and the wastage of man-power through casualties was on a scale never contemplated. Of volunteers to fill the gaps there was no lack. The *Sixth* had filled its ranks within a day or so of the declaration of War, and one more service battalion had thus been added to the strength of the British Army; but as yet no arrangements had been made to raise reinforcements which, ere long, the battalion would undoubtedly require. By the end of August, however, orders were issued for the formation of a second battalion for every Territorial infantry unit.

Major Stokes, who had remained at the battalion's drill-hall in Farringdon Road, when the *First* battalion marched away, was immediately overwhelmed with recruits, with the result that over 1,100 men were attested as fast as the necessary forms could be completed. Then, the *First* was instructed to dispatch four officers as a nucleus of the commissioned ranks, and Capts. Schwersee and Tucker, Lieut. Cooke, and Sec.-Lt. Sherrin* reported to Major Stokes on September 3rd, Capt. Tucker being appointed acting-Adjutant. During the ensuing weeks officers were gazetted to various ranks, but it was not until well into October that Col. Collinson, V.D., formerly C.O. of the 7th Bn., Middlesex Regt., was appointed to command the new unit.

Col. Collinson

Drilling and equipping the battalion proceeded as rapidly as possible, but the lack of facilities offered by London were so serious that a proposal made to the T.F. Association to rent Mount Felix, Walton-on-Thames, was agreed to, and thence toward the end of October the battalion marched. The change provided opportunities for training, but the cramped nature of the quarters

Walton-on-Thames

*Later, Colonel G. Tucker, Capt. Cooke, Capt. Sherrin.

will be realised when it is appreciated that 1,100 officers and men were accommodated in a single country house, even though it were a large one.

The 2nd/6th Bn., London Regt.'s stay here was short, however, for the brigade was ordered to concentrate in Sussex, and the battalion moved by train to Burgess Hill on November 18th. Here, in billets, N.C.O.'s and men received the utmost kindness from the householders who did everything possible to make them comfortable. Winter was approaching and no one relished the idea of living under canvas, and the temporary barracks being erected all over the country were as yet incomplete. *Burgess Hill*

Arms and equipment were still lacking, although both arrived during the winter, and in due course the organisation of the battalion into four companies was completed. Captain Tucker was appointed Adjutant, and after sundry changes, Capts. Sherrin, Hartley, Borthwick, and Browne,* were appointed to command A, B, C, and D Companies respectively. During the spring of 1915, other changes occurred through the formation of a *Third* or *Reserve* Battalion, and the creation of home-service units. To the latter were drafted all who were medically unfit for foreign service or unwilling to sign A.F. 624. During this period also, it was announced that the *Second* Battalion was destined for active service, and it became part of the 174th Inf. Bde., 58th Division, comprising the second-line units of the first twelve battalions of the London Regiment.

In April, 1915, the division was ordered into hutments at Crowborough, and a month later the 174th Infantry Brigade, comprising the 2nd/5th, 2nd/6th, 2nd/7th, and 2nd/8th Bns., London Regt., entrained for Norwich and took over the billets of a brigade of the 54th Division. Again the stay was short; one month later the brigade proceeded to Ipswich, where the Divisional Commander had at last been allowed to concentrate his division. By this time Capt. Collins had become Adjutant, and Capt. Tucker had been appointed Second-in-Command, and with Capt. Borthwick promoted to Field Rank. *Crowborough* *Ipswich*

No account of the early days of the *Second* is complete without a reference to the indefatigable R.S.Maj. Anderson, who, left behind on the mobilisation of the *First* as the member of the permanent staff detailed for duty at the depôt, worked unceasingly to assist in the organisation of the *Second*, and for two months never left 57a, Farringdon Road, by day or night, except when on parade.

Until the *Reserve* Battalion was in a position to supply drafts to the *First*, the *Second* was necessarily called upon to do so, and large drafts were

*Later, Major Borthwick, T.D., Major Browne, M.C.

sent overseas to join the *First,* in February and September, 1915, following the Battle of Loos. After that, it was announced that no further demands of Ipswich this nature would be made upon the *Second,* and that it was definitely intended that the 58th Division should proceed on active service as a unit. This intention of the Higher Command caused, without doubt, some tendency to misunderstandings. Officers and men fighting with the *First* in France could not understand why their depleted ranks were not filled up at once by those serving in the *Second,* and those in that battalion, already purged of all who were unwilling to volunteer for active service, keenly resented the imputation that they were shirking. From the Second-in-Command downwards, numerous applications for transfer were made, but with the exception of such drafts as were ordered, all applications were refused, for the very good reason, realised later, that the battalion had to be kept intact as an organised unit.

June, 1915, therefore, found the *Second* in billets at Ipswich. By this time complete equipment, including all transport horses and vehicles, had arrived, and the Divisional Commander was able to carry out more elaborate training. Exciting diversions were caused during this period by Zeppelin-raids, but many tedious hours were spent by junior officers picketing roads in order to stop motor-cars whose headlights were supposed to be guiding the raiders. Ipswich, however, owing to its situation in a hollow, and the strictness of its lighting regulations, escaped serious damage.

Chapter 6

LOOS

Meanwhile, the *First,* in France, after Festubert, remained in the battle area, at Noyelles and Vermelles (June 1st to 7th), and after relief by the 7th Bn., King's Liverpool Regiment, in reserve at Mazingarbe, providing working parties nightly at Grenay, where they remained until the 12th. The short stay in these places, although but a few miles from the line, was an excellent restorative after the previous strenuous month. The French civil population had not deserted their homes, and thus the amenities of shops and estaminets were available. It was even possible to obtain one-day-old copies of the " Daily Mail," and thus feel again a connecting link with the outside world. There was only one fly in this otherwise perfect tin of ointment, and that was the infrequency of pay-parades, which were held whenever circumstances permitted. The absence of ready money was not of great moment when the battalion was " in the line," but out on rest, or in reserve, as at Mazingarbe, there was little to do in spare time but to visit the shops and estaminets. Of course, much time was taken up in keeping clean, or to put it more bluntly, free from lice, and many hours were spent in running the seams of "greybacks," tunics, trousers, and underwear through the flame of a candle and listening to the crackle of exploding vermin and comparing it to a miniature bombardment. Exhilarating as was this activity, one tired of it in time, and diversion of a different kind was essential. That was the value of the estaminet; it made one forget the horror and the stupidity of the War. The light French beer never intoxicated or dulled the senses of anyone, but the comradeship of men caught in the net and under the shadow of death, enabled one to forget the filthiness, the tragedy, and the irksomeness of it all. But estaminet proprietors demanded payment for their wares.

Vermelles

Mazingarbe

Almost the first parade held out of the line was, therefore, the pay-parade, and officers would often ride twenty miles to draw five-franc notes for their men. Each usually received five francs, no matter the length of time that had elapsed since the last pay-day, and small as was the amount, it was looked for eagerly. The following is an account of a typical occasion:

" News quickly spread that someone had borrowed a horse to draw pay for the men. Francs were 28 to the £1, and after considerable trouble with the horse (the b——y thing won't go!) he returned at the gallop, hanging on to its neck, with the much-desired ' dough.'

" 'Five francs is the limit,' would shout the Company Quartermaster Sergeant, and then a man's name would be called, and strictly according to regulations, each would step smartly forward, salute the officer making the payment, step back, salute again, and retire in as orderly a manner as possible.

"Pay was distributed alphabetically. If the C.Q.M.Sgt. made a wrong cast-off, the last few would be unlucky."

* * * * *

Such a happy existence could not last long, and no one was surprised when orders were received to take over No. XI Sector of the line, then held by the 20th Bn., London Regt.

The relief was completed by 4.30 p.m. on June 12th, and the battalion found itself in an area which for the next three months was to remain familiar. The trenches now occupied, lay but a few miles south of the breastworks of *Loos* Givenchy, which the battalion had but recently vacated, but in totally different country. The ground was gently undulating, and forming part of the Lens coalfield, with its attendant slag heaps, factories, and rows of miner's dwellings, abounded in objects that had rapidly been converted into a connected series of fortifications, and the sub-soil of chalk made it possible to dig substantial trenches and sufficiently deep dug-outs. Where the trench-system ran close to houses, the cellars served the same purpose. The expenditure of ammunition had not reached the lavish scale that marked the fighting of the following year, but increasing damage by shell-fire was being done to the mining villages, machinery and plant. No. XI Sector was south of the Lens—Béthune Road, and faced the mining village of Loos, which lay to the east. It comprised a veritable net-work of trenches, many familiar names being given to them for distinguishing purposes, such as London Road, and Victoria Station. The German trenches were not more than five hundred yards away; and beyond them, two miles to the south-east, lay the mining centre, Lens, too valuable a prize to be lightly held or quickly surrendered by the German Army. After *Philosophe* four days in this sector, the battalion was withdrawn to Philosophe, a mining village which henceforth periodically provided billets for the battalion when in support.

A German attack from the direction of Loos had been expected on the night of June 16th-17th, and the battalion, which had been relieved and just settled into billets, had turned out and occupied the trenches near a slag heap *Fosse 7* to a pit known as Fosse 7. Now, German activity increased, and the village of Philosophe was shelled daily; and from June 20th (when the Second-in-Command, Major W. F. Mildren, was hit by shrapnel, but remained at duty) until 22nd, an intermittent bombardment was maintained. Much of the shelling seemed to be concentrated upon battalion headquarters, occupying a house in the village, and by 5.30 p.m. on the 21st, it was reduced to ruins. *Loos* Refuge for the time being was found in the cellars beneath the house, but these eventually had to be vacated. By great good fortune few casualties were sustained, but the officers' mess-cart was demolished by shell-fire, which, to add insult to injury, also destroyed the second-in-command's personal kit.

On June 22nd the battalion relieved the 8th Bn. in Sector XI, and remained in the line for a week, nightly patrolling no-man's-land, but happily suffering few casualties. When it was relieved by the 22nd Bn., it moved back into billets at Mazingarbe, and remained there, in support, until July 6th. Most of the remainder of that month was spent in that section of the front-line system known as Sector W.111, on the immediate right flank of the sector previously held. Here the enemy was far more active, and during this tour of duty, two riflemen were killed, and fifteen wounded.

In and out of the trenches, sometimes in support at Philosophe, and at other times at Mazingarbe—such was the life, with little variation, followed by the battalion; for supporting troops were called upon to form working parties at night, which more often than not brought them back into the front line from dusk to dawn. In the line itself, the troops were not idle, for continual improvements and repairs were necessary to the trenches. Where very muddy, bricks were laid in the bottoms of them, and wire defences were strengthened. Originally the trench-system had been dug by the French Army, which had built many well-constructed dug-outs, and some of them were lined with wood and papered; but on the whole, the trenches were anything but comfortable. However, some compensation was to be found when in support, for the villages of Mazingarbe and Philosophe had not yet been entirely deserted, although the inhabitants were daily leaving their houses as the latter became unfit, on account of shell-fire, for human habitation. Everything portable was, of course, carried away with them, but the fruit upon the bushes in the gardens remained for the lucky riflemen who happen first to chance upon it. The scene presented a strange contrast. The number of houses still standing was being rapidly reduced, but the birds continued to nest beneath the eaves; and miners remained in reduced numbers to descend the pits, whilst the very winding gear which lowered them stood in danger of demolition.

* * * * *

The 47th Division was withdrawn from the line at the beginning of August (1915), and the battalion, being relieved by the 13th Bn., Royal Scots, on the night of the 2nd/3rd, proceeded immediately to the corps reserve at Fouquereuil, where it remained for a fortnight. On the 10th, Lt.-Col. T. W. Simpson, who had taken the battalion abroad, gave up the command of it and returned to England. That day, in the morning, the battalion was inspected by the Brigade Commander, and all were complimented on their excellent conduct in the line. During the stay at Fouquereuil, the whole battalion was given a "refresher course," the fortnight's training being completed by a brigade route-march on August 16th.

Fouquereuil

Labourse

From Fouquereuil, the battalion moved to Labourse, a village lying a couple of miles to the north-west of Mazingarbe, where it remained for some nine days as supports for the Annequin Sector, nightly supplying working parties. Whilst at Labourse, Major W. F. Mildren, who since the return to England of Col. Simpson, had been commanding the battalion, was gazetted Lieut.-Colonel and appointed to the command. Major Mildren's promotion and appointment was well deserved, popular, and fortunate for the battalion, for not only had he long been recognised as an officer of outstanding merit, but with his intimate knowledge of the unit he was able to command it in a manner rarely equalled. He had joined the battalion shortly after the South African War, and ere long was commanding a company. In 1915 he had gone to France with the battalion, and in due course had been appointed Second-in-Command of it. His personal character was marked by a conscientiousness and devotion to duty clearly recognisable throughout his career; he was a realist, and could rapidly separate essentials from unessentials, was a stern disciplinarian, but compassionate, and was regardless of his own personal safety. A man of boundless energy, indefatigable, and tenacious, above all he was imperturbable in face of danger and privation alike.

Col. Mildren

Most of the second fortnight in August was spent by the battalion in Labourse, where a draft of one officer (Sec.-Lt. Noakes) and 100 other ranks from the 2nd/6th Bn., London Regt., joined it on the 22nd. From Labourse, too, representatives attended Divisional Sports, at Lapugnoy, held on the 25th, and carried away with them many prizes. As if to mark this success, the battalion, on the same day, moved closer to the line, into (north) Maroc, a mining village, east of Grenay, built on "garden-city" lines, from which on the following day it relieved the 7th Bn., K.O.S.B., in the W.3 Sector, due east of Maroc. It was whilst in this sector that the famous order was issued requiring all men with experience in the use of the sickle and the scythe to give their names in to company headquarters. Nearly half the battalion reported, everyone having visions of hay-making and harvest-fields, quiet lanes and estaminets well behind the line. But the agricultural workers were required

Maroc

not for rural France, but to cut down the long grass in no-man's-land to improve the field of fire. *Maroc*

The line was held on this occasion for seven days, during which covering parties in no-man's-land were supplied for working parties, digging trenches, extending saps. The tour of duty, although relatively quiet, was marked by a tragedy, happily less frequent than might reasonably have been expected. Sec.-Lt. Quilter, with Cpl. Ben Baker, and Rfm. Allen, returning from reconnoitring the ground between the British and German lines, was accidentally shot dead by a covering party belonging to a unit on the flank.

N. Maroc

William G. Newton. Redrawn March 1936

The 23rd Bn., on September 3rd, relieved the unit, which moved into billets at Les Brebis, thence on the following day it proceeded by motor-bus to Houchin, remaining there for a few days before returning to the now thoroughly accustomed task of trench digging in the equally well-known W.3 Sector. On September 11th, motor-buses carried the battalion, early in the morning, to Haillicourt, where it immediately became apparent to all that something out of the ordinary was in contemplation. Already there had been signs of some unusual activity, since three days previously orders had been received to remove the T and numerals from the metal shoulder badges. *Les Brebis* *Haillicourt*

Haillicourt Houchin

Now it was clear that a British attack was in preparation, for the ground between Haillicourt and Houchin had been planned to resemble a portion of the German trench-system, and over this ground the battalion was exercised on the 13th, in the presence of Brig.-Gen. Cuthbert, G.O.C. 140th Inf. Bde., and towards the end of the operation, in the presence also of Major-Gen. Barter, who commanded the 47th Division. As a result of suggestions made by the latter, the various objectives were changed and the operation repeated with modifications on the following day.

An attack on Loos was imminent. Preparations for an advance against Lens had been active for some weeks. Its object was two-fold; by drawing enemy reserves northwards, it would lighten the resistance to the French attack in Champagne, whilst the successful conclusion of the action would leave the rich Lens coalfield in the hands of the Allies. Accordingly, an attack immediately north of Lens had been decided upon, the intention being that seasoned troops should be used to overrun the enemy's defences, and that new troops, just from England, should be used to continue the advance, breach the line, and once more restore a condition of open warfare, when cavalry would be employed to exploit the initial success.

* * * * *

The plan of attack involved the use of troops of two Army Corps. The IV Corps, under Sir Henry Rawlinson, comprised the 47th Division, which, operating on the right, was to establish a defensive flank facing south, and the 15th (New Army) Scottish Division, and the 1st Division, which, operating in the centre and on the left, respectively, were to carry Loos, and the heights between Lens and Hulluch.

The I Corps (Lt.-Gen. Sir Hubert Gough), comprising the immortal 7th Division, and the 9th (New Army) Division, were to attack on the left of the 15th Division and link with the IV Corps at Hulluch, sweeping the enemy from the quarries, the Hohenzollen Redoubt and Fosse 8, at the same time threatening the La Bassée salient from the south. This, with the assaults of the 10th (French) Army on the right of the IV Corps would make a mighty gap in the German line in Artois, while General de Castlenau was hammering away with a similar object in the Champagne.

The 21st and 24th Divisions, both new to the field, with the encouraging support of the Guards Division, formed the XI Corps, and were stationed far enough from the battlefield to give the enemy little clue as to their ultimate destination. The 28th Division of the Second Army was also held in readiness to meet unexpected eventualities.

1

2

3

1. CHRISTMAS, 1914, AT WATFORD. D COMPANY AT DINNER IN "VI-COCOA" WORKS.
2. S.S. LA MARGUERITE WHICH BORE THE "FIRST" BATTALION FROM SOUTHAMPTON TO LE HAVRE.
3. OFFICERS OF THE "FIRST" BATTALION AT WATFORD, IN MARCH 1915.

Capt. GOORD.

Capt. POWELL.

Capt. LOWY.

Capt. BOOTH.
(Killed, Festubert)

Capt. COTTON.
(Killed, Festubert)

Capt. ASHBY.
(Killed, Loos)

Lieut. GREGORY.
(Killed, Festubert)

Lieut. CRAVEN.

Lieut. McLAUGHLIN.
(Killed, Festubert)

Plate 9

LIEUT.-GENERAL SIR CHARLES ST. L. BARTER,
K.C.B., K.C.M.G., C.V.O.,
G.O.C. 47th Division, 1914-1916.

Plate 10

THE BREAST-WORKS AT LE PLANTIN, NEAR FESTUBERT.
(Brig.-Gen. Cuthbert talking with Capt. Phillips.)

AFTER THE BATTLE OF FESTUBERT: THE BATTALION RESTING BEHIND THE LINE.

SIGNAL SECTION OF THE "FIRST" BATTALION.

SIGNAL SECTION OF THE "SECOND" BATTALION.

Plate 12

MAJOR-GENERAL G. J. CUTHBERT, C.B., C.M.G.
Commanding 140th Infantry Brigade, 1914-1916.

Plate 13

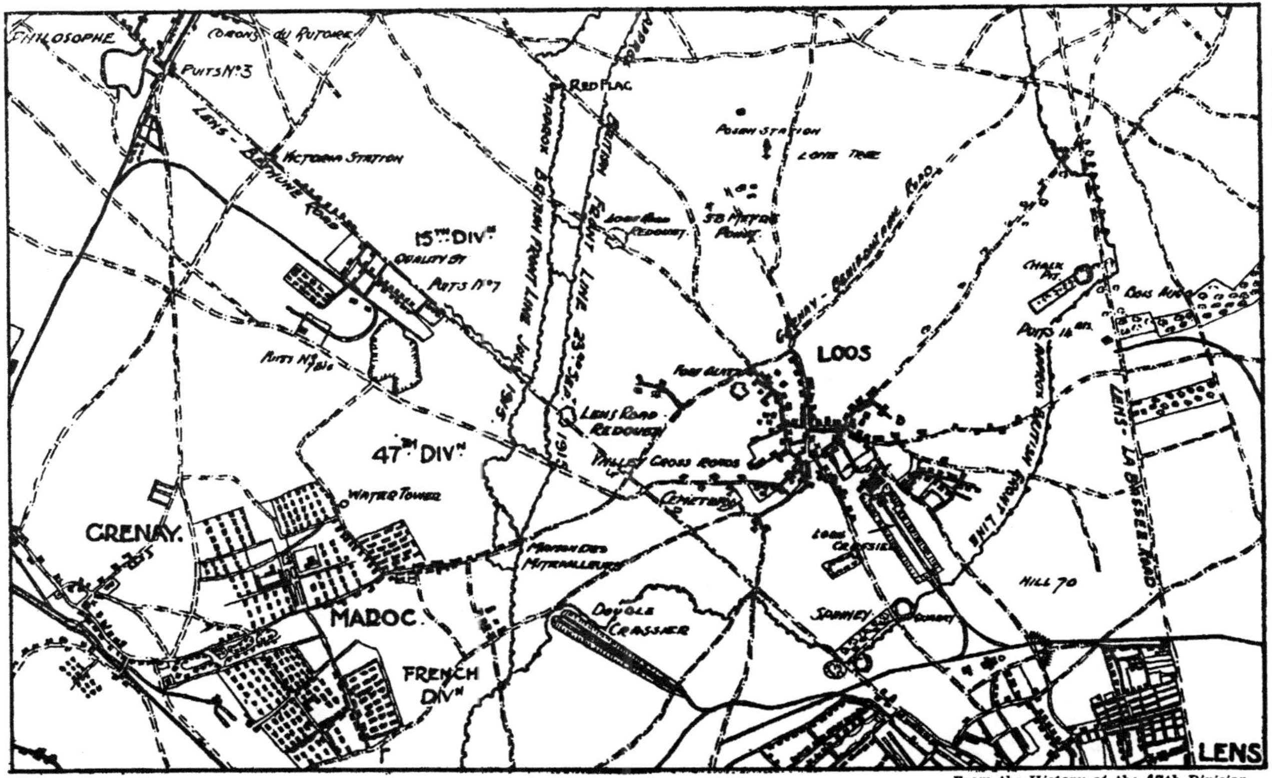

From the History of the 47th Division.

MAP 3.—THE BATTLE OF LOOS. THE MAP IS DRAWN ON A SCALE OF APPROXIMATELY ONE AND A HALF INCHES TO THE MILE.

To the *Sixth* and 7th Battalions, on the extreme right of the British Line, connecting with the French, fell the task of taking the enemy's trench system extending northwards from a large slag heap known as the Double Crassier, to the Lens-Béthune Road. The general direction for the advance was eastwards, on a frontage of about one mile, but the line to be consolidated was to face south-east to form the defensive flank. Captured German trenches were to be made defensible from this new direction, by " double-blocking " against the enemy where other portions of them were held by hostile forces. The operation was not an easy one, but the platoons, machine-gunners, and bombers, who then formed separate sections, had been well trained.

Double Crassier

As has already been mentioned, the *Sixth* previously practised the part they were to play in the attack. On September 15th, the exercise was again performed, on this occasion in the presence of General Rawlinson, commanding the IV Corps, who subsequently addressed the officers and emphasised the necessity of capturing and retaining all objectives assigned to them. That evening the battalion moved by motor-bus to Les Brebis, but machine-gunners and bombers remained at Haillicourt for training. Forty-eight hours were spent in digging and improving support and communication trenches, and on completion of the work the battalion moved to Houchin, where, on the same day (September 18th), a demonstration of a smoke barrage, memorable for its failure, was witnessed.

Les Brebis

Houchin

The brief stay at Houchin terminated on the 23rd, when the battalion moved to Noeux-les-Mines. Here, on the following morning, orders were received to concentrate at Les Brebis, where overcoats were to be stacked, tools drawn, and extra rations issued. The move commenced at 6.15 p.m., each platoon marching separately ; but progress was unexpectedly slow on account of obstruction by other units, and it was not until 9 p.m. that the leading company began to deposit its coats, and file along to pick up tools, sandbags, and rations. The battalion was clear of Les Brebis, however, shortly after 10 p.m., but it was 3.30 a.m. the following morning before all were in their appointed places, where a " cheese " ration was consumed and rum issued.

Noeux

Les Brebis

The Attack

Zero hour had been fixed for 5.30 a.m. Punctually gas and smoke were released, which had the immediate result of bringing an intense and accurate machine-gun, rifle, and artillery fire to bear on trenches occupied by the battalion. At 6.28 a.m. the gas was turned off, and precisely at 6.30 a.m. A Company climbed out of the trenches and advanced, to be followed by B Company, with C Company moving forward from the support trenches simultaneously. D Company followed C Company at a distance of about 200 yards.

The battalion was " over " and well on the move. The sight was magnificent ; the lines were absolutely steady, moving forward in quick time as if the battalion was performing a drill movement. Owing to the density of the smoke it was difficult at first to maintain correct direction, even such distinctive landmarks as the Double Crassier being almost obscured.

The Battle

The battlefield at this juncture must have offered a strange spectacle, as these weird-looking troops, who had donned the new gas-mask, moved forward. No face was visible. Tucked into the collar of the tunic each wore a thick flannel head-covering, and to add to this gruesome appearance the eyes were protected by large glass sections, giving the appearance of goggles. Thus attired, the waves of advancing infantry must have looked more like denizens of the underworld than British soldiers. A personal account follows :

" The extended first wave (A Company) under Capt. Ashby, encountered their first difficulties when passing over the rent-up ground caused by the British preliminary bombardment. Now the gunners were directing their fire ahead ; but shells were falling short. The enemy, too, were shelling the intervening ground, and as the Company Commander led his men towards the barbed-wire, he fell, and the battalion had lost its first officer in this engagement. As soon as the barrage on the German trenches lifted, rifle and machine-gun fire burst from the enemy lines, and with it came showers of stick-bombs.

" The men of A Company, with B Company following, were now close targets, as they hacked their way through the wire—in places destroyed, but elsewhere very much intact. Where the progress of the attackers was impeded on account of the wire, there the enemy wrought most havoc, and inflicted heavy losses. But on went A Company, staggering through the fire. Men were dropping on all sides. When Capt. Ashby had fallen, C.S.Maj. A. Yelf had gone forward and now he led the company towards the first German line. The air was still thick with gas and smoke, and splinters, shrapnel, shells, and bullets were flying everywhere, and the hand-to-hand fighting in and above the German trenches provided a terrifying spectacle."

Loos lay in a hollow, and the advance towards it was downhill ; there was practically no natural cover for the advancing troops, and enemy machine-guns wrought havoc in the ranks of A and B Companies. The German machine-gunners indeed worked their guns to the last minute, at least one being bayoneted at his gun ; but numbers of enemy infantry, although maintaining the fight until the leading company was upon them, retreated through their communication trench and across the open country.

The Battle It was then that an outstanding act of individual heroism on the part of a member of A Company took place. Rfm. F. Challoner, who had lost half his comrades in front of the barbed wire, charged along the communication trench after the fleeing enemy, and across the open stretch. He shot and bayoneted no less than nine of the enemy single-handed, and for this remarkable act was awarded the Distinguished Conduct Medal. C.S.Maj. A. Yelf received a similar decoration and the French Croix de Guerre for his prompt initiative on the death of his gallant officer, Capt. Ashby.

For the purpose of the action, some of the machine-guns and their teams, with those from other units in the brigade, had been grouped at Maroc, to give covering fire. Of those remaining with the battalion, one went over on the left flank with Lieut. R. Macdonald and Sgt. Brennan in charge, and another at the centre under Cpl. J. Dennett, who with his team succeeded in capturing a German machine-gun, afterwards using it with great effect upon the enemy. This gun was brought home to England and installed in the drill-hall at 57a, Farringdon Road, among other regimental souvenirs of the War. Sgt. J. Cox, who remained with the brigaded guns at Maroc, was awarded the D.C.M. for the part he had played in their effective use.

Bombers The bombers, under Lieut. Wylie and Sgt. Bidgood, were split up into sections of ten to a company, each man carrying ball and Batey bombs in horses' nosebags, and being armed with a terrifying cudgel in one hand and a dagger in the other. Before the battle, the bombers of the four battalions in the brigade had been formed into a single section for training purposes, and now, fighting with their respective units, their special training stood them in good stead. But their bombs were almost useless, many failing to explode, and for want of better ammunition they had to use the German stick-bomb, which, fortunately, lay in good numbers in the trenches captured from the enemy.

Both the first and second German lines were included in the battalion's objectives, and as a result of good timing and disciplined movement, not to mention personal bravery, all had been gained by 8 a.m. The 7th Bn., *Double Crassier* operating on the right, met with stiff resistance at the foot of the Double Crassier, Capt. Casson and his A Company of the " Shinies " being almost annihilated. With the aid of bombers from the 8th Bn., however, all the 7th Bn.'s objectives were held until reinforcements arrived. Three other battalions of the 47th Division, operating on the left of the *Sixth*, the 18th, 19th, and 20th Bns., were successful in their attacks, the 18th Bn. ultimately *Loos Cemetery* linking up with the *Sixth* near the Loos cemetery.

As soon as the positions were taken, the work of consolidation was commenced. The battalion signallers succeeded in laying telephone lines from Battalion Headquarters to them and thus communication was quickly established. Indeed, the work of this Section comes in for congratulation, particularly since throughout this and other engagements they discharged their duties without an officer to command them. Sgt. Houghton, Sgt. Montgomery, and Cpl. Sharp were the non-commissioned officers of it, and the section could not have had better leaders.

Signal Section

As the morning wore on a continual flow of refugees, prisoners, and walking-wounded straggled through to the nearby and inhabited villages of Les Brebis, Mazingarbe, and Noeux-les-Mines, where advanced hospitals had been established on the eve of the battle. The number of unwounded German officers and men taken prisoner approached two hundred, and the German officer commanding the enemy sector attacked by the *Sixth*, being wounded, surrendered.

Heavy rain, falling continuously during the afternoon, made the task of consolidating both strenuous and difficult, and equally handicapped the stretcher-bearers and parties sent out to collect the wounded and dead. Eventually the former were cleared to the hospitals at Noeux-les-Mines, Béthune, and Lillers; and to runners and members of headquarters fell the task of digging the final resting place at North Maroc for a hundred men of all ranks who had given their lives on that memorable morning. Rfm. Luce made a small wooden cross* to mark the burial place of the battalion's dead, and Rfm. Percy Garnsey painted an inscription upon it.

Apart from those who were identified and buried (many by the padre himself) in this cemetery, there were no fewer than eighty-seven officers and men who fell on the field of battle and who were interred near the Double Crassier, and after the War reinterred in the cemetery at North Maroc. A stone of granite, marking the position of the common grave, bears these words:

"In these Rows H, J, K, and L, are buried without individual identification eighty-seven officers and men of the 6th Battalion London Regiment, who fell on the 25th September, 1915, in the capture of Loos, and whose names are commemorated on the headstones placed round the walls."

Throughout September 26th, 27th, and 28th, fighting continued on the left of the battalion. Loos had been taken from the Germans, who continued to put up a stubborn resistance between that village and Lens, both on the rise

*This cross has since been installed in the Church of St. James, Croydon, by the padre, the Rev. A. E. Wilkinson, O.B.E., M.C., T.D., and annually a memorial service is held in that church and attended by members of the Old Comrades' Association.

known as Hill 70, and by the quarries. The Guards Division was ultimately called upon to crush the enemy resistance, and their attack on the morning of the 27th will be for ever remembered by those who witnessed their magnificent demonstration of disciplined movement.

So ended the Battle of Loos; and the commendation the battalion received was well merited. At Festubert it had shown its ability in defence; now, at Loos, it had proved its worth in offensive action.

FIRST BATTALION COMPANY COMMANDERS AND WARRANT OFFICERS AT

THE BATTLE OF LOOS—SEPTEMBER, 1915

	Officer Commanding:	Second-in-Command:	Adjutant:
	Colonel Mildren	Major Whitehead	Capt. W. W. Hughes
	R.S.Maj. Pettit		R.Q.M.Sgt. Percival
A Co.	Capt. Ashby (killed)	C.S.Maj. Yelf	C.Q.M.Sgt. Johnson
B Co.	Capt. Powell (wounded)	C.S.Maj. Bailey	C.Q.M.Sgt. Kent
C Co.	Capt. Goord	C.S.Maj. Cannon	C.Q.M.Sgt. Diggins
D Co.	Capt. Myer (wounded)	C.S.Maj. Stenner (wounded)	C.Q.M.Sgt. Cohen

Quartermaster: (Acting Quartermaster) Lieut. Neely
Machine-Guns: Lieut. R. Macdonald; Cpl. Dennett
Signallers: Sgt. Houghton; Sgt. Montgomery; Cpl. Sharp
Stretcher-Bearers: Capt. Bate; Sgt. Collins
Bombing Officer: Lieut. Wylie; Sgt. Bidgood (killed); Cpl. Newbury
Transport: Capt. Neely; Sgt. Gibbons
Cooks: Sgt. Britten; Cpl. Fleming; Cpl. H. Baldock

LOOS—SEPTEMBER, 1915.

Chapter 7

BROTHERS-IN-ARMS

Great as was the help rendered by the British Expeditionary Force to the allied cause in the critical years of 1914 and 1915, the brunt of the fighting, none the less, fell on the French Army. Little could be done without men—still less without adequate supplies of guns and ammunition. Until these deficiences could be made up, such a condition was bound to exist.

In a sense, Great Britain was unprepared for the War ; but no blame can be attached to her on that account. Before its outbreak, the duration of such a conflict had been freely spoken of as not more than six months. A long, drawn-out, bloody conflict, over a period of years had never been contemplated. Nor was it supposed that the size of the Expeditionary Force would not be adequate to reinforce the French. Indeed, French military opinion itself inclined to the view that a 100,000 men from Great Britain would be sufficient to turn the scales in favour of the Allies.

Slowly and painfully disillusionment was pressed aside, and Britain, already Mistress of the Seas, stoically set herself the task of building an army as great and powerful as any in the field, and supporting it with an arsenal capable, if need be, of equipping the world.

* * * * *

As has already been seen, the *First,* serving in France, at first received reinforcements from the *Second,* constituted at the end of August, 1914, which continued to supply them until the November of the following year. Before that time, however, the decision had been taken to convert the *Second* itself into a service battalion, and thus, in March, 1915, a *Third* battalion was raised to which later fell the task of filling the gaps caused by casualties in the battalion overseas. This new unit, at first commanded by Major Stokes, in its earliest days trained in Regent's Park. It was then about 1,300 strong, and was organised into two great companies and marched daily to the training area.

Regent's Park

The unsatisfactory nature of such training was felt by all ranks, whilst the lack of trained officers and N.C.O.'s made a hard task doubly difficult. Fortunately, some of the more recently joined officers had had previous military training, and in a remarkably short space of time something like order was created out of chaos. Under such conditions, and with little variations save the change of the training area to Victoria Park, the battalion continued its customary work when it marched, in August, to Hurst Park, and literally occupied the racecourse—stands, outbuildings, and stables being used as billets. The Royal Box itself was not excepted, being utilised right royally as the Sergeants' Mess.

The concentration at Hurst Park enabled immediate steps to be taken to reorganise the battalion and to systematise training ; but handicaps were great, for only fifty old .303 long Lee-Enfield rifles were possessed, and to fire the musketry course, parties had to travel all the way to Pirbright, and (later) to Rainham. Of the regulation infantryman's equipment there was virtually none, and khaki and service underclothing were almost unobtainable. At least one draft of reinforcements for the *First* was fitted out whilst waiting for the train on the platform of Esher Railway Station.

Early in September, Col. Simpson returned from France and took over the command of the *Third*. Indefatigable, tenacious, and imaginative, he was well fitted for an appointment which gave him an opportunity of displaying these powers to the full, and of initiating and elaborating new ideas and methods. The new officer commanding was fortunate, too, in the selection as Adjutant, of a remarkable man to whom more than anyone else, perhaps, belongs the credit of having built and maintained, in face of innumerable obstacles, a draft-finding unit of the highest efficiency and the finest *morale*. Captain E. Clay, M.B.E., a Regular soldier of many years' service in the K.R.R. Corps, first joined the battalion in 1906 as R.S.Maj., and after serving in France with the *First* in that rank, had returned to England in August, 1915, for the express purpose of taking up his new duties, his appointment being made early in October. Capt. Clay was a man of boundless energy, astute, determined, and reserved, highly efficient as a soldier and capable as an administrator. Above all, he was a disciplinarian, ready to lead or drive ; and if in consequence he was sometimes regarded as a machine, it was not because he lacked humanity, but because many years of soldiering had taught him to subordinate it, and because—though few suspected it at the time—he felt keenly the grave responsibilities of the task entrusted to him.

Hurst Park The *Third* remained at Hurst Park until the beginning of October, when it was decided that the unit should go into billets for the winter. The accommodation on the racecourse, adequate in summer, but regarded as unsuitable during inclement weather, suggested the change, whilst the fear of infection, ever present when large numbers of troops live on the same ground for any *Surbiton* length of time, supported it. Accordingly, the battalion moved into Surbiton, and there it stayed sufficiently long to make itself as heartily welcome as had been the *First* at Watford and the *Second* at Ipswich. Here it remained for two months, gathering strength in officers and men, and accounting for itself well, both in the direction of military efficiency and social activity. Here dances were given, dinners enjoyed, and a host of other events arranged which culminated in a public performance in the Assembly Rooms of "His Excellency the Governor," by the officers of the battalion, assisted by lady members of the local amateur dramatic society.

While much was gained by the transference from Hurst Park, much was lost. In Surbiton the battalion was scattered. Officers did not come to know their N.C.O.'s, nor the N.C.O.'s their men. A progressive programme of training was almost impossible, and what was worse, the corporate feeling, already discernible at Hurst Park, was beginning to be lost. Moreover, training at Surbiton was further handicapped by inadequate facilities, the nearest area being Esher Common. Whatever regret, therefore, may have been felt on leaving such pleasant surroundings, it was softened by the thought that in camp, at least, a three-mile march was not a necessary preliminary to a morning's drill. Hence, when the battalion moved early in January, 1916, to Fovant, on Salisbury Plain, it was with mixed feelings, which gave place gradually to a sense of gratitude for the change. *Surbiton*

On reaching Fovant, the battalion took over the northern section of some newly erected hutments, forming an immense camp on the southern slope of a hill facing the Compton Down, against the steep sides of which were built innumerable rifle, machine-gun, and bombing ranges. For the serious business of recruit-training no more suitable centre could be imagined. The camp was well arranged, and not overcrowded. It stood high, and was all but open on three sides. Above and behind it was a large parade ground, soon to be bounded on the north by a carefully planned bayonet-training course. The messing arrangements, both for officers and men, were excellent, and if the feet of a thousand men in winter churned the surface into liquid mud, and in summer raised clouds of choking dust, they carried the hearts of a thousand men who ere long had reached a state of military efficiency and developed a morale second to none in the British Army. *Fovant*

* * * * *

The 2nd/6th Bn., London Regt., remained in billets at Ipswich until October, 1915, when it moved about fourteen miles, to Stowmarket. Whilst at the latter place, rumours floated around to the effect that the battalion was shortly to be sent to Egypt, and various instructions from higher formations *Ipswich* *Stowmarket* proved that there was some justification for the rumours. Ultimately, nothing came of them, however, and a Kitchener Division went to Egypt, and the battalion moved only some twenty miles, to Sudbury, Suffolk. Arriving here at the beginning of January, it spent a somewhat independent existence in this old English market town, the original of Eatanswill, in "Pickwick Papers." Here, one night, an attack was made by a Zeppelin (March 31st), and somewhat serious casualties were sustained by the civilian population, but fortunately the battalion escaped with only one or two wounded. A noteworthy event was the award of the Military Medal to Sgt. May for gallantry in rescuing some members of his section from a burning house whilst bombs were still dropping. This, it is understood, was the first occasion such an award was made in inland parts of England.

Sudbury

On their return to Ipswich the battalion was accommodated in the artillery and old militia barracks until in July, 1916, it moved to Salisbury Plain. The period of East Coast defence work was over, and the final stages of training before proceeding overseas were begun. The entire 58th Division was now concentrated at or near Sutton Veny, near Warminster. Although a "London" Division, few other than the infantry were recruited from the Metropolis. Most of the gunners came from Glamorgan, the medical units from the Home Counties, and the squadron divisional cavalry from Hampshire. All these were first line units left behind when the major parts of their divisions went to India early in the War.

Sutton Veny

Salisbury Plain, in the summer, has many charming aspects, and the strenuous part of a soldier's training in peace-time is limited to the gentler months. The mud and rain of the autumn of 1916 made Salisbury Plain the reverse of comfortable, but for troops which had spent a long time in good billets, the Plain was undoubtedly the right place in which to harden them off a little before they were sent to France.

At last, after a period of waiting, irksome to those who wanted to pull their full weight in the struggle, final equipment was issued, and in the early hours of an intensely cold morning, the division marched quietly to Warminster Station, entrained for Southampton, and disembarked at Le Havre on the morning of January 25th, 1917.

* * * * *

The Battle of Loos definitely closed a chapter in the story of the *First* Battalion—as indeed it did of the War on the Western Front. Its partial success was sufficient to demonstrate that, without preponderance in man-power and gun-power, a break-through was unlikely ; that, with it, possible ;

and that in defence the new British Army could maintain its positions. Moreover, as a result of the action, it was clear that the German Army were beginning to recognise the ability and temper of the enlarged Expeditionary Force. The Battle of Loos was virtually over by September 28th, 1915, but desultory fighting continued, and minor operations were undertaken by both sides with a view to improving their respective positions. **Loos**

On September 30th, in bad weather, the battalion, then holding a sector, south-east of Loos, was relieved by a French unit, and withdrawing via the familiar Fosse 7, went into billets at Verquin, arriving on October 1st, to greet, later in the day, a draft of 144 " other ranks " supplied by the *Second*. Just prior to its withdrawal the battalion had had the good fortune of having posted to it as its adjutant an officer who was to become as highly popular as he was keenly efficient. Capt. H. L. Gilks, with many previous years' service in the " Artists," was at the time of his appointment, in France with the 1st Battalion of that unit. Amusingly enough, no one at Battalion Headquarters of the *Sixth* had been informed of his appointment, and his arrival was quite unexpected, and he was asked to remain at the transport lines until the necessary inquiries had been made. At Verquin, reorganisation was commenced immediately, and by the 6th of the month, when the battalion moved into billets at Noeux-les-Mines, the unit had virtually recovered from the effects of its recent fighting. Two days later the battalion was inspected by the IV Corps Commander, General Sir Henry Rawlinson ; and the inspection evidently gave sufficient indication of a good recovery, for within a few hours it received orders to move at once to Philosophe, to support units of the 1st Division, which had that day been heavily attacked. Here it remained for some days under the orders of the 2nd Infantry Brigade, which held a sector (O.B.1.) between Loos and Hulluch, lying to the north. Heavy shell-fire was encountered, and some casualties were suffered, R.S.Maj. Pettit being wounded. **Verquin** **Noeux**

With a view to improving the positions then held, the IV Corps attacked on October 13th, along a front between Hulluch and the Hohenzollern Redoubt, lying a mile to the north-west of it. The attack was unsuccessful, and after the operation, the 1st Division was withdrawn from the line and the 47th Division took over the sector. The trenches occupied were found not to be " traversed," and much hard work had, therefore, to be done by the battalion at night to improve defensive positions, and it found itself periodically occupying the front line opposite Hulluch until the end of the month. The monotonous round of defence and trench building which continued until the middle of November, was relieved once by a short rest at Mazingarbe, and **Hulluch** **Mazingarbe**

La Bussiere by an inspection on the 28th at La Bussiere by His Majesty the King, to which the battalion sent a party of two hundred officers and men to form a composite detachment representing the brigade, under the command of Lt.-Col. Mildren.

The physical conditions under which the battalion was fighting and labouring grew steadily worse. Rain fell in torrents during the first week of November, and the battalion, holding the line, deepening some communication trench, such as Tosh Alley, or carrying " duckboards " from " Victoria " to " Posen Station," found life almost unbearable, and the weather infinitely more unpleasant than the hostile shell-fire which was increasingly being directed against the new positions.

On November 1st, a further draft of two officers and one hundred and thirty " other-ranks " joined the battalion from the *Second*, and helped to relieve the strain which all by this time were feeling acutely ; but, as if annoyed at being thus cheated, the weather changed its tactics, and hard frosts added yet further discomforts, and perceptibly increased casualties. Liquid mud will localise the effect of high-explosive shells, whilst a frozen surface will increase their destructive power by delaying (ever so little) their burial in the ground. Thus the burst will take place nearer the surface, and its effectiveness as a death-dealer will be greater.

Tired and footsore, and covered with the mud of eighteen days of trench warfare, the battalion was withdrawn from the line on November 14th, and, Lillers resting for one night at Noeux-les-Mines, entrained in the morning for Lillers, where it arrived about 4 p.m., and soon settled into billets. Here for a blessed month it rested, trained and reorganised itself, receiving further reinforcements on the 23rd, Lewis-guns—for the first time—three days later, and competing and coming first in a brigade paper-chase on the 28th.

Divisional manœuvres took place during the opening three days of December, 1915, and in these General Sir H. Rawlinson took a keen, personal interest. Returning to Lillers upon their completion, the battalion continued to refit itself and undergo further training, especially in the handling of the Lewis-guns new weapons—the Lewis-guns—and of the rifle and hand-grenades.

On December 15, the battalion returned by rail to Noeux-les-Mines and, marching to Sailly Labourse, where it remained for three days, prepared itself for another tour of duty in the trenches. After such a long time out of the line—rare, indeed, for any unit—it was to be expected that some important sector would be chosen for the battalion to hold. Surprise was not great, therefore, when it found itself, on the 19th, in the trenches facing Cite St. Elie Hulluch (north of Hulluch), where much fighting had just taken place. The German artillery, still restless after the recent British assaults, became increasingly active and caused considerable damage to both front line and support trenches, all of which required constant attention by repair parties. On the 20th, a bombing assault by the 15th Bn., occupying the sector on the left, rapidly developed into a local action in which it became necessary for that battalion to attack briskly and in strength. Carrying parties, supplied by the *Sixth*, to maintain a continuous supply of ammunition and bombs, made a by no means negligible contribution to the success of the operation. **Hulluch**

As a consequence of this action and the threat of similar actions by the 1st Division, still farther to the north, the enemy became ever more restive, and liberally shelled the positions held by the *Sixth*. So heavy, indeed, was this retaliation, that the construction of arrowhead trenches at the ends of saps was decided upon; and although much of this work was undertaken by the Royal Engineers, covering and working parties had to be supplied by the battalion, to which also fell the wearying task of rebuilding traverses and keeping open such communication trenches as Fosse Way and Goeben Alley. When, therefore, the battalion was relieved by the 7th Bn. on the 23rd, the gaps in the ranks caused by casualties were noticeably wide.

Upon relief, supporting positions were occupied for the night, and on the morrow the battalion again entered the front line, now to occupy a sector lying a thousand yards to the south, opposite Hulluch; and in this new position it "stood to" at dawn the next morning to greet, not the enemy, but its first Christmas Day to be spent in France. Later during that day it was relieved and withdrawn into supporting positions; but the heavy work which immediately fell to it of carrying stores from Vermelles to the front line left little doubt that a more restful Christmas would have been experienced had the battalion remained in its front line positions.

The evening of Boxing Day, however, saw the end of this particular tour of duty and the battalion moved into billets in Sailly Labourse. Here it remained for three days, when, relieving the 20th Bn. on January 2nd, 1916, and marching in heavy rain through the thick mud, it returned to the Maroc Sector and took over the trenches from the French 132nd and 76th Regiments. Here, south of Loos, the battalion was on familiar ground, with the Double Crassier facing its positions, as carrying parties of rations and stores had shortly good cause to remember. The excellent field of fire which the slag heap provided gave every opportunity to the enemy of checking movement in the British lines. **Loos**

For six weeks the battalion remained in the area, energetically retaliating whenever enemy offensive action called for reply. A temporary lull had

Loos occurred upon the Western Front, and already the conception of a "war of attrition" was taking shape in the minds of the British military leaders. If a break-through were not feasible for one side or the other, perhaps the War would be won by that whose spirit of endurance would stand the greatest and the longest strain. Meanwhile, the British Army could do no more than inflict as severe casualties on the enemy as possible, and bear with fortitude whatever privations and sufferings the acceptance of such conditions might bring. In the discharge of such a task the qualities of perseverance and dogged determination were of greater value than in a war of movement where quickness of decision and resolute action are prime considerations. That nimble and witty Londoners should shoulder this responsibility with as much self-confidence as their northern and more stolid brothers was a matter of deep satisfaction. That the City of London Rifles was patiently waiting and conscientiously discharging all the duties entrusted to it during this phase of military operations was a source of constant pride for all who had its welfare at heart.

SLAG-HEAPS AT NOEUX-LES-MINES.

Chapter 8
VIMY RIDGE

In December, 1915, Sir Douglas Haig succeeded Sir John French in command of the British Army in France, and characteristically set himself the task of envisaging the whole of the immense task before the allied armies upon the Western Front. To him it seemed that the time was ripe for the formation of some generalised plan of operations upon a grand scale in which there would be concerted action, not only by the French and British Armies in France and Flanders, but by the Russians and Italians. A series of preliminary conversations with the French High Command led to a conference at Chantilly between the French and British staffs in February, 1916, at which the important decision was taken to commence the contemplated Allied offensive on July 1st.

A week later (February 21st) the German Army commenced its attack upon Verdun, the defence of which is rightly regarded as one of the epic achievements of the War. The defences had been as strongly built and as carefully planned as human foresight could make them, but with an enemy reckless in his expenditure of ammunition and ruthless in his sacrifice of men, it was not without heavy casualties to the French. The British Army, still undergoing the process of expansion, as new units crossed the Channel, was anxiously watching the struggle and ready to afford whatever assistance might be required of it. For many reasons, however, it was undesirable that individual units should be detached and sent south to reinforce the French, but when the suggestion was made by Joffre that British should take over a further section of the line and thus relieve the French divisions and enable him to reorganise his defences, no time was lost in acting upon it. Early in March, therefore, the First Army took over the French positions from South of Loos to Vimy Ridge, embracing the Angres and Souchez Sectors, and later in the month, the Third Army occupied those still farther to the south along the Arras Front. Finally, towards the end of March, the Fourth Army took over the ground held by French troops, from the Somme northwards, and thus at the end of approximately eighteen months warfare, the British line extended from Boesinghe, on the Belgian Coast, southwards to the Somme.

Extension of Front

The 1st/6th Bn., London Regt., was among the first of the British battalions to experience the results of the recent negotiations, and as if to signalise the one additional day of the year, it received orders on February *29th*

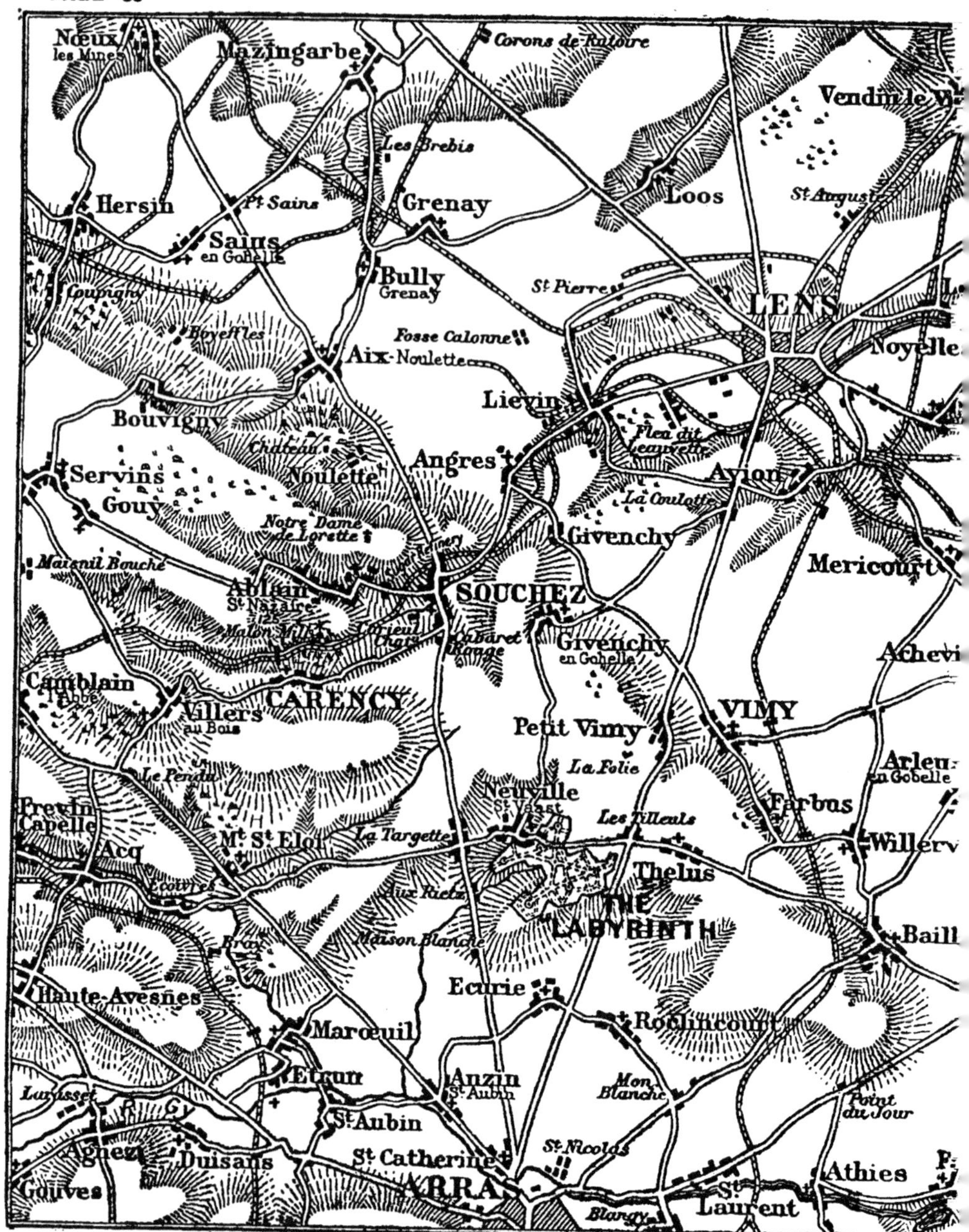

MAP 4.—VIMY RIDGE, LENS,

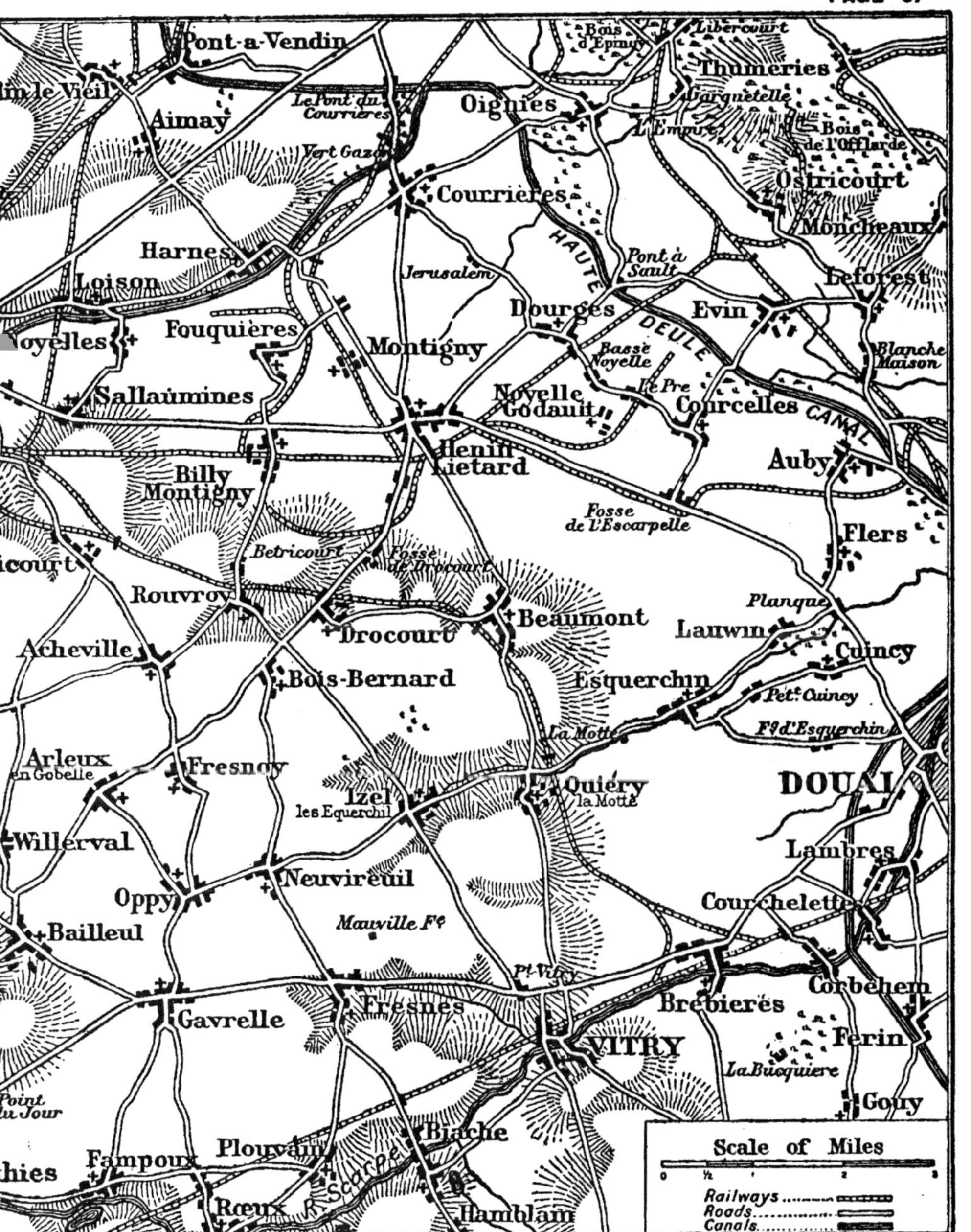

By courtesy of The Amalgamated Press, Ltd.

to move with other units of the 140th Infantry Brigade, and detachments of the 4th London Field Artillery, and No. 2 Company Divisional Train into the First Army training area, and to occupy billets at Equin-les-Mines, a village lying some nine miles west of the town of Lillers, where for the past two weeks the battalion had been engaged upon a reorganisation made necessary by the creation of Lewis-gun sections and a bombing platoon. The route chosen took the long column through the villages of St. Hilaire, Rely, La Tirmand, and Cuhen, all made picturesque through a heavy mantle of snow which had fallen a couple of days earlier. Here, and at Delette, where three days later the battalion was billeted, training consisted mainly of practising drill attacks, new formations being tried out, designed to give the Lewis-gun and bombing sections full scope.

Equin-les-Mines

The march to the new sector was continued on March 9th, the battalion arriving after a tiring day, at Amettes, where billets were found. The frozen condition of the roads made marching almost unbearable, and presented real difficulties to the horse transport. From Amettes it moved the following day to Divion, where it rested for a few brief days before continuing the march to the woods near Bouvigny. Here a large hutted camp, served by a light railway, had been constructed upon the crest of a ridge which ran north-westwards and south-eastwards, and in these pleasant rural surroundings, vastly different from the mining area of Lens, but a few miles away, the battalion saw the anniversary of its arrival in France.

Bouvigny

The high ground upon which the battalion now found itself, known as the Lorette spur, was part of a long ridge extending some thirteen miles south-eastwards from Bruay to a little north of Arras. When the Germans had retired in 1914, after the Battle of the Marne, they had allowed most of it to pass into the hands of the French, but they had retained that portion of it lying to the west of Vimy, which included Hill 140 and another rise known as Telegraph Station, and although little of the ground was of higher altitude than 140 feet (as the name of the hill suggests), yet the Germans from the Vimy Ridge had excellent observation in all directions. Indeed, Vimy Ridge was a natural defensive position ; to the south and west the ground sloped gently away from it, and to the north it was separated from the high ground running to Bruay by the Carency and Souchez Rivers. Thus, Vimy Ridge, dominating all the country to the south and west, and commanding the valleys which it overlooked, came to be regarded as almost impregnable, and in the popular imagination, the capture of it would be comparable to winning the War. Only in the extreme north-west corner had the French gained a lodgement on it, and here, separated from the Lorette spur by the two rivers, they maintained

Lorette Spur

precarious positions—precarious because nothing in the nature of an organised trench-system had been built, the front " line " being no more than a series of disconnected pits from which the foremost "poilus" had used their rifles and light machine-guns. Vimy Ridge, at its northern end, branched into two spurs, and it was on the westerly of the two that the French had gained a footing, and their patent insecurity must have been heightened by the thought that if they were driven from their posts there were the Carency and Souchez Rivers to be crossed before comparative safety could be reached. Fortunately, behind them lay the Lorette spur, which dominated even the formidable Vimy Ridge.

On March 20th, the battalion left the camp in the Bouvigny Woods for billets in Carency and Villers-au-Bois, and on the next day relieved the 19th Bn. in their positions on Vimy Ridge immediately east of Souchez. Here *Vimy Ridge* the forward platoons were scattered in isolated posts which could only be visited at night; but the British Staff, appreciating the tactical value of the positions, had given orders that they were to be maintained at all costs, and the first task, therefore, that fell to the battalion on reaching the line was the strengthening of these emplacements and the digging of new trenches. Snow was falling, but despite this everyone worked admirably, and by the end of their tenure of six days the battalion had made two continuous lines, both front and support.

So pleased was the Brigade Commander with the work done that immediately after a tour of inspection, he issued a special order expressing his appreciation of what had been accomplished. Evidently his approval was genuine, for although now in billets at Villers-au-Bois, the battalion was *Villers* required to furnish the Royal Engineers with large working-parties for work on the new defences being constructed under their supervision. On April 7th, the battalion returned to the line, this time holding a sector on the left of that previously held, and more to the north of the Ridge. Here the defences were even less organised; C Company, in the front line, occupied isolated posts, originally built by the French, which were described unofficially as the " Grouse-butts," and in support were B Company in the " Quarries," and D Company in dug-outs. A Company, more fortunately, remained in cellars at Ablain St. Nazaire. It was in this sector that troops belonging to a Saxon *Ablain St. Nazaire* Division had, during the previous Christmas, attempted to fraternise with the French, perhaps with the deliberate intention of masking the tunnelling then being done by the Germans—tunnelling which developed later into mining. That there had been fraternisation was clear enough. On one occasion Capt. Gilks was making a tour of the front-line trenches, when he came upon a German soldier who had crossed no-man's-land with the apparent intention of exchanging something for jam and tobacco. Capt. Gilks took him prisoner and handed him over to R.S.Maj. Bailey, who installed him for the night in a dug-out in which Sgt. Dommitt was at the time asleep. When the latter awoke he was more than a little surprised to see a German soldier by his side.

Vimy Ridge During the first tour of duty on the Ridge, the enemy had not been abnormally active, but as April wore on, shelling intensified, and casualties were more numerous on this account and from rifle-grenades. The battalion was relieved by the 22nd Bn. on the 13th, and the next day marched to Fresnicourt, where a brief rest was to be the reward for many strenuous days and nights spent in manning the line, strengthening and extending it; and here a weary but well-satisfied battalion read with considerable satisfaction a special order commending it for its work, issued by the Divisional Commander, who thus added his own appreciation to that already expressed by the Brigadier:

"The G.O.C. Division desires that his appreciation of the services rendered by his battalion in the centre and left sub-sections of the Carency Section in strengthening and improving the trenches be conveyed to all ranks."

Bouvigny The battalion returned to the hutments in the Bouvigny Woods on April 20th, and was here for a few days discussing a recent boxing tournament held in very wet weather, and enjoying the joke of no less than eighty-six men of D Company being isolated as a result of an outbreak of German measles.

Four days later it moved into supporting positions with two companies at *Carency* Carency, and two companies and Battalion Headquarters at Villers, and here, next day, heard the news that two great mines had been exploded by the enemy beneath the trenches occupied by units of the 25th Division, on the right. Mining operations had been going on for weeks in this area, and since similar activity was expected in the sector held by the 19th Bn., C Company, *Villers* then at Villers, was ordered, on the 26th, to move into the trenches as supports for that unit. No sooner had the platoons reached their positions, than the mine was exploded, the full force of it being immediately beneath the centre company of the 19th Bn., demolishing the front line trenches, making a crater forty feet across, and generally creating a state of chaos in the immediate vicinity. This was followed by a heavy artillery bombardment.

Meanwhile the remaining three companies of the *Sixth*, which had orders to relieve the 19th Bn. that night in the sector astride the Rabineau*

*Spelt also Robineau.

communication trench, had been " standing-to " since 9.30 that morning, and when the relief commenced they found everything disorganised. The guides lost their way, and it was not until the early hours of the morning of the 27th that the companies were in position. The order of battle was : left, C Company, Capt. Maynard ; centre, B Company, Capt. W. W. Hughes ; right, A Company, Major Elphinstone ; support, D Company, Capt. Neely. message of " relief-complete " to O.C. 6th Bn., from O.C. B Company reads :

Vimy Ridge

" The relief was completed by B Company at 2.15 a.m., and was carried out very badly by the 19th. The guides did not know their way ; very little work had been done, and they gave me no information and handed over no trench stores aaa I have only one platoon in the front line, the other three being in immediate support ; some progress was made with the trench surrounding the near edge of the crater aaa The enemy shelled our lines very heavily between 3 a.m. and 3.30 a.m., and we suffered three casualties, two killed and one wounded aaa I shall require ten boxes of bombs—we used four boxes this morning—and ten boxes of S.A.A., there being no S.A.A. store here, also 500 sandbags aaa Can a party be sent to remove the two bodies to-night, please aaa "*

A later message from the same company to the C.O. the same day reads:

" The enemy have detected our efforts to restore our sap in the centre of the crater, and are placing rifle-grenades there aaa Should be glad if rifle-grenades could be sent up, I have only one stand I can use aaa. Please ask A Company to work to their left round the crater, as my men will be working to establish the trench on the near side of the crater aaa Am supplying carrying party of ten men to R.E. Mining Company aaa "

To which a reply came from the C.O. :

" Please state how many boxes S.A.A. you have in your line aaa Have sent ten boxes each to left centre and right aaa Urgent aaa "

This was followed by another message from the C.O. :

" Is there an advanced German post on top of the New Crater aaa If so, can it see into Zouave Valley aaa "

*This and the following messages have been included in full to illustrate the kind of correspondence which passed between Battalion and Company Headquarters by day and night. The narrative is mainly by Col. W. W. Hughes. In the description of later engagements, only the most important messages have been included.

To which the Company Commander replied:

"Have detected no movement on the enemy's side of the crater aaa They appear to have three snipers' posts in their own front line, which is close up to the lips of the crater on their side aaa These posts could not possibly command the Zouave Valley aaa 3.10 p.m."

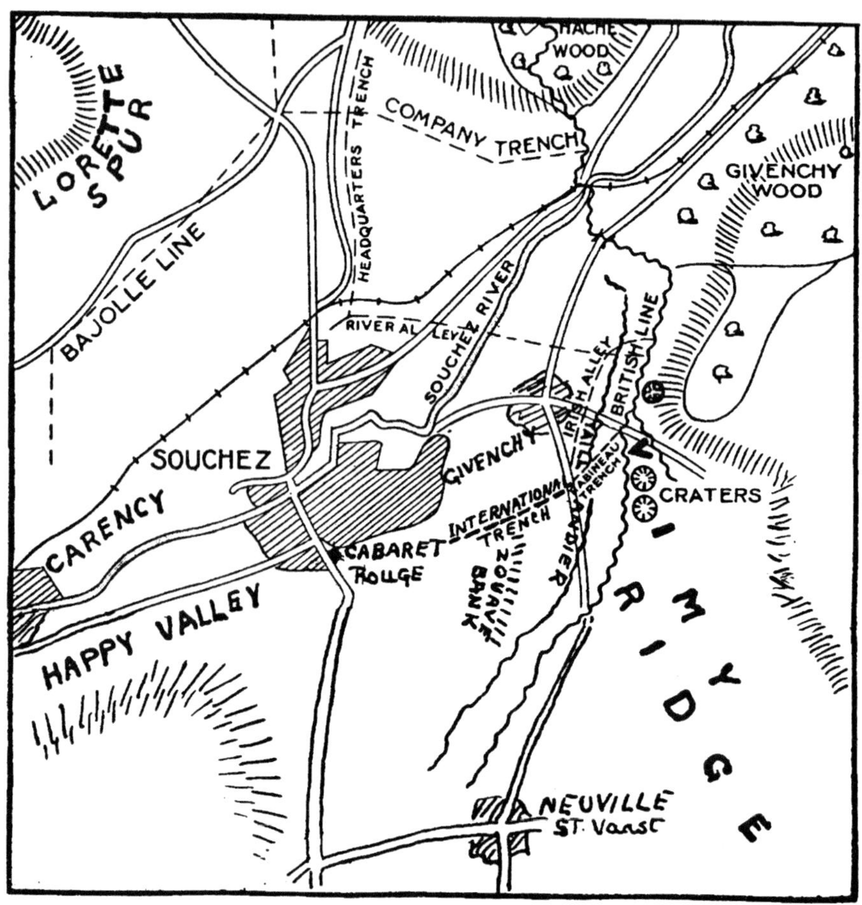

MAP 5.—SKETCH-MAP TO SHOW POSITIONS OF RABINEAU AND OTHER TRENCHES.
The scale is approximately one inch to one mile.

This was followed by a further message from the Company Commander: *Vimy Ridge*

" There was a considerable amount of work done on our trench surrounding the near edge of the crater aaa This position is under fire and controlled by the enemy's rifle-grenades and trench-mortars with rifle and machine-gun fire aaa The enemy displayed considerable activity between 3 a.m. and 3.45 a.m. this morning, covering our front and support lines with rifle-grenades, trench-mortars, and shells of light and heavy calibre. Our bombers, anticipating an enemy's advance on the crater, retaliated effectively with bombs on the far side of the crater aaa Three Germans were observed working on their side of the crater about 3.30 a.m. and returning to their front line trench aaa Throughout the day the situation was generally quiet, our trench-mortars fired during the afternoon and the enemy retaliated, particularly between 6 p.m. and 7 p.m, their fire with trench-mortars being very effective on the Rabineau Trench, and ours made no reply aaa 8 p.m."

The situation at this time was looking so dangerous that Lt.-Col. Mildren deemed it advisable to form a battalion reserve section of bombers, composed of the best bombers serving with the companies. A, B, and C Companies supplied three men each, and D Company, one man and L.-Cpl. Marrett. The command of the new section was given to Sec.-Lt. Keller.

The message to companies ordering the formation of the new bombing section was immediately followed by another from the officer commanding, which read: " Is Taillandier Trench wired ?" ; to which the officer commanding Centre Company replied: " Taillandier Trench, which is part of my support line, is wired, but owing to heavy artillery fire of yesterday and to-day the wire is badly damaged, although even now it would form a serviceable obstacle."

The morning of the 28th was fairly quiet, but a good deal of artillery activity developed during the day, and the final report of the 28th, timed 8.10 p.m., reads as follows:

" The enemy was fairly quiet throughout the night. During the day there was slight artillery activity which did no damage to our lines aaa At 7.45 p.m. the report of a mine on our far right was heard, and great activity by artillery and trench-mortars following this is still in progress, and the amount of damage done cannot be ascertained aaa The work of digging round the crater on my front was continued throughout the night and communication was practically established aaa The Taillandier Trench was repaired,

Vimy Ridge deepened, and fire-steps were begun aaa Very good progress was made by the wiring party in front of the Taillandier Trench aaa "

During the night of the 28th-29th, all the front line companies worked incessantly to repair and consolidate their trenches. Every man realised that good cover was essential, and that every minute mattered. Men never worked like it ; but this activity attracted the attention of the enemy, and they made a determined effort to stop it, which is shown by the following message from O.C. Centre Company to Battalion Headquarters :

" The enemy attempted to throw bombs into our front line at intervals during the night, but all were short, and our bombers retaliated from the sap aaa Few trench-mortars have been fired by the enemy aaa At present all quiet aaa. 3.21 a.m."

It was now generally known that the enemy was mining fiercely all along the Vimy Ridge, but the difficulty was to locate his mine heads, so that they might be destroyed. The tunnelling companies of the Royal Engineers were well aware of the fact that the enemy had gained a substantial lead in the matter of mining, and they also knew that counter-mining was the only effective reply, but in this respect the all-important element of time was well against them. They decided, therefore, to fire what they called " Camouflets "— small charges inserted in a single shaft directed at those of the enemy's galleries which were suspected as being tamped and ready for firing. These " camouflets " were intended to spring the enemy's mines, but it was not intended that the discharge should be followed by organised attacks on the craters so formed.

Several enemy mines were suspected astride the Rabineau Trench, and it was therefore decided to fire a " camouflet " to destroy the shafts to them, and thus destroy the enemy's work before it was completed. The operation was successful, and a crater, sixty feet wide, appeared in front of C Company between two saps known respectively as B 7 and B 8. The explosion was followed by considerable rifle and machine-gun fire, but the enemy was not aggressive, and being unprepared for such premature action, made no effort to occupy the crater. Hostile shell fire increased, however, and it became apparent that more batteries were being brought into the area. In point of fact, the charge was not intended to break the surface, but all were warned that if it did so, they were to be prepared to open fire and to capture the near lip. This was the message dispatched by O.C. Centre Company to the officer commanding :

"Our camouflet was fired at 4.30 a.m.; the explosion was fairly heavy, and a fair-sized mound has been formed in front of C Company's lines, blocking the trench on their right for approximately fifteen yards, and interrupting the communication with their front two platoons temporarily aaa My front and support lines and communications are intact aaa I opened rifle and machine-gun fire, and the enemy retaliated aaa Our trench-mortars fired, but some shots were short aaa The enemy's heavy and field guns retaliated for ten minutes chiefly in search of our mortars aaa At 5.10 a.m. the enemy's trench-mortars became active, and are still firing aaa 5.21 a.m."

A further report during the course of the morning stated that:

"All is quiet in B Company's lines." This applied also to the front line companies generally. During the day, the enemy became much more active with his artillery, trench-mortars and rifle-grenades; their fire was directed chiefly on our front and support lines, and we replied with trench-mortars and rifle-grenades. Work was pushed forward steadily on our trenches, a new trench was dug round the big crater, and Taillandier Trench transformed into a fire trench all along the line, good progress being made notwithstanding the damage that was repeatedly done by the enemy's mortars. Sounds of tapping were heard several times during that day near Sap 6, which indicated further mining activity, and O.C. Centre Company, in conjunction with O.C.'s A and C Companies, decided to request that the Royal Engineers might be asked to investigate.

This is the report of O.C. Centre Company on the morning of the 30th:

"There was considerable activity by the enemy with their artillery, trench-mortars, and rifle-grenades between 8 p.m. and 9 p.m. the previous evening" (i.e. 29th), "but otherwise there was no fire except rifle and machine-gun fire during the night aaa To-day the trench-mortars and rifle-grenades have again been active aaa The rebuilding of the front line was continued, the trench round the crater being deepened and a sap has also been made up to the lip of the crater and commands the interior of it aaa Barbed wire on iron uprights and interwoven with French wire has been placed all along the edge of the crater in front of our sap aaa Taillandier Trench is being built and made into a support trench and fire-stepped, and the wire in front was also strengthened aaa Rabineau Trench between the support and front line was built up in places."

During the whole of the afternoon of the 30th the enemy kept up a continuous bombardment with guns and heavy and light trench-mortars,

Vimy Ridge directing this fire mainly against reserve and communication trenches; and as if to presage the approach of a catastrophe, a German aeroplane flew over the line.

Evidence of further mining became more pronounced. Everything pointed to the fact that this concerted activity meant an attack. The Engineers replied that they would investigate the mining activity at 7 p.m. The men in the front and support lines endured hell throughout the day, the enemy's heavy mortars being particularly terrifying; four, five, and six of them could frequently be seen in the sky simultaneously. The Stokes-mortars replied, but the "heavies" were short of ammunition. The men replied with rifle-grenades, and succeeded in landing them repeatedly in the enemy's trenches, which gave them considerable satisfaction, and helped to maintain their full fighting spirit, so much so, that they were openly declaring that they wished the enemy would attack. Every bayonet was fixed and ready.

The storm broke at 6.45 p.m. when the enemy fired two large mines under the centre Company, demolishing the whole of the front line and all the occupants, with the exception of Lieut. Rose-Innes and three riflemen. Rabineau Trench, between the front and support line, was completely demolished. The explosions were instantly followed by intense artillery fire of all calibre and machine-gun fire from the Pimple, a small but prominent mound at the extreme north of the Ridge. Now, the enemy could be seen standing shoulder to shoulder in their trenches obviously ready for the assault, but the garrison manned their fire-steps and opened rapid-fire on the enemy's trenches with such good effect that the Germans were unable to advance.

The Vickers machine-gun, at the junction of Rabineau Trench and the support line, did admirable work until all the gunners except one were put out of action. Undaunted, he continued to fire to the end, whilst C.S.Maj. Jones and wounded men of B Company filled belts for him. During this active defence, casualties were numerous (the "Investigating-Officer" of the Royal Engineers was killed) and a gap in the line occurred between A and B Companies. Shortly after, a report was received that Germans had been seen in a sap which ran around the old crater to the right of B Company; but if any were there they failed to advance and were either killed or wounded.

The enemy artillery continued to fire for nearly two hours, and their concentration of communication trenches was particularly heavy. All telephone wires were cut; but Rfm. Murphy volunteered to take a message to Battalion Headquarters, asking for the assistance of D Company; and although he was never expected to reach his destination, he not only did so but returned, and collapsed through sheer exhaustion. For his gallantry he was subsequently awarded a Military Medal. The report from O.C. B. Company at the time gives an indication of the situation: *Vimy Ridge*

"The enemy blew up a very large mine (afterwards found to be two) from my sap 6, towards our small crater, at 6.45 p.m., and opened terrific fire on our lines aaa My front line is almost entirely blown in, and a large proportion of my support line aaa I opened fire and prevented them from advancing, and am holding the support line at present aaa I commandeered about twenty men from C Company and placed them practically in my old front line, and they are at work already aaa My men are also at work on my support line and at the top of Rabineau Trench aaa Have also asked for twelve men from D Company to help and perhaps it would be as well if a platoon of D Company was posted either on top or in the trench, such as it is, between me and Major Elphinstone aaa Should also like to have services of M.O. and any reserve stretcher-bearers available aaa My casualties amount to about thirty aaa" This number of casualties was, of course, in addition to the whole platoon killed in the front trench, with their Platoon Sergeant, Sgt. Jones.

Everybody fought splendidly. Some actually occupied holes between the four craters now formed and dug themselves in strongly. Others advanced up the lips of the craters and dug themselves in there, while others cut long strips of barbed wire and threw them into the craters to stop the enemy occupying them. Others, too, threw bombs into craters over the head of their comrades, to dislodge or kill the enemy in them, and to cover the men working on near side of the craters. This they continued to do under terrific fire. It seemed almost impossible that any man could live in such conditions, yet they did, and consolidated their positions. The enemy made a further attempt to advance towards the craters about 11 p.m., but they were repulsed immediately.

The work of digging near the lips of the craters continued through the night, in spite of interference from German patrols, so that by the morning all approaches had been barred, and the Rabineau, Taillandier, and Thiriet Trenches once more formed the main line of defence. During six terrible days the battalion had experienced a class of warfare that none wished to see again. Casualties had been heavy: twenty-four had been killed, seventeen were missing, and no less than fifty-one had been wounded; but when the battalion went out of the line on May 3rd, it was by no means down-hearted, and was conscious of having acquitted itself well. Many will remember the march-out, made notable by Sgt. Church, who played his violin as the troops trudged along, to keep up the spirits of the tried and tired men.

Vimy Ridge

The Divisional Commander, Maj.-Gen. Sir Charles Barter, proud of the gallant stand made by the *Sixth* against such tremendous odds, expressed his appreciation in a special order of the day, and offered his thanks personally to the Commanding Officer. On his way to Battalion Headquarters for that express purpose, he stopped as often as he saw men under his command and heartily congratulated them upon their achievement. Maj.-Gen. Barter was well-known by all ranks in the division. He had taken them to France in 1915, and thus was mainly responsible for their preparation for war, and he had already seen by their actions at Festubert and Loos that he commanded men of the finest calibre. The *esprit-de-corps* of the Army is made up of a number of loyalties—loyalty to the section, the platoon, the company, and the battalion; but another loyalty links all the units in a division—battalions, batteries, R. E. sections, signals, machine-guns, trench-mortars, transport, and R.A.M.C.—and sometimes makes it almost invincible. The 47th Division possessed such a spirit, and the high place in which it already stood in men's estimation, was largely due to General Barter.

After this active introduction to the Vimy area, the battalion settled down to three months of trench warfare, with little variation, save when it was out of the line resting, or when detachments were sent to the various schools of instruction which each army corps had established in order that the fullest use might be made of the new weapons now being placed in the hands of infantrymen. With the equipment of Lewis-guns, at first grouped as a section and operated under the direction of Battalion Headquarters, and of the Mills bomb and Hale's rifle-grenade, again used for the most part by riflemen forming a special bombing section, new aspects of offensive and defensive action emerged, and the tactical handling of the battalion and the companies required more detailed consideration.

Although equipped with novel weapons, existence was none the less stereotyped. Normally, the trenches were manned for about a week, during which time improvements to the system by digging, traversing, revetting, and wiring were continually made. Protection, both from attack and daily bombardment was essential, and trenches had to be capable not only of affording cover from shells and trench-mortars, but of providing the defenders with ample accommodation on the fire-steps, with commanding positions, and with ease of communication. When out of the line as brigade supports, such villages as Verdrel or Fresnicourt or the huts in the Bouvigny Woods supplied billets, from which working-parties, often to the number of two hundred N.C.O.'s and men, nightly returned to the trenches and continued for long hours the task of strengthening the positions on the Lorette Spur and adjacent sectors on Vimy Ridge.

The crater that had been formed by the mine explosion on April 26th had been named the "New Cut Crater," and that on April 30th, the "Mildren Crater," after the officer commanding the *Sixth,* and it was the trenches lying behind these two features that bore the brunt of hostile shell fire and thus required constant attention. Great activity continued on Vimy Ridge, where the R.E. mining companies steadily made up leeway with their counter-mining. Working-parties were in constant demand, even for battalions at rest, in particular to assist the tunnelling companies, and almost every night mines were fired, either by the British or the Germans. The latter had succeeded, early in the previous March, in driving the French out of their forward positions, and in gaining a certain amount of the observation they desired over the back areas, notably from the Pimple. This observation, however, did not enable them to control the Zouave Valley, or the areas behind Cabaret-Rouge, or the low ground around Carency. Still, they realised that an advance of comparatively a few yards would be sufficient to attain this end, and that the easiest and the least costly method of doing it was clearly to mine the British off the Ridge. This they had started to do in the most ruthless fashion, and the unexpected resistance of the *Sixth,* under such unequal conditions, may have had more far-reaching effects on the policy of the enemy than was generally thought at the time. The Germans had had the initiative in mining, yet, after six days of devastating explosions, they had not gained a yard of ground. Meanwhile, valuable time had been gained for our mining companies, who gradually gained the upper hand and enabled the British to meet the enemy on equal terms. In fact, nine British mines were successfully fired during the first fortnight in May. The enemy's intention, therefore, of blowing the British off the Ridge became impracticable, and some other plan of attack had to be devised. The historian of the German 86th Reserve Regiment, here holding the German line, confesses that they "could not fight the enemy any longer with his own weapons, for he was superior to us in men and material."

Mildren Crater

Behind the Vimy Ridge, on the Douai Plain, and amongst the scattered villages and slag heaps of the various coal-mines, and with the natural eastern slope of the Ridge, the enemy had the most magnificent cover for guns and for the assembling of attacking troops. He decided, therefore, that the only way to check the British was to assault the Ridge, and gain possession of their mineshafts. For this purpose, according to a summary of intelligence captured from the enemy, 650 pieces of heavy artillery were brought up and placed in what natural cover there was, rather than in fixed emplacements, in

Vimy Ridge

order to enable the attack to be made with a complete element of surprise. In this, it must be admitted, the enemy was completely successful.

The main direction of the German attack was directed against that part of the front overlooking the Zouave Valley, and astride of the International Communication Trench. This sector had been held by the 25th Division, who had not shown the same degree of aggressiveness and tenacity as their comrades of the 47th Division in the left sector. Consequently, when the 47th Division relieved the 25th Division in the right sector, they found themselves promptly up against a very aggressive and intensely active enemy. The 140th Inf. Bde. took over the front line on the night of May 20th-21st, with the following order of battle. Left front: 8th Bn., under Lt.-Col. Maxwell;* right front, 7th Bn.,

under Lt.-Col Green; the 6th Bn., under Major Whitehead,† being in immediate support, with A and B Companies, under the command of Capt. W. W. Hughes,‡ in the Zouave Valley; and C Company, Capt. Maynard, and D Company, Capt. Neely, at Cabaret-Rouge. The 15th Bn. was in support.

Other changes—not of man's doing—were noticeable. The weather, which since the beginning of the month had been wet and cold, turned fine, and the sun shone, and the trees and shrubs, slowly emerging from their winter sleep, awoke fully to greet the first promise of a hot summer.

*Later, Brig.-Gen. Sir A. Maxwell, C.B., C.M.G.
†Later, Colonel Whitehead.
‡Later, Colonel W. W. Hughes, D.S.O., M.C.

The morning of May 21st passed quietly, except for intermittent artillery fire, but, at 2 p.m., the most intensive fire, in which tear-gas shells were used, was directed on the whole of the British front and support lines, and on all the communication trenches in the Vimy Ridge, and a deadly barrage was placed on the Zouave Valley. This intensive bombardment—it is doubtful whether such intensive fire had ever before been directed at this particular part of the line—continued throughout the afternoon. During that time, the British infantry had little or no support from their own artillery, but this was afterwards explained as being due to the respective divisional artillery brigades being still in the process of changing over.

Zouave Valley

As the day advanced, the intensity of the bombardment increased, and during the late afternoon, it was ascertained that the whole of the British front and support lines were practically obliterated, and that very nearly all their defenders had been killed or wounded. The enemy were also aware of this, and when they had definitely decided that the infantry garrison were in no condition to put up an effective resistance, they made their assault at 7.45 p.m. Outnumbering the few remaining defenders, they swept over the front and support lines, practically without opposition, and in some instances, almost to the bank of the Zouave Valley. In fact, what remained of the 7th Bn., on the right, actually began to dig themselves in on the " bank " just above their own Battalion Headquarters. The position on the left was very uncertain. No one could get into touch with the 8th Bn., and their fate appeared to be sealed, although the ground they held afforded somewhat better means of resistance.

In the meantime, the two companies of the *Sixth*, in immediate support in the Zouave Valley, were terribly bombarded. Most of the shelters and dug-outs occupied by them were penetrated, several being directly hit, and there were a good many casualties. " All communications are broken," was the report from Cpl. Sharp, who had been out and found the wires broken, and thus, Major Whitehead, temporarily commanding the battalion, had no information whatever as to the position of the two battalions on his immediate front. He ordered, however, the two companies of the *Sixth* in the Zouave Valley, under Capt. W. W. Hughes, to " stand to " at about 8 p.m., and to be prepared to make an immediate counter-attack.

For very nearly an hour, these two companies " stood to " under very severe artillery fire, in particular from the " heavy howitzers," which were mostly directed at the steep western slope of the Ridge, since no other guns could reach it. At 9 p.m. they were ordered to line the " bank " immediately above their shelters; this they did, and in it dug themselves rifle pits. At 9.30 p.m. they were told to be prepared to take part in an immediate counter-

Vimy Ridge attack in conjunction with the battalion on the left (8th Bn.), and collective troops on the right. At 9.45 p.m., Capt. Hughes was informed that a counter-attack, supported by artillery fire, would take place at 10 p.m., and that he was to advance as far as he could in the centre, and that communication should be established with the battalions on the flanks.

Shortly before 10 p.m., a feeble artillery bombardment opened. The two companies of the *Sixth* advanced with their bayonets fixed, and promptly came in contact with isolated parties of the enemy. They swept forward, and carried everything before them, driving the enemy back and establishing themselves in an old disused French trench, some two hundred and fifty yards east of the "bank." But the troops attacking on the left and right appeared to make no progress, and the *Sixth* was unable to make contact with them. Although entirely in the air, with both their flanks exposed, the *Sixth* held their ground, and about 11 p.m. their actual position was reported to Major Whitehead. This information was passed to Brigade and Divisional Headquarters, with the result that a second counter-attack was decided upon to establish contact with the two exposed companies of the *Sixth*, and to gain, if possible, the whole of the ground that had been lost. For this purpose the 15th Bn. was brought up to attack on the left front, held by the 8th Bn.; the *Sixth* were to attack in the centre, although they had received no reinforcements; and on the right the 1st Cheshires were to co-operate. The 7th Bn., holding the right front of the 140th Infantry Brigade, were considered too weak in numbers to take part in the assault, and were ordered to line the "bank," so as to be in a position to cover a retirement if the counter-attack failed.

Zero hour was fixed for 2 a.m. (22nd), and after a short artillery bombardment the two forward companies of the *Sixth* again advanced, and this time gained a farther hundred yards of ground in the face of terrific rifle and machine-gun fire, and obtained a footing in another old trench, which they consolidated.

The 15th Bn., on the left, also made a determined effort, but their leading company, on their right flank, under Capt. Farquar, who was later found to have been killed in the action, met with devastating fire and were promptly repulsed. On the right the 1st Cheshires also attacked gallantly, but like the 15th Bn., could make little or no progress.

Meanwhile the two companies of the *Sixth*, although they had suffered heavily in both attacks, maintained their new positions, and got into touch with the International Communication Trench on the left (without, however, establishing contact with the 15th Bn.), and extended to their right for some

Colonel C. B. BENSON, D.S.O. (and bar).
Commanding 2nd/6th and Amalgamated battalion, 1917—1919.

Colonel WHITEHEAD, D.S.O., (P.O. Rifles.)
Commanding 2nd/6th and Amalgamated battalion for short intervals in 1917 and 1918.

Colonel COLLINSON,
Commanding 2nd/6th, 1916—1917.

Colonel SIMPSON, V.D.,
Commanding 1st/6th, 1915.

Plate 14

COLONEL C. B. BENSON, D.S.O. (AND BAR).
Commanding 2nd/6th and Amalgamated battalion, 1917—1919.

COLONEL WHITEHEAD, D.S.O., (P.O. Rifles.)
Commanding 2nd/6th and Amalgamated battalion for short intervals in 1917 and 1918.

COLONEL COLLINSON,
Commanding 2nd/6th, 1916—1917.

COLONEL SIMPSON, V.D.,
Commanding 1st/6th, 1915.

Plate 14

hundreds of yards across the Ridge, but did not come into contact with any British troops in that direction. Shortly after 2.30 p.m., Capt. Hughes reported to Lt.-Col. Green (7th Bn.), and to Major Whitehead, asking that one of the supporting companies of the *Sixth* might be brought into the line, and that the 7th Bn. might be pushed forward on the right flank of the *Sixth* to establish contact with the Cheshires. The second request was out of the question, however, in view of the losses of the 7th Bn. had already sustained, but just before 5 a.m., D Company of the *Sixth*, under Capt. Neely, crossed the Zouave Valley and advanced up the slopes of the Ridge, to continue the right flank of the two forward companies. The fresh arrivals were met by Capt. Hughes, and with Capt. Neely, they proceeded to extend to their right and to form a defensive flank. In this operation they encountered enemy bombing parties, but D Company bombers came to the rescue, and soon the line along the whole of the right of the 140th Inf. Bde. front was firmly established. No further progress was made on the flanks, but the centre was stoutly maintained, despite the fact that the new positions proved to be most awkward for the defenders, and, it was hoped, for the attackers. By this time, however, the Divisional Artillery was practically in position, and thus the infantry had very much more support. In consequence, the enemy became uneasy about his positions on the flanks, and having attained his main objective, which was to get possession of the British mining-shafts, or else to destroy them, he gradually withdrew, under pressure, so as to straighten his line; and to conform to this movement the flanks of both sides of the *Sixth* were advanced so as to be in line of the positions held in the centre. *Vimy Ridge*

A further counter-attack was contemplated, and the 2nd Division moved up in fighting order, to relieve the 47th Division, on the night of May 22nd-23rd. The *Sixth* were relieved by the 17th Bn. Royal Fusiliers, who had orders to counter-attack as soon as in position or as soon as the relief was complete. It did not take place, however, but an attack was actually made on the evening of May 23rd by the 21st and 24th Bns., London Regt., which was only partially successful; and it is noteworthy that in the centre, the line, as established by the *Sixth*, thereafter remained the front line, and was, in fact, the actual line taken over again when the 47th Division, later on, relieved the 2nd Division, and was the line held by it until the following July (1916), when the 47th Division left the Corps.

On leaving the line, the Brigade rested for a couple of days at Camplain and then marched to Bruay, the route taking it through the Village of Rebreuve, where the Corps, Divisional, and Brigade Commanders watched it march past, depleted in numbers, but undaunted. Indeed, as a result of the *Bruay* fighting on Vimy Ridge, and the losses sustained during the two counter-attacks, the battalions were abnormally low in strength. At Bruay, however, whilst reorganisation was taking place, several drafts of reinforcements arrived from the *Reserve* Battalion of the *Sixth*, numbering in all fourteen officers and over one hundred non-commissioned officers and men.

Bruay

In peace, Londoners frequently make the journey to see their Lord Mayor, and rarely, if ever, is he called upon to go far to visit them, but on the day before the battalion left Bruay, a message was received to the effect that the Lord Mayor was in France and would shortly visit the unit. The battalion was thereupon assembled on the " alarm " parade ground—the small " square " of the town. The Lord Mayor, Sir Charles Wakefield (now Lord Wakefield*) was accompanied by Maj.-Gen. Barter, the Divisional Commander, and by Brig.-Gen. Cuthbert, commanding the 140th Inf. Bde., and after inspecting the battalion, Sir Charles complimented it on its smart bearing and its steadiness on parade, and said that the City of London was proud of all its battalions, and commented upon the unit's past good work at Festubert, Loos, and its more recent exploits on Vimy Ridge. After the inspection, when the battalion had ordered arms, there was an amusing scene between General Barter and Brig.-Gen. Cuthbert. The former inquired why the battalion had not fixed their bayonets, which brought short, sharp replies, something similar to machine-gun fire, from the Brigadier: " Rifle Regiment, sir! Rifle Regiment, sir! Rifle Regiment, sir!"

The Divisional Commander was an officer of the K.O.Y.L.I., so that his lapse was immediately forgiven, and the incident closed, much to the amusement of those within hearing.

The battalion derived much pleasure from their stay at Bruay, for it was the largest town they had visited since the days spent at Béthune, and it was untouched by enemy action, and therefore helped all ranks to forget the War, at any rate, for the time being. Whilst at Bruay, a presentation of medal ribbons to recent recipients was arranged, and at Calonne Ricourt, nearby, to which the whole battalion resorted, the G.O.C., First Army, himself handed ribbons of the Distinguished Conduct Medals to Cpls. Wyman and Hassocke, and to L.-Cpl. Jackson, and of the Military Medal to L.-Cpls. Mills and Huson, and to Rfm. Millett.† Not that these were the sole awards for gallantry and good work. A few days later the King's Birthday Honours List contained the names of Capt. E. W. Hughes, to whom had been awarded the Military Cross;

*Lord Wakefield has crowded his life with progressive work and philanthropy, and it is interesting to note that he is a governor of St. Bartholomew's Hospital, where a " Mildren " bed has been endowed and dedicated to the memory of the battalion's fallen.

†Later, Lieut. Millett.

R.S.Maj. Bailey, and C.S.Maj. Cox, the D.C.M.; and Sgts. Houghton, J. Thompson, and Thorpe Tracey, the M.M., and a week later were published the awards of the M.C. to C.S.Maj. Jones, and the M.M. to Rfm. Bullock and Males.

On June 12th the battalion moved back to the line, and next day took over No. 1 Section at Souchez, where the waterlogged condition of the trenches prevented anything in the nature of systematic work upon them, but compensation was found in the thought that underground noises could best be heard when the ground was sodden. Tapping and picking could distinctly be heard, conjuring up visions of energetic Germans tunnelling beneath the British trenches to blow them sky-high; but anxiety on this score was allayed by the R.E.'s themselves springing a mine in the vicinity, and thus destroying whatever cause for apprehension existed. The soft soil, too, enabled good progress to be made with the erection of wire entanglements, and belts were placed from the right of the line to the Souchez River, west to the railway, and again west to a sunken road. *Souchez*

To the *Sixth,* which conscientiously lived up to the exhortation to leave the trenches in a better condition than when entering them, it seemed that the battalion was moved to whatever sector required most work done on its defences. With few brief intervals it occupied successively that to the right, covering Ablain St. Nazaire, then slightly to the north, the Souchez No. 2 Sector, lying to the south-east of Noulette Wood, then south again, this time to the Berthonval area, and wherever it went, it dug, it sandbagged, and it wired. June and July, 1916, quickly passed with such frequent moves, and August had been reached ere a rest was ordered, and to gain it the battalion had to march for many days, in blazing heat, almost across the small-scale map, known to the officers as "Lens II," before finally the village of Millencourt, many miles from the front, was reached. *Millencourt*

In this chapter certain messages from a Company Commander to Battalion Headquarters have been included in full, since they may be regarded as typical of those that daily, almost hourly, passed from one to the other. Such messages would range from a description of fighting or an urgent request for stores or reinforcements, to some trivial matter like the formation of a concert party. Needless to say, no man's life was ever risked with the carrying of an unimportant message, but when wires were intact, they hummed with messages grave and gay. One, emanating from the 4th Army Headquarters, announced the issue of solidified alcohol, and transmitted through Corps, Division, Brigade, and Battalion Headquarters, eventually was transcribed by the Company Signallers. The news leaked out, and all who heard it had visions of sucking a kind of solid beer or spirit. Great was the disappointment on finding that the term " solidified alcohol " was an Army description for the new " Tommy-cooker " and its solid fuel!

FIRST BATTALION OFFICERS, WARRANT OFFICERS and SECTION COMMANDERS at

VIMY RIDGE—MAY, 1916

Officer Commanding:	Second-in-Command:	Adjutant:
Col. Mildren	Major Whitehead	Capt. Gilks
Acting Officer Commanding:	Acting Second-in-Command:	
Major Whitehead	Capt. W. W. Hughes	

R.S.Maj. Bailey			R.Q.M.Sgt. Percival
A Co.	Major Elphinstone	C.S.Maj. Smale	C.Q.M.Sgt. Johnson
B Co.	Capt. W. W. Hughes	C.S.Maj. Jones	C.Q.M.Sgt. Kent
C Co.	Capt. Maynard	C.S.Maj. Diggins (killed)	C.Q.M.Sgt. Weedon
D Co.	Capt. Neely	C.S.Maj. Rush (wounded)	C.Q.M.Sgt. Cohen

Quartermaster: Capt. Denton
Transport: Sec.-Lieut. Noakes; Sgt. Pritchard; Cpl. Pollard
Cooks: Sgt. Britten
Stretcher-Bearers: Capt. Snowden; Sgt. Wade
Signallers: Sgt. Houghton; Cpl. Sharp
Machine-Guns: C.S.Maj. Cox; Cpl. W. Hunt
Lewis Guns: Sgt. Drage
Bombers: Lieut. W. Wylie; Sgt. F. Cuss
Orderly Room: Sgt. Dommit; Cpl. Peebles

Chapter 9

RESERVES AT FOVANT

The *Reserve* Battalion soon found, at Fovant (1916), that whatever creature comforts had been lost by the removal from Surbiton, distinct advantages had been gained. Officers and men had joined the Army for the express purpose of taking an active part in the War, and here, upon the wide but not unlovely expanse of Salisbury Plain, unique opportunities presented themselves for learning the rudiments of military training, and of making firm and lasting friendships. Of necessity, the principal items in the programme of training were musketry, square and arms drill, and physical and bayonet training, and whilst specialisation in the direction of signalling, sniping, and bombing was not overlooked, force of circumstances determined that it should take second place. The *Reserve* Battalion was there to feed both the *First* Battalion in France, and the *Second* Battalion, should it be called upon to go shortly on active service. Time was a consideration of the utmost importance. If in the space of thirteen weeks, officers and men could be thoroughly instructed in the use of the rifle, and made to realise the importance of immediate obedience to commands, and raised to an A 1 standard of physical fitness, then the primary objects would be achieved. ***Fovant*** ***Training***

So far as the first of these was concerned, the battalion was fortunate in having with it an officer whose long service in the ranks and unceasing devotion to duty had marked him out as a born leader, and whose exceptional experience as a non-commissioned and warrant officer had proved him a clever instructor. C.S.Maj. A. T. Cannon,* then serving in France, was given a commission and sent to England to assist in the training of the recruits; here, as a second-lieutenant, he took over the duties of musketry officer, and with the assistance of C.S.Maj. R. Hadley, soon had in being an efficient school of musketry. With the aid of an able band of instructors, most of whom were selected from those invalided to England on account of wounds or sickness, a 90-hour course was evolved, which covered all the preliminaries, as well as firing on the range, and even included instruction in fire-discipline and the indication and recognition of targets. The ardent band of teachers worked from morning to night, and, overcoming such difficulties as primitive butts, succeeded in making many of the raw recruits into marksmen. Night-firing was included in the course. One night the Brigade Commander paid a surprise ***Musketry***

*Later, Colonel A. T. Cannon, O.B.E., T.D.

Fovant visit to the range; he was puzzled at finding apparently no one on the 200 yards firing point where the practice was to begin, and was astonished when he learnt that the "details" were but ten paces behind him, so absolute was their silence. The recruits in question were from among the first of those who joined the battalion under the Lord Derby's scheme of enlistment, and the incident speaks volumes for their keenness and the quality of their instruction—the more so when it is remembered that they had had but one lecture on the importance of silence during night-firing.

Lord Derby's Scheme

The new recruits—and they were reaching the battalion at the rate of a hundred or more a month—spent many hours upon the square doing squad, platoon, and company drill, and arms exercises. The considerable amount of time thus occupied was desirable from a military point of view. Still more was it necessary in view of the special nature of the drill that recruits of a rifle battalion were called upon to perform. To the recognised drill of *rifle* as distinct from *line* battalions, certain peculiarities, by no means unpleasing, had been added. Formations were not called to attention before movements were made. Each exercise was commenced from the "at ease" position, and upon the halt, that position was re-adopted. Once mastered, the drill was both smart and graceful, but it required time and patience to learn, and out of the difficulties which recruits experienced, grew a system of training finally adopted by the entire British Army. From time immemorial it had been the custom of drill sergeants to shout out, by numbers, the different motions through which a squad had to go to complete a movement. To enlist the co-operation of those forming a squad, they were ordered by the Adjutant, Capt. Clay, to say these numbers at first silently, and later, when the value of the method was proved, out aloud. So efficacious as an aid to rapid mastery of drill movements did this method become, that its adoption was soon general, and eventually Capt. Clay's innovation became a recognised method throughout the Army.

Drill

Modifications in methods of training were becoming general, and nowhere was this more apparent than in the physical drill classes, in which men spent at least an hour every day. Medical opinion was soon to influence the abandonment of the early morning physical drill, and it became embodied in the programme of training for the morning or afternoon. But the many exercises in the long introductory and general tables tended to become stereotyped, and mental activity—considered as an essential accompaniment to them—was often clearly lacking. Before long, quickening exercises, designed to appeal to the quickness of the brain, became an integral part of them and transformed a wearing hour of regular, strenuous movements into a series of scientifically

Physical Training

arranged games, designed to exercise in proper sequence all the muscles of the body. The physical training staff, under the direction of Sec.-Lt. E. Stokes, was not slow to adopt every new method, and under such instructors as Staff-Sgts. Claxton, Andrews, and Wood, many new recruits found a very pleasant way to a robust health they had never known before.

Bayonet Training

Here a word must be said about the thorough-going course of bayonet training, for which the same instructors were responsible. From small beginnings, in which recruits stood for what seemed hours going through the motions of " In ; Out ; Up ; On guard," there developed a system in which a sense of reality was always present and mere exercises were reduced to a minimum. With bayonet fixed to rifle, a couple of sections in extended-order would line a trench, and on the command to charge, would race across a piece of imitation no-man's-land, giving vent to the most blood-curdling yells, and on reaching the " enemy " trench, where dozens of sacks of straw lay in inviting positions, would leap into it and slaughter the dummies. This done, the advancing line would get out of the trench, and at the double, attack a second and a third row of sacks suspended in realistic fashion from cross-beams, parrying the " enemy's " rifles (represented by five-foot sticks thrust out of the sacks) and go on to deal more death to straw and canvas ; until, after a hundred yards of thrusting and jabbing, the victorious but exhausted line, now anything but straight, would arrive at its objective and be given a well-deserved " stand-easy." The humorous Punch artist, Bateman, immortalised this exercise for the Army in his cartoon, " The recruit who took to it kindly "; and it was astonishing how kindly recruits did take to it.

Field Work

As may be supposed, with so much to be learnt about drill, musketry, extended-order work, and the bayonet, there was precious little time left for field work. Officers and non-commissioned officers might occasionally be given lessons in map-reading and field-sketching, and in wet weather lectures on advance-guards and pickets would be delivered by senior officers, many of whom had served in the Boer War and had seen years of service. But the battalion rarely left camp for field operations or even for route-marches, although one, along a Roman road on the crest of Compton Down, will for long be remembered. On this occasion every rifleman had to cook his own food, and soon the hillside was dotted with little piles of sticks, very few of which remained alight for more than a minute or two. Happy was the rifleman who as a Boy Scout or a lad in the Church Brigade had learned to lay and light a fire and cook a simple dish, for he alone that day had dinner.

It must not be supposed, however, that with so much to be done, there was little time left for recreation. Indeed, the reverse was the case. All work

Sport and no play makes "Tommy," no less than Jack, a dull boy, and no one realised this more clearly than the Adjutant, who fostered every kind of recreational activity. Those who wished to do a cross-country run before breakfast were excused the early morning parade, and if a man showed special aptitude or exceptional keenness in any activity, arrangements could usually be made for him to give additional time to it. Thus a first-class boxing-team was got together, and a very good concert-party. D Company held the boxing enthusiasts, and the contests held on March 11th brought to light a good deal of latent talent, developed later to the full by Drummer A Wheeler (who started professional boxing at the age of sixteen). Of the songsters, Sgt. Etherington and Cpl. Holmes, in regular demand at canteen concerts, will always be remembered, not only for their voices, but for their striking personalities. Never were there more cheerful singers, and never were there more appreciative audiences. Nor did the *Reserve* Battalion lack its scribes and artists. Whilst at Fovant, six monthly issues of a battalion newspaper were published, at first under the editorship of Rfm. F. J. Nilen, and later under that of Sgt. W. P. Flanagan, and in its pages, packed with topical jokes and sly digs, all the chief events were recorded. "The *"Castironi-cal"* Castironical," as the paper was named, must be remembered as much for its excellent pen-and-ink drawings by Rfm. Louis Knight, and its cartoons by Rfm. Sydney Carter, as for its amusing articles; and if at times the victims of its barbs called loudly for its suppression, yet they had to admit its humour and its truthfulness.

The *Reserve* Battalion, at its height in the summer of 1916, was certainly a very fine unit, and this was due as much as anything to the new class of recruit finding its way into the ranks. At the outbreak of war, the first enlistments had naturally been the younger, and generally single, men; but by now, Lord Derby's scheme, under which men attested and were called-up for service strictly in rotation, was beginning to provide the Army with somewhat older men, most of whom were married. Instructors who had handled many a recruit, used to say that the Derby men were the best that had ever come before them, and prophesied that they would become the backbone of the new British Army. Crime—the military term for petty misdemeanor or serious offence—was practically unknown amongst them, and they discharged every duty with forethought and energy, as befitting men who before the War were already responsible citizens. During the sojourn at Fovant, which ended in October, 1916, the opportunity was taken to mark for all time a permanent record of the battalion's stay in Wiltshire, and to this end a score of returned *First* Battalion men, recovering from wounds and doing light duty with the

Reserve, rose in the early hours of the morning, and crawling crab-like up the steep side of the facing hill, removed the turf and cut a large Maltese Cross —the battalion's badge—into the chalk. The example once set, other units were not slow to follow it, and in a remarkably short space of time, the face of the hill was decorated with various white regimental badges. That of the 8th Battalion was built on such a scale as to dwarf the badge cut by the *Sixth;* but nothing daunted, the indefatigable band, led by Lieut. Ball and Sgt. Hall, renewed their labours, and this time outclassed in dimensions anything that had yet been attempted. Cut in mother-earth, this badge remains to-day a permanent record not only of the battalion's stay at Fovant, but of the men who built it—the " Hall's and Ball's Light Infantry."

Chapter 10

THE SOMME

Thus read the first of the principles of war:

" The ultimate military objective in war is the destruction of the enemy's forces on the battlefield, and this objective must always be held in view."

Chantilly Conference

The Battle of the Somme, commencing on July 1st, as had been agreed between the Allied Commanders, at Chantilly, earlier in the year, was undertaken with this object in view. True, there were additional weighty reasons in support of it: the pressure against the French at Verdun, which the Germans had been attacking since February 21st, 1916, showed no signs of slackening, and relief was essential; most of the British battle-line lay but fifty miles from the sea, and movement behind the line would become restricted if any considerable advance was made by the Germans in the north. On the other hand, an advance by the Allies would give more room in which to operate. For these and other reasons the Somme was selected as the area for battle; but its main purpose was the " destruction of the enemy's forces on the battlefield."*

Owing to the losses sustained by the French at Verdun, and to the delay in sending British troops overseas, the original plans for the operation had to be considerably modified, and in the opening assault, the number of British and French divisions was reduced to nineteen and five respectively, whilst the frontage of the attack, abreast the River Somme, was much shortened. The Allied plan of attack finally provided for a simultaneous assault by troops of both the British and French Armies on a twenty-three mile front, stretching from Faucoucourt in the south to Serre in the north. The River Somme roughly marked the dividing line between the two Armies, and, incidentally, marked also the differences in the nature of the problems those Armies had respectively to solve before and during their operations. So far as the French were concerned, their effort was restricted to a frontage of eight miles across the relatively flat " Santerre " (as the Plateau of Chaulnes is called), but for the British, whose front was nearly double that of the French, the military problem

*There is considerable difference of opinion as to whether this really was Haig's object. Some historians maintain that he hoped for and expected a break-through and the restoration of a war of movement, and that only when the German defence made this impossible, did he claim his intention to be the infliction of losses and moral defeat of the divisions opposed to him.

was far more difficult. Here the Germans had the advantage in defence of a series of ridges running from the River Somme in a north-westerly direction, and on these they had organised almost impregnable lines of defences. Both first and second lines consisted of deep trenches, the fronts of which were invariably defended by thick belts of barbed wire a hundred feet or more wide. Immense dug-outs cut deep into the chalk sub-soil sheltered their garrisons, and well-placed machine-guns commanded every line of approach to their positions. Not a quarry or a cellar existed in the locality but what it formed a part of the defence, and not a single yard of the German front was left unprotected. So much care and attention had been lavished by the enemy of these defences, that he regarded them as affording him absolute security, and in the opening phases of the battle could not believe that the British were making a real effort to capture them.

German Defences

The offensive opened at 7.30 a.m. on July 1st, after a last-minute postponement of forty-eight hours, and before the day was out the British casualties had mounted to the appalling total of sixty thousand. Wave after wave of attacking infantry, far too heavily loaded, would rise up out of their trenches to be mown down even before the enemy's wire was reached ; for, heavy as has been the British preliminary bombardment, it had virtually succeeded only in levelling the enemy front line and support trenches, and had done no damage to the German dug-outs, not even to the extent of demolishing entrances. As captured German officers subsequently explained, their garrisons had but to wait patiently until the bombardment ceased, emerge from their dug-outs, man the nearest shell-holes, and catch the advancing waves of British infantry, either in the open of no-man's-land, or struggling in bunches through the half-cut German wire. Sometimes the first waves over-ran large numbers of the German garrisons still in their dug-outs, and when these emerged they found excellent targets both in front and behind them. No less than nineteen divisions were engaged in the assault, but only in the south, where the XIII Corps linked with the French at Maricourt, was any considerable progress made, and here, before the close of the day, Montauban Ridge was stormed and taken. Some slight advance, too, had been made by the XV Corps, north of Fricourt, but elsewhere along the front the positions of the opposing armies were much as they had been in the morning, except that, in the case of the British, thousands of dead and dying lay helpless in no-man's-land ; and it must ever be remembered with gratitude that the Germans freely permitted the collection of wounded by British stretcher-bearers. Indeed, the German 2nd Guard Reserve Division actually hoisted a red-cross flag as a signal to the British opposite them that the work of mercy might go on unmolested.

Opening Assaults

So far as the French were concerned, their attack across the Santerre was wholly successful; so that with the advance of the XIII Corps to Montauban Ridge, a considerable salient had been made in the enemy's line. Haig, therefore, decided to concentrate his offensive where most had been gained, having regard to the fact that German reinforcements could not be expected for five or six days, and to exploit this initial success attacks were delivered on successive days against Fricourt, Bernafay, and Mametz Wood, which for days defied capture. Thus, by July 13th, the line ran from Ovillers, on the left, to Contalmaison, thence in front of the Mametz and Bernafay Woods, and on to Hardecourt, and southwards to the River Somme, and in places these new positions represented an advance of between two to three miles from the line held on July 1st. The advent of rain and consequent low visibility put a stop for the time being to operations upon a grand scale, and the remainder of July and August was spent in consolidating and improving the positions then held.

The *First,* it will be remembered, was in the Vimy area when the battle began. Its period of rest at Bruay had seemed all too short, and thereafter it returned many times to the Souchez sector to hold the line on the Ridge. About the middle of July, while in reserve at Fresnicourt, it had orders to prepare for a raid on the enemy's trenches, to take place on the 20th of that month, but events farther south evidently suggested a curtailment of such offensive action except when that was absolutely essential, in order to preserve as much man-power as possible for use on the Somme. The battalion performed one final tour of duty in the left sub-sector at Souchez, relieving the 8th Bn. on the night of the 21st, before it was withdrawn to take part in the battle; and whilst in the line the fact that it was to be so employed seems to have become common knowledge. Lieut. J. S. Macdonald, writing while in the line on the 24th to an officer in the *Reserve,* said: " At the moment we are at a place that " (*here follows many names*) " remember well. But shortly we are going back for a rest, although we are not due for it. You know what that means, or we do, anyway, and we expect after that to travel light and quickly. Then watch the papers."

Change of Front

The relief he foreshadowed took place on the day after he wrote his letter, and on the 26th the battalion commenced its march southwards. At Maisnil Bouche it met the 7th Bn.; at Estrée Cauchie the 8th Bn. joined the column; and a little later the 15th Bn., to complete the Brigade, duly took its place in the line of march. The whole column marched past, first, General Barter, at Cauchin-Legal; and then the Corps Commander, at Ranchicourt. Arriving at Divion at about 5.30 p.m., it rested the night in billets, and on the following day, in almost tropical heat, it continued its march, when billets at Valhuon were found. On the 30th the journey was continued to Croissette, and on August 1st to Noeux. Here it rested for a couple of days, and here distinguishing arm-ribbons were sewn to jackets, A Company having blue, B Company, green, C Company, red, and D Company, yellow. On the 4th and 5th the march was continued, an early start to avoid the heat of the day being made on both occasions, and Millencourt, near Abbeville, many miles from the front, which was to house the battalion for a fortnight, was reached well before noon. *Millencourt*

An officer who took part in this long trek writes: "All who are still living will have happy memories of these marches through the countryside of Picardy. Hills and valleys, orchards and fields, kind people and kind weather, made the soldier's life a joy after the mud and filth of the Vimy trenches. The first day's march was a bad show, for feet that had been for so long in trench mud and water needed hardening, and the heat in the middle of the day was more than unseasoned beings could stand; so that although the spirit of the troops was very high some few were compelled to fall out. However, suggestions put forward by South African campaigners were happily accepted by 'the powers that be' and after the first few days, marching commenced soon after dawn and was finished in time for midday dinners."

At Millencourt the battalion settled down to the serious work of preparing for the part it was to play in the Somme offensive, and daily attacks on flagged positions were vigorously made in company with other units of the Brigade. The War Diary records (evidently with delight) that during one early morning exercise, the practice-attack "proved too much for ordinary imagination, with the result that in the absence of clearly defined trenches and objects to mark their position, the first and second lines, led by the Adjutant, gallantly swept forward and took the support battalion's objective, much to the excitement of the Brigade Major, who galloped wildly about in all directions." Training, however, was not confined to attacking flagged positions; there was practice in marching on compass bearings, out-post schemes, and with a coming event casting its shadow before it, a practice-attack by the brigade on the Forest of Crecy.

On August 20th the battalion left Millencourt, and marching by day, rested successively at L'Etoile, Naours, Mirvaux, and Franvillers, which it reached on the 23rd. Here, it continued to train and practise attacks, while Divisional, Brigade, and Battalion staffs reconnoitred the route to Mametz and the area in which the 47th Division would be operating. Step by step the battalion had been making its way into the battle area of the Somme, where, *Franvillers* in time, every unit of the British Army was to lend its aid. Yet another move took it to Black Wood, near Albert, where it encamped, while a conference at Brigade Headquarters discussed a forthcoming battle in which all ranks by now knew the battalion would be engaged. While marching to Black Wood, the battalion had its first sight of the new armoured-land-ship, so soon to be known the world over as the "Tank." Ponderous, but evidently mobile, comic, but awe-inspiring, several of these queer craft passed them on the way. This new weapon of war had been designed and built in the greatest secrecy, and now, for the first time in history, its value as a weapon was to be tested in battle.

Black Wood

While the *Sixth* had been training at Millencourt and marching to the battle area, deeds of the greatest heroism were being performed by British and Dominion troops in an endeavour to make victory absolute. The merest glimpse of the possibility of restoring a war of movement had been seen on July 14th, when the German defence collapsed around Bazentin-le-Grand and Bazentin-le-Petit, and mounted cavalry had been employed by the British in the neighbourhood of High Wood lying beyond these twin villages for the first time since 1914; but already German reserves were arriving to close the breaches, and thereafter the British offensive had to adopt a different character, partly necessitated by the consumption at an alarming rate of reserve stocks of ammunition. So far as the British were concerned, the Battle of the Somme now assumed the nature of a war of attrition in which, important as the capture of positions might be, the main purpose was the destruction of the enemy's forces. To do this necessitated the keeping up of a relentless pressure against the Germans by means of repeated attacks; and statistics were subsequently to show that for every German soldier killed the British lost two. However, in pursuance of the decision to wear away the enemy's *morale* and inflict casualties upon him, bitter fighting continued. Ovillers passed into British hands by July 16th; Delville Wood, stormed by the South Africans on the previous day, finally passed into their possession five days later; Guillemont, Trones Wood, and Pozieres, were repeatedly attacked, the last-named by Anzacs, so that by the end of July an advance of a farther mile or two had been made in a north-easterly direction. During August operations became even more fragmentary, although losses in killed and wounded continued on an unprecedented scale; but with the opening of September came a change in the fortunes of the British and French Armies. On the 3rd of that month, a combined assault from Chily, in the south, to Hamel, in the north, was almost everywhere successful, and by the 10th, after another advance by the French, it seemed to the Allied commanders that a break-through in the

Progress of the Battle

direction of Peronne and Bapaume was at long last in sight. By now the British were well-established on the ridge running from Guillemont north-west to the River Ancre, and could overlook the enemy's ground for miles. Nonetheless, the obstacles in the way of a final thrust were very great. On the right there was the Village of Morval, with its command on the Combles Valley; in the centre there was High Wood and Flers; to the left of them was Courcelette, and on the extreme left the German highly-fortified first-line at Thiepval. All these, as well as French objectives, to the south, had to be taken before the British Fourth Army, specially reserved for the purpose, might break through on the front between Morval and Le Sers, and restore a condition of open-warfare.

The third phase in the Battle of the Somme was about to begin. All the lessons learnt by British troops in previous attacks were instilled into battalions —such as the *Sixth*—new to the area. Mopping-up had become an art. By the most painstaking co-ordination, the creeping barrage of the artillery had reached an unimaginable precision coupled with an astonishing accuracy, and by its aid, advancing infantry, keeping close—but not too close—could be directed to their objectives when landmarks were obscured or obliterated. Its intensity, too, by sending the enemy trench garrison to cover until the very last moment, generally enabled the attacking infantry to get close to their objectives before active opposition was encountered.

The plan of attack, in which three army corps were involved, gave to the 47th Division the task of clearing High Wood; taking a line of trenches lying *High Wood* beyond it known as the Starfish Line; taking a third objective on the right, known as the Flers Line; consolidating the whole so as to link up with New Zealand troops operating on the right; and forming a defensive left flank, which, at the end of the operation, was to become a temporary front line facing north. The operation was both complicated and difficult—complicated because it involved a final alteration in direction, difficult because its success depended upon first taking High Wood, already renowned for its resistance.

High Wood had been attacked two months earlier by the 7th Division, and cavalry had temporarily occupied it; but most of it remained in enemy hands, and two months of continuous fighting had so far failed to give any firmer footing in it. There it lay, with the front line running through it, a devastated rectangle, having its broadest side measuring a thousand yards, facing south-west, the direction from which the British must attack. Like a tightly fitting cork in a bottle, it could neither be drawn out nor pushed in. Piece by piece it had to be crumbled away, and by the time the 47th Division had completed the process, High Wood was unrecognisable as such.

In making his plans, the Divisional Commander entrusted the frontal *High Wood* attack upon High Wood to the 141st Brigade, and to the 140th Brigade the threefold task of taking the first, second, and third lines of trenches forming the enemy's defence system, lying to the right of, and beyond High Wood. Respectively, the three series of trench-systems were known as the Switch Line, the Starfish Line, and the Flers Line, the last taking its name from a village partly incorporated in it.

This advance was to be in a north-easterly direction, and the success of it would be dependent to a large extent upon the complete capture of the wood by the 141st Infantry Brigade. If that were to fail, the advancing brigade on the right would be exposed to a deadly enfilade fire from German machine-guns concealed along the eastern edge of it.

Plan of Battle The plans made by the 140th Infantry Brigade were drawn up so as to provide each of the four battalions forming it with a definite task. With the 7th Bn. on the right, and the 15th Bn. on the left, an assault was to be made upon the first objective, the Switch Line, and upon its capture the 7th Bn. was to link up with the New Zealand troops operating upon the right, while the 15th Bn. was to work along the eastern edge of High Wood, with the object of suppressing machine-gun fire directed from it. Following the first assault, the 8th Bn. was to continue the advance, passing over the new ground then held by the 7th and 15th Battalions, and to attack and take the Starfish Line. Finally, the operation was to be completed by an assault by the *Sixth* upon the third and farthest objective, the Flers Line, the advance to which would be over all the ground taken by the other three battalions.

Black Wood The *Sixth* paraded in Black Wood at 3.20 p.m. on September 14th, stored its packs and greatcoats, and moved towards Bazentin-le-Grand, negotiating on its way a capsized tank, thereby experiencing a first taste of disappointment in the new weapon, and eventually occupied some half-dug trenches between two communication lines known as Elgin and High Alleys. Here it waited until movement forward permitted a farther advance into the front line, named Worcester Trench, then manned by the 8th and 15th Bns. The march to the assembly positions seemed interminable, and many wondered whether they and everyone else would not be too tired to attack, but a few hours rest worked wonders, and in spite of heavy shelling and the realisation that soon they would be " over the top," most got some refreshing sleep.

The arrival in Worcester Trench at 6.30 a.m. coincided with zero hour, when the 7th Bn. was at the point of launching its attack. Once the seriousness of the British assault was realised, the German artillery put down a heavy

1

3

4

2

5

1. AND 2. TRENCHES NEAR MAROC, 1915.
3. HOUSES IN THE "GARDEN CITY," NORTH MAROC.
4. "MACHINE-GUN HOUSE"—A STRONG-POINT ON THE LENS-GRENAY ROAD.
5. NO-MAN'S-LAND LOOKING TOWARDS LOOS, AS SEEN FROM THE TRENCHES AT MAROC.

Photographs by courtesy of Col. M. J. Macdonald

Plate 16

By courtesy of F. Ryland

The stone erected by the Imperial War Graves Commission in the cemetery at Maroc, near Loos, to mark the common grave of some of the officers and men of the FIRST battalion who fell in the battle.

Plate 17

C COY. H.Q. ON THE LORETTE SPUR.

NOTRE DAME, ABLAIN-ST. NAZAIRE

SOUCHEZ : THE RAILWAY STATION.

Photographs by courtesy of Col. M. J. Macdonald

Plate 18

From the History of the 47th Division

THE "MILDREN" CRATER, VIMY RIDGE—1916.

Plate 19

barrage, and although Worcester Trench came in for its full share of the shelling, casualties sustained on this account were surprisingly light considering the number of men taking temporary shelter within it. Early in this phase of the battle, a tank, ostensibly assisting in the attack, managed to get stuck close to where some of the *Sixth* were taking cover, and in the noise and excitement of battle, for some inexplicable reason opened fire upon the unfortunate Londoners who happened to be near it. A heated altercation between an infuriated company officer and the tank commander immediately followed, as a consequence of which the humiliated and gawky piece of mechanism refused to take any further part in the day's operations, and remained sullenly where it lay, an excellent target, no doubt, for German gunners. Nor was this the only machine that broke down; of the thirty-two employed along the whole of the battle-front, many developed mechanical defects or were "ditched."

High Wood

Tanks

As has already been mentioned, zero hour was fixed for 6.30 a.m. and punctually to the second, the 7th Bn. assaulted and captured the Switch Line. Meanwhile, the *Sixth,* in its assembly positions, awaited the order to advance. An officer with them writes: "Our guns intensified their fire, until the roar and explosions of shells was almost more than human beings could stand. The Switch Line was about one hundred yards in front of the assembly positions, and soon prisoners, dazed with fright and concussion, came drifting back. The *Sixth* was now experiencing what is probably one of the greatest tests a soldier has to face—waiting. We had to wait an hour before 'going over,' and the enemy's retaliatory barrage was hitting the trenches with unpleasant frequency. It was a most unnerving experience; officers were wondering if they would be alive to lead their troops, and, if so, would there be any troops to lead, and men were wondering if they would be alive to attack, and, if so, would there be any officers left to lead them. It was a most interesting thing to note the different reactions of different temperaments—some were laughing and joking in rather high-pitched voices, others were white and tight-lipped, with flashing eyes and jerky movements, but all were keyed up for the great moment."

News soon reached the *Sixth* that the 7th Bn. had taken their objectives, and at 8.30 a.m., Company Commanders whispered a few words of encouragement to those about them and up and away went the first waves. The battalion had commenced its long advance to the brigade's final objectives.

The Attack Launched

The attack, on a frontage of about five hundred yards, was made in four waves, each composed of one platoon from each of the four companies, and the order of battle was: C Company on the right, linking with New Zealand troops, B Company, D Company, and A Company, on the left, linking with

G

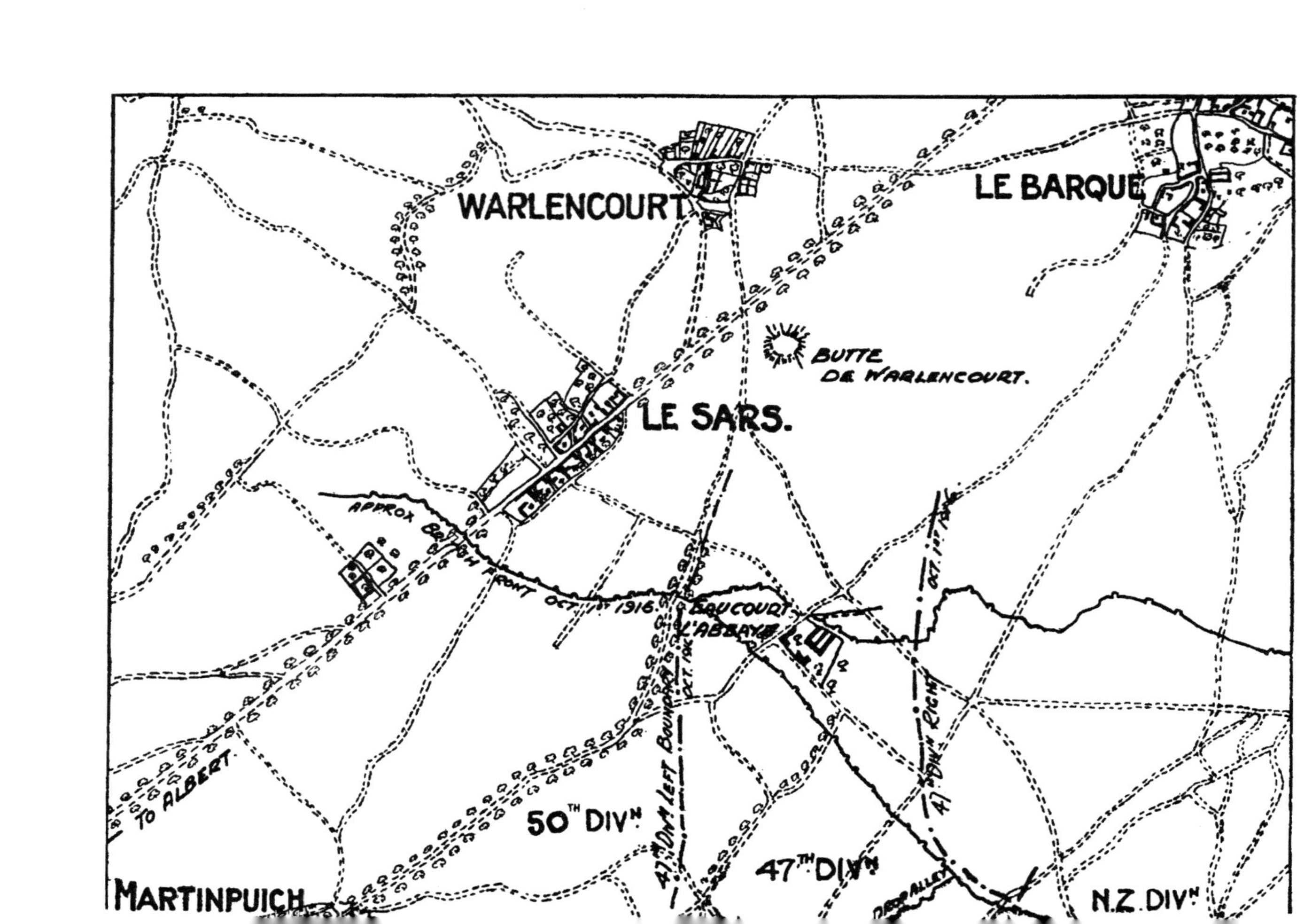

WARLENCOURT
LE BARQUE
BUTTE
DE WARLENCOURT.
LE SARS.
APPROX BRITISH FRONT OCT 1st 1916.
EAUCOURT
L'ABBAYE
OCT 1st 1916
47th DIVn LEFT BOUNDARY
OCT 1st 1916
47th DIVn RIGHT
TO ALBERT
50th DIVn
47th DIVn
MARTINPUICH
N.Z. DIVn

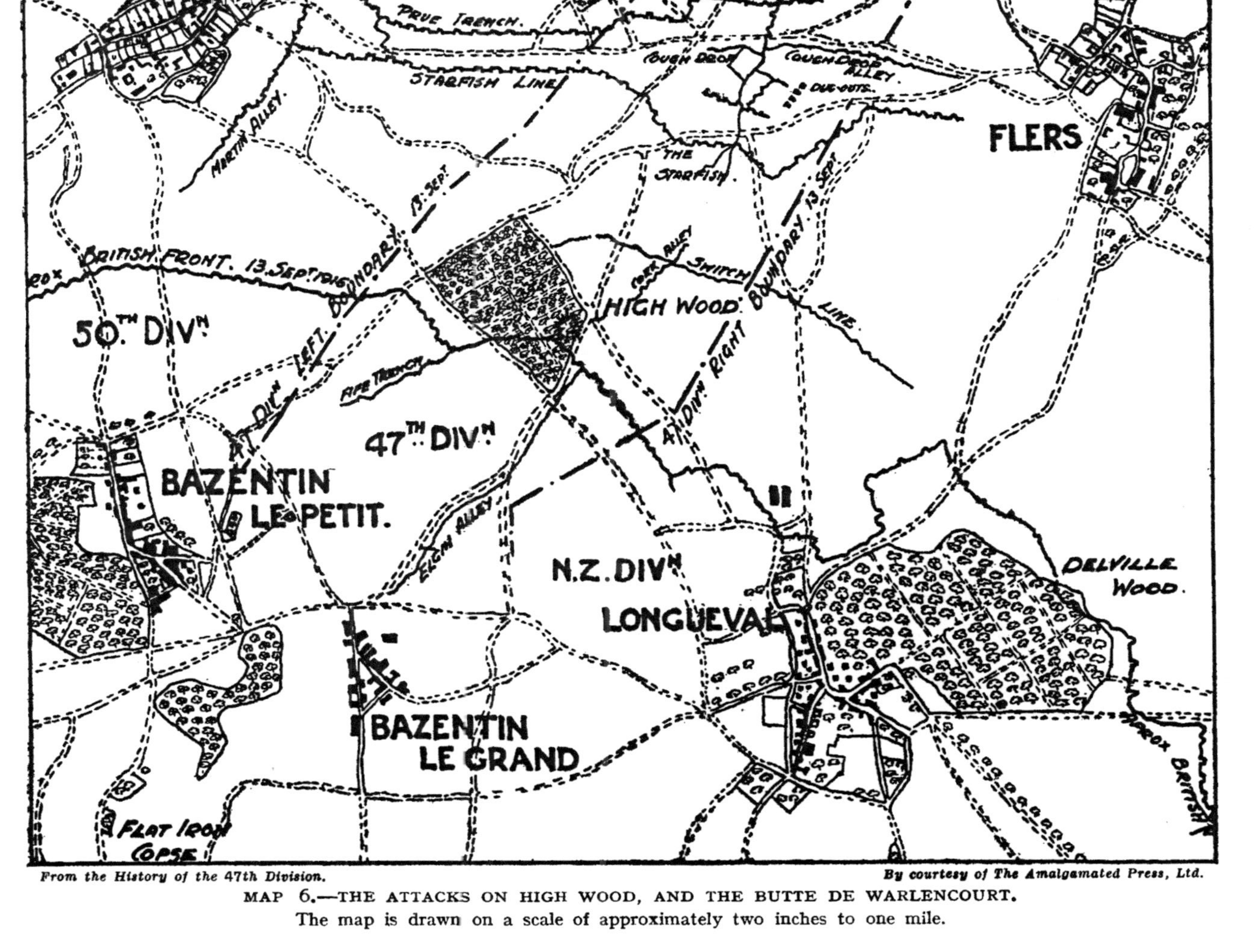

From the History of the 47th Division. By courtesy of The Amalgamated Press, Ltd.

MAP 6.—THE ATTACKS ON HIGH WOOD, AND THE BUTTE DE WARLENCOURT.

The map is drawn on a scale of approximately two inches to one mile.

the 15th Bn. Intervals of one hundred yards were maintained between waves, and platoons, about fifty strong, carried eight Lewis-guns. Platoon Commanders accompanied the first, second, and fourth waves, and Company Commanders, Company Sergeant-Majors, the third waves.

At first the advance was like a drill movement, but over such broken ground, everywhere pitted with shell-holes, this perfect formation was not long maintained. Almost at once it became apparent that the 15th Bn. had not succeeded in establishing itself along the eastern edge of High Wood, and that the 8th Bn. had been unable to get beyond the Switch Line. Parties of that unit had, with great dash indeed, reached their allotted objective, the Starfish Line, but the advancing waves of the *Sixth* encountered a stiff resistance from the German garrison there entrenched, which maintained an effective rifle and machine-gun fire. On the right, the Germans rose from their trenches to meet the advancing waves in the open, and in the open they were slain. Farther to the right, the New Zealand troops were checked, with the result that the enemy was able to concentrate on the *Sixth* from both flanks.

High Wood

The key to the success of the battle had early been recognised as the complete capture of the wood. The Germans realised this, too, and their resistance in it was desperate. Not before 1 p.m., after six and a half hours of continuous fighting, could the 141st Brigade report that the wood was clear of enemy forces. Meanwhile, the *Sixth,* making what progress it could in the absence of support from the left, suffered severely from enfilade fire from the wood, and from a strong point lying beyond it, known as the Cough Drop. This cluster of trenches and machine-gun emplacements had been allotted in the plans for the attack as a final objective of the 141st Brigade, but so heavy was the fire from this direction that there was no alternative for the *Sixth* but to deviate from the line of advance, not to avoid the Cough Drop, but to overcome it. This was done, and the strong point captured, mainly by C Company, but not before the defenders had exacted a heavy toll in casualties from the battalion. Remnants of the first wave did indeed reach their final objective—the Flers Line—but the numbers were too few to form a permanent lodgment in it, and the battalion had to content itself with the capture of the Cough Drop, and with the taking of many prisoners.

Cough Drop

Describing this advance, Capt. M. J. Macdonald,* who, although wounded, continued to command C Company, writes: " As a result of enfilade fire, whole waves were mown down in line, but some thirty of C Company, making use of what dead ground there was, fought on until held up at the Cough Drop, where a machine-gun was very active. A few lucky shots and this

*Later, Colonel M. J. Macdonald, M.C., T.D.

was put out of action, and a sudden assault with fixed bayonets captured the position. Some sixty prisoners were taken, as well as two machine-guns and quantities of ammunition and stores. A small party, under Lieut. Pickering, actually pushed on to the Flers Line, but this was very strongly held by a pocket of enemy troops, and Lieut. Pickering and his gallant little band all became casualties. I decided to consolidate on the Cough Drop, and while making arrangements for its defence, Capt. Brooke came up with twenty N.C.O.'s and men of B Company. This was fortunate, because it was found that only eighteen N.C.O.'s and men of C Company were unwounded, and thus, of the gallant *Sixth* there were left only two officers and thirty-eight ' other ranks ' to prepare and defend the captured ground against an expected counter-attack."

Cough Drop

There were no reinforcements, and when fifty men, normally employed on regimental duties in the transport lines had been brought up to the new positions, the total garrison was still lamentably weak. To their infinite credit, the Lewis-gunners, despite the severest casualties, had succeeded in bringing into the Cough Drop every one of the eight Lewis-guns with which the battalion was equipped. Immediate steps were taken to turn the newly captured system into a fortified stronghold, and to establish communication with the right. A small patrol was sent out and succeeded in locating the New Zealanders in a sunken road lying about five hundred yards to the east, and having satisfied themselves on this point, the small and almost isolated garrison settled down for the night, confident, and prepared to meet, if necessary, a counter-attack.

Early the next morning (the 16th) two hundred men of the 22nd Bn. arrived to strengthen the determined little force.*

---

*The party was led by Capt. Gilks, who writes: "It was a dark night, and as there were no landmarks progress was slow. After some considerable time the officer in charge of the party thought we must be going in the wrong direction, and eventually refused to go farther. I was confident that I was going right, and knowing the absolute necessity of our noble band of survivors having reinforcements, I persuaded the men to stay where they were, and with twelve men, including my runner, Bugler Woods, I went forward, dropping one man every hundred yards to act as a connecting-file. Finally only Woods and I remained, and, ordering him to act as the last file, I went on alone. After a considerable distance I came to a small brick edifice like a garden summer-house. I had seen this on the previous day from the Cough Drop, standing only a short distance in front and to the right of our trenches. Luckily, no enemy were in it, so I moved towards our trenches, and had gone only a few steps when I was fired on from them. I called out, but was not heard. I crawled forward, and then I heard 'Taffy' Hughes call out: 'There he is, have another shot.' Two or three more shots just missed me, and I shouted to Taffy, and you can imagine his surprise when he found out who I was. Returning, I picked up Woods and the other connecting-files, and at last reached the party of the 22nd, who, thinking I had failed to find the *Sixth*, and had probably walked into the German lines, were making their way back. Just before dawn, however, the much-needed reinforcements reached our trenches."

The final objective originally allotted to the battalion had been the Flers Line, and although it had been reached in places, the whole of it had not been captured. True, the *Sixth* had taken, of necessity, a most formidable stronghold, but the last objective—the trench-system running north-west from Flers—still remained in enemy hands. A further assault upon it was consequently decided upon by Brigade Headquarters, and during the evening of the 17th, the *Sixth* were astonished to learn that they were to take part in it. All that day, still manning the Cough Drop, the gallant little band had been subjected to severe bombardments, and although spirits were high, they were scarcely in a fit state to undertake another assault. However, in the early hours of the 18th, two hundred officers and men from the 8th Bn., and about half that number from the 15th Bn., all under the command of Major Whitehead, arrived to take up " jumping-off " positions a little to the left of the posts occupied by the *Sixth;* and punctually at 5 a.m., after a heavy bombardment, the Flers Line was assaulted. In this local attack, which everywhere proved successful, the *Sixth,* under Major Hughes, first took up positions in some trenches occupied by New Zealanders, and operating on the right of the 15th Bn., over-ran the German first-line trench, took, and retained his support trenches. A party of them, too, with men of the 15th Bn., occupied Drop Alley, a communication trench joining the enemy lines. At midday a detachment of New Zealanders relieved those of the *Sixth* occupying these positions, and withdrawing, the latter rejoined their comrades still in the Cough Drop, which now seemed to be the most " unhealthy " spot in the whole neighbourhood, hostile artillery fire being continually directed against it.

Flers

Drop Alley

Early in the following morning, Germans attacked the party of the 15th Bn. holding Drop Alley, and it looked as if this was but a preliminary to a larger movement, but beyond a good deal of shelling and sniping, nothing further occurred, and the 15th Bn. were later able to re-establish their positions. Still later, New Zealanders, in conjunction with the 15th Bn., made another assault upon the junction of Drop Alley and the Flers Lines in order to clear the enemy once and for all from this important point; but the attack was unsuccessful, and a German counter-attack restored the position in his favour. But the action was now virtually over. The 1st Black Watch relieved the *Sixth* in the Cough Drop early in the morning of the 20th.*

*With great difficulty. The *Sixth* had received no warning of the relief; and the Black Watch were in full marching-order and had to make their relief " over the top " because of the narrowness of the trenches. The garrison in the Cough Drop were very tired, some having been without sleep for six days and nights, and some of them were helped along the road by the A.S.C.

Meanwhile, what had been happening along the rest of the front attacked? It will be remembered that to the 47th Division had been entrusted the task of clearing High Wood, and against it the Divisional Commander had placed the 141st Infantry Brigade. In earlier Somme battles the Germans had been found to offer their stiffest resistance when fighting in wooded country, and thus a heavy concentration against High Wood was clearly desirable. Events proved the correctness of the decision, for here the enemy contested every inch of the ground he held. Four tanks had been allotted to the brigade to help in the assault, but they were soon found to be incapable of overturning the big trees growing in the wood, and at the last minute the infantry was robbed of their assistance. Further, the presence of the tanks in the fringe of the wood caused the British artillery to reduce their fire, with the result that the infantry, unaided by one or the other, were left to achieve the almost impossible task alone. The 17th and 18th Battalions, assisted by the 15th Bn. on the eastern edge, fought desperately against fearful odds, and the 19th and 20th Battalions, forming the second wave, soon found themselves amongst the men of the forward battalions, fighting with the enemy hand-to-hand. Casualties were enormous, and it was not until the afternoon that the wood was cleared of the enemy, the successful conclusion of the operation being largely due to the work of the 140th Trench-Mortar Battery. As has already been seen, progress on the right of the wood had been far more rapid, and the advance of the *Sixth* had been held up for some time by enfilade fire from it. A similar situation had developed on the left of the wood, and the necessity of clearing it, so as to advance the line in the centre, became hourly more urgent. Almost as soon as High Wood was taken, remnants of the attacking battalions launched an assault at 6 p.m. on the Starfish Line, lying about half a mile from the north-eastern edge of it. The attack failed, however, largely owing to ineffective artillery fire (for which no blame can be attached to battery commanders), and there was no alternative but to postpone further operations until the following day. The next morning (16th) companies drawn from the 22nd and 23rd Battalions launched an assault in the direction of the German defences lying between Flers and Eaucourt L'Abbaye, the first objective being the Cough Drop, already held by the *Sixth*—a fact apparently unknown to the Divisional Commander. Finding the *Sixth* in their first objective, the attacking companies of 22nd and 23rd Battalions were misled as to their positions, and went gallantly forward—towards the Flers Line. Parties indeed entered the enemy's trenches here, and aeroplanes reported having seen some of them in Eaucourt L'Abbaye itself, but they did not return, and it is to be presumed their end was a gallant one.

High Wood

Cough Drop

Elsewhere on the battle-front attacks had been uniformly and generally successful. The Canadians stormed and took Courcelette, and Scots troops the village of Martinpuich, to the right of it. Thanks to the 140th Infantry Brigade, and largely to the *Sixth,* the 47th Division had secured its objectives beyond High Wood, and to the right Flers was taken by New Zealand troops. Southwards from Flers the gains were not so considerable, but taken as a whole they were more than hitherto had fallen to British arms in a single day's fighting. More than four thousand prisoners and much material had been taken, and the enemy's *morale* was badly shaken. The French, too, had made good progress and passed beyond the Peronne-Bapaume road.

But the Battle of the Somme was not over, and weak though it was, the battalion had not finished with it. Eight days of rest and reorganisation were allowed it in the little village of Henencourt, when orders were received for its return to the battle area. Billets were found in Albert on September 29th, and bivouacs in Mametz Wood provided inadequate shelter from rain and wind three days later. From Mametz Wood the battalion moved on October 4th back to the trenches, to find, in consequence of consolidating actions taking place in their absence, that the new British line ran north-westerly from Flers and embraced the buildings around Eaucourt l'Abbaye and skirted the village of Le Sars, behind which, threatening and dominating, stood the Butte de Warlencourt, now for months a veritable mound of explosion.

Butte de Warlencourt

The positions taken up by the *Sixth* on October 4th, lay both in front of and behind Eaucourt, the front line being to the north-east of it and the support line to the south-west, and two companies occupied the former and two the latter. No proper trenches existed, and the ground was held only by outpost-lines. From these positions the Butte de Warlencourt could be clearly observed, since the surface of the mound had been bombarded into a chalky mass of whitish earth. The trenches manned by the outpost companies (they were really no more than lines of ditches) were so near the Butte that even slight movement by the occupants drew heavy machine-gun and trench-mortar fire upon them—so heavy that it is surprising that any lived to relate their experiences. In return, the British artillery continually bombarded the Butte, but despite the destructiveness of heavy shells, it stood as it stands to-day, a lasting memorial to those who died attacking and defending it.

When day came (5th), Germans were observed digging a trench at the foot of the Butte about four hundred yards in front of the positions held by the *Sixth,* and evidently the work they were doing was important, since neither rifle nor Lewis-gun fire caused them to stop. Continuous movement was observed also in the neighbourhood of an old mill about a couple of hundred yards in front of the battalion's left positions; and that night, after a patrol had reconnoitred and reported it was held, bombers and riflemen set out and surrounded the place. A short tussle ensued, and under cover of darkness the enemy garrison withdrew, whereupon it was occupied and incorporated in the battalion's defence system. The battalion had not long to wait for a renewal of the offensive. Orders were received on October 6th for a fresh assault. The 8th Bn. was to attack the new trench which the *Sixth* had seen being dug, and the 7th and 15th Bns. were to continue the advance to the Butte. To allow ease of movement, the *Sixth* were to withdraw from their positions, on the arrival of the 8th Bn., to the Flers Line, and to reoccupy them as soon as the attack had commenced. It was due to the *Sixth* that having already made such heavy sacrifices, it should be called upon to play no major part in the action, but events were to prove that the battalion was not to escape without severe losses. Moreover, heavy rain had been falling, and the condition of the ground was such that men sank up to their knees in mud, and their only shelter, owing to the impossibility of reconstructing trenches, was in the waterlogged craters.

Butte de Warlencourt

As an element of surprise, the attack was timed to commence at 1.45 p.m., and as soon as it was launched the enemy put down a heavy curtain-fire on the Flers Line, which now held the *Sixth;* consequently, no one was sorry when the order came to return to the battalion's former positions. However, when once more in the Eaucourt Trench, the bombardment seemed to intensify, and although casualties were probably less than they would have been had the battalion made the attack, they were considerable, and the nerve strain quite as exhausting.

By 4 p.m. so little reliable information had been received from the assaulting battalions, that a patrol was sent out to ascertain the real positions occupied by the attackers. It found, not far from the Eaucourt trenches, little groups of men gallantly endeavouring to connect up a series of shell-holes to form a defensive line, and it found, too, the reason of the enemy's effective resistance. Nature had placed in front of the Butte a gentle, unbroken valley, the whole length of which was covered by hostile enfilading fire. Immediate steps were taken to establish advance posts in front of the Eaucourt trenches so as to incorporate in the main system of defence the shell-holes which the attackers were holding.

The following day (Oct. 8th) was spent in securing what had been gained by filling in the gaps in the defence system. During these operations, patrols of the *Sixth* came in contact with the enemy, and one of them attacked and took a German post, bringing in four prisoners belonging to the 362nd Regiment.

Butte de Warlencourt

Needless to say, such activity as well as heavy shelling was taking its toll in dead and wounded of all battalions in the brigade, some of which were so disorganised and depleted in strength as to be incapable of operating as units. Accordingly, the Brigade Commander resolved to organise the defence into three groups, with the *Sixth* on the left, until such time as they should be relieved. It was only a temporary measure undertaken in the belief that the 142nd would take over the line that night. A last minute change of plans, however, necessitated the *Sixth* remaining in their positions and witnessing yet another assault on the Butte. At dawn on the 9th, the 142nd Infantry Brigade launched its attack. It had no great measure of success, but it brought down heavy fire from German artillery over the whole area, and the battalion suffered further casualties. Those who had witnessed the attacks brought away with them unforgettable memories of men in action. One particularly, on Le Sars, by tanks, is borne in mind: they were able to see the barrage lift, the tanks advancing, and the enemy leaving his trenches in large numbers and surrendering to the on-coming monsters, the commanders of which seemed not to know what to do with the crowd of prisoners whom they had captured.

Mametz Wood

Weary to the point of exhaustion, the *Sixth* was relieved that night by the Argyle and Sutherland Highlanders, and what was left of the battalion withdrew to the transport lines in Mametz Wood. It had seen the last of the Somme battlefield, and was not sorry to say " good-bye " to it. It had lived through moments when, had everything been foreseen, the occasion might have become historic. As it was, Press correspondents spoke of the final capture of High Wood as sharing " with Verdun the distinction of being the finest feat in the War." But the successful assault on the 15th and 16th might have been so much more ; in the words of one of the Company Commanders: "The attack of the *Sixth* and the surprise of the tank which entered Flers was not exploited. There is very little doubt that had fresh troops been thrown in, on the afternoon of the 15th, many months of weary fighting would have been saved. Indeed, it is conceivable that a vigorous attack by fresh troops might have had a decisive effect on the duration of the War. The Butte de Warlencourt was being evacuated, and it was stated that the Germans were actually leaving Bapaume."

This was the truth ; the September offensive might have proved decisive had the initial success been exploited, and the opportunity did not again present itself to the Commander-in-Chief. General Ludendorff judged that the approaching winter would put a stop to the British offensive. In this he was right, and after some further notable advances in November, the British offensive came to a standstill. Sir Douglas Haig subsequently claimed that the

British successes over the finest troops Europe had ever seen was a nail in the German coffin, and that when events could be judged in their proper perspective, it would be found that the Battle of the Somme definitely marked the turning point of the War. Whatever may be the final conclusions regarding that offensive, its immediate effect was to render untenable the German positions north and south of the salient formed by the British and French in their advance, and the story of one of the service battalions of the *Sixth* is intimately linked with the German withdrawal in the spring of 1917, rendered necessary by the Somme advance.

The total British losses in the entire Somme offensive in killed, wounded, and missing, were: Officers, 22,923; other ranks, 476,553; and the British gains were 38,000 prisoners, 125 guns, and an area of about a hundred square miles, increased to a thousand when later the Germans retired. The German losses were 444,933, all ranks. Posterity must decide whether the British gains were worth the sacrifice in lives they demanded.

FIRST BATTALION OFFICERS, WARRANT OFFICERS and SECTION COMMANDERS at

SOMME—HIGH WOOD, 1916

	Officer Commanding: Col. Mildren	Second-in-Command: Major W. W. Hughes	Adjutant: Capt. Gilks
	R.S.Maj. Bailey		R.Q.M.Sgt. Percival
A Co.	Capt. Terry (killed)	C.S.Maj. Smale	C.Q.M.Sgt. Johnson
B Co.	Capt. Brooke (wounded)	C.S.Maj. Good (killed)	C.Q.M.Sgt. Kent
C Co.	Capt. M. J. Macdonald (wounded)	C.S.Maj. Graysmark (wounded)	C.Q.M.Sgt. Weedon
D Co.	Capt. Jones (killed)	C.S.Maj. Sandison	C.Q.M.Sgt. Cohen

Quartermaster: Lieut. Daly
Transport: Lieut. Noakes; Sgt. Brown; Cpl. Pollard
Cooks: Sgt. Britten; Cpl. Hammond
Stretcher-Bearers: Capt. McGreggor; Sgt. Wade
Signallers: Sgt. Houghton; Cpl. Sharp
Lewis-Guns: Lieut. W. Perry; Sgt. Short; Sgt. Drage
Orderly Room: Sgt. Dommitt; Cpl. Peebles.

Chapter 11

RAIDING AND RAIDED

Although throughout the summer of 1916 the British Army in France had been attacking, the Allies were still strictly on the defensive. True, the situation appeared to be changing in their favour, but on the high seas, on the Western Front, in Macedonia, Palestine, and Mesopotamia, the first consideration was to prevent any farther advance by the common enemy, whether of Germans, Austrians, Bulgars, or Turks. So far as the Western Front was concerned, this necessity was of paramount importance. Already in the north the battle-line ran far too close to the coast, and from Nieuport to Arras the rôle played by the Belgian and British Armies was to prevent at all costs a further German advance.

Along this line, midway between these two bastions, stood the mediæval town of Ypres, already in ruins, watching again the nations of Europe engaged in battle. Since the repulse by the Canadians of the first German attacks in which gas was used, Ypres and the salient in the battle-line skirting it had become sanctified in the eyes of the British people and Army alike. More than anything else it represented one of their principal War aims—the liberation of Belgium—and the moral value attached to holding it was generally recognised. But if both tactical and moral considerations necesitated its being held at all costs, the task itself required both resolution and determination. Flat, bare, and low-lying, the surrounding country possessed naturally neither beauty nor shape; soon, after heavy bombardments, it wore the appearance, in summer, of an uneven desert; in winter, of a vast cesspool.

The 1st/6th Battalion arrived in the Ypres sector about the middle of October, 1916, and, staying a night in Westoutre and two in Victoria Camp, closer to the line, where a large draft of reinforcements from England was

Voormezeele

received, occupied the trenches in the neighbourhood of Voormezeele, and was soon actively engaged.* Two mines were exploded beneath some mine-craters incorporated in the defence system, and some attempt was made by the Germans to occupy the near lips of them; but the positions were shortly regained, and trenches and breastworks repaired, the sodden earth

*The *Sixth* relieved Australians who, rather than put on their boots and putties and wade through the deep mud in the trenches, moved out in their "Gum-boots, thigh," and left none for the battalion. Their action was the cause of endless trouble and voluminous correspondence between the battalion and the Higher Command.

greatly impeding the work. Before the month was out the battalion was relieved, and, in huts at Scottish Lines, near Ouderdom, reorganised and trained. The brief stay here was not without incidents. One night a small fire was promptly spotted, and as promptly put out by the quarter-guard ; a band was formed, and for the first time accompanied the battalion on a route march ; the new-pattern " box " gas respirator was issued in place of the almost useless P.H. helmet ; and medal ribbons were presented by the G.O.C., 47th Division, to those who had won decorations during the recent fighting on the Somme. *Scottish Lines*

By November 9th the battalion found itself in the " Hill 60 " sector, lying south of Zillebeke, to the east of the Ypres-Comines Railway. Here for the most part military activity took the form of artillery duels, the luckless infantry, confined to their trenches, bearing the brunt of the enemy's return fire. Time after time Marshall Walk and other trenches were blown in, and work upon clearing them was incessant. Nor was it possible to do much by way of retaliation ; but the battalion's snipers made the most of every opportunity and inflicted an ever-growing number of casualties upon the occupants of the opposite trenches, and the small fighting patrols sent out nightly by the four companies turned no-man's-land into *Sixthland.* Otherwise life consisted of long periods of boredom interspersed with moments of intense fear. The monotony was varied by periodical reliefs, and when in support at Battersea Farm and in the railway dug-outs, or in reserve at Scottish Lines, the most would be made of the change, and a concert or a sing-song would be held. Sometimes the sector opposite the steep western side of Hill 60 would be occupied, and for hours on end the enemy's trench-mortars, the " rum jars " and the " toffee-apples," would come hurtling through the air, clearly visible to the practised eye, to blow gaps in the wire-entanglements, to demolish a dug-out and its occupants, or to level a piece of newly-repaired trench. Then the light Stokes guns, and the medium and heavy mortars, firing from cunningly-contrived places in the British lines, would smother the hostile fire with well-aimed shots, which at night would be the immediate cause of a shower of coloured rockets, fired from the enemy's lines, as a signal to his artillery to retaliate. In such surroundings the battalion spent its second Christmas on active service in France and Flanders, and here is the entry in the diary for the occasion: " Marked quietness prevailed. Enemy snipers inactive, but ours maintained alertness. During the night the enemy indulged in shouting and singing. A patrol went out from B Crater and found enemy sap strongly occupied. No hostile patrols were met. Ground very muddy and difficult. Work proceeded with

Zillebeke

Hill 60

building-up parapet at entrance of tunnel, cleaning, repairing, and draining trenches. Weather fresh and misty. Casualties: 1 O.R. wounded."

Scottish Camp

Poperinghe

So it went on from day to day, and it was a week later, on January 1st, 1917, at Scottish Camp, that the battalion ate its Christmas dinner. Then, of course, the tension was relaxed for a while and the most made of the welcome break in a sordid routine. One day the new Brigade Commander, the Viscount Hampden, gave a dinner to the sergeants of the battalion in the mess at Poperinghe, and had the satisfaction of learning that full justice had been done to his generosity. The story goes that Sgt. Jimmy Britten alone could describe faithfully all the events of that memorable evening.

Arduous and strenuous as was this garrisoning of the trenches, it was less exhilarating than a war of movement, and the fear that it might lead to a deterioration in the fighting spirit of the Army gained ground. Consequently all units were urged to seize every opportunity of demonstrating that the British defence was active and not passive. A booklet, " Am I as offensive as I might be," showing how the enemy might be continually harassed, was printed and distributed to all platoon commanders ; and in pursuance of this policy higher formations undertook local actions often involving considerable preparation. Sometimes these would take the form of an attack, with a strictly limited frontage, on a clearly-defined objective, with the object of securing a trench or two, a strong point, or a mine-shaft. Thus the line would become straightened, the enemy deprived of a commanding position, or robbed of the fruits of many weeks' labour. More often these offensive actions took the form of raids upon the enemy's lines by which much damage could be inflicted on his defences, his personnel and their moral. By them, too, identification of the defenders could be secured, and thus the movements of German units checked. Occasionally these actions took the form of a reconnaissance in force, when two or three companies would make a sudden assault upon the lines of trenches opposite them, capture or destroy their garrison, and return within an hour or two, bringing prisoners and material with them.

In this third category came that undertaken by the 1st/6th Battalion on February 20th, 1917.

" The raid was planned and rehearsed long before its actual execution ; in fact, it was reported that the proprietors of any estaminet in Poperinghe were prepared to tell you the date, time, and personnel of the projected operation for some months before it took place. If this was so, either the German Intelligence Service had deteriorated or the accuracy of the information was doubted, because when the raid was eventually carried out after a week's wire-cutting, extending, it is true, over a wide area, the prisoners admitted that they were completely surprised by the attack.

" The plan was to raid the enemy trenches in the map-square I.34 in daylight, with the object not only of inflicting casualities, capturing and destroying war material, dug-outs, machine-gun, and minenwerfer emplacements, but of gaining information in regard to the hostile front system and its garrison, and also to look for, and, if found, to destroy any mine-shafts in the vicinity, to search for gas-cylinders, and to destroy a light gun which had been the cause of considerable annoyance to us, and had been located not far behind the German third line.

" Zero was fixed at 5 p.m. with the idea of ensuring more efficient control and taking advantage of the dusk to cover the withdrawal of the attackers an hour later.

" The troops employed consisted of four companies of Lt.-Col. Mildren's 6th Battalion, with six Lewis-guns, one officer, and twenty sappers of the 520th Company, R.E., and one officer and four other ranks of the 2nd Australian Tunnelling Company, making a total of twenty officers and six hundred and forty other ranks. With the object of deceiving the enemy as to the actual point of the attack, a dummy raid by the 22nd Battalion of the 142nd Infantry Brigade, who were holding the Hill 60 sector, was arranged to precede the actual raid, a small mine being fired in no-man's-land five minutes before, and a second two minutes before zero.

" The firing of the first mine was to be followed by a barrage of field-guns and 2 in. trench-mortars, which lifted at zero to form a box barrage in rear of the craters until zero, plus ten minutes. Trench junctions and strong points behind the line were bombarded by howitzers and 2 in. trench-mortars, and smoke-bombs were fired at Hill 60 and the Caterpillar. Various coloured rockets were fired behind our lines. Other coloured rockets were collected in the Bluff craters and were fired in salvos, six, nine, and twelve minutes after zero, while the 41st Divisional Artillery kept the high ground south of the canal under heavy fire throughout. Finally Stokes mortars were borrowed, for over eighteen were in position to barrage the enemy's front lines on the actual front to be raided, most of which was too close to permit of wire-cutting by the 18-pounders. The usual artillery and machine-gun co-operation was arranged, and smoke-grenades and trench-mortar smoke-bombs were used to isolate the raided portion of the enemy's lines and prevent accurate enfilading fire being brought to bear from the high ground on their side on either flank.

"This plan worked out admirably. The enemy was evidently very nervous of the situation at Hill 60, and, as this had been included in the previous wire-cutting, mistook the dummy raid for the real one, as his counter barrage was prompt, and, of course, descended upon almost empty trenches, the garrison, with the exception of the minimum number of sentries, having been withdrawn into the tunnels. The firework display from the Bluff also contributed, as another barrage descended on that area. The hurricane bombardment of the eighteen Stokes mortars not only cut the enemy's wire, but forced the garrison of the front line either to get into their concrete dug-outs or stop outside and be killed.

"In consequence the attackers met practically no hostile fire when going over.* They captured the front line almost without resistance, the hostile machine-guns in their concrete recesses not being ready for action. The only officer captured in the raid was found in one of the dug-outs, which was solidly built and almost undamaged. He proved to be the officer in command of the sector, and had been caught on an ordinary tour of inspection without a revolver or even a stick. He was a brave man, and it was only the lack of something to do it with that had prevented his putting up a fight. The intermediate line, which did not appear to be used, was badly flattened out, and the main support line was also badly damaged, and yielded a considerable haul of prisoners. There were no gas-cylinders, and only one mine-shaft was discovered, which was destroyed.

"The light gun was not found. Enemy dug-outs and machine-gun emplacements were wrecked by firing mobile charges in them, and this very nearly caused us severe casualties, as during the noise and confusion of the raid the R.E. company had the greatest difficulty in diverting triumphant raiders returning dragging machine-guns and other loot from the neighbourhood of dug-outs containing a fizzling charge of ammonal. The withdrawal was carried out according to plan, the red rockets that were fired behind our lines proving a useful guide and signal.

"The total results were: One officer and one hundred and seventeen other ranks captured, two of whom died in our trenches ; two heavy and three light machine-guns and large quantities of documents, maps, and papers. A large number of the enemy were also killed or wounded when escaping to the rear. A great deal of destruction was carried out in the enemy's trenches at a total cost of eleven other ranks killed, three died of wounds, two missing, with four officers and fifty-six other ranks wounded, a total of seventy-six. The number of prisoners broke all existing records,

*They were led by Capt. Neely, sounding a hunting-horn.

Lord WAKEFIELD OF HYTHE.

As Sir Charles Cheers Wakefield, Lord Mayor of London, he inspected the battalion at Bruay, 1916. He is a Governor of St. Bartholomew's Hospital in which the "Mildren" bed has been dedicated to the Battalion's Fallen.

Plate 20

By courtesy of The Amalgamated Press, Ltd.

GENERAL LORD HENRY SEYMOUR RAWLINSON, G.C.V.O., K.C.B., K.C.M.G., G.O.C. Fourth Army.

General Rawlinson early in his military career served in the "60th Rifles" (K.R.R.C.) and before the war was A.D.C. to Lord Roberts, Honorary Colonel of the SIXTH. The SIXTH was one of the first Territorial battalions to serve under him on the Western Front.

Plate 21

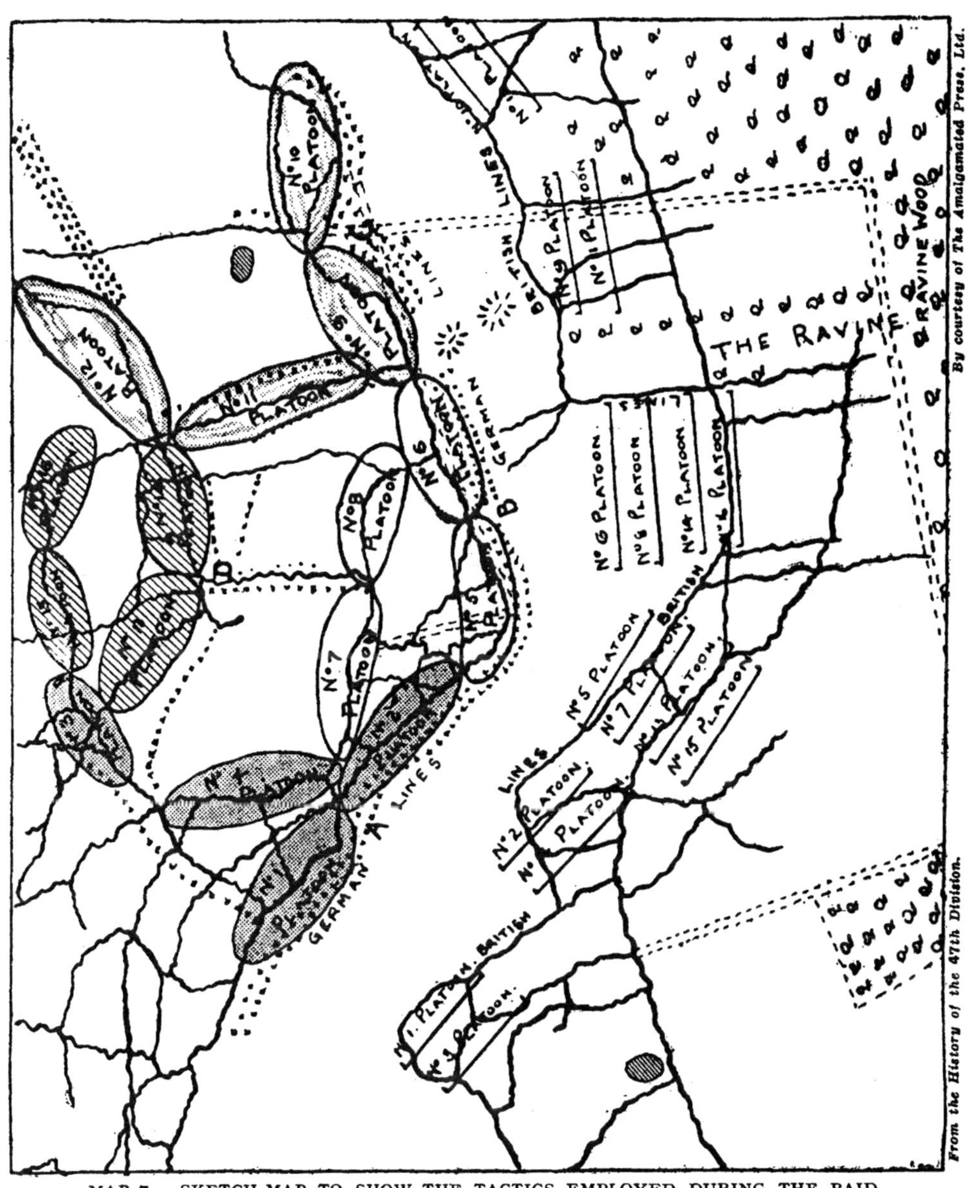

MAP 7.—SKETCH-MAP TO SHOW THE TACTICS EMPLOYED DURING THE RAID ON THE 20TH FEBRUARY, 1917. THE MAP, P. 126, ALSO SHOWS THE SECTOR RAIDED AND THE MAP, P. 124, THE AREA OF OPERATIONS.

and was never equalled in a raid by a single battalion during the whole of the War. The large number may be attributed to the fact that the enemy were largely surprised, while the attacking troops had few casualties going over, and also succeeded in cutting off the bulk of the garrison of the enemy salient. The official German account of this extraordinarily successful raid, circulated to the German Press of February 22nd, 1917, was as follows: 'Strong English patrols which attempted to advance after exploding mines on both sides of the Ypres-Comines railway were checked by our barrage fire. Some few did reach the German lines, but were driven out again, losing prisoners. It is significant that the unwounded British prisoners captured here were so absolutely intoxicated that it was impossible to interrogate them.' "*

If intoxication there was, it was the intoxication of success, for as events were to prove this raid was the most successful ever undertaken by any unit on the Western Front, and is to-day regarded in military circles as a classic example of careful preparation and resolute action. All who took part in it deserved the highest possible praise, and the number of decorations bestowed subsequently marked the appreciation of the higher command of a singularly fine performance.

Lt.-Gen. Sir T. L. N. Morland, then commanding the division, visited the battalion on the next day, personally congratulating those on parade on their fine performance, and three days later, after church parade, the Army Commander, General Sir Herbert Plumer, added his own appreciation, ending with the words: "Fine performance; very good, very good. But—er—we haven't won the War yet." Subsequent testimony was just as congratulatory, if a little more polished. Mr. Frank A. Mumby, in the *Great World War,* wrote: "In one brief, crowded hour the Londoners had also succeeded in wrecking the whole area, including mine-shafts, stores of grenades, and every machine-gun they could not carry back."

No account of this remarkable achievement would be complete without some reference to the officers primarily responsible for its success. To Capt. Neely, and to the Adjutant, Capt. Gilks, upon whom largely fell the task of organising the raid, under Col. Mildren's direction, must the chief credit be given. It was they who supervised the rehearsals over taped positions, and saw to it that every man knew what was expected of him. These rehearsals had not been without anxiety, since enemy aircraft hovering overhead must have noted every movement and reported this activity. But by giving every platoon a particular task, and by seeing that all were well-equipped—bombers with

*From the "History of the 47th Division."

special jackets in which to carry their bombs, others with wire-cutters and blankets to throw over uncut wire, some to assist the R.E.'s with high-explosive strapped to their backs, and all with a sandbag into which anything of military value, such as maps and papers, might be put—provision for every eventuality was made. To the maintenance of communications they gave equally careful consideration, and under Sgt. Houghton, the Signal Section laid lines on the flanks, both of which remained intact throughout the engagement, and assisted the R.E.'s to carry a wireless transmitter (subsequently destroyed by shell-fire) into the captured positions.

George Neely was a pre-War officer, and served at first as Signal Officer. Later, shortly after the outbreak of War, he was appointed Transport Officer, and showed remarkable aptitude for handling both men and animals. Tall, and always immaculately clad, in both speech and bearing his manner was charmingly foppish. None at that time thought for a moment that such a languid and disdainful exterior could cover the heart of a lion, yet, when at Vimy, he was promoted to Captain and appointed to command D Company, he showed that to all his other virtues he could add one of great personal bravery. Lucky, indeed, were those who came most closely in contact with him. Affectionately nicknamed " Kate " by the members of the Transport Section, none had any but the happiest recollections of serving under him, and none tires of relating amusing stories about him.

" On one occasion, when escorting rations up the line at Vermelles, Lieut. Neely bemoaned the fact that he had vermin in his shirt. 'Where the hell do these things come from?' he inquired of his groom.

" 'Mules, sir.'

" 'Animal lice cannot exist on human beings,' drawled the officer.

" 'Well, sir. I'm *chatty* myself, and I shall be glad to return your breeches when my issue comes along.'

" 'Confound you, man! Who gave you permission to wear my breeches?'

" 'You told me to borrow a pair, sir, until I could get a pair from the stores.'

" 'I didn't tell you to take mine,' fumed the officer.

" 'Sorry, sir. I didn't know anyone else with more than one pair.'

" 'Consider yourself under arrest!'

" The rations they were escorting were to be dumped at a point known as Lone Tree. On went the limbers, but no tree could be found, and Lieut. Neely decided to take another track alone, the limbers continuing on their way. They crossed over one trench-bridge, and soon came to another. Here they were challenged by the garrison in the trench, and found that that was their destination, and the quartermaster was told where to dump the rations. When this was done, the limbers returned at the trot, for the spot where the Lone Tree *used* to stand was anything but quiet. At about four o'clock in the morning the groom was awakened by a terrific banging on the stable door.

" 'Confound you, man! Where have you been?'

" 'Here since midnight, sir.'

" 'I've scoured the whole ruddy battle-front looking for you and the damned tree. Where are the limbers?'

" 'Home, sir.'

" 'Did you find the battalion?'

" 'Yes, sir; where the Lone Tree was.'

" 'Well, where is the Lone Tree?'

" 'They've cut it down, sir.'

" 'I don't see anything to cackle about; consider yourself under open-arrest.

" Needless to say, nothing followed this frequent display of authority and punishment rarely, if ever, followed the arrest of the accused."

Such was George Neely, whose wit and gallantry became bye-words throughout the *Sixth*, and later, the 18th Bn., London Regt., when, in 1918, he was given the command of that unit. After the War he continued his military career, serving in India with the Highland Light Infantry, and his death, in 1934, greatly distressed all who had served with him, for he had many friends and no enemies.

FIRST BATTALION OFFICERS, WARRANT OFFICERS and SECTION COMMANDERS at

YPRES RAID—FEBRUARY, 1917

OFFICER COMMANDING:	SECOND-IN-COMMAND:	ADJUTANT:
COL. MILDREN	MAJOR W. W. HUGHES	CAPT. GILKS
R.S.MAJ. ABERY	ACT.: MAJOR NEELY	
Act. R.S.MAJ. S. JONES		R.Q.M.SGT. PERCIVAL
A Co. CAPT. EVE	C.S.MAJ. PHILLIPS	C.Q.M.SGT. JOHNSON
B Co. CAPT. ORDISH	C.S.MAJ. BITTEN	C.Q.M.SGT. KENT
C Co. CAPT. MAYNARD	C.S.MAJ. BAKER	C.Q.M.SGT. YOUNGS
D Co. CAPT. DALY	C.S.MAJ. BITTEN	C.Q.M.SGT. J. GOOD

Quartermaster: LIEUT. LOVETT
Transport: LIEUT. NOAKES; SGT. BROWN; CPL. POLLARD
Cooks: SGT. BRITTEN; CPL. HAMMOND
Stretcher-Bearers: CAPT. HOPE-CARLTON; CPL. WADE
Signallers: SGT. HOUGHTON; CPL. SHARP
Lewis-Guns: LIEUT. MAXTED; SGT. DRAGE; SGT. SHORT
Bombers: LIEUT. SMITHER; SGT. KINNINGDALE
Orderly Room: CPL. PEEBLES

Meanwhile, the *Second*, restless in its wooden huts at Sutton Veny, grew more and more impatient at its enforced stay in England. Of the original battalion most had been drafted to the *First* in France, but the depleted ranks had long since been made up to strength, and it remained with other units of the 58th Division, trained to the point of staleness, self-conscious, and a little disheartened, patiently awaiting orders to go on active service. Two years of progressive training had resulted in a battalion of high efficiency, marred only by the lack of its first early enthusiasm for soldiering. It could march twenty miles in a day and carry out an attack at the end of it without a man falling out by the way. It had mastered the intricacies of advance and rear guards, and of outposts, so that every man knew what was expected of him before the order was given. It had done its tours of duty in local trenches, and understood the routine of the garrison. Its discipline was excellent, and crime was practically non-existent. Its daily prayer was that it should see something of the War before peace was made. It was destined to see much of it. *Sutton Veny*

Early in January, 1917, unmistakable signs that the battalion was going overseas manifested themselves. Steel helmets were issued, and clothing inspected and replaced where badly worn. Finally, on January 23rd, the battalion marched to Warminster, entrained about 9.30 a.m., and moved slowly to Southampton, where it arrived about 4 p.m., and waited for hours on the quayside to embark. The channel crossing was made in two vessels, the s.s. Highland Brae, carrying the Headquarters Staff, details, and two companies, and the s.s. Viper* the remainder of the battalion. The first stank vilely of horses and cattle, an earlier cargo, and was the cause, rather than the smooth sea, of whatever sickness occurred.

Next morning, at Le Havre, the battalion disembarked, and in the early hours marched, with band playing, up the steep hill to a reception camp at Harfleur. Col. Collinson, proudly at the head of his long column, led the way with firm, quick steps up the hillside, and in a very short while outstripped the battalion. No pack was on his shoulders, and before long the tired troops, doing their best to maintain the pace he set, were literally panting by the wayside. Lieut. Halford, a deservedly popular officer, forged ahead and informed the impatient C.O. that the battalion "couldn't keep up." There followed a heated altercation between the two, during which the straggling unit was able to pull itself together, and by the time it reached the crest it had recovered itself sufficiently to march into the tented area with its usual self-possession. The weather was bitterly cold, *Le Havre*

*According to some, the s.s. Archimedes, an old boat used for carrying live-stock.

and the high altitude of the camp, exposed to a biting wind, lowered the temperature still further. There was snow upon the ground, and some hitch occurred with the ration supply. The water tanks were frozen, and the tentage accommodation totally inadequate. Taken all together, the conditions were so unpleasant that when orders to move came two days later they were received with great relief.

The first step brought the battalion to the village of Frevent. Thence the battalion marched to Buire-au-Bois across snow-covered country, arriving at 5.30 a.m. Here it rested for a day, and on February 1st, motor-lorries arrived *Souastre* to carry the battalion to Souastre, a village lying some thirteen miles south-west of Arras. From this centre the four companies were directed to various parts of the line to be attached for purposes of instruction to two units of the 138th Infantry Brigade (the 1st/4th Lincolns and the 1st/5th Leicesters) who were manning the trenches at Fonquevillers *Hannescamp* and Hannescamp. The trenches, however, were not built to accommodate such strong garrisons, and all but one platoon of each company were withdrawn to St. Amand, a village in which some French peasants were still living, although it was well within the range of even light guns.

At the end of the week the battalion had had a pleasant enough introduction to trench warfare. Some of the positions occupied had been as much as a thousand yards from the enemy's front line, and, except for occasional shelling, the sense of danger was rarely present. The cold was still intense, but the snow upon the ground presented a picturesque appearance, and the breath of cold east wind against the cheek as each morning the dawn came up over the white expanse beyond the parapet added to the personal enjoyment of a novel experience. It was good to be alive, and in such surroundings. Could it be that these were the appalling conditions of active service so often described? So far, very little hostile activity on the part of the enemy had been experienced, and it seemed as if the War, except when actual fighting should take place, might become bearable. Irksome and tiring as carrying rations or working for the Royal Engineers might be, there were times when life was exciting and exhilarating, as when patrolling in no-man's-land, and none could say that the *Sixth* was not bold. Mastery of no-man's-land had been taught as essential, and nightly patrols went across the ground between the British and German trenches, thereby attracting a good deal of attention to themselves.

For the next fortnight the battalion remained in this area holding various *Bienvillers* parts of the line, or in support at Bienvillers ; then, moving to Humbercamps, it took over some trenches, a little north of those formerly occupied. They were situated on the crest of a hill and overlooked the village of Ransart; then in German hands. Here the conditions were vastly different. A thaw set in, and, despite their elevation, the trenches rapidly filled with water. In many places the revetments gave way before the pressure of the frozen earth, and the fallen soil churned everywhere to the consistency of newly-mixed cement by dozens of half-imprisoned feet, removed at once all false impressions of life on the Western Front. Gum-boots, thigh-high, were issued, and soon found to be a boon to the wearers so long as the liquid mud in the trenches did not go above the tops of them. In other directions, too, the War was seen to wear more serious aspects. Enemy shellfire increased, wire was cut, and communication trenches became blocked. Ration and ammunition parties as a consequence found their way at night, above ground, to the front line, and the tracks thus made were soon spotted by hostile aircraft. At 3.30 a.m. on March 6th, after a short but intense bombardment, an enemy raiding party, bent on identifying the British troops opposite them, entered the line, inflicted casualties, and carried off two riflemen alive or dead. Not knowing the precise nature of the assault, a hastily-organised counter-attack was launched; but the front line, when reached, was found to be intact, and the garrison, mystified, alert, and angry.

Ransart

One of the battalion scouts, writing of these incidents in a diary he himself kept, said: " . . . I had come off an observation post in the front line at midnight, after reporting an enemy plane passing over our lines . . . and making signals. At 2 a.m. we were awakened by the bursting of enemy shells about our dug-out, and the firing became so fierce that it was unhealthy outside at all. As all was quiet half an hour later, we settled down to rest.

"After what seemed a few minutes we were rudely awakened by the Intelligence Officer rushing in, crying: 'Come on, my bonny lads, the Bosche is over the top,' and we were soon out in the open and formed a line of defence along the support line . . . Soon our officer reported 'all clear,' and while the reserve company at Bellacourt was rushed up, we retired to talk, not to sleep, until dawn. On the following day, and again three days later, a lateral-patrol, consisting of an N.C.O. and a rifleman, moving along disused trenches, was ambushed. On both occasions one was killed and the other 'missing.'"

These incidents made a deep impression on the battalion. The true meaning of trench warfare was beginning to be understood. Why, during its training, had no instructions been given to officers and men to prepare them for such emergencies? Why had so much time been devoted to training the unit for a war of movement, when the actual situation required, not a general knowledge of field operations, but a detailed study of the craft and

Ransart cunning of the paid assassin? Such unspoken questions arose naturally; they were shortly to be answered. A lesser unit might have been dismayed by these events; but not so a battalion of the *Sixth*. By way of retaliation the snipers redoubled their efforts, and the scouts nightly led fighting patrols into no-man's-land, the ground being reconnoitred right up to the enemy's wire. From the reports of these nocturnal expeditions it soon became clear that the enemy's garrison was being substantially reduced in strength. On March 17th the Scout Section went boldly across no-man's-land, in daylight, and, entering the opposite trenches, found them vacated. Immediately two companies were thrown into them, and on the next day positions east and south-east of Ransart were secured.

The Germans were retiring. As a direct result of the Battle of the Somme they were moving back to prepared positions running south-east from Arras, to Bullecourt, and to Laon. Now it became apparent why the 58th Division had been allotted this part of the battle-front. A condition of open warfare existed. The advance was continued, and on the 25th the battalion took up positions in the new outpost line between the villages of

Boyelles Boyelles and St. Leger, feeling far more at home in this type of warfare than in the muddy garrison duty of the trenches.

YPRES.

Chapter 12

FAILURE AND SUCCESS

The opening months of the year 1917 saw profound changes both in the political and military situations. In March, the Russian Tsarist Government fell, to be replaced by a provisional administration headed by Kerensky, and whilst at the time no one foresaw that this revolution was to be followed by a still greater upheaval and the withdrawal of Russia from the War, shrewd observers realised that many months must pass before the Russian armies under Kerensky's schemes of reorganisation would again become a menace to the eastern frontiers of the Central Powers. Disappointing as was this first sign of Russian collapse, British troops on the Western Front were heartened by the clear realisation that man for man they were as good as, if not better than, the troops of the greatest military machine the world had ever known. As has already been seen, the first fruits of the Battle of the Somme were already being reaped. British divisions were following closely on the heels of the German armies as they withdrew from their untenable positions on the Somme to carefully prepared lines of trenches, the Hindenburg Line and the Droucourt-Queant Switch. The *Second,* taking part in this advance, crossed no-man's-land on the evening of March 17th, and established themselves in the enemy's apparently deserted lines. Although late in the day, there was sufficient light to show that the enemy trenches were infinitely superior to those the *Sixth* had just vacated, and when morning came, and the defences of Ransart could be examined, it was seen that, at all events, the Germans believed in bodily comfort as well as safety. The trenches were ten to fifteen feet deep, and from them steep shafts led to dug-outs constructed forty feet below the surface, some of which were capable of housing sixty or more in comfort. A little behind the front-line trenches, wherever sunken roads would permit of their construction, were shelters of a different kind, airy and picturesque châlets, gracing the road-embankments, in which it was conjectured German officers and warrant officers lived their lives. The contrast with the conditions in the British lines, where men were sometimes up to their waists in water, was profound, and the question was asked over and over again whether it would be possible to get British troops to expend so much energy for their comfort and safety as had evidently the Germans.

Ransart

Two days later the *Second* was withdrawn from the outpost line and, resting at Basseux for the night, it moved, on the 21st, to Bienvillers, and on the 24th relieved the 2/4th Bn., London Regt., then in reserve at Boiry St. Martin, and on the following day took its place again in the outpost line between Boyelles and St. Leger. To take up this position it was, of course, necessary to traverse much of the ground recently surrendered by the enemy, and many were the genuinely shocked remarks at the wilful damage done to property of all kinds. That roads should be mined was understandable enough, but that cottage property should be razed to the ground and even cemeteries desecrated, seemed both wicked and stupid. Scarcely one stone stood upon another; the whole area was a shambles. Not until later was it realised that the systematic removal or destruction of everything likely to afford shelter or protection to the advancing troops was in accordance with the elaborate plan of defence associated with the Hindenburg Line, so sited as to give, with the removal of interrupting objects, an extensive command over all approaches to it.

Bienvillers

Boyelles

The outpost line between St. Leger and Boyelles was within a couple of miles of the Hindenburg Line and the strong points established in front of it, and for the suppression of the latter, cavalry (Bengal Lancers) were employed to locate and overpower them. Unsuccessful as were these minor actions, they enabled the advancing British to consolidate their positions before moving closer to the German strongholds. In this forward movement the *Sixth* was spared, not to save them from offensive action, but because there was apparently more important work to be done. Hurriedly, on the 27th, it was withdrawn from the line, moved to its former billets at Bienvillers on the 28th, and on the next day the whole battalion, with its transport, marched some ten miles westward to Lucheux. Early the following morning it continued its march in a westerly direction, reaching Fortel at the end of the day; and again on the following day, continuing the march, the village of Tollent, on the River Authie, was reached. Westward-ho! The march was resumed next morning, and rumours were afoot that the division was to return to England to repel a projected German invasion. Caumont was reached by the night of April 2nd, and everyone speculated on what would be the morrow's orders. Another day's march would bring the battalion very nearly to the coast, and then that lying jade—rumour—would at last be vindicated. But it was not to be. True to Army tradition, motor-lorries arrived at Caumont on the morrow, and carried the battalion, not to the coast, but all the way back almost to its starting-point! In fact, de-bussing took place that evening at Mailly-Maillet, a small village in the Somme area, close to the River Ancre, but eight miles from Bienvillers. Here it remained for three days, and then

Caumont

Mailly-Maillet

moved a little closer to the new line into bivouacs at Bihucourt, a village lying between Achiet-le-Grand and Bapaume, where, in snow and rain and bitterly cold winds, it cursed the War and all pertaining to it. **Bihucourt**

Why was it here? As has been seen, the *First* had already established a name for itself, both as a first-class fighting unit and a hard-working battalion, and not infrequently it bemoaned the fact that wherever it went it was under the necessity of doing other people's work with pick and shovel. Perhaps something of the reputation it had established had been heard of in the 58th Divisional Headquarters, for here at Bihucourt the *Second* was to discharge similar tasks. Reference has already been made to the destruction wrought by the enemy during his retirement, and nowhere was this more noticeable than at road junctions and crossings. At such points the ways were virtually barred to all but infantry by enormous craters, in which moderately sized houses might easily stand without their roofs reaching road-level, and wherever houses stood along the highways, they had been razed to the ground in such a manner that most of the débris fell across the thoroughfare. Hence the amount of labour required to clear the roads and make them passable for horse-drawn vehicles was stupendous, and it seemed as if the *Sixth* was called upon to do most of it.

A change in command took place whilst the battalion was at Bihucourt, and Colonel Collinson, who had commanded it almost since its formation in the early days of the War, was succeeded by Lt.-Col. A. Foord, of the Manchester Regiment. Colonel Foord had for some time been employed as Brigade-Major of the 173rd Inf. Bde., and his being posted to command the 2nd/6th Bn., London Regt., helped to strengthen the ties that bound the battalion to other units in the division. **Col. Foord**

Meanwhile, the *First,* after its astonishingly successful raid on February 20th, 1917, for which Colonel Mildren had received the D.S.O., and no less than four M.C.'s, two D.C.M.'s, and sixteen well-deserved Military Medals had been awarded, remained in the Hill 60 Sector, south-east of Ypres, doing garrison duty in the trenches, and when relieved, resting in huts at Scottish Camp. Two years had passed since this battalion had last set foot on English soil, and to mark the anniversary of its sailing, a football match was played on March 17th with the 7th Battalion, always regarded as the battalion's most friendly unit.

Early in May, however, it left the area, and marching, on the 13th, from Ontario Camp, Reninghelst, through Boeschepe to Abeele, near which it found billets for the night, and on the following day through Steenvoorde,

Ebblingham St. Sylvestre, Hondeghem, and Staple, it reached the large village of Ebblinghem, some six miles to the east of St. Omer. The battalion's march was continued on the 15th, through Renescure, Blendecques, Wizarnes, Setques, and *Acquin* Lumbres, to its destination, Acquin. This was no forced march, but in three days it had covered nearly forty miles, most of which had been done in the last two. Here it remained until the end of the month.

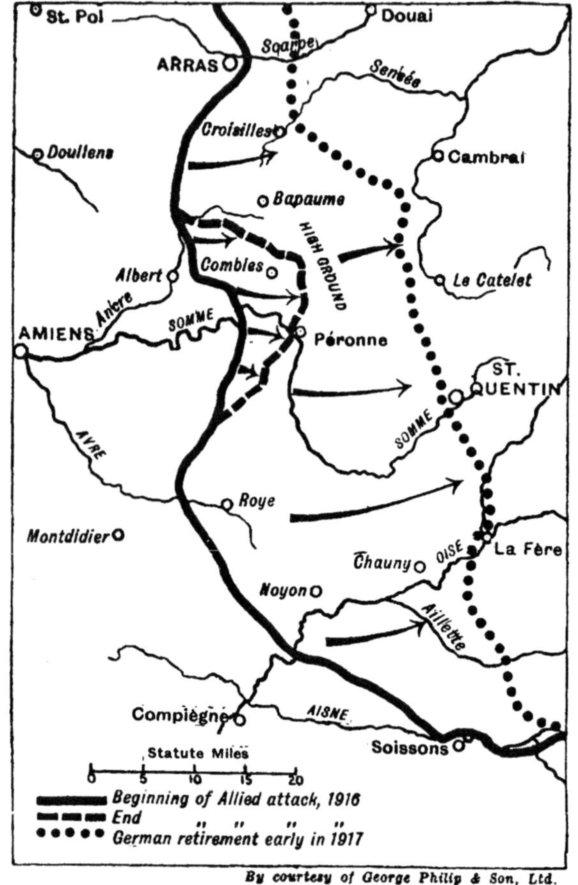

MAP 8.—THE GERMAN RETIREMENT, 1917.

Whilst the *First* was moving away from the line for a period of well-earned rest, the *Second*, many miles to the south, was packing up its bivouacs at Bihucourt preparatory to assisting in a task that was to defy the stoutest efforts of English and Australian troops. Bullecourt, lying at the junction of two massive German trench systems running, roughly, north to Arras, and south-east to Laon, had so far proved an unyielding part of the Hindenburg Line.

Bihucourt

Why were the two battalions, like hundreds of others, preparing for offensive action? The answer is interesting only because it illustrates how in democratic countries public opinion may dictate military activity. Distressed as were the British people at the appalling losses on the Somme battlefields and disquieted at the thought of possible incompetency in the higher command, they were none the less quietly proud of the prowess of their new armies, especially when the retirement of the enemy, in March, seemed to suggest that the much-vaunted German Army was beginning to show the first signs of defeat. The truth was, of course, that despite the optimistic reports from the British G.H.Q., the Germans were anything but feeling themselves beaten. Ludendorff's retirement to the Hindenburg Line was merely in obedience to the military principle of the conservation of strength, or in other words, to save his men unnecessary losses and fatigue. By shortening his front fewer divisions were required to man the trenches. But the reaction of the British people was that they were beginning to reap the early fruits of ultimate victory.

Pronounced as was the effect of the Somme battles on the British people, it was greater on the French, who before the end of 1916 were beginning to demand increased activity on the part of their armies. In November of that year, the Allied Commanders-in-Chief had met to draw up schemes for a continuation of the offensive in 1917, and as though to show their earnestness in the part the French were to play, Joffre was dismissed and Nivelle appointed in his place. Three conferences were held, at which it was eventually decided largely to meet the wishes of the French the main thrust should be made by the French armies operating in Champagne, after the British had first struck a blow east of Arras with a view to breaking through the established German defences, as well as the half-finished northward extension of the Hindenburg Line, the Droucourt-Queant Switch, lying five miles beyond them. The retirement of the Germans in March, 1917, in reality removed the strategic object of compelling a retreat, but, nevertheless, the plan of a double thrust from north and south was retained, and on April 9th British battalions assaulted the German defences facing Arras on a twelve-mile front, from Croiselles in the south (about six miles north-east from Bihucourt, where the *Second* was in

French High Command

Hindenburg Line

bivouacs) to Vimy Ridge in the north. The first day's fighting, though not everywhere successful, was generally encouraging, and on the 11th, to divert
Bihucourt attention and attract German reinforcements farther south, Gough's Fifth Army struck a little to the right, the Australians attacking Bullecourt, which they overran, only to find large numbers of Germans who had remained in their massive dug-outs until the tanks and first waves had passed over, reformed in their rear. The battle ended on the 14th, and if a break-through had not been accomplished, at least thirteen thousand prisoners and two hundred guns had been captured. But Bullecourt, a key position, remained in enemy hands, and although, on the 11th, parts of it had been penetrated, it was not until May 7th that a footing had been gained in the village itself, and not until the 17th that what was left of the village had passed into the hands of the three Australian divisions which had repeatedly attacked it. Not even now could it be said that Bullecourt had been taken, for Bovis Trench, lying just beyond the north-eastern outskirts of the village, was still actively defended by a most tenacious enemy, and not until that was cleared, and Bullecourt freed from its menace, could the general advance east and west of the village be made.

To capture Bovis Trench was the task given to the *Second;* and,
Mory apprehensive, the unit marched from Bihucourt to Mory on May 15th, and into Bullecourt on the 18th.

Bullecourt For six weeks now, Bullecourt had been subjected to heavy bombardments by guns of all calibres. It had early passed through the stage of looking as though an army of housebreakers had been at work upon it, and was now entirely demolished. Nothing remained but heaps of stones and piles of débris, and these, constantly shifting by the hourly bursting of thousands of shells, were daily giving to Bullecourt the appearance of a wide plain of heaving desolation. Of all the buildings only the church could be identified, a white mound of crumbling stone, higher than the rest, marking the centre of the village. Over all hung perpetually a cloud of dust, and through it passed continually every missile that modern weapons could throw. One object alone remained almost intact. An isolated crucifix to the west of the village, partly sheltered by a sunken road, had so far escaped destruction.

From this crucifix ran a sunken road north-eastwards, cutting through Bovis Trench to another road coming south, which it joined near an isolated factory. This southern road, too, came to Bullecourt, entering it at the north-east, first cutting the Bovis Trench at its eastern end. Between these two roads lay the objective allotted to the attacking battalion, whose plan provided that both roads should be used as defensive flanks. The principal action, performed by A (Major Collins) and B (Capt. Hartley) Companies, was to consist of a direct frontal attack to be delivered immediately after a four-minute hurricane barrage on the main objective. White tapes were laid during the night 200 yards in front of Bovis Trench, the Intelligence Section, under Sgt. Grundy, being entrusted with this task. One of them, who kept a diary, wrote: *Bullecourt*

"We started at 9 p.m. and went north into no-man's-land, eventually finishing up fifty yards from the enemy line. Working on compass bearings, we crawled along over a succession of shell-holes. Now and then the whole

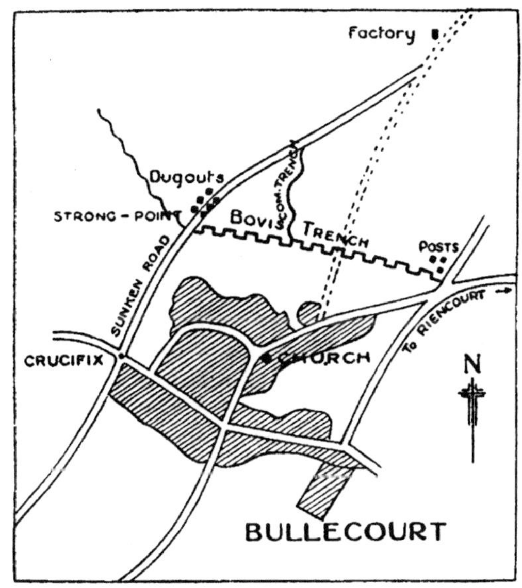

MAP 9.—BULLECOURT.
Scale approximately 3 inches = 1 mile.

ground lit up with Verey-lights, but strange to say, we were not disturbed, though we were probably watched all the time . . . Thoroughly exhausted, we arrived at Battalion Headquarters and begged for water. Never before had we realised the want of it (so much) . . . I was told to go out again and put a company on to the tapes, and although I was almost dead-beat, it had to be done. Once again through the shelling. I reached B Company, ready, but shaking with the results of barrages, and totally lacking in that dare-devil

Bullecourt confidence which is necessary at such times. The men were heavily laden, so it was only possible to go slowly, and with great difficulty I eventually got the company in position one minute before zero-hour."*

Coinciding with the main frontal attack on Bovis Trench were four minor tasks. A Company was to detach a platoon to clear enemy posts on the road to Riencourt, and to establish a Lewis-gun post in the communication trench running northwards from Bovis Trench. D Company were to provide a strong flanking patrol on the right, moving up the Bullecourt-Factory road, and one platoon of C Company was to protect the left flank of the advance by working up the Crucifix-Factory road, and bombing the dug-outs built in its banks.

At 4 a.m. the hurricane bombardment commenced, and four minutes later A and B Companies moved forward. Almost at once the enemy put down a heavy defensive barrage of high-explosive shells and shrapnel, whilst nests of machine-guns which, theoretically, should have been destroyed, sprang into activity. Before many yards had been covered severe casualties had been suffered, particularly in the centre, where the two companies touched, and in the darkness, intensified by the smoke and dirt, the gap thus caused was invisible. The two companies continued the advance. Shells were falling and bursting so thickly that it was impossible to tell where the enemy defensive barrage ceased and the British began; but the objective had been clearly described beforehand, and the attackers believed that once Bovis Trench was reached they had but to destroy or capture its defenders and consolidate their positions. Their information was that the trench was only lightly held and would offer little or no resistance.

But where was Bovis Trench? On the right, of what had once been Bovis Trench there was now no sign, and the right-hand company advanced over its objective, which, under the severe shelling it had suffered, was like the rest of Bullecourt, completely demolished. Instead, therefore, of halting, it continued the advance and seems to have lost direction and swung slightly right. Two hundred yards farther on it commenced to dig in, but enemy machine-guns and well-posted snipers caused heavy casualties, and eventually the depleted ranks, in danger every minute of being surrounded, were ordered to withdraw, all but one becoming casualties in the attempt to do so.

The left company met with unexpected opposition from machine-guns behind the objective (which was partly discernible) and from posts near the German dug-outs on the Crucifix road. A slight swing towards them, in the circumstances, was bound to take place, and thus, with the right company's swing to the right, a gap occurred between the two, and soon enemy machine-guns

*The War Diary states that companies were in their jumping-off positions one hour before zero.

BRIG.-GENERAL VISCOUNT HAMPDEN, K.C.B., C.M.G.,
Commanding 140th Brigade, 1916-1917.

Plate 22

AN INSPECTION BY GENERAL SIR IAN HAMILTON, IN DECEMBER, 1914, ON CHAILEY COMMON.

OFFICERS OF THE "SECOND" AT IPSWICH, 1915.

MAJOR TUCKER, WARRANT OFFICERS, AND SERGEANTS OF THE "SECOND," IPSWICH, 1915.

COL. COLLINSON WITH WARRANT OFFICERS AND SERGEANTS AT CROWBOROUGH, 1915.

had found their way into it. Then, the advance was brought to a standstill, and although in isolated groups they stood their ground, a German counter-attack in the evening forced the remaining handful back.

The personal experiences of a wounded corporal of the company operating on the left, throws some light on the reasons for the failure:

"Every available man was 'roped in,' and we seemed to be so hard put to it that even wounded men were sent back from the dressing station to take part in the attack. I well remember one N.C.O., who was wounded by shrapnel in the leg during the afternoon—not badly, of course—had to report back in the evening. We lost quite a lot of men getting through Bullecourt. Jerry was dropping 'whiz-bangs' pretty frequently. We arrived on the tapes about two a.m. I remember the officers shaking hands just before the whistle went. We were told that the trench we had to take was only sparsely occupied, probably by a machine-gun or two. As soon as the whistle went, however, and we got under way, the most awful inferno broke out. Jerry simply swamped us with shell-fire, machine-gun, and rifle fire. It seemed as though they knew all about this business. To me it seemed more like 600 yards than 200 yards, and afterwards, when discussing it with other prisoners, we were all agreed that the distance was wrong, as was the information that the trench was only partially held."

So much for the two companies involved. What of those performing the minor tasks? The platoon of A Company, which was to protect the right flank by working up the Bullecourt-Factory road, suffered severely, and influenced by the swing of the main attack, also slightly lost direction. The platoon of A Company, detailed to clear enemy posts from the Riencourt road, seems to have been successful, and afterwards mixed with the right of the main attack. The platoon of C Company, working northwards along the sunken road from the Crucifix, met the same stern opposition as did the left-hand company, and after suffering heavily, delivered a frontal attack, with no success, on enemy posts by now discovered in the neighbourhood of the dug-outs which the platoon was to bomb.

A rifleman of C Company (No. 2 Platoon), writes in connection with its task:

"Although I was in the second wave, we soon caught up with the first. We arrived at our trench (objective) but there was no enemy about, but we slung our bombs down dug-outs. Then we went to a big shell-hole and fortified it, making a parapet and position for the Lewis-gun. When daylight came we began to receive attention from Jerry's snipers, and some of the team

Bullecourt

were wounded, and that night I went back to report where we were . . . and later I guided an officer and Lewis-gun team of the 7th Battalion to the position which they consolidated. My impression of the action is that the Germans withdrew all their men from the front line and fired on us from his support or reserve trenches."

One company-sergeant-major, writing shortly after the event, said:

"I don't think many actually reached the trench,* most of our men, at all events, seem to have stopped in the shell-holes about thirty yards away, and to have done more rifle firing than anything else. The casualties were so many that they were reduced to mere groups, and they retired as best they could during the darkness of the ensuing night. Everybody behaved splendidly, and it is a real treat to hear the commendation which the fellows give to each other."

The attack was a failure, and in his report of the action, the Commanding Officer attributed it to three main reasons; the impossibility of recognising objectives and over-running them on the right, where the enemy evidently retired to fortified shell-holes in their rear; severe casualties from machine-gun fire from the left, and in the centre, where the gap had occurred consequent upon the loss in direction; and heavy losses early in the attack, particularly among officers. He concluded his report by saying: "Of the 111 men reported missing, four have since reported, and evidence points to the fact that the remainder were either killed or so severely wounded as to be unable to get back to our lines. Of eleven officers who went over only three have returned, all of them wounded." More eloquently than any written report speaks the aeroplane photograph of the area, which showed that weeks before the *Second* went to its death, not one stone was left unturned, and scarcely a mark remained by which anything could be recognised.

Since going into Bullecourt, the battalion had lost no less than thirteen officers and two hundred and twenty-six other ranks, in killed, wounded, or missing. In the space of a few hours it had been reduced in numbers by one-half; and later events were to prove that it had been sacrificed in a vain endeavour to secure a few more square yards of a grimly contested key-position. No reflections could be made on the quality of leadership, nor on the loyalty and skill of the troops employed. Acts of individual heroism proved that to the hilt, and devotion to duty was beyond all praise. Had the attack been ordered for a later hour, when there was more light, or had the artillery preparation been effective, another story might have been told. Perhaps if

---

*Doubtless, the attackers had gone well beyond their objective owing to its obliteration, and then realising it, they halted.

fewer officers had been killed in the early stages of the attack, and if the exact positions of the enemy had been known, the tale might have been different. If, in fact, it had been possible to foresee the possible combination of all these adverse circumstances, the attack might have been successful; but it must always be remembered that eager as were the British to advance their lines north-east of Bullecourt, the Germans were equally determined that not one yard should be conceded. *Bullecourt*

Bitter as was the humiliation of defeat, the battalion was not slow to recover its normal composure, encouraged as it was by the knowledge of superhuman individual efforts on the part of those who took part in the attack. Some measure of their staunchness and loyalty to one another can be gauged from the authentic story, learned later, of two wounded N.C.O.'s captured by the Germans, who learned on their way to the German dressing-station that a British officer was out in front of the German lines apparently badly wounded. Without a moment's hesitation the two went out and brought him in, and later, in captivity, managed to visit him occasionally, until his death from the wounds he had received freed them from such service. Such incidents were the redeeming feature of a ghastly episode, the horror of which can best be imagined. Let it be recorded here that the Germans themselves spent many hours collecting the battalion's wounded.

The month of June (1917) saw the battalion still in the same area, although Bullecourt itself was not again held. Indeed, the losses sustained scarcely warranted the battalion's being considered a fighting unit, and until it was made up by drafts from England, it was forced to play a subsidiary role. But although small in numbers, it was still able to do its part in operations undertaken by other units, and by the 13th found itself attached to the 173rd Inf. Bde, then commanded by General Freyberg, V.C., who had received orders to attack the Hindenburg Line at points known as the Hump and the Knuckle, a little less than a mile north of Bullecourt. This brigade's attack was delivered on the 15th, B and C Companies of the *Sixth* co-operating with it, whilst A and D Companies were used as supporting troops, occupying positions during the operation along a railway embankment south-east of Croiselles. Towards the end of the month the 58th Division was withdrawn from the area, and in the first week of July, moved south into a part of the front but recently held by the French. *Croiselles*

* * * * *

Whilst the *Second* was undergoing its first great ordeal by battle, the *First* was training to take part in yet another great British attack. By May 31st its

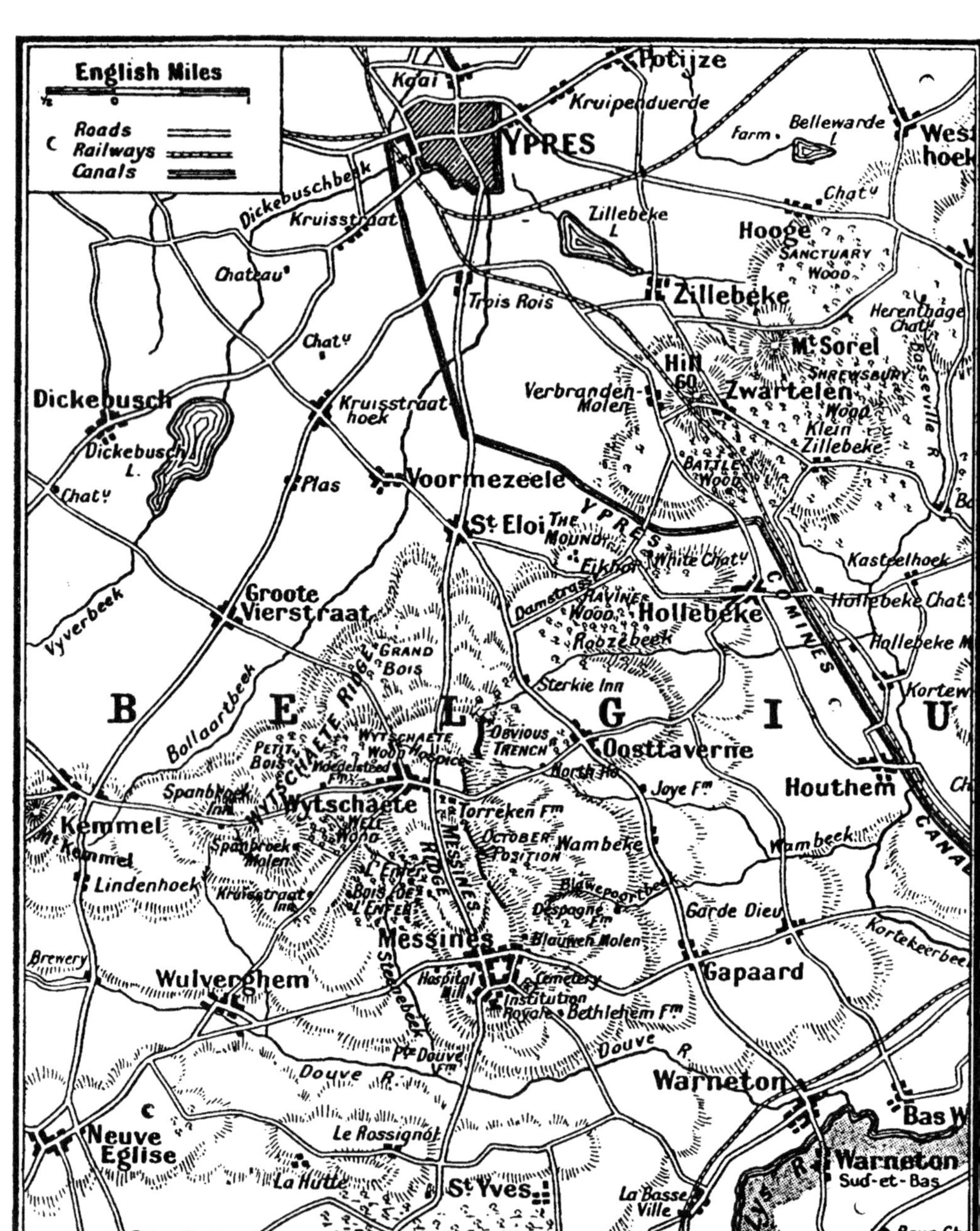

By courtesy of The Amalgamated Press, Ltd.

MAP 10.—THE MESSINES RIDGE.

very pleasant stay in Acquin was brought to a close, and its return to the line commenced. After marching to St. Omer, the battalion entrained for Poperinghe, and on arrival marched to Ouderdom. **Acquin** **Ouderdom**

The Battle of Arras had been undertaken in co-operation with the French Army, now commanded by the enthusiastic and optimistic General Nivelle, whose plan, it will be remembered, consisted of two converging attacks to be delivered simultaneously by the British, eastwards from the direction of Arras, and by the French, northwards from the Aisne. However, the chisel, although hammered with terrific French blows, encountered hard obstacles; and as a result of disaffection amongst the French troops and political influence, the offensive was discontinued, and the whole vast project brought to naught. Indeed, had Ludendorff been aware of the condition of the French troops, and ordered a counter-stroke, the War might have ended disastrously for the Allies.

To give the French time to recover and to attract German attention to another part of the line, preparations for the Battle of Messines, already included in the general plan of advance to come into operation upon the French southern success, were hurriedly pushed forward; and with an artillery preparation in which over 2,300 guns, throwing 90,000 tons of ammunition, were employed, an assault on a nineteen-mile front from Ypres to Armentieres was launched on June 7th.

In this battle the 47th Division was employed attacking in a south-easterly direction astride the Ypres-Comines canal, the 1st/6th Bn., London Regt., with other units of the 140th Inf. Bde., operating on the right, south of the canal. The objectives allotted to the brigade were the White Chateau and its stables to the south of it, and a portion of the Damstrasse Trench flanking it. In the plan of attack the 7th and 8th Battalions were to make the initial assault, taking the first objectives, including the White Chateau, whilst the *Sixth* and 15th Battalions were to pass through the newly won positions to the assault of the final objectives.

On June 5th, the battalion paraded in fighting order, and moved from Ouderdom across country by platoons at fifty yards intervals, to Ecluse Trench, whence on the following day to the first assembly point—Old French Trench—which it reached by 11.30 p.m. The battle commenced at dawn on the 7th with the firing of twenty-two mines and a terrific bombardment, in which guns of all calibre took part, while aeroplanes dropped bombs on the enemy positions. At 5.30 a.m., two hours after the battle had commenced, the leading company filed out of Old French Trench, and in due course crossed no-man's-land and arrived in the German third-line trench, having suffered few casualties. Indeed, the slackening of hostile shell-fire had been noticeable

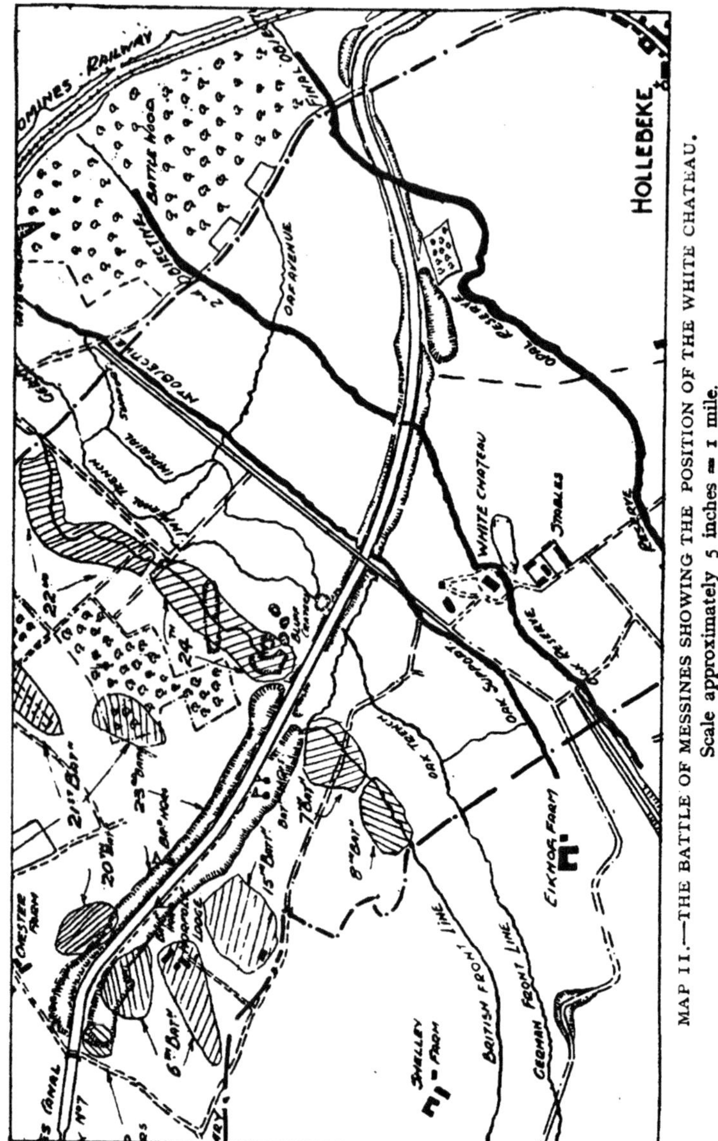

MAP II.—THE BATTLE OF MESSINES SHOWING THE POSITION OF THE WHITE CHATEAU.
Scale approximately 5 inches = 1 mile.

within an hour of the commencement of the attack* and it only intensified when a German observation balloon was apparently able to indicate valuable targets to the German gunners. No difficulty was found in maintaining direction during the advance, a compass bearing having been given to each company before it commenced.

On arriving at the German reserve line it was found that the 7th Battalion had failed to secure the White Chateau, and that hostile fire covered all approaches to it; also that there were enemy machine-guns in the grounds of the chateau which were enfilading the *Sixth* and the battalion on the right. At this point in the battle an extraordinarily daring act was performed by C.S.Maj. C. Bitten which must be recorded, if only to show what, single-handed, a brave man can do. Running to the company on the right he quickly ascertained the position of affairs from Cpl. Girling, and then climbed to the top of the chateau, from where he could see two enemy machine-guns firing steadily from positions a little beyond it. He threw two bombs, scattering the crews of the guns, and then, his ammunition exhausted, continued to pelt them with bricks, and waved to Capt. Ordish and Major Maynard to advance. Acting on these signals the two companies continued their forward movement, and soon the German third line was captured, and covering cross-fire arranged behind the chateau.

White Chateau

The chateau having been effectively isolated, the assault upon the out-buildings was undertaken. Behind an effective artillery barrage the attacking platoons advanced, cleared the first set of stables, and making good use of their Lewis-guns when the barrage lifted, rapidly gained and surrounded the second set of stables and an adjacent wood, and there captured two German officers and sixty-one men.

The task that now remained was to capture the trench system beyond the buildings. At Acquin, where the plan of attack had been prepared, and every movement practised, special attention had been given to the final advance, and this attention to detail was well repaid. A specially trained bombing party, formed to clear the front line and support trenches of this system, entered the first with ease, cleared the enemy from the battered trench and shell-holes, and following closely the lifting barrage, took the support line, silenced a machine-gun whose team took refuge in a dug-out and were bombed, captured many prisoners, and, more important, established communication with the troops operating on the left. Meanwhile two companies detailed to make the final assault upon Opal Reserve Trench, made their way through the stables, deployed, by sections, to the Opal Support Trench, which by now

*The result of effective counter-battery work by the British "heavies."

White Chateau

had been secured by the special bombing party, and there assembled for the battalion's last task. A frontal attack, made in two waves of two lines each, immediately the barrage lifted, was completely successful, and the leading men had the satisfaction of seeing the remainder of the German garrison leave their positions and retire in disorder down the gentle slope towards the little village of Hollebeke.

Immediate steps were taken to consolidate the gains made, the usual protective screen being thrown out in front, whilst the work of digging and sandbagging was carried out. Earlier in the day Battalion Headquarters had been established in the ruins of the White Chateau, an act of audacity conforming exactly with the *élan* that so characterised every movement performed throughout the day. Two officers and thirty other ranks were killed, and eighty-one (all ranks) wounded during the action—numbers which, though heavy in themselves, were comparatively low, and which testify to the thoroughness of the preparation for and delivery of a determined stroke.

So ended the first day's fighting; but there was more to be done. On the following day, spent in consolidating, the Divisional Commander visited Battalion Headquarters, and discussed a scheme whereby the *First* should advance its line slightly to form with a battalion of the 24th Division, acting on its right, a line of outposts stretching from Opal Reserve Trench southwards to the most advanced posts on the right. The attack launched later in the day is very briefly dismissed in the War Diary, which states laconically: "Scheme was unsuccessful owing to the battalion on our right being unable to reach their objectives on account of shell-fire. We established three posts, the garrisons of which were withdrawn at dawn."

The battalion was relieved that night (10th) by the 15th Bn., and found shelter and rest in dug-outs in Ecluse Trench, and on the 12th moved out of the line to Ontario Camp.

Ontario Camp

The actions at Bullecourt and the White Chateau, coming as they did within a month of one another, but under totally different circumstances in widely separated parts of the front, must serve as examples of courting failure and inviting success. The material was largely the same; but in the one it was called upon to attack ill-defined objectives held by resolute opponents, without preparation and without adequate support; and in the other, to carry out a nicely conceived attack, repeatedly rehearsed, and supported with an immense weight of accurately-timed artillery fire which had already paralysed opposition. Small wonder that the one should be a lament and the other a proud boast.

FIRST BATTALION OFFICERS, WARRANT OFFICERS and SECTION COMMANDERS at

MESSINES—1917

Officer Commanding : Col. Mildren	Second-in-Command : Major Neely	Adjutant : Capt. Gilks
R.S.Maj. Abery		R.Q.M.Sgt. Percival
A Co. (I) Capt. Eve	C.S.Maj. Phillips	C.Q.M.Sgt. Sandison
(II) Capt. Cooke		
B Co. Capt. Ordish	C.S.Maj. Bitten	C.Q.M.Sgt. Kent
C Co. Capt. Maynard	C.S.Maj. Murphy	C.Q.M.Sgt. Weedon
D Co. Capt. Green	C.S.Maj. Snow	C.Q.M.Sgt. Good (J)

Quartermaster : Capt. Lovett
Transport : Lieut. Noakes ; Sgt. Brown ; Cpl. Pollard
Cooks : Sgt. Britten ; Cpl. Grant
Stretcher-Bearers : Capt. Hope-Carlton ; Sgt. Wade
Signallers : Sgt. Houghton ; Cpl. Sharp
Lewis-Guns : Sgt. Short ; Sgt. Drage ; Cpl. Ryland ; Cpl. Paxton
Orderly Room : Cpl. Peebles ; Cpl. Wade ; Cpl. Stapleton

SECOND BATTALION OFFICERS, WARRANT OFFICERS and SECTION COMMANDERS at

BULLECOURT—1917

Officer Commanding : Col. Foord	Second-in-Command: Major Tucker	Adjutant : Capt. Crofts
Act.-R.S.Maj. Catlin		R.Q.M.Sgt. Parish
A Co. Major Collins (killed)	Act.-C.S.Maj. Macey	C.Q.M.Sgt. Williams
B Co. Capt. Hartley (killed)	C.S.Maj. Godfrey	C.Q.M.Sgt. Martin
C Co. Capt. Lathbury	C.S.Maj. Palowkar	C.Q.M.Sgt. Davies
D Co. Lt. Smart	C.S.Maj. Morris	C.Q.M.Sgt. Leat

Quartermaster : Lieut. Goodger
Transport : Lieut. Webb ; Sgt. Russell
Cooks : Sgt. Buckland
Stretcher-Bearers : Major de Muth ; Sgt. Yelland ; Cpl. Iveson
Signallers : Lieut. Tew ; Sgt. Wilson
Lewis-Guns : Sgt. Webster
Scouts and Snipers : Lieut. Godfrey ; Sgt. Grundy ; Cpl. Larkworthy

Chapter 13

IN THE SALIENT, I

After their exertions at the White Chateau and Bullecourt respectively, both the *First* and the *Second* deserved periods of rest, but some weeks of duty in the line lay before them ere they could be released for that purpose. Of the two, the former was the more fortunate, for after a few days as supports in Ecluse Trench, that battalion was moved back to

Ontario Camp
Ebblingham

Ontario Camp, whence, on June 15th, it marched to Caestre, and on the following day to Ebblinghem, a village some six miles west of Hazebrouck. There it remained for twelve days, fairly comfortable in billets, barns, and outhouses, training and reorganising; and there, as if to mark the approach of midsummer's day, trousers were cut, turned up, and thus converted into "shorts." The month was hot, and the change in costume much appreciated, as was also the daily visit by motor-lorry to Blaringhem, through which passed the Canal de Neuf Fosse, in the cool waters of which the battalion bathed again and again. The tenth day of their stay was marked by attendance at the divisional aquatic sports, the "odd-craft" race and greasy-pole competition affording considerable entertainment. A torch-light tattoo in the evening brought a memorable day to a close.

Ridge Wood

But the fine weather couldn't last for ever; and it was in a deluge of rain when, on June 28th, the battalion marched via Hazebrouck, Borre, and Strazeele to Meteren, and on the following day, in fairer weather, via Schaexton, Berthen, Westoutre, Scherpenbourg, and La Clytte, to Ridge Wood, where in bivouacs it rested the night. Before midnight on the last day of the month the battalion was back in the trenches of the Ypres Salient. On this occasion a sector between Bois Confluent and Bus House, south of the

White Chateau

Ypres-Menin road, near the White Chateau, was occupied. For the first fortnight little occurred to make the tour of duty memorable, but during the latter half of the month events moved swiftly enough.

Following the Battle of Messines there were, as usual, many local actions undertaken with a view to straightening the line or securing some point of vantage. Part and parcel with them went interminable patrolling, and not a little raiding. It was fully expected that the Germans would make some attempt to recapture the ground they had lost, and the desirability of securing prisoners who might be willing to give information as to the movements of their own formations was understandable. All men work better when they see a good reason for their work, and there seems to have been a ready acceptance of tasks imposed upon the battalion. On July 14th, after a few days in support, the *First* went into the front-line again, this time on the left of their former positions. D and C Companies were forward, with A and B in support, and Battalion headquarters were established in Norfolk Bank Tunnel. Patrolling commenced at once, and nightly parties, consisting of one N.C.O. and six men, crossed no-man's-land from each of the forward companies to obtain all the information they could, and if possible to secure prisoners.

To straighten the line in the neighbourhood of Junction Bridge, the 19th Division, on the right of the *Sixth*, made a small advance on the night of the 17th. In this minor operation the battalion co-operated, as was usual, with units on the flanks, and under cover of an artillery barrage two fighting-patrols, furnished by C and D Companies, entered the enemy's trench-system through an unoccupied bombing post at the head of Oblique Trench, which, as its name implies, ran crosswise towards the British line. After entering it the patrols worked up Oblique Trench and another trench running south-east towards a small wood until resistance was encountered, which took the form of a heavy shower of canister-bombs. The patrols replied with Mills, but unable to dislodge the enemy they opened-out and endeavoured to surround the defending garrison. The supply of bombs running short, however, compelled a retirement, and the patrols returned to their companies, having themselves suffered no casualties.

Oblique trench

The attack by the 19th Division was successful but short-lived. On the following day the Germans counter-attacked and retook their positions, only to be evicted later, and still later to counter-attack once again, and again successfully. Such stern defence on the part of the Germans was significant. Nor did it take the form solely of counter-attacks. There was heavy and persistent shelling of both forward and back areas, in which gas was used freely. Further, German planes began to fly low over the British lines. Something was afoot, and the necessity of obtaining at least identification of the German troops holding their line became urgent. That afternoon (22nd) Sec.-Lt. Shepherd and a small party of picked N.C.O.'s worked their way over no-man's-land and entered Optic Trench, another work running obliquely towards the British lines, hoping to take a few prisoners. They found the trench strongly held, and an exciting bombing duel took place, but they could secure no prisoners.

Optic trench

To achieve this object, therefore, the Commanding Officer decided immediately to prepare a more elaborate undertaking, and issued detailed operation orders with maps for a raid on the enemy's lines, to take place at 10 p.m. on the following day (23rd). There was, of course, no time for preliminary training. For ten days the battalion had been in the line holding posts in shell-holes, where no trenches existed, and working hard to provide communication trenches, and conditions were anything but pleasant; but the *First* had already established a reputation for itself as a raiding battalion, and the Commanding Officer judged aright that the operation would prove successful.

Raid on Oblique and Optic trenches

The objectives selected were Oblique Trench and the ground as far as the Comines canal beyond it, and a little to the right, the trench running in front of the small wood already referred to, and beyond that to a road lying some two hundred yards farther away. Two parties were formed: that for attacking Oblique Trench was commanded by Sec.-Lt. A. C. Sampson, and that for the wood, by Sec.-Lt. Shepherd. An experienced officer has expressed the view that of the two the former task presented the greater difficulties, and bearing in mind that Oblique Trench had twice before been assaulted, it is to be supposed that the enemy would be on the alert and ready for any eventuality. The operation orders provided for an intense bombardment by 18-pounders on the objectives themselves, to last for five minutes, after which the artillery fire was to lift and smother the areas immediately behind those to be raided. Artillery retaliation and a defensive barrage was to be expected, and if this fell upon the raiders the success of the venture would be jeopardised. All holding the shell-holes, therefore, were instructed not to look at aircraft flying overhead during the day-time, and on no account to fire at the planes, and thus disclose their positions. This wise order completely justified itself, for when the action commenced and the enemy barrage descended, most of the shells fell well to the rear of the forward positions, and few casualties were suffered on that account.

Each man in the raiding parties was armed with rifle and sword, and two Mills bombs, and each was instructed in the task he was to perform, and each was ordered to bring back one prisoner. Personal belongings, indeed everything that might identify the raiders should the undertaking prove a failure, was left behind. In all, the raiders numbered fifty-seven.

Punctually at five minutes to 10 p.m. the barrage commenced, and the raiders moved into their respective positions behind it. When it lifted, Sec.-Lt. Sampson's party rushed Oblique Trench before the enemy had time to man the trench, and quickly overcoming all opposition, secured twenty-nine prisoners. The assault had been delivered with such dash that the

German garrison was taken completely by surprise, and although offering some resistance, were unable to prevent each man of the raiding party from securing his prisoner. Rockets were fired from the British lines to recall the raiders, and when the left party returned with their prisoners, twenty-nine in all, belonging to a Bavarian Regiment, a most embarrassing situation arose, for they numbered more than A Company's garrison. It was solved by crowding them all temporarily in the large shell-hole that did service as A Company's Headquarters, and by covering the prisoners' heads with P.H. gas-helmets, with the eye-pieces to the back, so that none might see how big was the number taken.

The party furnished by D Company, assaulting the trench by the small wood, under Sec.-Lt. Shepherd, was not so fortunate or successful. Half-way to their objective they encountered, as soon as the barrage lifted, very strong opposition, and although they reached the German trench, heavy fire greeted them; and when the recalling coloured lights were fired from the battalion's lines, a fierce hand-to-hand struggle was still going on, and no prisoners were secured. This was a disappointment, but taking the raid as a whole it had been brilliantly successful, for it not only secured the required information, but considerably lowered the German *morale* in this sector. After the action was over, the General Staff of the Fourth Army issued extracts from a conversation with a wounded prisoner—an officer—captured during the raid. Apart from useful information he was willing to impart, he said he had fought in several different portions of the British front on the occasions when the British assaulted, and added that the raiding party attacked with great dash and determination, and that they moved across the open to the assault so close up to the artillery barrage that as it lifted they were on top of the German parapet, and gave the garrison no chance to man the trench or get their machine-guns into position.

Shortly afterwards a German document fell into the hands of the British which, when translated, proved to be a divisional order relating to the raid:

"The English succeeded, during the night of the 23rd-24th, after a short, intense bombardment, in penetrating that part of our front line occupied by the R.I.R.8., and in regaining their own lines, after capturing 31* prisoners. I am of the opinion that this very regrettable incident would have been impossible if each commander, and each man in the front line of the 12th Company, R.I.R.8., had completely carried out his duty . . . The

*Two more than the number recorded in the War Diary and quoted above.

R.I.R.8. will submit a report about the incident, showing to what extent a Court of Enquiry should investigate the conduct of individual commanders and men. I also command the R.I.R.8. to wipe out the stain as soon as possible by a powerful raid . . . Commanders of all ranks will . . . take care that the moral and fighting spirit of the troops does not suffer, and that the incident, which is very harmful to the reputation of the division, remains an exceptional case."

The *First* was naturally enough elated by this success, particularly since very few casualties had been suffered, the dead numbering three, and the wounded, mostly slight, only nine. Moreover, a valuable lesson had been learnt, to be taught subsequently in Army schools, that at the risk of suffering casualties from a covering barrage, raiders would be more likely to find an enemy unprepared and less likely to suffer losses from hostile fire, if they kept close to the barrage, and thus reduced the distance to be covered before reaching an objective.*

Similar actions were taking place all along the Ypres front, and were the usual preliminaries to some big offensive. But the British Army had already delivered its stroke at the Battle of Messines. Could it be that another offensive was about to be commenced ? And if so, why was Flanders selected as the area for the operations ? To answer these questions satisfactorily is perhaps impossible, for although the main facts are known, controversy still rages around the necessity of attempting an assault in the historic cock-pit of Europe, whose very soil already stank of blood spilled in former battles. In the first place, the general war situation had changed, and was no longer in favour of the Allies. Whereas, in July, 1917, both the Russians on the Eastern Front, and the Italians in the south, had been attacking, by September these offensives had collapsed. Thus the German High Command was in a position to devote all its attention to its Western Front, and since the British Armies were now the chief menace, to that part of the line held by them. Had the success of Messines been followed immediately by offensive action elsewhere on the front, the German position would have indeed been serious ; but it takes time to plan a campaign, and still more to organise it, and every day's delay meant a strengthening of the German position. In the second place, whereas the Battles of Arras and Messines had been undertaken

*A Field-Officer of the *Sixth* gives it as his opinion that B Company's success was due as much as anything to the extreme care taken before the raid to keep the enemy ignorant of Company's positions. Hostile aeroplanes frequently flew low to discover them, but the Company had been as frequently told never to look upwards at them lest the airmen should spot the faces showing white against the dark earth. It may be that D Company had not exercised such care, that their positions were known, and that fire was directed against them as soon as the raid commenced. In that case they were bound to suffer heavy casualties.

largely to afford relief to the French, the need for that was passing, for under General Pétain, the new French Commander-in-Chief, the French armies were steadily recovering both their discipline and fighting spirit. In the third place, no isolated action in the north (or, come to that matter, on either flank) could in any event prove decisive. Further, Sir Douglas Haig had been warned that if the elaborate system of dykes and drainage canals were destroyed by bombardment the area would be flooded, and meteorologists had informed him that statistics showed that fine weather rarely lasted for more than two or three weeks at a stretch. His reason for selecting the Ypres area as the theatre of operations is, therefore, difficult to understand, although it is only fair to say that the Admiralty, worried by the success of the submarine campaign, urged that an attempt should be made to turn the Germans out of those Belgian ports they held. True that, in April, the Royal Navy had partially sealed Zeebrugge, and thereby reduced its usefulness as a submarine base, but there were other ports on the Belgian coast still in German hands that could harbour them; and although it was known that most of the submarines operated from German ports, the Admiralty was apprehensive, and certainly supported Haig's proposals. Again, the liberation of Belgian territory was in itself a laudable aim, would give him more room for movement, and the action he proposed would certainly have the good-will of the British people behind it. In planning a big advance eastward of Ypres, Haig was doubtless influenced by all these factors.

Despite inevitable delays the offensive commenced on July 31st, over a wide front, stretching from Steenstraat, about five miles north of Ypres, in a great semi-circle eastwards and southwards to Deulemont, lying about nine miles south of the city. The chief objective was the high ground lying to the north-east, possession of which would command the country eastwards for many miles; but to mislead the enemy as to the real intentions of the British, an advance over the whole front was planned. The French First Army, and the British Second and Fifth Armies, were engaged in the operation, and by the end of the first day the line had been advanced from half a mile in the south (where the attack was only a feint) to a couple of miles in the north. La Basse Ville, Hollebeke, Sanctuary Wood, part of Shrewsbury Forest, Verlorenhoek, Pilckem Ridge, Pommern Redoubt, and Bixschoote were all taken, and Westhoek, St. Julien, and the Steenbeek* were reached, as also were Inverness Copse and Glencorse Wood. These successes appear to have given the Commander-in-Chief satisfaction, but they were not what were hoped for, and doubts as to the wisdom of continuing with the plan were

*See the map, Page 144.

immediately raised. Indeed, General Gough, commanding the Fifth Army, usually optimistic, urged that the battle should be broken off. Why was this? Since zero hour, at 3.15 a.m., rain had fallen steadily, and there seemed no prospect of its abatement. For ten days heavy and light artillery had thrown an ever-increasing number of shells of all sizes upon and behind the German defences, and in doing so had completely destroyed the elaborate network of dykes and ditches by which the low-lying ground was drained. The Belgian authorities had questioned the wisdom of doing this, but the British G.H.Q. had evidently considered the risk worth while, for had the weather remained fine, both infantry and tanks would have met with little resistance, except from concreted strong points, the whereabouts of which were, for the most part, exactly known. As it was, both men and machines were greatly hampered by mud, the latter often becoming completely bogged and presenting easy targets to enemy gunners. For four days it rained solidly, and in those four days the fate of the enterprise was sealed. It was not until August 15th that the offensive was resumed, and by that time the Germans, now fully aware of the real intentions of the British, had constructed, or were constructing, still more concreted "mebuses."

Meanwhile, the *First*, after its successful raid on Oblique Trench, was relieved by a battalion of the Royal West Kents, and moved by small parties to Curragh Camp, where in the comparative comfort of corrugated-iron huts, it remained for the next fortnight, when not employed as supports. On such

Ridge Wood

occasions Ridge Wood was occupied, and tents, bivouacs, and dug-out shelters did service as sleeping quarters. At both places, although well within artillery range, and frequently subjected to bombing from the air, it suffered, fortunately, few casualties. Aerial activity was indeed constant, and falling observation balloons and crashing planes were frequent sights. Two planes forced to land near the camp in Ridge Wood had to be guarded until personnel from the Royal Flying Corps could be sent to salve them.

On August 12th, the battalion was relieved in Ridge Wood by the 11th and 13th Bns. of the Royal Sussex Regiment, and marched back to Kempton Camp at Westoutre. From here, on the 15th, it moved to Abeele and entrained for St. Omer, where it arrived in the afternoon; and marching

St. Martin-au-Lert

Tatinghem

to St. Martin-au-Lert, it found billets there for a couple of days, when it occupied the adjoining village of Tatinghem. Withdrawal to the rear could mean either of two things—to enjoy a well-earned rest after strenuous fighting, or to prepare for battle. It was to practise a forthcoming attack that the change had been made. Here, then, as at St. Martin-au-Lert, and Kempton Camp, training took the form of extended-order work and open-fighting

LIEUT.-GENERAL SIR G. F. GORRINGE, K.C.B., K.C.M.G., D.S.O.,
G.O.C. 47th Division, 1916-1919.

Plate 25

From the History of the 47th Division

From the History of the 47th Division

ABOVE: THE "COUGH DROP" LOOKING TOWARDS EAUCOURT L'ABBAYE.
BELOW: THE RUINED VILLAGE OF FLERS (TAKEN IN SEPTEMBER, 1916).

Plate 26

Left: THE WOODEN CROSS ERECTED AT HIGH WOOD IN SEPTEMBER, 1916, TO MARK THE LAST RESTING PLACE OF MANY WHO FELL IN THE ASSAULT ON HIGH WOOD.

Right: THE DEDICATION BY THE REV. A. E. WILKINSON, O.B.E., M.C., OF THE STONE CROSS ERECTED IN 1936.

generally, and instruction to officers and N.C.O.'s in semaphore signalling, and musketry practice on a local range completed the preparation.

Whilst at Tatinghem, the battalion twice marched to the neighbouring village of Longuenesse, on one occasion to take part in a Brigade church parade, and on the other for inspection by the Commander of the Second Army, under whom the unit had now come. After the service on the Sunday, in the grounds of the Chateau de la Croix, medal ribbons were presented by the Brigadier to eight recipients of decorations. *Tatinghem*

The move to the area of forthcoming operations took place on August 24th. Motor-buses carried the battalion from St. Martin-au-Lert northwards to Vlamertinghe, via Arques, Hondeghen, Steenvoorde, Abeele, and that veritable " capital " of the Salient, Poperinghe. From Vlamertinghe it marched to inadequate accommodation in Vancouver Camp, with headquarters and some details in the adjoining Montreal Camp. No time was lost in preparing for action. A big ground plan, built at Vauxhall, was carefully studied by officers and N.C.O.'s on the following day, and on the 26th, a Sunday, eleven officers actually reconnoitred the trenches and their approaches, from which the attack, east of Dickebusche, was to be delivered. *Vancouver Camp*

On the next two days the battalion practised the forthcoming attack over the taped course, and extra ammunition and equipment was issued to companies on the 28th. Again, with disciplined movement, it went over the course, and on the 31st, as if to mark the very last day of the month by giving a final touch to such careful preparations, it once more attacked over the tapes, and in the afternoon listened to a lantern lecture on the forthcoming operations. All was ready. Provision had been made for every contingency —but one. Driving rain, wholly out of season, was again turning the Salient into a quagmire, and further operations were for a time out of the question. That evening, the extra ammunition and equipment issued to companies three days before, were withdrawn.

Chapter 14

IN THE SALIENT, II

During the latter part of the time spent by the *First* in the Brickstacks and in the Westoutre area, the *Second* was engaged in somewhat similar activities, and when its time came for rest, the relaxation was in pleasant surroundings. Like the *First*, it, too, following a battle, found itself called upon to perform a strenuous routine trench duty, and it, too, lent active supports to units operating on the flank. The attacks by all units on Bullecourt having failed to break the German defence, the decision was made to attempt a breach in the Hindenburg Line immediately north of

Croiselles the village, in the neighbourhood of Croiselles. To the 173rd Brigade, under the command of Brig.-Gen. Freyberg, V.C., fell this task, and on June 16th, the *Second* was detached from the 174th Inf. Bde. to support the attacking troops. The action took place on June 16th, and C Company of the *Sixth* being allotted an objective in the Hindenburg Front Line, took it with little loss to themselves.

The remainder of the month was spent training, while acting as divisional supports at Courcelles; but early in July a slight change of position was ordered, and the battalion occupied the front line trenches at Beaucamps. Later in July, when the whole division was moved southwards, it found

Ytres itself doing regular tours of duty near Ytres, where the beauty of the country-side and almost complete absence of enemy action recalled the daily and nightly manœuvres of Warminster and Ipswich days, now, alas, after fighting at Bullecourt, remembered by few only of those who had sailed with the battalion in January, but six months earlier.

One of the battalion scouts, writing shortly afterwards, gives a good picture of the almost ideal conditions under which the War was now being waged by the *Second :*

" We had six of the most interesting days I have spent in the line. We lived in a little cubby-hole dug into the side of the trench, and at sunrise I was at the (observation) post, while my friend cooked the bacon. When he finished, I went down for a while, and thus we worked it all day. We had maps, prismatic compasses, and field-glasses, and reported on anything in the way of movement, artillery, and aerial activity, etc., and our scope of observation was very great. In the distance we could see, through our glasses, the trains running into the inhabited town of Cambrai . . . Daily we sent in long and often useful reports." Ytres

After recording a few days spent out of the line, the diarist continues: " This time we . . . manned a support-trench called Stafford Reserve. We had another post here, and all went well until the Company Commander started men working on the top of the trench in broad daylight. This gave the enemy a chance to reply to our gun-fire on a new trench we had discovered, and next morning he set up a furious bombardment lasting six hours, sending over three hundred and seventy-five rounds of 5.9's. Our post became too warm, and at 11 o'clock we deserted it, and found the trench a mass of great holes and duck-boards standing on end, and in crawling over the debris to Company H.Q. an enemy gun tried to find us."

The description out of the line is equally good: " We were relieved by the 5th London . . . and went to Ytres by light-railway. We alighted right outside the camp, and at 5.30 were having tea in tents. Such an easy time and novel manner of leaving the line made one think that perhaps it wasn't such a terrible War, after all. While at Ytres we had a good bath and were able to visit the well-stocked canteens, Y.M.C.A., Church Army Hut, etc., which were the only signs of civilisation. There were no civilians, as the Germans had destroyed every house, every crop, and every tree—anything of the slightest use."

At Ytres, the War, such as it had earlier been known, was far removed; at Berneville, some ten miles south-west of Arras, to where the *Second* moved on July 29th, for a month of blessed rest, it was almost forgotten. Berneville

August was ever the time for holiday-making, and like all good Londoners, the *Second* enjoyed their stay here to the full; but all good things come to an end, and no one was surprised when orders to move north were received. On the 24th, the battalion moved by buses to Bapaume, entrained, and were carried to Godewaersvelde, ten miles south-west of Poperinghe, and marching to that town, stayed there for a couple of days. On the 27th it moved by rail to Reigersburg, occupying New Camps 1 and 2, and on the following day, at dusk, to the Yser Canal, cut into the banks of which it found by no means uncomfortable dug-outs about a mile and a half north of Ypres itself. For most, however, such pleasant quarters were but temporary. On the first day of September—a month to be for ever memorable—the battalion relieved the 2nd/7th Bn., London Regt., in their positions north of St. Julien. St. Julien

Since the first advance on July 31st, some further slight progress had been made, and the outpost system here lay beyond the River Steenbeek by

about half a mile, and faced north-east in the direction of Poelcappelle. The trench-map of the sector confidently marked the river as being ten feet wide, and having in places banks five feet high. The intense bombardment to which it had been subjected by British artillery, and the continuous shelling it now received from the German, levelled the banks and diverted the waters a
St. Julien hundred times a day, with the result that the whole area was one deep bog over which progress was possible only if the several duckboard-tracks crossing it remained intact. These much frequented boards, needless to say, invited and received constant enemy shelling.

The danger from high-explosive shells was not nearly as great as was that from shrapnel, since the former would bury themselves well in the mud before exploding, and their effect would be localised. From shrapnel, however, there was no protection, unless the forward rim of an extra big and recently made shell-hole was at hand, and if it were not, a choice of a wound, or worse, or a plunge into liquid mud (from which sometimes there was no escape) had to be made. Trenches were practically non-existent, and defensive positions were but fortified shell-holes, sometimes linked together by a little scraping, in which men stood often waist-high in mud and water, their greatest care to keep arms and ammunition clean, their greatest fear to be wounded and so unable to save themselves from sinking beneath the slime.

In consequence of these foul conditions, which made movement equally impossible for foe or friend, as few as possible were detailed to man the shell-holes, and as many as possible accommodated in the concrete mebuses built by and wrested from the Germans. Ranging from quite tiny emplacements to block-houses capable of sheltering a hundred or more, these massive houses were proof against almost every kind of shell, unless, unhappily, one should pass through the low doorway, now, of course, facing the enemy, to burst inside. Some of the largest had been constructed within farmhouses and cottages, the roofs and walls of which, collapsing under bombardments and falling on or about the mebuses inside them, afforded additional protection to the defenders and proved real obstacles to attacking troops.

It was into such shell-holes and emplacements that the battalion moved on September 1st. Winding their way by half-platoons along the duckboards,
Steenbeek A and B Companies crossed the Steenbeek and took up positions close to Triangle Farm, in a line running parallel to the Langemarck-Zonnebeke road. Those not in the shell-holes were accommodated with the two Company Headquarters in an enormous concrete box called Mon. du Hibou. C Company, in support, occupied shell-holes facing the Steenbeek, and D

Company, in reserve, some disused German trenches close to Alberta, another massive concrete box, which became Battalion Headquarters, and housed runners, signallers, and stretcher-bearers. In front of Alberta ran a low concrete gallery nearly one hundred yards in length, and into this the Brigade machine-gunners packed themselves and their guns to cover the whole front should occasion arise, with a veritable curtain of bullets.

From their posts in the shell-holes the men in the forward platoons, caked with mud and often wet through, could see only a watery waste, relieved here and there by the stumps of a row of trees, or a mound where a house once stood, and where protected by four of five feet of ferro-concrete, machine-gunners now sat waiting for any movement that might be made. Facing most of the battalion's front these pill-boxes were widely spaced, but on the right there appeared to be a number very close together. As far as could be judged, they were not merely a cluster of boxes formerly occupying the interiors of a farm and its outhouses, but specially constructed and sited so as to command the ground in all directions. If, as was expected, a British advance was to be made as soon as the weather improved, special attention from heavy artillery would have to be given to them.

Blunt Salient

Evidently the position—the Blunt Salient, as it came to be called—was regarded by the Germans as important. It was with astonishment, however, that three days later the battalion received orders to make a night raid upon it, with the object of discovering, if possible, how far the system extended, and of obtaining prisoners.

Accordingly, two platoons of B Company, numbering forty-seven in all, and commanded by Capt. Webb and Sec.-Lt. H. V. Hart, made the attempt on the night of September 6th-7th. Sec.-Lt. Hart's party was to provide covering fire for the raiders under Capt. Webb. All went according to plan. A hurricane bombardment was thrown on to the " Blunt," and a box-barrage put round it. During their advance, the raiders, keeping close to this curtain fire, early lost their leader, whose death may have been due to one of our own shells falling short, but his last encouraging words: " Go on, boys," sent them forward into what was virtually unknown. Arrived at the mebuses, they found themselves first confronted by barbed wire, and then fired on from posts at the flanks, whose presence had never been suspected. Here was a new situation, and it was dealt with in the only possible manner. While some attacked them with bomb and bullet, others ran to the back of the foremost box in an endeavour to get prisoners; but for this the Germans were ready, and their defence at the rear was as virile as it was at the flanks, and consequently, when the rockets recalling the raiders soared into the sky, nothing definite had been achieved, and a loss of seven " missing " was the only definite fact that could be recorded.*

Nothing? Perhaps this is an overstatement. At least the Blunt's importance as a defensive position had been confirmed, and the knowledge that the Germans were placing reliance on adjoining earthworks was valuable. None the less, it is difficult to escape the conclusion that the raid was foredoomed to failure, and should never have been attempted. For the parts they took in it, Sec.-Lt. Hart was awarded the M.C., and Rfm. Chamberlain the M.M.

The severe conditions under which the front-line platoons existed necessitated frequent reliefs, changes in dispositions usually taking place every two or three days. Thus, on the following day, the battalion moved back to

Dambre Camp

Dambre Camp, and there soon commenced training for a coming attack. During the last week the weather had been steadily improving, and if the offensive was to be renewed, no time should be lost, or the summer months would be over. Accordingly, plans were made for a simultaneous assault by divisions from the Second and Fifth Armies, along a front of about eight miles from the Ypres-Comines canal, northwards to the Ypres-Staden railway. Objectives were limited to those within about a thousand yards of jumping-off points, and included the remainder of Shrewsbury Forest, Inverness Copse, St. Julien, and some high ground between this village and the Stroombeek, which flowed north-east of it.

St. Julien

To the 58th Division was allotted the task of capturing the village and the higher ground beyond—ground that was studded with concrete houses and pill-boxes. The assault on the village itself might be successful, but to attack up-hill against such fortifications as were to be encountered later was obviously a course to be avoided. Fortunately, an alternative was possible, although the manœuvre would be complicated: briefly, it was that, simultaneously with the attack on St. Julien, an advance by the 174th Inf. Bde. from the positions north of it, recently held by the *Second*, might be made, with the object of securing some portion of the higher ground, from which, by a turning movement, the whole might be taken from the flank. In conception the plan was bold, but its successful execution would depend upon the ability of the attacking troops, in the last phase, to wheel to the right and

*A sergeant who took part in the raid states that most casualties were suffered during the advance, after the barrage had commenced. He adds that all were convinced that British shells were frequently falling short, and that the few who reached the Blunt mebuses could do nothing owing to their smallness in numbers. He and another sergeant tried to deal with enemy posts in front of the mebuses by firing and throwing bombs. Incidentally, he mentions that at first they couldn't understand why their fire wasn't effective, and then discovered that they had forgotten to remove the pieces of " four-by-two " which they had inserted in the muzzles to keep out the mud.

deliver briskly the final assault. After long debate, the alternative was decided upon, and the unit selected for the last intricate movement and farthest objectives was the *Second*.

Whilst the battalion, at Dambre Camp, was preparing for its forthcoming ordeal, the most careful plans were being made by the Brigade Commander, Brig.-Gen. G. C. Higgins, and his Bde.-Major, Capt. R. M. Barrington-Ward, to ensure the success of the operation. Nothing foreseeable was overlooked, and in collaboration with the Commanding Officer, every conceivable eventuality was provided for. Objectives were most clearly defined, and artillery and machine-gun fire co-ordinated with the infantry movement. The fighting troops were to be supplied with ammunition and food by means of pack-animals, and to make the troops easily recognisable by commanders, guides, and reinforcements, coloured patches were affixed to the haversacks of the assaulting companies, so that when in battle-order with the haversack on the back, the colours might be easily spotted from the rear. *Dambre Camp*

One further precaution was taken by the Commander of the 174th Inf. Bde. An Advanced Brigade Headquarters was established in the front line immediately before the attack, at a mebus, named Springfield, and into and around this were crowded Brigade Signallers, Power-buzzers, dogs, rockets, and pigeons, with the Intelligence Officer of the *Sixth* in command, charged with the responsibility of keeping touch with the advancing infantry and reporting back all information as he secured it.

A rifleman of the *Sixth* attached to the brigade as the brigade pigeoneer, has the following comment on these preparations: " In the first place, miles of cable had to be buried in shallow trenches, dug by parties drawn from the infantry, supervised by the R.E.'s, and this was carried out at night, not without casualties, as the enemy's machine--guns kept up a heavy fusillade on all suspected points, the shells, too, taking their nightly toll. Every available man was employed in this work, even the clerks, runners, batmen, and waiters of the Brigade Staff . . . We used to parade under our Brigade Signal Officer, and start off up the duckboard tracks, loaded up with huge drums of armoured telephone cable, sometimes weighing a hundredweight or so, past Hilltop, Mousetrap, to Alberta, which was Battalion Headquarters, arriving there as it got dark, and commencing operations, laying the line from there, forward to Mon. du Hibou, and beyond, into no-man's-land . . . This work went on for about ten days or so."

The same infinite pains were taken in the preparation for the battle by all divisions in the Second and Fifth Armies taking part in the assault; but a special responsibility rested on the 58th Division, since it was operating as

By courtesy of The Amalgamated Press, Ltd.

MAP 12.—YPRES, AND COUNTRY TO THE EAST AND NORTH-EAST.

part of the XVIII Corps (General Sir Ivor Maxse) on the extreme left, and had among other tasks, to watch the flank. The divisional plan of attack provided for the assault to be made by two Infantry Brigades, with the 173rd Inf. Bde. on the right, to take the village of St. Julien, now represented only by a dozen huge concrete houses and many smaller and similarly protected posts, and the 174th Inf. Bde. on the left, to climb the rise, north-east of the village, and wheel and take the ridge. The success of the latter's operation depended upon the punctual arrival of the 2nd/5th Bn. and 2nd/6th Bn. at the point where each was respectively to continue the assault. It was a daring manœuvre to start the *Sixth* off at zero so far away and to count on its reaching its assault position on time, and then to expect it to execute a right-wheel in the very face of the enemy, and its successful execution was truly one of the most remarkable exploits of the War.

St. Julien

The offensive commenced at 5.40 a.m. on September 20th. At 1 a.m. on that morning the leading company of the battalion left camp, and by 5 a.m. the whole unit was in Canoe trench to the rear or south-west of Kitchener's Wood. The first objective was allotted to the 2/8th Bn., whose task it was to overcome opposition from the German forward positions, including, amongst others, the formidable Blunt Salient, which the *Sixth* had raided earlier in the month. This they did with some assistance from the 2nd/5th Bn., who "leap-frogged" them, bore slightly to the right, and captured their objectives.

Wurst Farm

It was now the turn of the *Sixth*. As if on the parade ground, the advance was steadily made, and the turn executed; then, with speed and determination, assaults were delivered on the final objectives—Cluster Houses, Wurst Farm, Olive House, and Clifton House, and all were taken quickly and decisively. At the outset tanks had contributed to the initial successes, but as time wore on such targets, even though moving, could not escape the well-directed German gunnery, and they were soon left behind in so rapid an advance.

The turn and the flank attack took the Germans completely by surprise, and most surrendered when they found the British troops behind or alongside them. Indeed, more were taken than were killed, and an amusing sight was to see the surrendering Germans pulled out of craters, turned in the direction of the British lines, and kicked squarely on their behinds. Some, indeed, did not wait to suffer this indignity, but, throwing away their arms, ran as quickly as possible from the attackers towards the former British positions.

St. Julien

The delivery of the assault, resulting in such a rapid and easy victory over the enemy, is well described by two members of the battalion, from different angles. The first, by Rfm. Hammer, ensconced in relative safety with his pigeons at Springfield, tells of the commencement of the battle: " Punctually at 5.40 the attacking waves went forward. There were three waves, and a wave of men wearing yellow arm-bands as moppers-up. I had obtained a post of vantage close to one of the loopholes, from which I could see all that was taking place as the waves passed us on their way forward. They were cheering as they went, and a line of four tanks kept pace with them. Several shells burst amongst them as they went, but still they went forward." The second, by L.-Cpl. Cowherd, of A Company, tells of the battle itself: " Our first difficulty was to get through the enemy's protective barrage, which, though not heavy, was very skilfully placed. We saw a platoon receive a direct hit just in front of us, and found some poor chaps killed when we reached the spot. . . . Our Platoon Commander went out in front to find a gap in the barrage, and was hit; but ' carry-on ' we did, of course, the Company Commander now leading us. Soon we found that the 5th and 8th had captured most of their objectives with slight losses, and Germans in hundreds were running by us like little children, motioning to us to point out to them the way back. Round about lay scores of dead Prussian Guards, struck down by our terrible artillery fire.

" We had to wait a few minutes for the barrage to lift, and sent two or three men to aid a sergeant of the 8th Londons to capture a large and obstinate mebus, with forty-seven prisoners (for which he was afterwards awarded the Victoria Cross).

" It was now our part of the picture, and we were soon only fifty yards behind our terrible crawling barrage. Enemy machine-guns rattled at us from afar, and our company sergeant-major*—my old sergeant of 1914—was hit by a stray bullet in the mouth, and dropped dead. Brave enemy snipers still held their ground, and one after another fell as they were slowly but surely outflanked by us in reaching our objective. We found all concrete emplacements beaten to the ground, and we formed ourselves in shellholes round about, secure from artillery-fire for the time being.

" By carefully crawling from shellhole to shellhole, I reached our Company Commander (Captain Anderson), who, cool and collected, was assuring some timorous mortals of the comparative security of our position on a ridge, from which we could see for miles into enemy lines. I shall never forget his brave words: ' We've got here, and we're going to stop here.' "

*C.S.Maj. Carr.

On account of the very rapidity of the advance information as to the progress made was not immediately forthcoming, as doubtless it would have been had there been serious checks; and by a quarter-past nine it was possible to send backwards from Advanced Brigade Headquarters only the briefest information, and this a pigeon carried: *St. Julien*

"Can get no definite information from wounded or prisoners aaa Power-buzzer can receive but not send aaa About 30 wounded men behind this mebus mostly shell-fire cases aaa Signal arranged between UNDER and this post to show UNDER H.Q. at Advanced H.Q. not yet reecived aaa Large parties of prisoners seen moving in direction of Triangle Farm aaa Enemy still heavily barraging Triangle Farm—St. Julien road aaa Sgt. Preston of UPSHOT says battalion reached objective."*

It was not long, however, before more precise information was received. Major H. M. Brown, who as Second-in-Command of the *Second* had established Advanced Battalion Headquarters at Mon. du Hibou, after reconnoitring part of the line himself, was able to send a message from Springfield, reading as follows:

"Following from C Company UNBOLT aaa WURST FM. and CLUSTER HOUSES taken and being consolidated aaa Strength of Coy. 30 O.R. and 1 Officer aaa Wants S.A.A. bombs, rifle-grenades, verey-lights, & pistol, and water aaa Lt. Smith 4th Section UNION in WURST FM. and consolidated also CLUSTER HOUSES aaa Strength of Section 40 O.R. aaa Wants nothing aaa UMBALA (Springfield) reports THORNTON gained position no casualties aaa Disposition maps per runner."* *Wurst Farm*

This message, with its code words and abbreviations, reads to-day almost unintelligibly, but at the time it was full of meaning, and signified that not only were all objectives taken, but that relatively few casualties had been suffered, and that consolidation was proceeding apace. This information was confirmed by others, as, for example, by Cpl. Cowherd:

"The task of sending back a message was very difficult. This officer asked me to get back to a mebus about fifty yards away and dictate a message myself, as one written was unsafe.

*UNDER code word for 2nd/5th Bn., London Regt.
UPSHOT code word for 2nd/7th Bn., London Regt.
UNBOLT code word for 2nd/6th Bn., London Regt.

" While discussing this a man . . . dropped in on us and, between his terrified gulps, informed the officer that the mebus was occupied by Germans and that communications were cut off at the rear. Some clamoured for an immediate withdrawal, but the officer refused. I believed the latest news impossible, and said so ; but, of course, immediate action was necessary. I set off crawling like a snake, but it was so ' warm ' that it took me an hour to go fifty yards, and at last I reached the mebus, which at first seemed deserted. After a careful search I found two dead Germans and two wounded beyond recall, and at the bottom of the mebus . . . was our company signaller. I heard the good news that he was in touch with the rear, and dictated him a message of my own composition, and, as I could see the enemy massing for a counter-attack, put that in as well.

" Then I crawled back safely, and made our cool officer's face light up with the good news. I got a very welcome drink of tea for my pains. About fifteen minutes afterwards the reply to our message came in a terrific barrage from our artillery on the massing enemy, and we amused ourselves by peeping over and seeing the enemy scattering in panic."*

Others, too, had noted the enemy forming up for assault. The Intelligence Officer, crawling from post to post to get the latest information, reached D Company (Capt. Kidson), and with him watched this significant hostile movement. He returned at once to Springfield, and, writing a hurried report of the threatened counter-attack, saw it entrusted to a messenger-dog, which, on release, made a beeline for the enemy positions. The message was immediately duplicated, and entrusted this time to a pigeon, and, to make trebly sure that brigade artillery should lend immediate aid, the forward observation officer of the supporting battery, fortunately near at hand, was told of what had been seen, and in no time effective shelling commenced over the whole area in which the enemy had been seen assembling, and the counter-attack was frustrated. It is only fair to record, however, that the message-dog must soon have recognised his initial error, for it reached its kennels in record time, bearing faithfully the message entrusted to it.

The Germans made several fruitless attempts that day to recover their lost ground, but the ridge which had now passed to the *Second* and other British units operating on the right, dominated the surrounding country, and every enemy attempt to form up preparatory to delivering an attack was seen, reported, and dealt with by the artillery. So ended the day, and the

*Needless to say, when L.-Cpl. (later Sgt.) Cowherd wrote his diary, he had no idea that excerpts would, many years later, be incorporated in a history of his battalion.

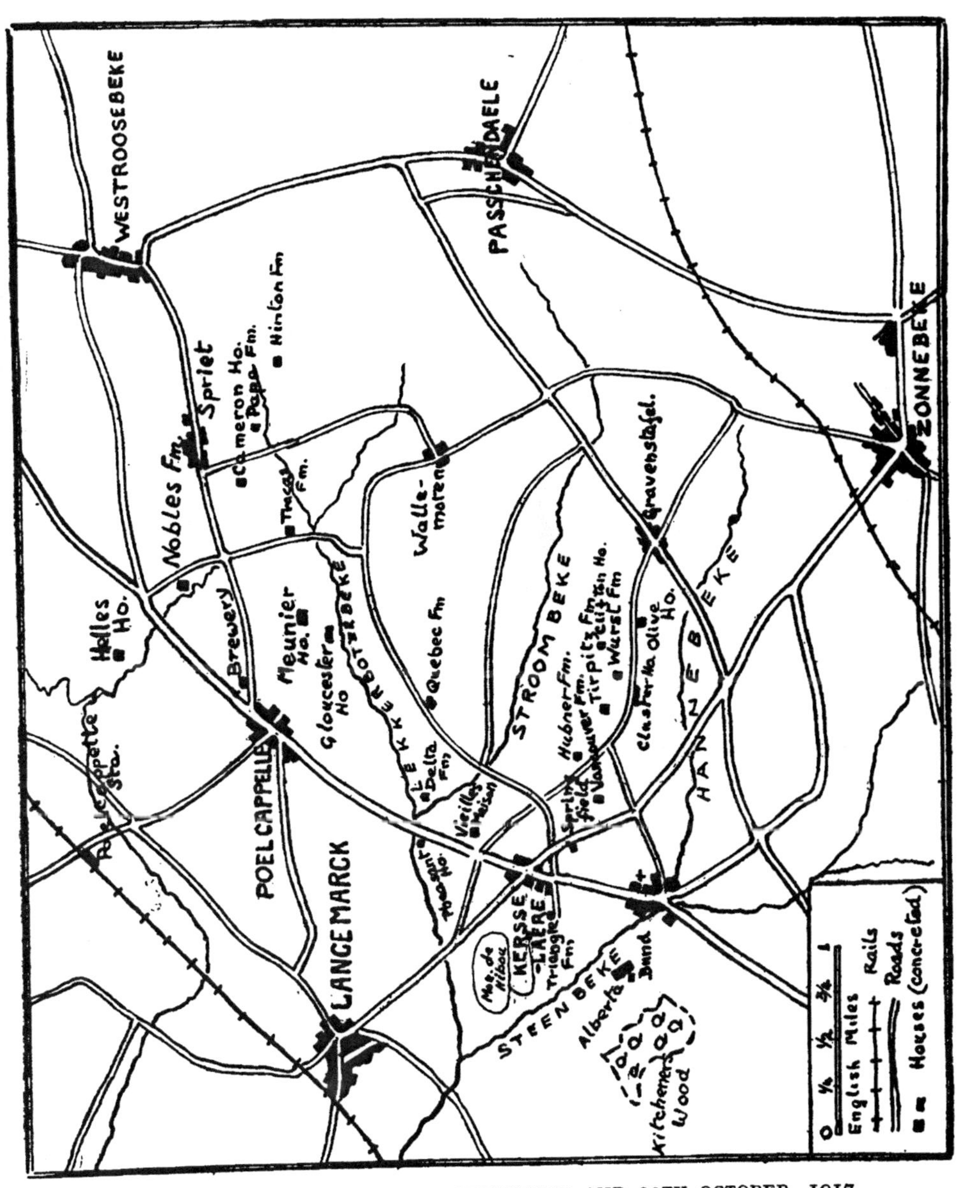

MAP 13.—OBJECTIVES ON 20TH SEPTEMBER AND 30TH OCTOBER, 1917.

night of the 20th-21st was spent everywhere in improving the positions occupied by the victorious troops, and the several showers of rain that fell did not hamper the progress being made. The following day passed without major incident; evidently the Germans realised that further attempt to wrest the conquered ground from the British would be useless; they had behind them the Passchendaele Ridge, everywhere studded with concrete mebuses and emplacements, and, since theirs was a defensive battle, and time and weather were on their side, they could afford the loss of territory rather than men. During the night of the 21st-22nd the battalion was relieved by the 11th Bn., and, moving back to Kitchener Wood, was carried to the rear by a light railway that the Royal Engineers had quickly extended to that point. Here, too, to greet them, was the Corps Commander, General Sir Ivor Maxse, who, elated with the success of the whole operation, clapped all and sundry on the shoulders, and kept repeating "Thirteen bloody battles, thirteen bloody victories." To his personal congratulations came later those of the Army Commander, General Gough, and finally, on the 22nd, those of the Brigade Commander, Brig.-Gen. Higgins, whose efforts, and those of his Brigade-Major, Capt. Barrington-Ward, in planning the attack, had been crowned with such success.

Kitchener Wood

"Please express to all ranks under your command my thanks and admiration for their great efforts on the 20th and 21st September, which ended in such an unqualified success.

"The fighting spirit and discipline shown by the whole brigade in capturing and holding this most important position against determined attacks was beyond all praise."

This praise was, indeed, well deserved, for the brigade had been confronted by General von Armin's best troops—the 2nd Reserve Division of the Prussian Guards, with the 234th Division held in reserve to counter-attack; and the enemy's positions had been carried without undue sacrifice. The 5th and 8th Battalions suffered more heavily than the *Sixth*, which, happily, had to report the loss of only two officers and seventeen "other ranks" killed, and just over one hundred wounded, including the Commanding Officer, Colonel Foord. It had brilliantly achieved a notable success, and out of the line, at Reigersburg Camp, it was able to reflect on its achievement, and was conscious of the fact that if at Bullecourt it had met defeat, at Ypres it had been victorious. And this satisfaction was heightened by the knowledge that elsewhere along the front attacked on September 20th the same proud story could be told.

Reigersburg Camp

* * * * *

A contributor writes: " Whenever I hear Passchendaele mentioned my mind drifts back to the memory of my one and only German prisoner. I had the job of escorting him to a concentration camp, and in silence we both walked the long trail of duckboards from Kitchener's Wood to find the nearest ' cage ' beyond the Canal Bank.

" There was something about this ' Jerry ' I had to admire. He carried an air of pride, and certainly did not care a jot for anyone in the Allied Armies.

" Having crossed the Canal Bank, we made for the Elverdinghe Road, and at a quiet spot I decided to halt for a rest and smoke, and bade my prisoner sit down.

" Offering my companion a cigarette (' Red Hussar '), he surprised me with a pleasant: ' Thank you! I hope we will meet again some day!'

" ' You speak good English, Fritz!'

" ' That is my name—the other half is Lukie!'

" ' Ever been to England?'

" ' It is my home!'

" ' Where?'

" ' London!'

" ' Called to the colours, eh?'

" ' Nineteen-thirteen — joined the " Cockchafers," crack German regiment!'

" ' What do you think about the War, Fritz?'

" ' Not much! And you?'

" ' Same as you. Want some bully beef and biscuits?'

" ' Thank you! Is there a dressing station where you are taking me?'

" ' Yes; why?'

" ' Am wounded in the back!'

" ' Show me; I have some dressing!'

" His shirt and trousers were saturated in blood, and he had a shrapnel gash as big as an egg in his back. He'd walked about seven miles without a grouse. Game fellows, some of those ' Jerrys.' "

* * * * *

On September 27th the *Second* moved by rail to rail to Audenfort, where, in the separated villages of Le Poirier, Fouquesolles, and Quinsole, it rested. Life at Audenfort and its neighbouring villages was most pleasant, partly on account of the excellent billets occupied and partly (need it be said) because companies were sufficiently far removed from Battalion Headquarters to make them feel conscious that they were, if not separate units, certainly distinct entities. Never perhaps had spirits been higher. Elated by their **Audenfort**

Audenfort

success in the Salient, sure of the officers and non-commissioned officers who commanded them, the rank and file, whose military prowess was now matching that of the *First*, were supremely self-confident. Further, and by great good fortune, they were not kept waiting for a new Commanding Officer.

Col. Benson

Four days after the attack on September 20th, Major G. B. Benson, of the Oxford and Bucks Light Infantry, had assumed command in succession to Colonel Foord, now in hospital, wounded. His unostentatious arrival was typical of the man. Wearing a "Burberry" over his uniform, he visited the battalion, then resting at Reigersburg Camp, and, without disclosing his identity, chatted and joked freely with officers and men, in such a manner that when, later, it was learned that he was to command them all felt instinctively that they had a friend. Nor were they mistaken; every day by some act or decision it became clearer that the new Commanding Officer was someone who was watching their every interest, their comfort, their leisure, and their training. He expected and received immediate and implicit obedience to his commands, not because of the military discipline that required it, but because he knew, and his officers learned, that he never gave an unnecessary order. In a short time he became unquestionably the most popular man in the battalion, and his closest companions soon came to love him. Gay, but never irresponsible, strict, but rarely stern, he led as much as commanded, and by his human sympathy won a place in everybody's heart.

Thus, with Colonel Benson's advent, the battalion was well commanded and well officered. In command of A Company was Capt. Anderson, a man of quick action, never cooler than when facing the enemy; in command of B Company, Capt. Godfrey; in command of C Company, Capt. Hill, a man who, as a sergeant in another unit, had won the Military Medal as well as the Medaille Militaire; and in command of D Company, Capt. Kidson, an officer of the first rank, who through many engagements had displayed good leadership and great bravery. As its Second-in-Command the battalion now had Major H. M. Brown, who had served with the unit since its formation in 1914, first as a Platoon Commander, and later in command of D Company. Lieut. Halford had followed Major Collins as Adjutant, in the spring, and, being wounded at Bullecourt, his place was taken by Capt. Crofts, an officer of experience, originally gazetted to the 15th Bn., London Regiment. For some time his assistant was Lieut. I. H. W. Idris, of the 19th Bn. London Regiment, whose name recurs again and again towards the end of this history. Lieut. Goodger was now the Quartermaster of the unit, and the stories told of him would fill many pages. Then, too,

Sgt. DRURY.

Sgt. GROSS.

Sgt. ALEXANDER.

Sgt. FRAILEY.

Sgt. FRASER.

THE CAMP OCCUPIED BY "RESERVES" AT FOVANT LOOKING TOWARDS COMPTON DOWN.
Note the badge cut out in chalk on hill in background.

RETURNED WOUNDED FROM FESTUBERT AND LOOS, 1916.

Plate 28

Colonel W. W. HUGHES, D.S.O., M.C. (C.L.R.), O.C. 17th Bn. London Regt., 1918.

Colonel M. J. MACDONALD, M.C. T.D. (C.L.R.), O.C. 20th Bn. London Regt., 1918; and 6th Bn. London Regt., 1928-1933.

Colonel G. NEELY, D.S.O., M.C. and Bar (C.L.R.), O.C. 18th Bn. London Regt.

Colonel A. FOORDE, D.S.O. (Manchester Regt.), O.C. 2nd/6th Bn. London Regt., 1917.

Sgt. L. GORDON,
D.C.M.

C.S.Maj. A. YELF,
D.C.M., C. DE GUERRE.

C.S.Maj. J. ALLEN,
D.C.M.

C.S.Maj. F. THORNDYKE,
M.C., D.C.M., M.M.

Sgt. J. BUTLER,
D.C.M.

Sgt. J. WEBB,
D.C.M.

C.S.Maj. H. PALOWKAR,
D.C.M.

Sgt. B. BAKER,
D.C.M.

L.-Cpl. HYNEMAN,
D.C.M.

CPL. J. DUDLEY,
D.C.M.

SGT. W. CHURCH,
M.M. AND BAR.

CPL. J. MILLS,
M.M. AND BAR.

CPL. A. GOLD,
D.C.M., M.M.

C.S.MAJ. C. BITTEN,
M.M.

RFM. J. LUMSDEN,
M.M.

SGT. E. ELLIS,
M.M. AND C. DE GUERRE.

SGT. F. BRUIN,
M.M.

SGT. W. WORBOYS,
M.M.

Plate 31

there was the Medical Officer, Capt. Laurence Geraty, M.C., R.A.M.C., of whom it was said at the end of the war no doctor had served longer on active service with any front-line unit. Audenfort

Strong as was the battalion in its officer personnel, it was, if anything, even stronger in warrant and non-commissioned officers. Of the company sergeant-majors the names of Thorndyke (B Company) and Palowker (C Company) were to become by-words for personal bravery and indefatigable attention to official and unofficial duties.

To complete the picture of an almost perfect infantry battalion it needed only the stiffening of tried and seasoned soldiers to strengthen the platoons now largely filled by young, enthusiastic, if untrained, lads. Fortunately, drafts from England now brought in increasing numbers non-commissioned officers and men who had already seen service in France with the *Sixth* or some other London battalion. After recovering from war-wounds, these old soldiers had spent some months with their respective reserve units, and in due course found themselves, after medical inspection, marked A 1 and drafted into the " overseas " companies which each reserve battalion maintained. Soon—all too soon—their time would come to return to the front, and apprehensively they would parade, be innoculated, equipped, and given a few days' leave, and shipped abroad. The dangers they would have to face were nothing, they knew, as compared with the discomfort and physical exhaustion to be endured, and life would be bearable only if they " got in with a decent crush " when they reached " the other side." It was joy when they " landed-up " with a unit that had some thought for their physical requirements, and, what was more, some respect for them as persons. The following account records the reception of such a draft by the *Second :*

" Detachments from each section of the great Base camp at Harfleur were marched to the railroad to the skirl of Scottish pipes. In most cases members of the drafts welcome the change owing to the strenuous nature of the training at the ' Bull Ring.' The journey to the front was conducted with a certain element of tact as the train slowly rumbled along with innumerable halts. Throughout the process of manœuvring and transporting troops by rail enemy planes had to be taken into account. Late at night, so slow and disjointed, was the journey made, the mileage of which was, nevertheless, absurdly small. The train came to a final halt, and the draft ultimately found themselves welcomed by a captain of the 2nd/6th Bn., London Regt., at the small village of Le Poirier, in the Pas de Calais area. Le Poirer

" When comfortably billeted, the party took advantage of a good night's rest, and, after a well-cooked breakfast, sorted out their surroundings. One small contingent of the party comprised men from the ' Kensingtons,' another from the *First*, and a few men came from the Civil Service Rifles. The officers realised the men were seasoned troops returned from wounds and sickness. The Kensingtons were men who had served with that regiment in 1914 at Ypres.

" It was later discovered that the *Second* was a sportsman's battalion. Many members were boxers of ability, amongst them being : Rfm. J. Lumsden, Sgt. E. Ellis, Sgt. G. Sparks, and the only coloured member of the battalion, Rfm. Harris. Most of these men received decorations for work in the field. At football the battalion team was almost unbeatable, and at athletics in general they claimed a champion in C.Q.M.Sgt. Sired, the Highgate Harriers runner. Another athlete was Rfm. Hammond, the Brighton walker.

Audenfort

" Shortly after arrival the party was paraded before Colonel Benson, who at once put the men at ease with a short speech of welcome. ' Hoping,' he said, ' you will find many friends in your new surroundings, and give your best services to us as you have done in the past with your mother units.'

" C.Q.M.Sgt. Maxwell Davis took one half of the newcomers, and C.Q.M.Sgt. George Sired the remainder. All trooped off to the cookhouse of Sgt. Buckland and partook of the ' best meal they had had.' "*

Kempton Park Camp

After about three weeks at Audenfort the battalion returned to Poperinghe, and on the 26th moved to the camp at Kempton Park preparatory to taking up positions in the outpost line now established about a mile beyond those which it and other units of the 58th Division had established in September. Since then the offensive had been resumed whenever conditions had proved favourable, and by the end of the month progress had been made along the Ypres-Menin road and in the direction of Poelcappelle. Important as were these successes, the advance to the Passchendaele-Staden ridge was anything but according to plan, for it had been expected that the ground now won would have been British within a fortnight of July 31st. Another attack was therefore planned for October 4th, and by a coincidence the day selected was the very day on which the German High Command had decided upon for an attempt to recover their lost positions. Consequently, when the British barrage was put down at 6 a.m. it caught the assembled German troops and completely disorganised them. The advancing infantry, meeting a demoralised enemy,

*R. G. Emery.

took over five thousand prisoners and gained all their objectives; only along the Ypres-Menin road itself was the issue in doubt, but by the end of the day Poelcappelle had been reached, the Stroombeek had been crossed, Gravenstafel, Zonnebeke, Reutel, and Polygon Wood had been captured, and a footing gained on the Passchendaele ridge.

Successful as had been this operation, there was still much fighting to **Poelcappelle** be done if the campaign as originally planned was not to be abandoned, a necessary preliminary to which was the capture of the ridge running north from Passchendaele; and, despite the shocking weather conditions, the advance was continued on October 9th, and 12th, and again on the 26th, so that by the time the *Second* was about to leave Audenfort the outpost line had been established slightly to the east of Poelcappelle. The mebuses, shellholes, and emplacements they were about to hold lay along a front of about one thousand yards, stretching from Tracas Farm, to the south, northward to Helles House, with Meunier House, and the Brewery at Poelcappelle as intermediate defensive positions. Into these posts the battalion moved on October 28th, relieving the 2nd/7th Bn., London Regt.

The line now held by the battalion faced north-north-east, in the direction of Westroosbeke, lying about a couple of miles away at the northern end of the Passchendaele Ridge. In front of it, on lower ground, stood the village of Spriet, and in front of this a number of concrete houses and mebuses built in **Spriet** and around Moray House, Hinton Farm, Para Farm, Cameron House, and Nobles Farm, the last a little nearer than the others to the British positions. If, as might be expected, an attack was to be delivered from the southern end of the Ridge, northwards to Passchendaele and beyond it, some support from the British positions west of the Ridge would be required, if only to divert the enemy's attention and confuse him as to the direction from which the main effort was being made. Not that he could have had much doubt in the matter, for between his positions and the British a slight depression in the ground made all the difference between mud and bog, and rendered movement all but impossible. Indeed, there was little to choose, for that matter, between high or low ground, conditions everywhere being appalling.

Despite the mud and water, the forthcoming operations provided for the delivery of a direct assault on the German positions lying beyond the bog. Whilst the Canadians worked up the Ridge, two companies of the 8th Battalion, and one of the *Sixth* were to undertake this frontal attack. Originally B Company had been allotted the task, but owing to severe casualties being suffered by that unit on the 29th, and to the fact that their Company Commander had been taken by Colonel Benson to form with him and the Adjutant an advanced Brigade Headquarters, A Company were detailed for it, much to everyone's surprise and annoyance.

Poelcappelle

Writes a corporal of A Company: " We thought we were in for a fairly quiet time as all the shell-fire was poured into Poelcappelle on our left. But we received an order to move at 4 p.m. to relieve B Company at the Brewery to enable them to make an attack . . . I had to relieve a platoon at Helles House . . . across a flooded waste, and it took us an hour to get there. We found B Company in a terrible state, having had twenty casualties, and in the mebus were ten seriously wounded cases. We squashed our shaken men in, and looked forward to twenty-four hours rest before relief.

" But alas! we were doomed to disappointment. About midnight two runners, one of whom had been wounded on the way, rushed in with the message that we two corporals were wanted at once. We knew it must be urgent to leave our platoons, and with great misgivings we found Brewery Farm . . . Then the details of the last fight for Passchendaele Ridge were unfolded to us. The barrage was to extend over a front of five miles, and the 8th Londons were attacking on our right, and the Canadians to the south of them. We were to capture Noble's Farm, which was in a very peculiar position, and had been captured and lost a week previous . . .

Noble's Farm

" With weary limbs we went through all that mud and rain again to Helles House and our hard task of telling the men what was in store for them. To my surprise and relief they took the news quite quietly, but I am inclined to think they thought they would not come back, and I, who knew we were being sent only to draw fire from the Canadians, and that it didn't matter twopence whether we reached our objective or not, heartily agreed with them, and I didn't trouble to take any rations with me."*

The attack was delivered at 5.50 a.m. on the morning of October 30th, and under the superb leadership of its commander, Capt. Anderson, M.C., A Company took the objectives allotted to it, including Noble's Farm, which, with its cluster of mebuses to the south-east, lay fortunately not beyond the depression, or shallow valley, flanking the Ridge. The objectives of the 8th Battalion, however, lay beyond it, and the attack by that unit, heroically delivered, was brought to a standstill by the mud. Pitifully the gallant sections struggled towards their objectives—Moray House, Hinton Farm, Papa Farm, and Cameron House—to cease only when machine-gun fire put an end to their heroic endeavours and their misery. If consolation there could be for such

*The attack was the subject of protests beforehand from the Brigade, the Division, the Corps, and the Army; but G.H.Q. insisted that it was necessary for larger reasons.

pitiless sacrifice, it was to know that the Canadian attack from the south had been successful, partly perhaps on account of their very gallant effort.

By the action on October 30th, the Third Battle of Ypres was over. The offensive was not renewed; but as if to give an opportunity to say farewell to the many comrades whom they had left behind in the stinking mud of the Salient, one more tour of duty was done by the battalion, in the same sector, from November 10th to 12th. It was without incident; and on the 26th, the battalion marched to Proven, entrained, and was carried to Wizernes, and the next day found billets in Quesque and Verval, where it rested for ten precious days. It had not, however, said "good-bye" to the Salient. By December 8th, it was back, at first in huts at Dirty Bucket Camp, and later at Turco Huts and Hulls Farm; but the circumstances were different—the weather, if cold, was now fine and sunny, the mud was frozen hard, and the offensive had come to an end. Further, hours were more or less regular, for the brigade was working for the Royal Engineers, consolidating the positions gained, making roads, and generally achieving order out of chaos, and if work was strenuous, it was exhilarating, and casualties were few and far between. Christmas was spent under these conditions, and a fortnight later (January 8th, 1918) the Salient was left for good and all.

Quesque

Dirty Bucket Camp

This is not the place to discuss the wisdom of the Commander-in-Chief's decision to attack in Flanders, nor the merits and demerits of the Staff's plan of campaign, nor yet the tactical handling of the various situations as they presented themselves. Suffice it to say that the Third Battle of Ypres cost the British Army 350,000 casualties, and the victory, if victory it could be called, was of no permanent value. Two days after the *Second* had left the Salient, secret instructions were issued to prepare for a withdrawal from the Passchendaele Ridge, in the taking of which so much blood had been spilled.

* * * * *

There were noteworthy incidents in the life of both service battalions of the *Sixth* whilst they were in the Salient—incidents which are worth recording, although they had no direct part in the actions in which the *First* and *Second* were engaged. There was, for example, the incident of the receipt by the *First* of orders from 140 Inf. Bde. to furnish a guard for his Majesty King George V, at Cassel, during one of his periodical visits to the British Front. To Sgt. J. Allen, D.C.M., fell the honour of taking, by lorry on July 3rd, the smartest and most willing guard the battalion ever mounted, to the house of M. Deschodt, at 32, rue de Lille, Cassel, where his Majesty had made his headquarters. The orders for the commander of the guard issued by the Camp Commandant of the Second Army, made provision for every eventuality —fire, suspicious characters, or unusual occurrences—as also for the soldierly bearing of the sentries on duty. Does it detract in any way from their smartness and watchfulness to mention that the orders providing for the guard to " turn-out " whenever his Majesty left the house, included the tip to the sergeant in command to " ascertain from the house at what time he is likely to leave, so as to be prepared " ? The *First* had had the privilege of being inspected by the King at Watford and already once in France, and it appreciated the signal honour conferred upon it by being ordered to guard his Majesty's person. There was a final occasion when, still on active service, the battalion, then amalgamated with the *Second*, had close contact with his Majesty; but that story is told towards the close of this history.

The declaration of war by the United States of America at the beginning of 1917 did not mean that help in the form of officers and men would all at once be forthcoming, but as early as possible American doctors had been enlisted, and before all the fighting in the Salient was over, some were serving with British battalions. One of these—Lieut. Frost—joined the *Second* just before the end of the year, and soon became one of the most popular officers in the battalion, identifying himself completely with it. " Thundermug " Frost—as everybody called him, as soon as this technical expression was understood—arrived in American Army kit, with knickerbockers, high-necked tunic, and cowboy hat, wondering very much how he was going to be treated by his English companions. He need have had no fears; before very long he was wearing breeches, collar and tie, British officer's tunic, with black regimental buttons, and in his headdress, now the regulation peaked-cap, he wore not the badge denoting his connection with the medical services, but the red boss with the silver bugle superimposed upon it. Dr. Frost's advent followed the return to England for a few months of the war-weary Capt. L. Geraty, M.C., R.A.M.C., to whom a reference has already been made. The Military Cross was awarded to him while he was serving with the *Second*, and was richly deserved, for few medical officers could have been more devoted to the troops entrusted to them. Stories told about him are legion; one must suffice in these pages to preserve his memory. Capt. Geraty had seen service with the *Second* at Bullecourt, Croiselles, at Ytres, and in the Salient, where, whether in the firing-line or in reserve at some corrugated-iron encampment, the battalion was always under fire, if not from field artillery, certainly from the German " heavies " and from aircraft, whose nightly visits sometimes took a heavy toll in the lives of men and animals. Because of these nocturnal visits, elaborate precautions were taken to render the camps invisible, and to minimise casualties. Not a light was permitted to be shown; walls of sandbags were placed around huts and tents; parties occupying the accommodation were kept as small as possible; and officers messed by companies, and not all together, as they would, and did, when farther from the front, and when a suitable room could be found. Colonel Benson was never really happy about this segregation of officers, and on one occasion gave permission for all to dine together. Aerial activity during November had been less than usual on account of heavy rain, and the risk was not very great. Warrant and non-commissioned officers were informed of the forthcoming events, passed many a good-humoured remark, and prepared for the best—or worst! The eventful night arrived. Ominously the skies cleared. About twenty officers sat down to dine. Half-way through their meal the sound of aeroplane engines was heard droning overheard. Were they friendly or hostile? Half a dozen terrific explosions in the immediate vicinity answered that question. The camp was being bombed. Quietly Colonel Benson told two officers to leave the hut, investigate, and report whether any huts had been destroyed or casualties suffered. Meanwhile the officers waited motionless and in silence. They were thinking not of their own safety, but of what would be said by the Higher Command, if by some cruel turn of fate a bomb should find its mark where they were dining altogether. It was at this moment of acute tension that Capt. Geraty rose, and in his inimitable drawl, said: "I think this is when I tell my story about the commercial traveller who called on a farmer to show him a wonderful powder he had, a powder guaranteed to increase the productivity of the farm enormously." And then he told his story slowly, but without hesitation, his eyes twinkling, an impish smile over the whole of his face. Without once faltering he continued his story to the end, to the point where the farmer's boy couldn't draw water from the pump because the donkey was there; and by the time it was told and the laughter was over, the bombers were past, and the tension was relaxed. The two officers returned, reported on the slight damage sustained, and the evening was quietly brought to an immediate close.

Not long after Lieut. Frost's arrival, some American infantry officers arrived, ostensibly to learn something of modern warfare on the spot, and they were attached for instruction to various companies. They were keen, capable, and anxious to learn all they could, but the mere fact that they were novices caused some amusement, and many stories were told of their dry humour in tense situations. One Company Commander to whom an American officer had been entrusted was returning from Battalion Headquarters with his charge along the duckboard track, when a dozen or more " whiz-bangs " were neatly placed just in front of the two of them. Both took cover, the English officer, in no great hurry, selecting a shell-hole a little drier than others in the immediate neighbourhood. He knew the " strafe " would be over in a minute or two, and that there was really no danger. But to the uninitiated the " whiz-bang " was a fearful thing, and often its actual explosion was mistaken for the sound made by a heavier shell landing in the mud. When, therefore, the English officer emerged from his hole and could not see the American, he shouted out that all was clear, and clambered back on to the duckboard track. From here he looked over the soddened waste, and presently saw a mud-covered face peeping above the crumbling lip of a water-filled shell-hole, which asked cheerfully, and in inquiring tones: " Say, Bo', has the darned thing gone off yet?"

One other incident is well worth preserving for posterity as typical of the kind of person who served in the *Sixth*. It will be remembered that at the last moment A Company had been ordered to take Noble's Farm on October 30th, and that the action had been completely successful. In point of fact, the final assault on the cluster of mebuses known by that name had been made by a mere handful of men led by their Company Commander, Capt. Anderson, and one of his subaltern officers, Sec.-Lt. Foulds, who with Sec.-Lt. Spink, of B Company, was killed in that action. Two days after the battle, when the battalion was at Siege Camp, several officers, including Capt. Anderson, and non-commissioned officers, obtained permission to visit Poperinghe for an evening's amusement. A good meal at Skindles was a wonderful restorative after weeks of campaigning in mud and blood. On this particular night the word came from Brigade Headquarters that the battalion which had relieved the *Second* denied that Noble's Farm was in British possession. This was a very serious reflection on A Company, since it implied that not only had it not taken the objective allotted to it, but that it had claimed it had.

Siege Camp

On receiving this information Colonel Benson found one of the other Company Commanders and sent him to Poperinghe, there to find Capt. Anderson and to intimate tactfully what the relieving unit had reported. This he did. Capt. Anderson was found at Skindles dining with other officers of the *Second*, and in a very little while the news was broken gently to him. For a moment he was dumbfounded; then, putting aside his knife and fork, he rose and said: " I'll show those b—— whether I took Noble's Farm." With that he left the restaurant, returned to Battalion Headquarters, went straight to the headquarters of the battalion then holding the sector, and from there to the company in whose defensive area Noble's Farm lay. Precisely what happened thereafter is unknown, for when he returned to the battalion, Capt. Anderson would not discuss the matter; but this much is certain, the battalion in question could no longer claim that Noble's Farm was unoccupied by them, for Capt. Anderson had assured himself before he left them that they were there.

Noble's Farm

To conclude this chapter on the fighting at Poelcappelle and Passchendaele is appended a typical operation-order written by the Commanding Officer himself in Army Book 153, and issued to all Company Commanders on the occasion of the battalion's going once more into the sector east of Poelcappelle on the night of November 10th, to relieve the 2nd/7th Bn., London Regt. The orders are not remarkable, except as showing the care and thought given to an eventuality before it arose. To understand them properly, the reader must imagine a bleak expanse of mud rising almost imperceptibly eastward to Westroosbeke. There were no organised posts other than the concrete houses and emplaces wrested from the enemy, and the platoons, when placed in positions best suited tactically to defend the ground held, merely sought the driest shell-holes, and, motionless, for fear of attracting attention to themselves, remained in them for forty-eight hours, during which it was not unusual for men to die of cold and exposure. Movement about or away from these positions during daylight was impossible for the reason already noted, and at night equally impossible on account of the mud. It took a Company Commander the best part of the night to travel the two or three hundred yards necessary to visit his platoons, and when posts were widely separated, he was often unable to visit them all in the time at his disposal. There they remained with only such water and food as they had brought with them until their two-day vigil was ended.

Secret. Copy No. 2

UNBOLT ORDER No. 3. November 10th, 1917.

1.—Division on our right have taken all objectives, including VOCATION and VOID farms and VAT COTTAGES. The enemy may consequently withdraw on our front.

2.—The role of companies will be as under.

3.—If reconnoitring-patrols find the enemy have withdrawn battle-patrols will at once be pushed out as follows:

(a) by B Company to PAPA FM. and HINTON FM.
(b) by C Company to CAMERON HO. via the SPRIET ROAD.
(c) by D Company to WHITECHAPEL and round junction V 14 b 4.0.

4.—These patrols will be supported by a complete platoon from their respective companies, as soon as it is found that a patrol has reached its objective.

4a.—As soon as it is known that the supporting platoons have reached their objectives by receipt of the code word GOOD and letter of company (example: GOOD C CAMERON HOUSE) by me, I will issue the word MOVE when the following moves will take place:

B Coy.—Two platoons from Tracas to PAPA and HINTON FARMS. Fourth platoon and Coy. H.Q. to MORAY HO.

C Coy.—Two platoons to the line PAPA FARM-WHITECHAPEL (SPRIET ROAD exclusive). Fourth platoon and Coy. H.Q. to CAMERON HOUSE. *Note.*—V 21 a 8.3 and V 21 a 7.7 would appear to be suitable posts for the above-named two platoons.

D Coy.—Two right platoons to line Whitechapel (inclusive)-Road Junction V 14 b 4.0, as far as V 15 a 3.0. *Note.*—WHITECHAPEL and HUTS (V 15 c 4.3) would appear to be suitable platoon posts.

Two left platoons (via road to SPIDER Cross-roads) in continuation of this line to Road Junction V 14 b 4.0, gaining touch with division on left.

Coy. H.Q. to HUTS V 15 c 40.45. *Note.*—Mebi at V 15 a 2.0 and Road Junction at V 14 b 4.0 would appear to be suitable platoon posts.

A Coy.—Two platoons at GLOUCESTER FM. to TRACAS MEBUS and MEUNIER HO. respectively.

Two left platoons at BREWERY to NOBLE'S FM. and HELLES HO. respectively.

Coy. H.Q. to remain at BREWERY.

PHEASANT TRENCH COY. UNDER.—Two platoons to GLOUCESTER FM.

Two platoons and Coy. H.Q. to BREWERY.

BATTN. H.Q. remains at NORFOLK HO.

5.—If above moves take place A COY. UNBOLT and Support Coy. UNDER will detail all working parties, to supply same, and inform me of action taken and strength of Coy.

6.—*Moves of Machine-Guns.* (Here follows dispositions).

7.—On arrival at new line patrols will again be pushed forward to get in touch with enemy.

8.—Lamp communication on completion of above moves will be established as soon as possible with PAPA FM. and WHITECHAPEL.

9.—Earliest possible information of any move forward is to be sent to me so that necessary alterations in S.O.S. lines may be made.

10.—Frequent situation reports and sketches showing dispositions will be sent to me as soon as the situation is clear.

11.—Reports to NORFOLK HOUSE.

12.—My designation is UNBOLT.

13.—Give necessary orders so that you may move at once when ordered.

14.—Acknowledge.

Copies:

No. 1—A Coy.
No. 2—B Coy.
No. 3—C Coy.
No. 4—D Coy.
No. 5—Support Coy. UNDER*.
No. 6—M.G.Coy.
No. 7—UNCLE†.
No. 8—File.

(Signed) C. B. Benson, Lt.-Col.
UNBOLT.
12 noon. 10/11/17.

SECOND BATTALION OFFICERS, WARRANT OFFICERS, ETC., at POELCAPPELLE—1917

	Officer Commanding:	Second-in-Command:	Adjutants:
	(1) Col. Foord (2) Col. Benson R.S.Maj. Morris	Major Browne	Lieut. Crofts and Capt. Wylie R.Q.M.Sgt. Parrish
A Co.	Capt. Anderson	C.S.Maj. Montier	C.Q.M.Sgt. Williams
B Co.	(1) Capt. Worral (2) Capt. Godfrey	C.S.Maj. Thorndyke	C.Q.M.Sgt. Sired
C Co.	Capt. Hill	C.S.Maj. Palowkar	C.Q.M.Sgt. Davies
D Co.	Capt. Kidson	C.S.Maj. Worrall	C.Q.M.Sgt. Grundy

Quartermaster: Capt. Goodger
Transport: Lieut. Brasher; Sgt. Price; Cpl. Dorling
Cooks: Sgt. Buckland
Stretcher-Bearers: Capt. Geraty; Cpl. Parker
Signallers: Lieut. Tew; Sgt. Wilson
Lewis-Guns: Sgt. Webster
Scouts and Snipers: Capt. Morrow; Sgt. Larkworthy

*Support Coy. UNDER—One company furnished by 2nd/5th Bn.
†UNCLE—H.Q. 174 Inf. Bde.

Chapter 15

BOURLON WOOD

With the cancellation of the attack planned for August 31st, in which the *First* was to have taken part, that battalion's stay in the Salient virtually came to an end. There was, however, some garrison

Zillebeke

duty yet to do at Half-way House, Zillebeke, but on September 22nd, about the same hour its sister battalion was returning from its successful action, it paraded at 7.15 a.m., marched to Caestre, and entrained for Aubigny, and,

Acq

again marching, found billets in Acq,* five miles north-west of Arras. Needless to say, no one was sorry to leave the Ypres area with its intense military activity, and everyone noted with satisfaction that the front they were now to occupy appeared to be relatively calm. Two days later the battalion moved into huts and tents at Wakefield Camp, near Roclincourt,* a little closer to the line, and on the following day, relieved the Hood battalion of the 63rd

Gavrelle

(Naval) Division in the trench system skirting the village of Gavrelle.* Here, as wherever the battalion went, work was commenced at once on strengthening and improving the trench system, constructing shelters, and generally making the front, support, and reserve lines as strong and as comfortable as possible, in preparation for the coming winter. For the moment the weather was fine, and enemy activity negligible. Thus, the time was opportune for such work; and life in the line, if safe, was strenuous.

After a week in the trenches at Gavrelle, the battalion was relieved by the 1st/19th Bn., London Regt., and spent a few days again in Wakefield Camp before moving, on October 10th, into the reserve trenches, on the left, opposite

Oppy

Oppy,* a small village within the German lines. Accommodation here was in dug-outs and tunnels, but the object of putting the battalion in reserve was evidently not because of the excellent protection they would afford, but because while at Gavrelle all ranks had shown such energy in building and repair work. Day and night, therefore, working-parties were provided to strengthen defences and make trenches habitable, with such success that when the battalion moved up into the front line a week later, an entry could be made in the War Diary to the effect that a vast improvement was apparent. But even in the front line the good work continued. Trenches were improved, wire erected, shelters built, and a drying-room commenced—all in preparation for a " winter-post " scheme that was to come into operation in November. The

*For map, see pages 56-7.

scheme had for its object the establishment of a series of self-contained "defensive localities," to be manned by companies in place of the more usual fortified front line running the width of a battalion sector; and the adoption of it had been necessitated by the shortage of troops. Two armies were fully engaged at Ypres, and thus the rest of the line could only be lightly held; and the XIII Corps Commander had decided upon this method of defence in preference to manning the front line trenches thinly along the entire sector. The one obvious disadvantage of the method was that sooner or later the enemy would locate the fortified localities and direct his artillery against them. Indeed, to some extent he was already doing that, and frequently the newly constructed positions would receive attention from his artillery, and heavy and light trench-mortars. Casualties, fortunately, were not heavy, and the damage done was almost as quickly made good. *Oppy*

Despite the long hours of heavy labour, life at both Gavrelle and Oppy was very pleasant, and it was with real regret that the division moved from the area in the middle of November. The battalion was back in the Gavrelle sector, still working, either at the Millpost or in Thames Alley, and when the time came for the move, it left them on November 18th with feelings something akin to affection. On the 20th the huts at Ecoivres, where there were civilians, shops, and a cinema, were occupied; and on succeeding days the battalion marched south and east through devastated country just north of the Somme, via Ransart, Achiet-le-Grand, Bihucourt, and Bapaume—all well-known to the *Second* during its advance to the Hindenburg Line in the spring of 1917—and very great interest was shown on the march in the systematic destruction of villages, isolated houses, and indeed, anything that might provide shelter for man or beast. *Gavrelle* *Ecoivres*

Beaulencourt was reached late on the 25th, and here for a couple of nights the battalion rested. So far the move to a new part of the front had been done in a leisurely fashion; indeed, at times progress had been tediously slow, for roads were congested and the battalion's transport frequently delayed by reason of the abnormal amount of traffic on them. Then suddenly all was activity; buses arrived at 2 p.m. on the 27th, and carried the battalion to Laboughiere, whence it marched immediately to Doignies. At 10.30 the next morning it moved into the line, and that night occupied half-built trenches west of Bourlon Wood, and by the 30th, all ranks were fighting for their lives. *Beaulencourt* *Doignies*

What was the nature of the operation now taking place, and what part in it was the *First* going to play? The answer to the first question can be quickly told, but that to the second must be a full account, since it tells the story of one of the most heroic incidents in the history of the regiment.

Doignies The Germans had retired to the Hindenburg Line. Soon it would have to be crossed, and to Colonel J. F. C. Fuller, General-Staff-Officer of the Tank Corps, must largely fall the credit of devising a successful means of doing it. Since the Somme days, tanks had been considerably improved, and when used over solid ground had done more than was expected of them. Despite the mud, they had made possible the capture of Poelcappelle. Again, at times they had proved invaluable in carrying supplies and stores where no roads existed.

But hitherto in an attack, tanks had been used singly or in small numbers for a specific and limited purpose, such as crushing machine-gun nests, or flattening wire. Colonel Fuller's proposal was nothing less than a tank raid on a big scale, in which these engines should play a major role and not act merely as useful adjuncts to an infantry assault. General Byng, on whose front the proposed action was to take place, early grasped the real significance of the new weapon, and enlarged the scheme into a sudden frontal attack across the Hindenburg Line in the direction of Cambrai, with the main object of seizing the high ground in the neighbourhood of Bourlon and its wood, some ten miles to the east of Bullecourt, and thus, by dominating the country for miles to the north, compel a substantial German retirement. An attack on a wide front was, of course, out of the question in view of the limited number of troops available for the operation, the very nature of which necessitated the choice of an area where the attackers' flanks, which were bound to be deep, could be stoutly defended. The St. Quentin Canal, on the right, and the Canal du Nord, on the left, provided such flanks. A further reason for selecting the Cambrai sector was the existence of the Havrincourt Wood, covering a total area of about three square miles, which on their retirement to the Hindenburg Line, the German had allowed to pass into British hands. In the natural cover of this wood could be concentrated men, guns, material, and tanks, invisible to hostile aircraft.

On the very night (November 19th) then, that the battalion had reached Ecoivres, the troops of seven divisions were moving up to their jumping-off positions facing the Hindenburg Line along the front to be attacked, and nearly five hundred tanks, most of them carrying bundles of brushwood, ten feet long, to assist them in crossing the deep German trenches. Most noticeable was the almost complete absence of shell-fire. To preserve the element of surprise the usual preliminary bombardment had been entirely dispensed with, reliance being placed entirely on the tank to flatten wire and so make infantry movement possible. At 6.30 a.m. a single gun spoke. It was the signal for the advance. Tanks, with infantry close behind, moved quickly towards the German trenches. Every available gun burst upon the enemy's batteries and paralysed them, and the bewildered German garrisons, taken completely by surprise in the absence of a barrage, fled, surrendered, or were slain. Mile after mile the advance continued unimpeded, except at Lateau Wood and Flesquieres, and by nightfall the St. Quentin Canal had been reached, and at places, crossed. Never before had the enemy's defences been penetrated to such a depth in a single day's assault. The invulnerable Hindenburg Line, and its support, had been carried, and five thousand prisoners taken; and only the check at Flesquieres had prevented the capture of the entire Bourlon Ridge. *Doignies*

But the check was serious. Moreover, although a footing had been obtained beyond the St. Quentin Canal, the villages of Crevecourt and Rumilly were still held by the Germans, and until their capture, Byng would be without his southern defensive flank. There were, however, at least twenty-four hours before substantial German reinforcements could arrive, and thus the position was that either a halt must be called to the advance and gains consolidated, or fresh attempts to reach objectives made the following day. The latter course was decided upon; and by the evening of the 21st the edge of the wood, and the village of Fontaine, to the south-east of it and about three miles from Cambrai, had been reached, and some further progress made in the effort to secure good defensive positions east of the St. Quentin Canal. For two days now the British had been on the offensive, and a pause was imperative to rest them and relieve those divisions which had suffered most severely. It is a moot point whether, now that German reinforcements were arriving, the offensive should not have been broken off; but the temptation to complete the victory was too keen, and on the 23rd renewed efforts to capture the Bourlon Ridge was made; and after bitter fighting, the whole of the wood passed into British hands. Attempts to take the village, however, finally proved unsuccessful.

Byng's divisions now manned three sides of a square of territory, having as its fourth that portion of the Hindenburg Line which had been stormed on the first day of battle. The north-east corner, containing Bourlon Wood, was thus exposed to attack from the east, the north, and the west, and against the British positions around it the Germans were already launching counter-attacks. On November 24th, and again on the 27th, desperate efforts were made by the British to seize the ridge before it should prove too late, and the action of the Guards on the latter day, will for ever be remembered as one of the most heroic episodes of the whole war. Forcing their way yard by yard, they cleared the village and established themselves to the east and

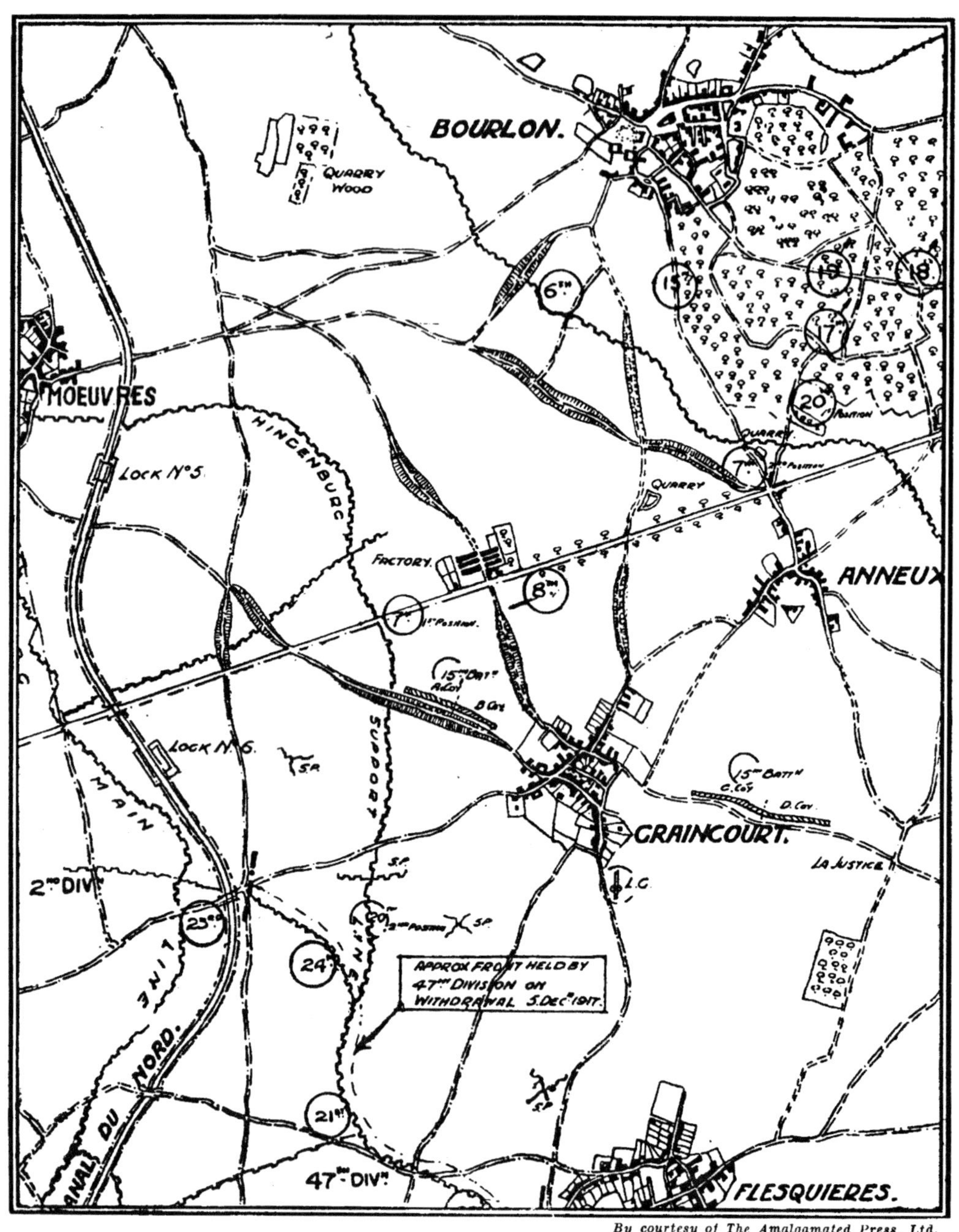

By courtesy of The Amalgamated Press, Ltd.

MAP 14.—BOURLON WOOD, SHOWING AREAS HELD ON NOV. 29TH-30TH, 1917.

THE BROTHERS MONTIER; SGT. G. MONTIER; RFM. J. MONTIER; RFM. E. MONTIER.

"THE THREE MUSKETEERS." C.S.MAJ. JACK FOX; SGT. J. THOMPSON, M.M.; SGT. F. HALL, M.M.

A TYPICAL DRAFT OF OFFICERS ABOUT TO PROCEED OVERSEAS FROM THE "RESERVE" BATTALION AT FOVANT, JULY, 1916.

Standing, from left to right: PICKERING (*killed*), ALLAN (*killed*), DREYFUS, WESTCOMBE, ODAM (*killed*).

Seated, from left to right: FRENCH (*killed*), JONES (*killed*), MACDONALD, ORDISH (*killed*), COPPING (*killed*).

Major H. D. MYER,
1st/6th Battalion.

Major E. A. MYER, second-in-command 1st/6th Battalion.
(Killed.)

Major H. M. BROWNE, M.C.,
second-in-command 2nd/6th
Battalion.

Major W. S. BORTHWICK, T.D.,
2nd/6th Battalion (later R.E.).

Plate 33

Sgt. B. SAVILLE,
MÉDAILLE MILITAIRE.

Sgt. H. WADE, M.M.,
C. DE GUERRE (BELGIUM).

Rfm. L. FREEMONT,
M.M.

L.-Cpl. C. PARNALL,
M.M.

L.-Cpl. S. WILLIAMS,
ALBERT MEDAL.

C.S.Maj. R. STENNER,
M.S.M., O. OF ST. STANISLAUS.

C.Q.M.Sgt. A. W. JOHNSON,
M.S.M.

R.Q.M.Sgt. T. PERCIVAL,
M.S.M.

Cpl. W. GREENSLADE,
M.M.

Plate 34

Sgt. PASSMORE.

Sgt. RYLAND.

Col.-Sgt. PAPWORTH.

Sgt. STAPLETON.

Rfm. HARRIS.

MEDICAL STAFF AND STRETCHER-BEARERS OF THE "FIRST" BATTALION.

C.Q.M.Sgt. YOUNGS.

Rfm. A. MORRIS, M.M.

Capt. MERRETT.

C.Q.M.Sgt. BAILY, D.C.M.

C.Q.M.Sgt. MARSHALL

Sgt. GARSTIN.

C.S.Maj. STILLWELL.

Sgt. THORPE-TRACEY, M.M.

Sgt. BUCKLAND, M.S.M.

Lt. COWNLEY.

west of it, and beat off counter-attack after counter-attack, until overwhelming numbers of fresh German troops forced the newly established line slowly back to its former position. Yet Bourlon Ridge, with the wood at its centre, had to be indisputably in British hands if the Germans were to be driven from their positions to the north of it, and if, in fact, the whole operation was not to be abandoned as a failure. It was to man this ridge and so hold the north-east corner of the salient—the key position—that the 47th Division had been summoned on the 28th, and it was to occupy this key position that the *First* had been moved, as has been seen, on that day to Doignies.

At 1 p.m. in the afternoon of the following day, the battalion took up positions in a part of the Hindenburg Line that had passed into British hands on the first day's fighting, and there it rested for a few hours, while its officers reconnoitred the positions on the ridge which the battalion was to occupy at nightfall. The relief of the West Yorks, then occupying these positions, commenced at 8.30 p.m., and an hour or so afterwards the battalion found itself holding the high ground to the left or west of the wood and just south of the village itself. The front-line trench—if trench it could be called—was nowhere more than four feet deep, and it ran quite straight along the crest of the ridge, facing north-east, for about six hundred yards. Some three hundred yards to the rear and south of it was an even shallower trench, which had to do duty as a defensive position for the right-hand supports; and to the left, facing more north-west than north, was a longish trench which had to serve the double purpose of supporting the left of the front line and of forming a defensive flank. This was necessary, because the right-hand battalion of the division on the left was not as far forward as the *First*, and without such protection, the battalion's left flank would have been exposed. On the right, however, the battalion was protected, for it linked with the 1st/15th Bn., London Regt., occupying the western half of the wood. In these positions the order of battle was: D Company (Capt. Cannon) held the right half of the front line linking with the 1st/15th Bn., London Regt.; A Company (Sec.-Lt. Simcock) held the left half. Supporting this line was C Company (Major Maynard) with two platoons under Sec.-Lt. Farringdon on the right, and two platoons under Sec.-Lt. Plunket on the left. B Company (Capt. Brooke), in reserve, found accommodation in a sunken road a little to the rear of the supporting positions.

Hindenburg Line

Bourlon

The night of November 29th-30th was spent, as may be supposed, in a desperate endeavour to improve these defensive positions before daybreak should reveal to hostile aircraft the weakness of them. Front-line trenches were dug to a depth of six feet, and such wire as could be collected was hastily

Bourlon placed in front of them, but there was no time in which to construct new trenches in echelon, so as to link effectively with the battalion on the left as had been intended. Indeed, almost before it was light the Germans made it clear that they were not going to wait until the British had consolidated their positions before recommencing their attempt to thrust them from the ridge. By 7.30 a.m. they started shelling the wood and a sunken road to the west of it, as well as the platoons in the support trenches, which received a good many gas and smoke-shells. An hour later intense artillery fire opened upon the back areas, and soon an S O S signal put up by the 1st/15th Bn., London Regt., made it clear that an assault was being made on the right. Already two hostile balloons were in full view, and German planes were flying low over the ridge in an endeavour, evidently, to locate the exact positions held on it. At 9 a.m. the battalion on the left put up the S O S signal. Clearly, the enemy's tactics were to attack on both flanks of the *First* on the ridge; and this intention was soon confirmed by messages from the front line from where large numbers of Germans could be seen emerging from Quarry Wood, behind the village of Bourlon, massing in front of it, and moving into assault positions. The attack quickly developed; more and more Germans were thrown against the positions on the flanks of the *First*, which was, of course, able to inflict considerable losses on the troops advancing to its right and left.

Probably the Germans had never appreciated how easily their waves of infantry could and would be thus enfiladed; but when this became clear a frontal attack upon the ridge itself was evidently decided upon, since, shortly before noon large numbers of Germans were seen to be massing directly in front of the battalion's positions. The attack developed, and as was to be expected, met with some success, and on the right where the Germans penetrated the front-line defence, a gap occurred between the *First* and the 1st/15th Bn., London Regt. On the left, too, some ground was given. Little as were these gains, they were enough to give the Germans direct observation on the trenches held by the battalion, and in a very little while the front line was rendered almost untenable on account of the cross-fire from both flanks. In the morning it had been the turn of the *First* to enfilade the attacking enemy, and now he was giving the battalion a dose of its own medicine. To make matters worse for the front-line defenders, the Germans succeeded in bringing a light gun through the village of Bourlon, still intact, to its south-eastern end, and from some convenient point overlooking the whole length of the front line, they maintained a steady fire upon it. Casualties increased rapidly; and to strengthen the garrisons in the front line, the two platoons in the right-half of the support trench were sent forward to join them, while to deal with the menace from the left, the left-hand company in the front line threw back its flank. **Bourlon**

Soon after 2 p.m., following a heavy bombardment, partly from field-guns brought into the open, the Germans delivered powerful attacks against both the front line and from the left, rolling up the left company by attacking from front and rear. Needless to say, the ground was not given without desperate resistance, and not taken before almost all the defenders had been either killed or wounded.

To dwell on the tenacity of the defenders is not necessary, and only those who faced the withering fire from three sides and retired at the last moment, or were wounded and captured, can recount the heroic episode; and whenever they do, it is to speak of the last man to leave the crest of the ridge, Cpl. F. Ryland, who single-handed worked his Lewis-gun until almost surrounded, and then, without haste, withdrew from the untenable position, bringing his gun with him.

To restore the position, a counter-attack by three platoons of the reserve (B) Company, together with all available men at Battalion Headquarters, including signallers, runners, and police, was immediately launched, and, led by Colonel Mildren himself, succeeded in establishing a line on the ridge along a wide front approximately in line with the support positions. A company of the 1st/8th Bn., London Regt., arriving soon after, helped in this protracted effort; and another attack made by two further companies of that unit later resulted in the gain of some further ground on the right. Several German prisoners were taken in this counter-attack, and were found to be in possession of metal numerals which they had taken from the shoulder-straps of those of the *Sixth* who had been captured by them during their assault.

To quote the Commanding Officer's report, made at the end of the day's fighting: " . . . The position held by the 6th Bn., London Regiment, on the morning of the 30th November, was a very exposed one, and it was to be expected that if a resolute attack was delivered in force after previous preparation, it would be very difficult to hold the high ground on the immediate left of Bourlon Wood.

" The Germans did undoubtedly gain ground on the front of the 2nd Division, with the result that the left flank of the 6th Bn., London Regiment, was enveloped, and it became impossible without very strong supports to maintain the position intact. The enemy observation must have been very good all day, his three observation balloons being close up and his aeroplanes constantly flying over our lines until dusk. In his final assault in the afternoon, two flights of enemy planes, one of them consisting of eight

Bourlon machines and the other of six, co-operated with the infantry flying low and using their machine-guns with considerable effect, particularly when the reserve company and details counter-attacked.

" The German troops engaged were massed and in great numbers, well turned out, and appeared first-class troops. The enemy undoubtedly suffered considerably before he succeeded in overwhelming the two and a half companies in the front line. The two platoons of the support company on the left maintained their original positions throughout the day and until they were relieved early the next morning, in spite of severe losses. They were engaged all day in both the assault on the 2nd Division and on the 6th Bn., London Regiment, and although at times surrounded, were successful in holding on.

" The artillery support received was not adequate in the circumstances. It is possible that this was due to the fact that they were heavily engaged with the enemy attacking the 2nd Division, also to the fact that once the enemy attack had developed on the left, the extremely dangerous position of the 6th Battalion was not perhaps appreciated . . . The position at nightfall was that although the Germans had secured the front-line trench and right-support trench, the 6th Bn., London Regiment, assisted by the 8th, still held positions on the hill on the southern side of the plateau, and this line was firmly established.

" The casualties incurred in the fighting totalled thirteen officers and three hundred and sixty-nine ' other ranks,' of which two hundred are missing and unaccounted for at present, but it is hoped many may have been wounded and reached our own advanced stations and will be traced later. The majority of the missing were undoubtedly casualties, and prisoners would not be many—possibly thirty or forty."

Such indeed proved to be the case. Many were traced subsequently at the dressing stations, and of those made prisoner, very few were unwounded. But the death roll had been all too heavy; some of the bravest and most popular having lost their lives, amongst them Capt. F. W. Brooke, M.C., fearless to the last. The Divisional Commander expressed his view of the defence thus: " I heartily thank all ranks of the 140th and 141st, and the R.A., for their gallant and stubborn resistance this day to all enemy attacks. The enemy have clearly suffered heavily and have failed in their attempt to recapture Bourlon Wood, the honour of defending which tactical feature has been entrusted to us. I rely on you to hold the ground we occupy, and am confident that if the enemy renews his attacks he will suffer still greater losses than he has to-day."

In his report, the Commanding Officer had referred to two factors which had largely contributed to the German success—enemy aerial observation and the use of his planes in the assault, and the inadequacy of the British artillery support. Neither his balloons nor his planes had been engaged by British craft, and so far as artillery support was concerned, there had been virtually none. Happily, the reasons for this dual lack of activity reflected no discredit on either of those two arms, both of which were in fact at the time doing super-human work elsewhere along the new Cambrai front. *Bourlon*

As has already been noted, an essential condition of the success of the whole operation was to be the establishment of an impregnable right flank along the St. Quentin canal, without which the new positions to the north would be in constant jeopardy, and the units operating there in danger of being captured. Although in the early fighting the canal had been reached and at places crossed, not all of the final objectives had been secured, and thus no impenetrable line existed. This fact was as clearly realised by General Snow, commanding the VII Corps, holding the flank, as by the experienced German Chief-of-Staff, General Ludendorff, who was quick to take advantage of the situation. Simultaneously, therefore, with the assault on Bourlon Ridge, stronger and more determined German attacks were delivered against General Snow's VII Corps. Striking at dawn from Honnecourt, and expanding north and south, a salient of a couple of miles deep by four wide was soon made in the British defences, and had it not been for the heroic work of the 29th Division, and a successful counter-attack by the Guards, who recaptured Gouzeaucourt and the high ground beyond it, the day would have been lost. November 30th was full of surprises, and this attack of the Guards must, for the Germans, have been one of the greatest. It was delivered, of course, with legendary calm and was strongly supported by artillery fire—fire which came from one of the artillery brigades (235th Bde., R.A.) of the 47th Division. That brigade had been just about to come into action on the Divisional front, when it received orders to go south and cover the Guards attack; and the subsequent operation, perfectly executed in every detail, will always be recalled with pride. General Fielding, commanding the Guards Division, wrote to the 47th Divisional Commander, in the most appreciative terms of the help he had received, and the Commander-in-Chief himself wrote that the steady conduct of the division had "contributed very largely to the security of the divisions engaged on the whole front of attack." This was no exaggeration; while the 47th Division's infantry was holding the Bourlon Ridge, its artillery was helping to regain lost ground elsewhere. Together they can claim largely to have saved the day.

* * * * *

But what had happened to those unfortunate enough to be taken prisoner? Perhaps it would be better not to particularise, but to quote from the published experiences of a soldier who suffered captivity. It is a proud boast of the *Sixth* that very few of their numbers were lost in this way, and that of those that were, most were wounded. Nearly all reports say that the treatment they received at the hands of the enemy was not too harsh. Shortage of food was the greatest hardship, but all agree that captors and captives suffered equally in this respect. Work, and often very hard work, was found for the able-bodied and for those who recovered from their wounds, which included farm-work, road-making, and coal-mining.

GEFANGENERS

Arbeit! Alles arbeit!

Had that diabolical ditty, "Ain't it grand to be blooming well dead," been published during the days of the War, "Gefangeners" (prisoners of war) in Germany would certainly have acclaimed it as an anthem! There are memories within our lives that time cannot efface, and to those who had the misfortune of "taking the wrong turning" and finding themselves "Somewhere in Germany" behind the lines, or in an isolated compound miles away from habitation, had experiences that can never be forgotten. It had its tragedies, but let us look on the lighter side.

Mesum Venn—a tiny village miles from Munster, and in it a compound classified as "Drei Z," the equivalent to a convalescent depot in England, but not a bit like one.

What a collection! Russians, Frenchmen, Italians, Mongolians, and our own little band of Cockneys. There was only one slogan in this godforsaken spot on the marshes that it was situated on. "Arbeit! Alles arbeit!" (Work! Always work!) So long as you could stand, ill or well, "arbeit" was the order. One morning we paraded, my chum, a Cockney, was genuinely queer, and begged to be excused from "arbeit" (work), as he was "krank" (ill). The guard explained to the unter-lieutenant the request, but the usual command came: Nicht! Arbeit! Alles arbeit for the Fatherland!" Poor old Smith, semi-starved and "fed-up" with the stereotyped saying, shouted:

"—— the Fatherland!"

"Yah! Yah!" answered the guard.

But he did not understand English.

"Regen! Alles regen!" Torrential rain did not deter the modus operandi of those in command of this hell hole. Many occasions we marched miles across the marshes to work on road-making. Soaked to the skin and semi-starving, little wonder we waxed indignant. One morning it teemed down, and after working through it, the order came to cease work. Under the impression we were being marched back to compound we were elated. But the hopes were shortlived.

A new order came along and the guard told us it was " Kartoffell's for Kinder " (potatoes for children). The recent rain was spoiling one of the very few things they could get, and we were ordered to dig for potatoes. During the operations a guard came up to our party, and remarked:

" Regen! Alles regen! Nicht Gut for Fatherland!"

Jock Hamilton, of the Argylls, turned to me, and shouted:

" Send it down and drown the square-headed ——"

Immediately the guard turned on Hamilton with the butt end of the rifle, and said:

" Englander! Swinerund! Regen kom Nord Sea!"

He even blamed England for the rain! But he understood English.

" Nicht brod! Nicht Arbeit!"—(No bread! No work!) Pandemonium on parade! Trouble had been brewing for days, and the climax was reached on the morning when our ration of three ounces of black bread was missing. With the exception of a few Russians, the men refused to work without food. Guards raised their rifles in a threatening attitude. The ober-lieutenant shouted: " Arrestzellen!" So we were marched to the cell which had only the space to place three prisoners and their guard.

Realising the ridiculous position they were in, the prison authorities gave fresh orders. Frenchmen were ordered " stillenstand," with their face to the walls of the compound. A real French farce! Italians were placed on fatigue. We Britishers were marched around the prison for hours. We must have circled the compound thousands of times during this Marathon march!

" Mit-tag " (midday) arrived to save the situation. Whistles were blown for resumption of " arbeit," but not a man went on parade, and to mark the occasion, an entertainment was held. According to the tastes and talents of the mixed company that was present, merriment was made. Some scream!

" Morgen! Brod!" (To-morrow! Bread!) The ober-lieutenant on his last visit of the day, promised prisoners a double ration, but we had been " fed-up " with promises, and ordered him out of the room. " Schlafen " (sleep) was his last order, and we retired on empty stomachs. Seven o'clock precise! Parade for " brod " (bread). If perchance an incursion by rats had been made through the bread at night it was wild speculation as to what your allotment would amount to, as no allowance was made for these trivialities! You may wonder how the men did exist under such trying conditions. Occasionally we had a " joy day," which took the form of a special meal-soup, jocularly termed " sand-storm." No one ventured to eat the meal, which looked like silver sand and tasted terrible. By a curious coincidence, these days synchronised with the visits of neutral representatives and Red Cross reporters, who went away favourably impressed.

Frogs for food! In the closing stages of the campaign throughout Germany, the problem of providing food was more acute than in any part of the war zone. " Gefangeners " had to find other channels to satisfy their appetites. At great risk, we each in turn would steal away from the working party and make our way to the stream, where there was a likelihood of finding frogs. A queer sight to see us marching back to barracks with a long string dangling, and on it fine fat frogs ready for the pan. For safety sake we consulted the Frenchmen, who would advise us which were edible. Only the legs! And very nice, too!

Pat's party! We had an Irishman from the Munster Regiment in compound with us. It mattered not how black things were, he was always the optimist. His humour acted as a tonic during these trying times. One night he issued invitations to a party, which consisted of a " high tea " !

Imagine our surprise, when, after spreading the table with brown paper, he produced a hedgehog! For a day or two he had secretly prepared it in clay and baked it under a boiler in the washhouse. Although in a state of semi-starvation, I could not make myself a participant in Pat's party. The variegated colours in the flesh proved too much for my taste. Pat and his pals thoroughly enjoyed it.

There are many readers who will read these reminiscences and doubt the genuineness of them. As I remarked in the opening of these true incidents, it is only the lighter side of the life, or existence of a prisoner of war, but, nevertheless, true in every detail. As to the real tragedies that happened from time to time, perhaps it would be wiser not to relate. You may think I hold an enmity against these people. No! War is war! Let us hope the children of to-day will not undergo similar experiences. Considerable time and money is now being spent on the League of Nations. Is it worth the while? Yes! If they are sincere! But who knows?—" ADSUM."

* * * * *

The German attacks on November 30th, against the southern flank of the newly formed Cambrai salient, were sufficiently successful to compel a British withdrawal from the most advanced positions, and General Byng wisely determined to give up Bourlon Wood and make the Flesquieres ridge his defensive line. Thus, when the *First* was relieved on December 1st by the 1st/7th Bn., it was not to move out of the battle area, but to take up positions *Graincourt* in a sunken road north-west of Graincourt in conformity with the general plan. *Havrincourt Wood* Here it remained until December 4th, when it moved to Havrincourt Wood, there to camp for a couple of nights, in order to clean-up and to refit, preparatory to occupying the new front line, north-east of Havrincourt village, established on December 5th. The new front line in the neighbourhood of this village was none other than the Hindenburg support-line, and the trenches, if deep, were wet and muddy. Apart from shell-fire, there was little enemy activity, however, and the battalion suffered no further casualties. On December 11th, it moved to new positions astride the Havrincourt-Metz road, *Bertincourt* and on the next day, into billets and huts at Bertincourt, not for the rest it so well deserved, but to enable all ranks to clean the caked mud from their uniforms and equipment. On December 14th, the battalion marched by companies again into the Havrincourt sector, which it had come to know so well, but on this occasion it occupied trenches north-west of the village, not primarily for defensive purposes, but because they had ample dug-out accommodation, and the battalion was to work and not to fight.

Work! It seemed always that the *Sixth* was to do the lion's share of both fighting and manual labour. At Ypres, at Oppy and Gavrelle, and now at Havrincourt, picks and shovels were the order of the day. Nightly the four companies moved towards the Flesquieres ridge to dig a new support line. Fortunately, the weather was now turning cold, and the eternal rain had ceased, and there were deep, warm dug-outs to return to after the night's labours, so life was not too bad. Perhaps it would have been a further consolation to the *First* to know that their brothers-in-arms in the *Second*, after their fighting, were performing precisely similar tasks in the Ypres Salient. But this tour of duty was not to last long. On December 21st, the battalion was withdrawn, and after marching through Havrincourt Wood, it was met by the band, and was played into its billets at Bertincourt. A short period **Bertincourt** of bliss was before it, for on the next day the battalion marched to Etricourt, entrained, and, after a long and very cold journey, arrived at Miraumont, and from there marched to Ribemont, a village east of the devastated area and quite **Ribemont** close to Amiens, a busy provincial city which so far had escaped the ravages of war. It was now Christmas, and a real Christmas holiday was spent at Ribemont. Snow began to cover the ground; and although the traditional Christmas dinner had to be postponed until the 27th, owing to there being insufficient time in which to prepare it, full justice was done when the day arrived to turkeys, beef, ham, pudding, nuts, apples, and beer, not forgetting a packet of cigarettes. The Sergeants' Mess had its dinner on the following day, and, as may be supposed, it was an even greater success. Happy indeed were the days at Ribemont; training was not too strenuous, there were periodical visits to the baths at Senlis, and passes to visit Amiens were easily obtained. To these creature comforts were added others of a different quality —praise from all quarters was being showered upon the battalion for the magnificent part it had played at Bourlon. The Divisional Commander personally congratulated all ranks after divine service on Christmas day, and several officers, N.C.O.'s, and men were awarded decorations or were mentioned in dispatches. There was only one regret, other than the continual recollection of lost comrades, and that occurred on January 4th (1918), when a wire reached Battalion Headquarters from the III Corps, ordering "Lt.-Col. W. F. Mildren, C.M.G., D.S.O., 1st/6th Bn., London Regt., to assume command of the 141st Infantry Brigade, with temporary rank of Brigadier-General." Colonel Mildren had commanded the battalion since August, 1915, and whilst, of course, everyone was delighted and proud to learn that their Commanding Officer had gained well-deserved promotion, none thought of his leaving the unit without feelings of personal loss.

FIRST BATTALION OFFICERS, WARRANT OFFICERS and SECTION COMMANDERS at

BOURLON WOOD—1917

OFFICER COMMANDING:	SECOND-IN-COMMAND:	ADJUTANT:
COL. MILDREN	MAJOR NEELY	CAPT. GILKS
R.S.MAJ. PHILLIPS		ACT.: LIEUT. MARTIN
		R.Q.M.SGT. PERCIVAL

A Co.	CAPT. M. J. MACDONALD ACT.: LIEUT. SIMCOCK	C.S.MAJ. ALLEN (J)	C.Q.M.SGT. SANDISON
B Co.	CAPT. BROOKE (killed)	C.S.MAJ. BITTEN	C.Q.M.SGT. KNIGHT
C Co.	MAJOR MAYNARD	C.S.MAJ. CASTLEMAN	C.Q.M.SGT. YOUNGS
D Co.	CAPT. CANNON	C.S.MAJ. SNOW	ACT.-C.Q.M.S. PASSMORE

Quartermaster: CAPT. LOVETT
Transport: LIEUT. NOAKES; SGT. BROWN; CPL. POLLARD
Cooks: SGT. BRITTEN; CPL. GRANT
Stretcher-Bearers: CAPT. HOPE-CARLTON; SGT. WADE
Signallers: SGT. HOUGHTON; CPL. SHARP
Lewis-Guns: SGT. F. SHORT (killed); SGT. DRAGE; CPL. RYLAND; CPL. PAXTON
Intelligence: CAPT. SMITHER
Orderly Room: CPL. PEEBLES; CPL. WADE; CPL. STAPLETON

Chapter 16

FROM RIBEMONT TO RIBECOURT

"Rest" at Ribemont came to an end on January 10th. On that day the battalion commenced its return to the Cambrai Sector, travelling by rail to Etricourt, thence marching to camp at Lechelle. On the 12th, another short journey by rail brought it to Trescault, from where it marched to the newly constructed trench system on the Flesquieres ridge, **Flesquieres** north of Ribecourt. Here, like calm after the storm, there was little hostile activity except spasmodic shelling, but almost at once the frosty weather came to an end, and as the frozen earth thawed, trenches became water-logged and impassable. There had naturally been no time to revet and drain, to sand-bag, and lay duckboards, and trenches were, therefore, in a deplorable state. In consequence of these adverse physical conditions some rearrangement of the brigade front was decided upon. Battalions held a narrower front to enable at least one of their companies to be placed, as reserves, in drier quarters. To the *First*, this meant that one company could remain in reserve at Ribecourt, where also the whole battalion was housed when in support. The glutinous mud of the trenches made it virtually impossible for the front line companies to do anything more than render their immediate surroundings habitable, but some patrolling was done at night, and in the daytime, the battalion's snipers busied themselves with picking off their "opposite numbers" in the German trenches. Later in the month the right-sub-sector was held for a few days, and here the conditions were just as deplorable and constant work just as necessary. If there was any similarity at all between the villages of Ribemont, where the battalion had spent Christmas, and Ribecourt, to where it repaired when not in the front line, that similarity lay only in their two names. In all other respects the one was the antithesis of the other.

On January 24th, the *First* was withdrawn from the line and moved to Bertincourt, but eight miles away to the west, where on Sunday, 27th, after **Bertincourt** church parade, at which the Divisional Commander was present, it heard with astonishment and dismay that the 140th Infantry Brigade was to be reduced to three battalions, and that it, the *First*, was to be disbanded. This astounding piece of news—only credible because it was given by the Divisional

Bertincourt Commander himself, when addressing the battalion after the parade—had a numbing effect on all. That the losses sustained by the British Army on the Somme, at Messines, at Ypres, and at Cambrai, should compel this reorganisation was understandable enough, but that the choice of the unit to be disbanded should fall on the 1st/6th Bn., London Regt., was unbelievable; and it was not until stores began to be collected and nominal rolls of those to join other units began to be prepared, that the dire truth fully dawned. An impassioned speech by Major Neely, during a battalion concert a couple of days later, exactly expressed the feelings of every officer, non-commissioned officer, and man serving in it.

The *First* had been in France since March, 1915; had taken part in every engagement of importance; had fought at Festubert, at Loos, at Vimy, on the Somme, in the Ypres Salient, at Messines, and at Bourlon Wood; it had made the " record " raid of the whole British Army; and it had a reputation throughout the division for efficiency, bravery, and tenacity. Why, then, should it be disbanded?

There is no adequate answer to this question, nor is any useful purpose served by making an inquiry into the matter. But whatever the official reasons, it is agreeable to think of two, wholly adequate, which the Gods in their wisdom must have known. After their sacrifices at Bullecourt and at Ypres, the *Second* badly needed the strength and spirit which only the *First* could bring to it. That was one; and the other was this: that now that the *First* had lost by promotion the officer who had for so long commanded them, led them, and shared their miseries and privations, it was fitting that the battalion should no longer exist. Colonel Mildren and the *First* were interchangeable terms; and it is almost poetical to think that when the one went the other should go, too.

The *First* was to be disbanded; six officers and one hundred and seventy " other ranks " were to join the 1st/18th Bn. (London Irish), eight officers and two hundred and fifty " other ranks " were to join the 1st/15th Bn. (Civil Service Rifles), and fourteen officers and two hundred and fifty " other ranks " were to join the *Second*. On January 30th, 1918, at 1.45 p.m., the battalion paraded as a unit for the last time, and heavy in heart the first two of the contingents marched away. Three days later, on February 2nd, the third embussed, at 8.45 a.m., to join its sister battalion, and standing to say " farewell " to them as they went were the Adjutant, Capt. Gilks, and six warrant officers, C.S.Majors Bitten, Allen, and Castleman, and C.Q.M.Sgts. Howell, Weeden, and Young. For some inexplicable reason they were considered surplus to requirements, and had no unit to join. Apparently unwanted, they yet had the distinction of representing the last of the *First*, and none was more worthy of that honour.

* * * * *

When the *Second* moved from the Ypres Salient on January 8th, 1918, the general supposition was that, after the usual period of rest for training and reorganisation, some quiet sector on the western front would be found for it, and that there it would remain until some sudden military emergency demanded its virile presence elsewhere. Events proved the correctness of the forecast, although no one—not even the wildest imagination—predicted the astonishing events the battalion was to see during the next three months. The first occurred at Proven, where the battalion was cleaning-up and where medal-ribbons were presented. Here, on the 19th, it received movement orders for Demuin, a tiny village away to the south, close to the untouched market town **Demuin** of Villers Bretonneux, and only about ten miles east of Amiens, where it was known life was going on much as usual. The battalion's luck was evidently in. The village of Demuin was reached at 5.30 a.m. on the 20th, the billets were comfortable, estaminets inviting, and villagers kind and attentive. The very countryside with its undulating fields and green hills, in sharp contrast to the flatness of the salient, was exhilarating. Spirits were high; and when on February 2nd, eight officers and one hundred and ninety-six non-commissioned officers and men* arrived from the disbanded *First*, everything was ready to give these veterans a hearty welcome. Of course, many in both battalions were already well-known to one another. Earlier, drafts from the *Reserve* in England to the *Second* had contained many *First* men, and some of those who now came to join the *Second* had seen service with it in 1915, when it was the draft-finding unit for the *First*, before the *Reserve* had been formed.

Thus, although there were complications arising from the fact that the battalion now had to settle questions of seniority and command, there was very little difficulty in wedding the two units, and Colonel Benson's complete understanding of human nature overcame whatever friction there might have been. It ought to be recorded, too, that sensing possible difficulties, everybody sportingly accepted the Commanding Officer's decisions and did their best to help him solve his problem. As an indication of its magnitude the following contribution is a good description of what had to be done:

" Perhaps in the case of the officers the task was not so big, but with the 'other-ranks' and the riflemen it was a different matter. For example, the

*See above. There is a discrepancy between the War Diaries of the two battalions as to the number joining the *Second*.

Demuin *Second's* Transport was complete in strength, and the question of fitting in a dozen *First* Transport men offered no mean task. Cpl. Pollard and Cpl. S. Williams, with a few others, were attached to the companies, but Cpl. Shillingford, Drivers New, Halford, Hilliard, Hitchcock, Crook, Stewart, Doubleday, were all merged into the section.

" R.Q.M.Sgt. Percival, of the *First*, was co-opted with R.Q.M.Sgt. Parish, of the *Second;* Cpl. Davis, of the *First*, going into the ' Stores,' too. Positions had to be found for Sgt. Britten, who had been sergeant-cook of the *First* for three years, and the solution there was for him to join Sgt. Buckland, sergeant-cook of the *Second*, and together these two stalwarts co-operated to prove that two heads are better than one. Sgt. Wade, with Cpl. Brett, were merged in with the Stretcher-bearer Section, Wade ultimately taking charge; and Cpl. Sharp, who had been in charge of the *First's* signallers, and who had the reputation of having been in every engagement of that battalion until the amalgamation, became the sergeant of the *Second's* signallers.

" The remaining sergeants, corporals, and men were attached to companies—old ' Festubert ' warriors like Sgts. Alexander, Zeeman; Cpls. Wicken, Gold, Viney, and Neyland, and others too numerous to mention, all throwing in their lot with their comrades of the *Second*.

" Major George Neely had come with the contingent, and had made sure of bringing his horse, ' Nigger,' with him, and soon spied his old groom serving in the Transport Section as the medical cart driver, and made a valiant attempt to claim him."

Those were the kind of contacts made, and by the time the battalion came to leave Demuin, the " *Sixth*," as it could now be called without the distinguishing " 1st " or " 2nd " to precede it, was truly one. The move took place on February 8th, the battalion marching to Villers Bretonneux—a village it was soon to see again in very different circumstances—and entraining,
Chauny was carried to Appilly, and reached Chauny by bus later in the day.

The area in which the *Sixth* now found itself was new to the British Army which after the campaign of 1917 had been asked by the French Commander-in-Chief to extend its line southwards. During that year, and so long as it had to bear the main burden of the offence, the length of front that it held had necessarily to be shorter than that of the French, who had over three hundred miles to protect as against the round hundred of the British. But now, at the beginning of 1918, the international situation had changed. The Russian collapse and subsequent treaty of peace with Germany meant the release of hundreds of thousands of German troops for use on the Western

Front, and since November division after division had been carried across Central Europe to augment the German armies in France and Belgium. In the face of this reinforcement the role which the British and French would have to play was pretty clearly indicated. At least, for the time being they would have to act on the defensive, and in the circumstances an extension of the British front southwards was equitable. Just how far this extension should be, however, was a matter of considerable dispute, not between the respective Commanders-in-Chief of the Allied Armies, who apparently reached early agreement in the matter, but between the British and French Governments. The dispute was settled eventually by the adoption of the original plan for the British to extend southwards as far as the River Oise, and thus to hold a front of about one hundred and twenty-five miles. To be precise the allotted British line extended beyond the River Oise (for which the British accepted responsibility) the junction of the two armies occurring at the village of Barisis, lying about four miles beyond it. The whole of this extension was over ground surrendered by the Germans at the time of their withdrawal to the Hindenburg Line in the March of the previous year, and bore all the customary marks of systematic destruction which the *Sixth* had noted when earlier operating in more northerly sections of it. All the villages were razed to the ground, bridges destroyed, and mines sprung systematically to cause the utmost inconvenience to the occupying forces, and nowhere was this calculated destruction so evident as in the towns and larger villages. Chauny, where the battalion passed the night of February 8th-9th, wore the appearance of having been visited by an earthquake. Of many of its buildings only the outer shells remained, and in others, more solidly constructed, great cracks were visible from roof to ground. Bricks, tiles, and beams littered the ground, and where the feet of men and horses had made undulating paths over the wreckage, the pulverised bricks and mortar were stirred, during fine weather, into clouds of dust, during wet, into sticky slime. *Chauny*

While the battalion "details," quartermaster's stores, and transport remained at Chauny, the rest of the unit moved closer to the front line, relieving the 18th Bn., Manchester Regiment (9th), in the forest of Coucy. To the 58th Division had been allotted the defensive positions north and south of the Oise, and the 174th Inf. Bde., south of the river, was thus on the extreme right of the British Army. The whole country was magnificently wooded, and the war seemed strangely remote. Even in the "line"—which was nothing more than a series of connected posts lining the edge of a clearing in the forest—the impression of peace was rarely disturbed, except when on rare occasions the Germans fired a few "whiz-bangs" into the ruined village *Coucy Forest* of Barisis. It was, if anything, too peaceful, for it gave a sense of false security, and at least one party from another battalion, marching quietly along a country lane, oblivious to every hostile sound, fell victims to machine-gun fire from a marauding plane.

Barisis At Barisis itself, where the right-hand company made contact with the French, there were indeed trenches of a kind, and the German and British lines were not far apart, and occasional shelling and sniping acted as reminders that a war was being fought. But it is noteworthy that from the 9th to the 24th, during which the battalion was holding the right-hand sector, only one casualty occurred. Apart from the novelty of the surroundings, interest was centred as much as anywhere else on the French troops and their methods of defence. Relying almost entirely upon the counter-attack as a means of maintaining their positions, the front line at Barisis was very nearly deserted. An occasional sentry, carefully hidden in a partly demolished cottage, represented their front line, and all routes to his post were equipped in some way or another to ensure that anyone approaching it would give audible signal to him. A few pieces of iron on a wire, or a loose board, would sound the alarm, and bring forth a whispered: "Qui va la?" There were French "regulars" as well as Colonial troops in the neighbourhood, and the great caves at Carrieres-Bernagousse seemed to contain them all. There was, of course, considerable fraternisation between the French and the *Sixth*, and some brisk business was occasionally done in the exchange of bully-beef for vegetables.

On the last day of the month (February 28th) the battalion was relieved *Pierremande* in the Barisis Sector by the 12th Bn., and resting one night at Pierremande, a tiny village lying some five miles west of Barisis, it took over the left sector from the 7th Bn., and had its first real experience of holding the line against a silent and invisible enemy. The Coucy Forest was a westward extension of the larger St. Gobain Forest, still in enemy hands, and in it grew deciduous trees of all kinds, as well as innumerable small shrubs and bushes, and in places the vegetation was so dense that movement was confined to horse-drives and such footpaths as lateral patrols and ration parties might make. *Coucy Forest* No war of movement in it was possible, and the French, when following the Germans after their retirement in 1917, had wisely halted at an edge of the forest where a wide belt of grassland separated it from its larger neighbour. The presence of Germans in the St. Gobain Forest was indicated by a narrow strip of wire on their side of the clearing, but no-man's-land seemed to be deserted by the enemy, and nightly patrols of the *Sixth* passed unmolested about it, often approaching right up to his wire without drawing fire. The

BRIG.-GENERAL H. B. P. L. KENNEDY, C.M.G., D.S.O.,
Commanding 140th Infantry Brigade, 1917-1919.

Plate 36

From the History of the 47th Division

From the History of the 47th Division

ABOVE: PART OF THE "BLUFF CRATERS" SECTOR NEAR TO HILL 60.

BELOW: THE WHITE CHATEAU, CAPTURED BY THE "FIRST" IN THE BATTLE OF MESSINES ON JUNE 5TH, 1917.

Plate 37

Royal Air Force

BULLECOURT (looking north).

The photograph taken in April, 1917, three weeks before the attack by the "Second" battalion. From left to right the distance measures nearly one mile. The trench running east and west at the top formed part of Bovis trench.

Coucy Forest

Germans, of course, realised that there was no real danger in holding their line so weakly, for effective action by either side was out of the question in such closely wooded country, and in all probability the British garrison was no stronger than the enemy's. Indeed, upon occasion the situation was positively alarming to the company commanders holding the front line, particularly when Major Neely, who had joined the battalion from the *First* as its Second-in-Command, saw fit to prowl around no-man's-land on his own, and to greet a company commander later with the sickening remark: "I've been through your wire and passed your posts three times in the last hour, and none of your damn fellows has seen me!"

This was serious but understandable. Companies, although now strong, held half a mile of front; and that could only be done by dotting posts at intervals along its entire length and patrolling between them. Gaps of a hundred yards or more sometimes occurred between the sections, and the wire between them was rarely more than a few strands twisted around bushes and tree-trunks, and the forest was so full of natural sounds (it was said that the wild boar still lived in it) that the rustle of leaves or the crack of twigs underfoot went unnoticed. The defensive system, exactly suited to the French temperament from whom it was a legacy, was not designed to repel the single invader, and when the *Sixth* inherited it there was a distinct feeling in the companies that they were being unfairly asked to apply trench organisation and trench discipline in circumstances wholly different from normal conditions of defence. It was impossible to watch every inch of the line, and everyone knew it. The Commanding Officer was perhaps the first to appreciate this situation, and with characteristic realism, soon had the company in reserve and the Pioneer Section, cutting long alleys through the undergrowth so that by means of cross-fire from rifles and Lewis-guns, every post and locality was fully protected. For the first week in this sector bill-hooks were handled far more freely than rifles, and soon, from every post, appeared narrow paths through the forest, radiating like spokes in a wheel. An effort, too, was made to strengthen the wire wherever it seemed particularly thin, or wherever some glade separating the trees might tempt an enemy patrol to penetrate by night into the battalion's outpost system. The forward zone was defended by C and D Companies, with A Company in support, and to complete the defence the reserve company (B) which remained at Pierremande with Battalion Headquarters, and "details," had to know the whole front sufficiently well to enable it to counter-attack in any direction at a moment's notice. On the day it took over the defence of this sector, the strength of the battalion on paper was fifty-eight officers and nine hundred and seventy-six "other ranks."

Transport at Autreville

When the battalion had moved into the Barisis Sector, it had left behind at Chauny its Transport Section and Quartermaster's Stores, both of which comfortably established themselves in some chemical works where water could be readily obtained for men and horses. All its machinery had been destroyed, and few roofs were intact, but sleeping accommodation was available in some of the factory's offices, and apart from the inconvenience of piles of broken glass and a thick covering of red and black powder which lay in almost every part, the billet was considered highly desirable. It was with some regret, therefore, that they left these quarters for Autreville, on February 24th, so as to be nearer the battalion, which since going into the Coucy Forest, had been making heavy demands on men, horses, and vehicles, in consequence of the wide front it held.

Far too little thought was often given by the companies to the tireless energy of Company Quartermaster-Sergeants, storesmen, and drivers, in keeping them supplied with food, water, and ammunition, to say nothing of post-bags. Theirs was work which went on day and night, and often when the men in the line were having a quiet time the supply personnel was experiencing exactly the reverse. Frequently, when the companies had no hostile activity to report, the back areas would be receiving persistent attention from the enemy's artillery; but no matter how heavy the shelling might be, how impassable the roads, or how wet and dark the night, the long journey from stores to companies had to be made. As one of the drivers puts it:

Coucy Forest

"From a life of quietness gradually the nightly journeys through one of the main roads of the forest to the line became veritable nightmares. For a distance of two miles the road itself was impassable, and to avoid this section we had to deliver supplies by means of pack-animals. For miles through the horrible stillness and darkness of the forest the pack-animal leaders would plod on, ankle deep in mud, the horses at times being startled by some weird noise. Occasionally, the silence would be broken by a screech, followed by a deafening roar, as some "coal-box" burst near at hand to echo for half a minute through the forest. Once, a shell—fortunately a dud—actually struck the road between the back-half of a cooker and the medical-cart."

"It was quite clear to those who made these nightly journeys that the routes to the advanced positions were under pretty close observation, and as each night passed so the shelling increased, and it was obvious that if things continued to get worse, it might be impossible to get vehicles away from the foremost posts."

The increase in enemy artillery fire, which the Transport Section had noted with apprehension, signified something more than mere local activity. Similar action was taking place along almost the entire British and French fronts, with this difference, that whereas in the Coucy Sector, for example, little attention was being paid by the Germans to the British front-line, elsewhere they were subjecting it to fairly steady bombardment. That a German attack in strength would be made against the British or French, or both, along a wide front, as soon as sufficient reinforcements had arrived was already known to both Commanders-in-Chief, who could not be expected, however, to divine exactly where the blow would fall. But experience had shown that one almost infallible clue was the disposition of the enemy's front-line garrisons, and if they could be identified and checked against the reports of Secret Service agents, the enemy's intentions could often be correctly gauged. In accordance, therefore, with instructions issued to all front-line troops, every effort was made to secure prisoners, and thus identify the German regiments facing the British; and it was largely with this object that the companies did so much patrolling in no-man's-land. True, one German infantryman had strayed into the area held by the *Sixth,* and had been captured by Capt. Lathbury, but that was hardly sufficient for the purpose, and if the required information was to be obtained, a special effort would have to be made.

Coucy Forest

Such an effort could only take the form of a raid, and about the middle of March this measure was decided upon. Capt. Sampson, already decorated for the highly successful raid he led* on Oblique Trench, when the *First* had been in the Ypres Salient, and now in command of the special battle-platoon which every battalion had formed, was selected for the task on hand, and with him went Cpl. Gold, M.M., Cpl. Viney, and a handful of stalwarts. Their task was simple and difficult enough—simple, because the enemy clearly never expected such action against them, and permitted free movement by night about no-man's-land, difficult because owing to the thinness with which the Germans held their line there could be no set objective. Large-scale maps indeed showed both enemy wire and trenches, but they could, of course, give no indication as to the whereabouts of the German garrisons, and to find an occupied post to raid in such dense forest might be like looking for a needle in a haystack. Early investigation by the patrol revealed that the German line was protected by far more wire than was the British, and an attempt to cut a path through it showed that that part of the task alone would require more time than one night could give. Resuming this laborious work when darkness fell the next day, the patrol found no less than five narrow belts of wire, through each of which a clearing had to be made.

*See page 132.

Coucy Forest

So far the enemy's attention had not been attracted to what was going on, and the patrol wondered if their luck would hold. It did. When the last strand was clipped, they moved quietly forward until a trench was reached, and were greatly surprised to find it completely deserted. Dropping noiselessly into it, they followed the trench until they came to a sentry-post from which the sentry had absented himself, leaving, however, his arms and ammunition hanging in the trench. These they hid, and continuing their midnight stroll, they came first to a German latrine (unconcernedly made use of by one of the patrol) and then to a German dug-out, against the entrance to which and on either side of it, stood rifle-racks, and in them a number of rifles, giving a clue to the size of the garrison.

There were painted wooden notices, too, which indicated that the occupants of the dug-out were machine-gunners, and Capt. Sampson wisely decided in view of their number not to enter it; so, contenting themselves with hiding the rifles and taking down the notices, the patrol continued its way until another, but smaller, dug-out was reached. Here, the single rifle-rack contained only eight rifles, and judging that that was the number of the occupants, Capt. Sampson decided to seek his captive here. First, the rifles were hidden, then the painted notice removed, after which Cpl. Gold, who spoke German well, descended the dug-out steps and shouted out something to the effect that there were officers in the trench, and that the occupants were to turn out. Perhaps the Germans inside were not entirely convinced that they were wanted, for they were slow in obeying the order, but after a few moments they began to move towards the staircase and slowly mounted it, Cpl. Gold retreating before them.

The first German to reach the top was seized and told by Capt. Sampson, who also spoke German, to make no noise and to go quietly with the patrol. But he shouted out—doubtless to warn his comrades—and there was no alternative but to shoot him, as well as the other Germans, who by this time were well up the stairs. That done, the first German's shoulder-straps, bearing the name and number of his regiment, were removed, and with these and the painted notice-boards, the patrol returned the way they had come and reached the battalion's line without themselves sustaining any casualties. This successful raid was a very clever and daring piece of work, and for the part each took in it, Capt. Sampson received a bar to his Military Cross, Cpl. Gold the D.C.M., and Cpl. Viney the M.M.

By now everyone was talking about the projected German attack. The observers daily manned their vantage points (one of which, constructed in the branches of the tallest tree in the forest, overlooked the country for miles around, and was rivalled only by a similar post in enemy territory) and with their glasses searched the countryside for hostile movement. Companies were allotted their battle-positions, and March 21st was freely spoken of as being the day when the enemy would launch his great offensive. Elated by these recent minor successes, the battalion remained quite unconcerned, but became more and more vigilant, the alertness being by no means confined to the men in the line. An amusing story is often told of the Transport Section in this connection, although it reflects nothing but credit upon those who composed it. One day at Autreville, Capt. Brasher and Sgt. Price, the Transport Officer and sergeant respectively, disturbed by the presence of a British "Heavy" which, firing at intervals of ten minutes on each occasion brought down slates and brickwork on to the heads of their men and animals, billeted in a partly ruined farmhouse, crossed a civilian cemetery which separated the gun from the transport lines, with perhaps the intention of lodging a protest. The account continues:

Coucy Forest

"When they arrived at the wall which bounded the cemetery and which screened the gun, they found that they were not alone. A huge man, immaculately dressed as a French officer, was close beside them, and was watching the gun with intense interest. Now, the nearest French troops were several miles away, and there was nobody living in the village. Who then, could this elegant fellow be, and why should he be watching the gun from behind the wall? Suspicions aroused, Cpl. Shillingford and a driver were instructed to keep the man in view and follow him when he went away. This soon he did, and the two of them sauntered along after him as far as Chauny, where he was seen to enter a dilapidated estaminet. Quickly taking counsel together, it was decided that the corporal should keep watch while the driver should find the Provost Marshal and tell him the whole story.

"The driver had no difficulty in performing his task, and soon was discussing plans for further action with the Provost Marshal and the French Provost; then, in accordance with decisions taken, he returned to the estaminet, entered it, seated himself at the same table as the suspect, and ordered a bottle of *vin blanc*. But, alas! he had no money with him, and while he was wondering what to do, the suspicious character promptly paid the bill. At this moment, however, the Provost Marshal and the French Provost entered the inn and ordered the suspect to accompany them to the gendarmerie. There followed the customary altercation between Frenchmen whenever a difference of opinion arises, and after considerable cross-questioning and examination of papers, there were expressions of mutual esteem and apologies from both sides. The 'spy,' it appeared, was a highly placed

Coucy Forest

French artillery officer, whose home, now razed to the ground, was in Autreville. Both his parents lay buried in the cemetery, and it was natural that being near at hand he should visit their graves to see if the tombstones had been in any way disturbed. While there, he had heard the gun firing, and his professional interest being aroused, he had gone to watch it.

"' All's well that ends well.' The French officer was delighted that such precautions were being taken, brushed aside the driver's apologies and his thanks for paying the wine bill, and gave him a letter explaining the whole matter to the Commanding Officer. The *entente cordiale* was saved."*

With so much front to hold, and so few men to hold it, there was little chance of sleep by night for any of the forward companies, or for that matter, for the reserve company, to whom largely fell the odd jobs of fetching and carrying for the whole battalion. But in the day-time sleep was permissible, and nearly everybody after mid-day dinner turned day into night and slept the sleep that only tired soldiers know. Yet not all; at least one indefatigable officer, Sec.-Lt. Metzler, an able musician, used the afternoons more profitably, and his daily request to his Company Commander: "If you don't want me this afternoon, sir——" aroused a good deal of interest among his brother officers, and there was coarse speculation on what he did in the depths of the forest into which he was seen to ride on a borrowed signal-section bicycle every afternoon. He had been doing this for ten days or more, when on March 20th, his Company Commander thought fit to inquire where he was going, and by way of reply he invited his "skipper" to accompany him, and the two set off together, the senior wondering into what kind of mischief he was being led. The answer to this unspoken question lay surprisingly near at hand, for in a short while the couple arrived at a tiny church buried in the forest, where the attendant curé, an aged man, still said his mass and his matins. The Germans in their retirement had left the church intact, taking from it only such metal as might be useful to them. From the musician's point of view, however, this was disastrous, for the church's melodious organ had been stripped of all its copper pipes, and from them came the sweetest notes.

Disconcerting as this was, Sec.-Lt. Metzler, like a true musician (who lacking his instruments will make music with a reed), had soon found ways and means of making the organ speak again, and now, seated before the keyboard, he was at home and at peace with all the world. And very beautiful it was as the notes were played and the woods responded to the wind gently fed to them by the old curé. It was a pity, of course, that only half the organ

*R. G. Emery.

remained, but the great composers had evidently foreseen such a situation as this, and Sec.-Lt. Metzler knew exactly what was suited to the wooden pipes.

"You want stuff with plenty of bass in it to hear it at its best."

"Such as?"

"Oh, the 'Dead March' in 'Saul.'" And he struck the notes, and the organ boomed out, and the forest reverberated with it.

The "Dead March" was never finished; before he was halfway through a breathless runner arrived, hot and tired. In his hand he carried a field-telegram, which he passed to the Company Commander.

"Man battle-stations," it read.

OFFICERS, WARRANT OFFICERS and SECTION COMMANDERS at

COUCY FOREST (ST. GOBAIN)

Officer Commanding:		Second-in-Command:	Adjutant:
	Col. Benson	Major Brown	Capt. Wylie
	R.S.Maj. Boss		R.Q.M.Sgts. Parrish and Percival
A Co.	(1) Capt. Anderson (2) Capt. Burt-Smith	C.S.Maj. Montier	C.Q.M.Sgt. Williams
B Co.	Capt. Godfrey	C.S.Maj. Thorndyke	C.Q.M.Sgt. Sired
C Co.	Capt. Hill	C.S.Maj. Palowkar	C.Q.M.Sgt. Davies
D Co.	Capt. Maxted	C.S.Maj. Worrall	C.Q.M.Sgt. Grundy

Quartermaster: Capt. Lovett
Transport: Capt. Brasher; Sgt. Price; Cpl. Dorling
Cooks: Sgt. Buckland; Sgt. Britten
Stretcher-Bearers: Maj. De Muth; Sgt. Wade; Cpl. Brett
Signallers: Lieut. Bubb; Cpl. Sharp
Battle Platoon: Capt. Sampson; Cpl. Gold; Cpl. Viney
Scouts and Snipers: Capt. Morrow; Sgt. Sutton

Chapter 17

VILLERS BRETONNEUX

Although the companies had been warned on the afternoon of the 20th to occupy their battle-stations, there was no indication of any hostile intention during the remainder of that day and night on the battalion's front. The dispositions had been unaltered, with C and D Companies in front, A in support, and B in reserve, and waiting for any eventuality, the platoons ' stood-to ' all night. For some days heavy shelling north of the Oise had been distinctly heard, and companies had learnt from their C.Q.M.Sgts. that "things were getting a bit unhealthy " in the back areas; none the less, when the storm actually broke at 4.30 a.m. on the morning of the 21st, surprise was almost as great as if there had been no knowledge of its coming, and that was due partly to the fact that troops had learnt that situations rarely developed as they were predicted, and also to the fact that on the battalion's front there was no change. The day dawned much as any other day, except that the morning was misty and it was a little difficult to tell the exact direction from which the sound of greatest gun-fire was coming. One thing was certain, however; while that part of the 58th Division north of the Oise were "getting it in the neck," the two battalions of the 174th Inf. Bde. south of the river were so far untouched.

Coucy Forest

The sound of heavy gun-fire on the left, across the Oise, continued throughout the day, but towards the evening, judging from the direction where there seemed to be most noise, the German artillery had ceased, and only British guns were firing. Where ignorance is bliss! Some were saying that that was only the first day of the enemy's final bombardment; some, that on no account would the Germans move forward from their Hindenburg Line once they had retaken the parts they had lost; and some again, that the real attack, if attack there was, would be against the French. All were wrong, and none knew that on that day the Germans, profiting by the mist,* had overrun the first defences, killing the flower of the Fifth Army, and were even then in places five miles beyond their jumping-off positions. Just across the Oise the advance had been not less than three miles, and there, contesting the ground inch by

*But German commanders claimed that the mist handicapped the advance and that without it more progress would have been made. British officers after the battle on August 8th, 1918, made a similar claim (see page 223 below).

inch, were the other two brigades of the division fighting a losing battle, the result of which in the circumstances was a foregone conclusion.

Why was this? The decision by which the British extended their line southwards has already been noted, as also the fact that in the Coucy Forest companies were holding lengths of front out of all proportion to their strengths. The peculiar circumstances obtaining in this sector warranted the use of so small a force in its defence, but north of the Oise, where the country was open, and where no reserve trench-system existed, adequate defence depended upon the presence of far greater numbers. Yet the numbers were no greater. Along the whole of its forty-mile front, General Gough's Fifth Army had only twelve infantry divisions (excluding three in reserve) to oppose over treble that number launched by the Germans in their initial assault. Assuming that the usual number of battalions in each British division were in the forward zones, and that in turn each had two companies in the front line, then each of those companies would be holding on the average a front of about one third of a mile. Probably the strength of companies did not each exceed one hundred officers and men, and if this high figure is assumed, it will be seen, bearing in mind the numbers invariably employed elsewhere than in the front line, that each rifle was responsible for something like ten yards. Forty miles of front held so lightly invited attack and received it; and the marvel is not that the Germans were able to break the British front, but that the Fifth Army was anywhere able to hold them. The "thin red line" which Napoleon was unable to break at Waterloo was dense in comparison with the Fifth Army's thin khaki line of the morning of March 21st. Moreover, it had been made very much thinner by the intense bombardment to which for hours before the attack the German artillery had subjected it.

Coucy Forest

Of course, it is not to be assumed from this analogy that the companies were so disposed. The whole front was held by "isolated posts, in irregular and zig-zag lines, so laid out that the posts, and machine-guns in particular, could fire along belts of wire and take an attacking enemy in enfilade. The posts were drawn back in the valleys, with the object of firing across and sweeping the opposite spurs."*

Behind the men who manned these posts there were, apart from battalion, brigade, and divisional reserves, and the three infantry and three cavalry divisions, which General Gough had wisely kept in hand, nothing on which the Army Commander could call to form anything in the nature of a second line of defence. What British and French support might be forthcoming as the battle wore on, would be days before reaching him, and the possibility of such

*"The March Retreat." *Gough.*

Coucy Forest

a situation arising had not been overlooked. Repeatedly General Gough had expressed the view that the major German effort would be made against his front and convinced of this he had laid his plans for a delaying action by means of a co-ordinated retirement should the circumstances warrant that; and this course had the approval of the Commander-in-Chief.

To return to the *Sixth*: very little was learnt even by Battalion Headquarters of the situation which had developed by the evening of the 21st, but by noon of the following day, after information had filtered through (C.Q.M.Sgts. were often bearers of good or evil news) the principal fact about the battle was known. Curiously enough it did not appear to concern anyone greatly, and the fact that the battalion's front had not been attacked was the one solid piece of satisfaction which it was able to enjoy. It was not, however, to remain in ignorance as to the seriousness of the position for very long. Soon shells from a northerly direction, fired from light German guns north of the Oise instead of from the east, were falling into the Coucy Forest, and as the days passed this shell-fire increased. On the 24th, Company Commanders were apprised of the situation, and were told that an evacuation of the forest might be ordered at any moment, and that they should prepare for that move without delay. Thereupon everyone set to work with good heart, destroying anything that might be of possible use to the enemy, and laying as many "booby-traps" to catch the unwary as time and ingenuity would allow. Trip-wires attached to hidden bombs were laid with gusto, and shelters so adjusted that an uncautious step would either blow them up or bring them down.

On March 26th the evacuation commenced. For the companies the task was simple enough; they had merely to move away from their posts in single file; others had sterner work to do. There was the Transport Section, which had to remove ammunition limbers, two cookers, and the water-cart; the last

Pierremande

brought out by Cpl. Dorling and Dvr. Harris to Pierremande, was along roads which were being shelled, and across which lay heavy trees, victims of German high-explosive.

"The cart was full of water; all taps were turned on, and the best four horses in the section rescued the vehicle in a most spectacular manner. Along the tree-strewn road through the forest, with shells bursting everywhere, this team did the journey at full-stretched gallop. As each tree across the road was met, so the water-cart leapt a couple of yards into the air. At the edge of the forest the offside wheel was smashed to pieces. Nothing daunted, the team carried on. Pulling up on the Pierremande road, the axle was found to be worn to a razor-like edge, and far too hot to handle; but there was Merryfield, the wheelwright, who quickly effected repairs, and the team once more galloped off."

The temporary departure from the Coucy Forest on the 26th was occasioned by the fall of Chauny on the previous day, followed by an attempt on the part of the enemy to cross the Oise at this point, doubtless in order to secure the southern flank of his attack. Had it been successful, the *Sixth*, in the forest, would have been in a most precarious position, and the obvious move was to withdraw the battalion to positions where they would be of more use in stemming the advance. West of Chauny, and southwards from the Oise, flowed the Oise-Aisne Canal, and behind this natural barrier the battalion formed an outpost-line as soon as it had crossed it. But not the whole of the battalion; the 'knotcher' patrol, under Capt. Sampson, was left behind in the forest as a kind of spearhead to be brought into action should the Germans attempt an advance through it, and there the patrol remained for three days with ammunition and bully-beef, and enough of the latter to last a lifetime!

St. Paul au Bois

Others, too, were left in exposed positions. There were, for instance, the various guards which the Battalion Headquarter Company had mounted over the many bridges crossing the River Oise and the St. Quentin Canal running parallel to it. Occupying positions on the farther, or northern banks, to give warning of any German attempt to cross the bridges, these men were withdrawn only when demolition of the bridges was finally decided upon, and one of them relates how his attention was attracted to a British soldier, standing on the bridge he was guarding, who was shouting and waving his hands. Wondering what he wanted, he walked back towards it, and presently broke into the double, as he realised he was evidently wanted in a hurry. Reaching the bridge, he found the soldier to be no less a person than a sergeant of the Royal Engineers waiting to blow it up. He continued to run, and behind him a few seconds later, he heard the bridge go "sky high."

Colonel Benson, who earlier had been placed in command of all 174th Inf. Bde. troops south of the Oise, made his headquarters at St. Paul au Bois, a village just west of the canal, and from here directed the defence. French divisions had been rushed from the south to the theatre of operations, and were now on either flank of the 58th Division, which then came under French command; and the story of the intermingling of French and British soldiers in a common endeavour to stem the tide is worthy of full-length treatment; but it must suffice to say that the scene on the 26th, when the battalion took up its positions west of the canal, is one that will ever be remembered by all who saw it. On the roads and in the fields, blue and khaki uniforms were shoulder to shoulder. French 75's, firing in the open, had in front of them perhaps French, perhaps British infantry. What mattered? Everybody was determined not to give ground, and the spirit of energetic resistance seemed to pervade the very air. All available men—headquarters staff, cooks, drivers, and storemen—were there to do battle.

For the moment, the situation south of the Oise was in hand, and on the 28th and 29th the battalion continued to consolidate its positions west of the canal. Some casualties had been suffered on the earlier of the two days on account of shell-fire, but, having regard to the extent of the losses sustained by other units of the Division, the battalion had been remarkably fortunate. Had the Germans renewed their attempts to cross the Oise, the tale would certainly have been different, but by the 29th, it was clear that they were concentrating upon their westward march north of the river, and were making no effort to occupy the Coucy Forest. That being the case, there was no reason why it should be given to them gratuitously. The 7th Bn., London

Barisis Regt., was still at Barisis, in the centre of the forest, and as has been mentioned, the "knotcher" patrol had remained for some days in its northern section. But the 7th Battalion was now required for use elsewhere on the divisional front, and was withdrawn from Barisis, and it fell to the *Sixth* to reoccupy that village. This it did on the 29th, B and C Companies being sent forward to hold it that and the following nights (April 1st), when the whole battalion, the remainder of which had moved forward on the previous day, was withdrawn to Pierremande, its place being taken by the French 215th Infantry Regiment. Here, at Pierremande, it passed the night, and on April 2nd, was carried by lorries to Vic-sur-Aisne, where it entrained for a destination which

Longeau proved to be Longeau, a railway junction about three kilometres south-east from Amiens. Longeau was only five miles from Villers Bretonneux, and towards the little market town it had come to know so well during its stay at Demuin, the battalion commenced to march late in the afternoon of April 3rd.

Meanwhile, along the more northerly British fronts events had not been standing still. The original assault by the Germans on March 21st, had extended from Arras to the River Oise, with the object of breaching the line north of the Somme, wheeling to the north-west, and thus forcing the British backwards to the sea. But it was north of the Somme, and particularly at Arras, where the defence held (or gave little ground) and it was south of the Somme where the German advance was greatest. Without anything to stop it except Gough's reserves and his hastily improvised "forces" (such as Hunts, Watt's, and Carey's), which the Army Commander had foreseen as likely to be necessary and had told his Corps Commanders to form, it had reached by the 29th, a line drawn roughly from Montdidier to a point a few miles east of Villers Bretonneux. Such an advance was not apparently what Ludendorff either expected or intended, and instead of exploiting this success, he delivered attack after attack against the Arras front in a vain attempt to break the line there; and later, as a diversion, he ordered an assault against the British between Vimy and La Bassée. Not meeting in this sector with the success he hoped for, he turned his attention to the southern advance with a view to taking the important railway junction of Amiens. Between him and his objective stood the Australian Army Corps contesting every inch of the ground and now at the point of exhaustion. It was to help in repelling a further encroachment in this direction that the *Sixth* had been moved.

Villers Bretonneux

The march by companies with intervals between them along the Amiens-Villers Bretonneux road on the afternoon of April 3rd, gave some indication to both officers and men of the seriousness of the position. On either side of the road without protection or even camouflage stood groups of field-guns, and close to them teams of horses ready to limber-up and drag them away to other positions. Exhausted gunners sat around the guns waiting for the evening S O S signal that would call them to instant and frenzied activity. Some few, astounded at the spectacle of a complete battalion marching resolutely towards the enemy, rose from the ground and cheered the companies as they passed; others, too tired even to speak, stood dumbly by the roadside, nodding their heads, as if the sight they saw was not to be believed. Nearer and nearer came the battalion to Villers Bretonneux, passing on the way groups of wounded and dazed men as they stumbled more than walked away from the eight days and nights of continuous fighting in which they had been engaged. There was a section of Australian infantry, dream-walking, through exhaustion, away from the town, who watched the battalion pass, and then turned and followed it back into the hell from which, stupefied, they were trying to escape, and there were small parties, sole survivors of complete battalions, stumbling along, too weary to notice what was coming to their aid; and there were drawn-faced civilians wheeling or carrying their household possessions, and cattle and other farm-stock wandering aimlessly about.

Dusk had fallen by the time the battalion entered Villers Bretonneux, so that its appearance presented much the same spectacle as it had worn when the battalion had seen it in February. Houses and shops were intact and roads were unmarked by shell-fire; only the darkness, the absence of civilians, and the presence of so many soldiers suggested the altered circumstances. Guides took the companies to different parts of the town, and soon the battalion had settled into billets and was enjoying a meal. Some were accommodated in the cellars of houses, others in a cloth factory, and others again in a school,

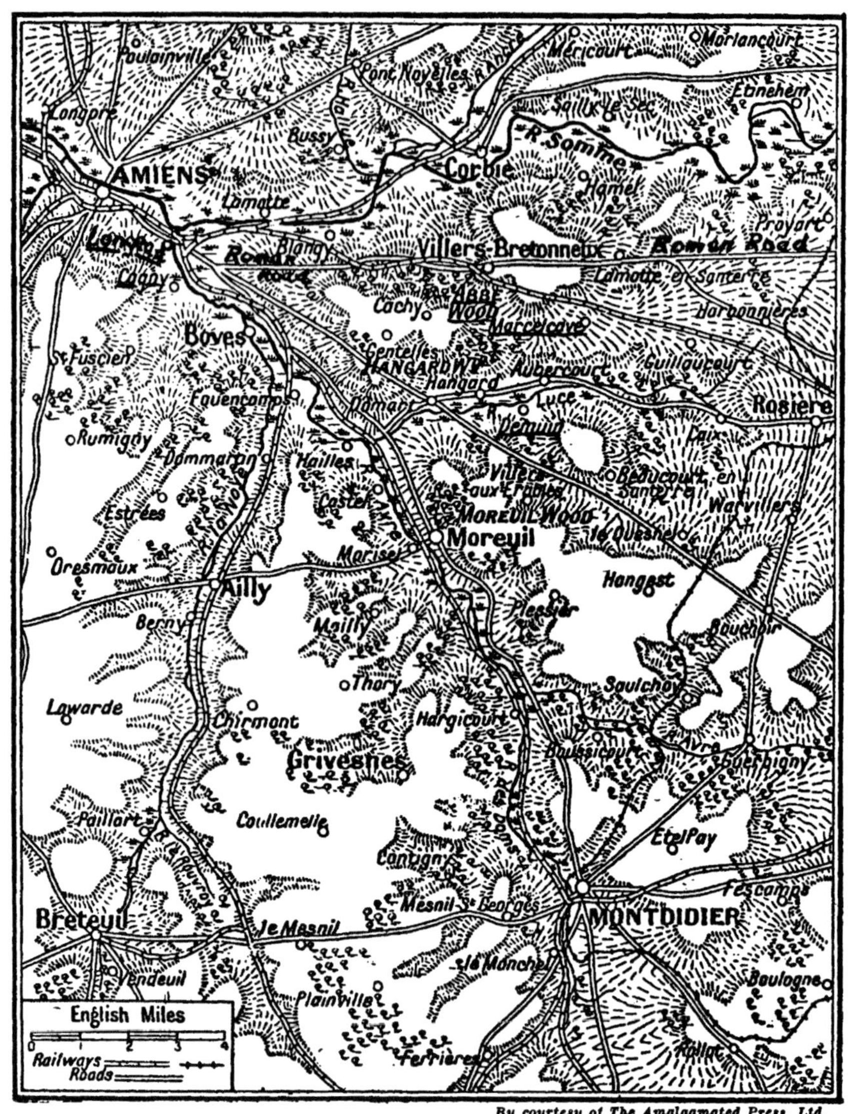

MAP 15.—THE DEFENCE OF AMIENS.

and all felt secure in view of the assurance that company commanders had received to the effect that the Germans had outstripped their supplies, and that their artillery was miles behind their infantry. Their rapid advance had been across the devastated area of the Somme battlefield, and the assumption that it would be twenty-four hours before they could bring their guns forward was not unreasonable. Some Australian infantry were clearly making themselves very much at home in a town that had only just been evacuated and that, too, suggested that there was no immediate danger to be faced. Bitter experience taught infantrymen to be chary of occupying houses when hostile shelling was likely, but when this danger was remote they were the first to seek such protection from wind and rain as only bricks and mortar could provide; and here in Villers Bretonneux there was more, for the French civilians, in their hurried evacuation, had left behind them a hundred and one things that could make a billet comfortable.

Villers Bretonneux

By about ten o'clock the battalion had retired for the night—it seemed like that, so complete were the domestic surroundings—but at 4.30 a.m. the following morning (April 4th), it was awakened suddenly by the noise of bursting shells and falling masonry. No more efficient alarm-clock than an unexpected bombardment has ever been invented, and in no time platoons were seeking safer if less comfortable accommodation in cellars; but in directing their men to them many officers became casualties, amongst whom was Major W. Whitehead, D.S.O., the battalion's Second-in-Command. The bombardment continued throughout the day bringing destruction upon a town which so far had escaped the ravages of war, and although no heavy shells were thrown into it, the place soon changed its outward appearance.

Nor was the war outside Villers Bretonneux standing still. In pursuance of Ludendorff's belated decision to secure the railway centre of Amiens, attacks in that direction had been renewed on March 27th, 28th, 29th, and 30th, but by the last of these dates, as a result of increasing British and French resistance, the German advance was virtually brought to a standstill. Thus, by the time the *Sixth* reached Villers Bretonneux, the line ran northwards from the Roman road, Amiens to Estrées, and south of it, faced south-east. The Germans were already in Demuin—the village in which the officers and men of the *First* and *Second* had been united in one unit but two months earlier. The situation immediately in front of the *Sixth* when it marched into the town was that the 35th Australian Battalion held positions east of it, but south of the Roman road, with the 7th Buffs on their right, and the 8th Bn. Rifle Brigade on their left.

Villers Bretonneux

The early morning bombardment of April 4th presaged a renewed attempt to wrest Amiens from the Allies, but the possibility of such action had been foreseen both by General Foch and the British Commander-in-Chief, and arrangements made to meet it. So far as the *Sixth* was concerned, there was nothing to do but wait in the cellars, into which all had hurried early in the morning, until the companies should be sent forth to meet the oncoming tide of invaders. The stretcher-bearers, it is true, were busy throughout the day carrying wounded to the battalion aid-post, but for those unwounded there was only to sit and listen to exploding shells and the sound of rifle and machine-gun fire getting nearer and nearer to the town as the day wore on. An Australian, Colonel Goddard, was in command of the defence of Villers Bretonneux (he commanded the 35th Bn., Australians) and the *Sixth* had been placed at his disposal. During the day, his battalion was attacked three times by the 9th Bavarian Reserve Division, comprising troops quite fresh to battle, and three times repulsed the assaults; but north of its positions, some ground was given, and there was no alternative but for this gallant Australian unit to retire to a line about half a mile east of the town.

During the day attacks of similar intensity were delivered against positions south-east of the town held by the 18th Division, and the spirited defence of them in which cavalry played a major part deserves a story to itself. At 4 p.m. these attacks were renewed, and meeting with some success, caused a gap between that division and the Australians to the north of them. It was just for such an emergency that Colonel Goddard had kept the *Sixth* in hand, and with it and the 36th Bn., A.I.F., he decided to restore the position and fill the gap caused, by counter-attacking south of the railway running almost eastwards from Villers Bretonneux.

On receipt of Colonel Goddard's request, Colonel Benson placed the Adjutant, Capt. Wylie, in command of the operation. Conferring with other officers (Capts. Morrow and Lathbury, and Lieut. Hodges) it was decided to move out of the town, turn south, cross the railway bridge, and then deploy, and in sectional rushes advance until the enemy should be met. D Company had earlier in the day been detached to reinforce the Buffs, on the right, and some of the battalion's Lewis-guns had already been sent to the Australians, whose own weapons were unserviceable on account of the mud. Thus the action was largely entrusted to the riflemen, and worthily they responded to the call, and simple as was the plan, it was entirely successful. The advance in section-rushes, without artillery support, and with little opposition, continued for about half a mile, when Germans were encountered. They retired, however, on seeing fresh troops coming into action, and after covering parties

BRIG.-GENERAL CHARLES GRAEME HIGGINS, C.M.G., D.S.O.,
Commanded the 174th Brigade, 1917-1918.

Plate 39

Capt. F. H. H. THOMAS, O.B.E., T.D., Quartermaster 1st/6th Bn.

Rev. A. E. WILKINSON, O.B.E., M.C., T.D.

Capt. T. W. BROOKE, M.C., 1st/6th Bn. (Killed)

Capt. E. PHILLIPS.

Capt. BATE. M.O. 1st/6th Bn.

Capt. BRASHER. Trans. Officer 2nd/6th Bn.

Capt. M. A. MYER.

Major S. SHORT, T.D.

Capt. S. T. COOKE, M.C.

Plate 40

Capt. E. G. GODFREY, M.C.

Capt. H. L. GILKS, M.C., ADJUTANT 1ST/6TH BN.

Major J. THOMSON.

Capt. T. J. BOOTH, M.C.

Lieut. TERRY. (KILLED)

Lieut. WILLIE.

Major VENNING, D.S.O., M.C.

Capt. I. H. W. IDRIS, M.C.

Capt. MORROW.

Plate 41

had been pushed forward for a hundred yards or so, digging was commenced along a line at right angles to the railway, and astride the Villers Bretonneux-Marcelcave road, running parallel to it, in order that the battalion might be in secure positions to meet further German attacks in the morning. During the night, the 36th Bn., A.I.F., made a silent advance north and south of the railway, capturing some prisoners, and Capt. Lathbury extended D Company farther to the south to link effectively with the troops on his right. Thus, by the morning of the 5th, the line was restored, with D and A Companies in the front line, facing south-east, C a little to the north, with B Company in reserve. Thinly as it was held, the defence was adequate, for when the enemy was seen massing in the early hours of the morning, he was dispersed by machine-gun, Lewis-gun, and rifle-fire; and although there was no proper trench system, nor wire, the companies felt secure despite the fact that there would be little, if any, artillery support for them. The absence of artillery was, of course, regretted mainly because so many good targets had presented themselves and had not been engaged.

Marcelcave Road

Two excellent pen-pictures must be included with the story of this action to complete the picture. " A Company, with fixed bayonets, started down the road to meet the enemy. We reached the eastern end of the town, dashed through the enemy barrage, and formed a line astride the Marcelcave road in remarkably quick time. We then saw lines upon lines of the enemy advancing, and they stopped about four hundred yards from us. A few Australians joined us, and we started a rushing attack which surprised the enemy into a sudden but orderly withdrawal by stages to his old line. After a lively machine-gun and rifle contest, our advance stopped at twelve hundred yards, and we started to dig in. The attack had been so swift that casualties had been slight, and the good order was marvellous."*

" B Company, after crossing the bridge (at the east end of the town) left the road and got into extended order, and advanced across a ploughed field, meeting with slight machine-gun fire and a few shells, and having a few casualties. I took cover behind a haystack, and it was here, just on my left, that a troop of cavalry galloped up and dismounted on the blind side of some farm buildings. We then advanced farther, and the company mustered in a kind of sand quarry. Patrols were sent out, and some time afterwards we went forward again and occupied some shallow trenches, which were not connected and were actually on the aerodrome, the hangars still standing and the place littered with camp equipment, which we made use of."†

---

*Sgt. Cowherd.
†Rfm. Lumsden.

O

The work of the battalion was done for the time being. The assault was not continued, and " thus on April 5th, the sixteenth day of the great struggle, the German offensive between Barisis and Arras came to an end, just as so many of the Allied offensives had done, in spite of early success, closing with a few spasmodic attacks, the sure signs of an expiring effort. The assault had failed to attain a break-through."*

* * * * *

The story of the failure of the Germans to take Amiens might very well be left here, but for the fact that after the collapse of Ludendorff's next effort to break the British front, he turned his attention once more to the Somme area. Since the opening of the battle, German attacks had spread northwards, the Arras sector had been vainly assaulted, and failing here, the offensive was carried into Flanders. On April 9th the Germans attacked in the Lys area against the British First Army, and met with what appeared to be considerable success, but the resistance stiffened, and before the end of the month they were brought to a standstill.

Meanwhile, after their action at Villers Bretonneux on April 5th, the *Sixth* remained on the ground for another day, and on April 6th and 7th, was withdrawn to Boves, a village on the River Avre, about seven miles west of the line, the Transport Section moving at the same time from Glisy to Cagny. Two days later, after refitting and reorganisation, it returned to the battle-area, relieving the 10th Bn., London Regt., then in support south of Villers Bretonneux, and on the 13th relieved the 12th Bn., London Regt., in these positions south-east of the town which the *Sixth* had established on the 5th astride the Marcelcave road.

Boves

Marcelcave Road

This tour of duty, however, lasted only three days, and on the 16th, the battalion was withdrawn from the line and became Brigade *Reserve* in Villers Bretonneux. All ranks being very tired, or rather sleepy, after their three nights' vigil, were soon asleep, not in billets, but in the open, sheltered by a bank (which in emergency would do as a defensive position) in the Bois l'Abbé, west of the town.

Bois l'Abbe

At 6 a.m., almost before some of the platoons had returned from the line, the enemy commenced shelling the town and its immediate neighbourhood with gas. Those asleep were wakened, masks were adjusted (some using only the nose-clips) and the battalion waited patiently until this early morning greeting should cease. The shelling continued until about 8 a.m., many shells falling directly on to the position occupied, and before long many men

*Official History, France and Belgium. 1918. Vol. II.

were showing acute symptoms of gas. About noon, owing to the increasing effect of the bombardment, fresh positions were sought about two hundred yards north of those formerly occupied, and in these the battalion was again subjected to gas bombardment, the effect of which, coupled with the similar treatment of the morning, was to put half the battalion out of action,* rendering most of them temporarily blind. No gas-mask will render its wearer immune for ever, and those with which the battalion was equipped had been in use for some considerable time. The most experienced soldiers suffered with the least, and Sgt. Weir, who throughout the day had been making tests for the presence of gas, was himself an early victim. It was a pitiful sight to see officers and men led in single file away from their positions, gasping, vomiting, and unable to see where they were going. The evacuation of the gas cases to Cagny was fortunately completed before the end of the day, and what was left of the battalion marched to Boves, there to rest in billets until the following morning (19th) when it moved to Boutillerie, a neighbouring village. *Bois l'Abbe* *Cagny*

Here, at Boutillerie, for a blessed week, the non-commissioned officers and men of recently received drafts had an opportunity of settling down in the companies and platoons to which they had been sent. Many, of course, had seen previous service in France with the *Sixth*, but there were some key-men and specialists who had been retained in England that now joined it, and there were many young men below the age of nineteen, made available as a result of the British Cabinet's decision to lower the age for active service to eighteen and a half years, who came with them. Reorganisation and training commenced almost immediately on arrival, and a very necessary medical inspection held. Those whose eyes had not been affected by gas often had raw blisters on their bodies where the poison had penetrated their dress and come in contact with their skin, and proper treatment of these sores was essential. This particular medical inspection is memorable on account of the extraordinary sight presented to the Medical Officer when he came to examine them. The battalion had been in action more or less continuously since April 4th, and there had been no opportunity of issuing clean underclothing; but soldiers are nothing if not resourceful, and while at Villers Bretonneux they had salved anything likely to be of use as wearing apparel from ruined houses, and now were clothed beneath their service dress in a remarkable variety of garments, ladies " undies " predominating. The Medical Officer gave one look and exclaimed: " What's this? A battalion of women?" *Boutillerie*

*Casualties numbered 10 officers and 390 Other Ranks. The Australians were similarly affected, the total gas casualties amounting to over 1,000.

A battalion of women! The remark was made as a jest; but inasmuch as heavy casualties had rendered it useless for the time being as a fighting unit, it was not without point, and thus at Boutillerie the battalion assumed the role temporarily as the 58th Division's last hope. Since the day it came north from Barisis, other units comprising the division had been following it into the battle-area, and it was now their turn to bear the brunt of the fighting. Nor had they long to wait. The failure of the German offensive on the Lys persuaded Ludendorff to make a final effort to secure Amiens, and the drenching of the Villers Bretonneux area with gas in which the *Sixth* had lost so heavily, was but a preliminary to a stroke which proved to be the last. By the middle of the month the enemy's intention was divined. Artillery fire and aerial activity had been increasing steadily, and on April 21st, the German *Ace*, Richtofen, was brought down behind the British lines, quite near to some men of the *Sixth*, who tried to reach the plane before enemy shell-fire destroyed it.

Boutillerie

The storm broke on the 24th. The 58th Division, south of Villers Bretonneux, and once again on the extreme right of the British Army, took with the 8th Division the full force of the attack in which the Germans used tanks, the advance of which was, luckily for the enemy, concealed by fog. Despite this handicap, the 173rd Inf. Bde. made a magnificent stand in the forward zone, and was brought back to the reserve line only after the key-positions of Villers Bretonneux, on its left, and Hangard Wood, on its right, had fallen to the enemy. For neither of these positions was the 58th Division responsible, but when later that day (to be precise at 10 p.m., by moonlight) the 8th Division and 5th Australian Division launched a counter-attack to recover the town, units of the 58th Division co-operated on the right in an endeavour to regain the ground it had been compelled to relinquish earlier in the day. This action, continued on the following day and the next, had the successful result of restoring virtually to the British the line originally held.

So ended the enemy thrust against the British right. The attacks against Villers Bretonneux were not renewed by the Germans, and with their defeat on the Somme came their defeat also in the Lys area, the result of both actions being that they were left with two big salients in their western front, both of which necessitated the employment in defence of far more men than Ludendorff could afford to use if he were to continue the offensive. A year earlier Hindenburg had shortened his line to economise his forces. Now, the Germans were back, indeed beyond, where they had been twelve months earlier, and although still more numerous than the Allied forces, they were losing this advantage, for American troops were arriving in great numbers.

Before leaving this all-too-brief account of the Fifth Army's defence of the Oise-Somme front and the part the *Sixth* played in it, a comment ought to be made on the bitter resentment felt by all ranks who outlived the War, at the suggestion that they had unnecessarily retreated before the enemy. Of recent years, as the full facts have become known, less has been said about the fact of the retirement and more of the stubborn resistance put up by the divisions forming General Gough's Army in their rearguard action, which from first to last had been foreseen as necessary and controlled by him. Those who lived through the days of March 21st to April 27th, through attack and counter-attack, without respite, without sleep, and often without food, and worst of all, in the knowledge that they were without succour, felt keenly the implication that they had failed to "play the man," and that their commander, by his recall to England, had in turn failed them. It must be with a feeling of solid satisfaction that those who took part in the battle can now read the recognised view of the Fifth Army's effort: "The Fifth Army grew smaller owing to casualties; it bent, but it never broke; and its components all remained in being . . . Spread out over a front too long for its strength; crushed and poisoned by a bombardment, the intensity, if not the duration of which, was never experienced before or after in 1914-1918; assaulted and pursued by a numerically superior and specially trained enemy, the officers and men of the Fifth Army carried out a most difficult retirement, as planned by General Gough, without being even morally defeated and without losing heart."* **Boutillerie**

OFFICERS, WARRANT OFFICERS and SECTION COMMANDERS at

VILLERS BRETONNEUX—1918

OFFICER COMMANDING:	SECOND-IN-COMMAND:	ADJUTANT:
COL. BENSON	MAJOR WHITEHEAD	CAPT. WYLIE
R.S.MAJ. BOSS		R.Q.M.SGT. PARRISH
A Co. CAPT. ANDERSON	C.S.M. TEMPLAR	C.Q.M.SGT. WILLIAMS
B Co. (1) CAPT. GODFREY (2) LIEUT. HODGES	C.S.MAJ. PALOWKAR (wounded)	C.Q.M.SGT. SIRED
C Co. CAPT. HILL	C.S.MAJ. THORNDYKE	C.Q.M.SGT. DAVIES
D Co. CAPT. LATHBURY	C.S.MAJ. WORRALL	C.Q.M.SGT. GRUNDY

Quartermaster: CAPT. LOVETT
Transport: CAPT. BRASHER; SGT. PRICE; CPL. DORLING
Cooks: SGT. BUCKLAND; SGT. BRITTEN
Stretcher-Bearers: CAPT. FROST; SGT. WADE; CPL. BRETT
Signallers: LIEUT. ALDEN; SGT. SHARP; SGT. BURKE
Scouts and Snipers: CAPT. MORROW; SGT. SUTTON

*_Official_ History of the Great War, Military Operations, France and Belgium, 1918. Vol. II, p. 458.

Chapter 18

THE HOME FRONT

Quite early in the War, when enemy action took the form of shelling unprotected parts of England's eastern coast, and making Zeppelin raids over London, service with the *Reserve* was popularly known as " on the home front." Nor was this without reason, for as time wore on, that unit, although organised primarily for training officers and men for service overseas, had to hold itself in readiness for any eventuality. The air menace was becoming serious. Zeppelins had been paying intermittent visits since February, 1915, and before the close of that year were bombing the Capital, and on one occasion (September 8th, 1915), dropped two bombs on Messrs. Frank Stadelman's warehouse in Farringdon Street, adjoining the drill hall. The damage to both buildings was considerable, that to the latter being largely attributable to falling masonry from the warehouse, and indicated what London might look like if daylight raids on a more extensive scale were made. For such the populace did not have long to wait. In the summer of 1917 fleets of hostile aeroplanes (Gothas) commenced the regular visitation, first of English southern seaside resorts, and later of the Capital, creating something akin to panic in the East End. At any day, therefore, the *Reserve* might have been called upon to do special duty in what had become essentially a military area, and although, in fact, it was not called upon for help in this connection, there was an occasion of a different nature, as will be seen later, when it had to act as a fighting unit.

Hurdcott Otherwise, as month succeeded month, little change was noted in the daily routine, except when programmes were modified to meet some special training requirement of the fighting-forces, or varied to fit in with a change of quarters. Before it left Fovant, at the end of 1916, the *Reserve* had already established a first-class reputation for itself, and it retained the good name it had earned when in turn it moved to Hurdcott, to Newton Abbot, and finally to Blackdown. **Newton Abbot** At Newton Abbot many made their first acquaintance with the " west country," and the kindliness and generosity of the Devonshire people on whom they were billeted is a lasting memory to all who had the good fortune to winter with them.

At Blackdown, throughout 1918, the battalion was at the hub of the military machine, and worthily it took part in all the activities of the Aldershot Command, establishing a reputation for itself which to-day senior officers of the Regular Army have not forgotten. The battalion ran like a well-oiled machine; instructors had completely mastered their art, time was never wasted, diet was regulated scientifically, and the soldier's leisure was amply catered for; thus few, if any, of the young men now called up for military service had cause for regretting their first introduction to training. Sport continued to be encouraged by the Commanding Officer, Colonel Simpson, and the Adjutant, Capt. Clay, and under Lt. Amos and Sgt. Wood one of the finest teams of boxers the Army has ever known was formed, no reference to which would be complete without the mention of Rfm. Coveney, a welter-weight, who fought two hundred fights, and was never known to have been knocked out. *Blackdown*

Not everyone was able to attend the Command contests in which these men won renown for the unit in which they happened to be serving, but all felt that they had a share in the honour these successes brought, and their pride in the unit showed itself in increased eagerness to learn, and willingness to perform all tasks allotted to them.

Then, too, there was the concert party, organised by Lieut. Hammond, which periodically gave real pleasure to all fortunate enough to be free from duties to attend its performances. Some of the battalion's most popular instructors were members of the troupe, amongst whom should be mentioned Sgt. Etheridge, Sgt. Lloyd, Cpl. Nimmo, and Cpl. Holmes, whose singing and dancing and acting was as popular as themselves.

Appreciative as were the younger and newly joined men of all that was done to make life interesting and enjoyable, the older soldiers who had returned to the battalion after recovering from war wounds were probably even more grateful, although, being " old soldiers " and thus entitled to grouse, they rarely had much to say by way of thanks. Discipline was strict, and after the freer and easier modes of the battlefield and the hospital, many found the frequent inspections, the necessity for keeping uniform and equipment clean, and square-drill, irksome in the extreme. Nor was discontent limited to such very necessary military practice; there was a feeling, perhaps without much foundation, that while some of their comrades with little or no active service to their credit remained at home in " soft jobs," they were called upon to return again and again to the battle-front; that drafts for overseas were not made up systematically and having regard to a man's previous service abroad, but haphazardly, from all and sundry who happened to be available when orders to send reinforcements were received. This unrest led eventually to a protest being made on parade by a soldier to a General Officer inspecting a draft about to proceed overseas; and as a result a regular comb-out followed, and many who had not seen previous service found their names substituted for those whom it had been intended to send.

The year 1918 was a time of great searching of heart, not only for soldiers but for civilians. Many were asking whether the sacrifices they were being called upon to make were worth a victory which before the summer of the year was looking more and more remote. Industrial workers of all kinds were feeling intensely the strain of continuous overtime and restricted food supplies, and if earnings were high, they could not compensate the worker for his lack of time for recreation or loss of nervous energy. Strikes from one cause or another were not infrequent, and after three years of war an appeal to national patriotism had lost largely the force it once had. In July, 1918, the miners of the Welsh coalfield came out on strike, and negotiations for once failed to bring about an immediate settlement of the dispute. There was no real danger that the men would damage the mines in any way, nor that any assembly would result in rioting, but there was an urgent necessity to get them back to work. To help them to realise, therefore, that their work in providing the country with an essential commodity was intimately linked with the work of their fellow-men who were in arms, the battalion was ordered to move

Newport to Newport and there make a display of armed strength. For the *Reserve*, the visit to Newport, lasting a week, came as a welcome diversion, and the route-marches through surrounding villages were thoroughly enjoyed. Happily, no untoward incidents occurred, and the strike was soon settled, for no one relished the possibility of being called upon to intervene in a civil disturbance.

The battalion remained at Blackdown until the end of the War.

* * * * *

From Blackdown to the base, and from the base to the front! Often it seemed as if the whole world conspired to send a man there as quickly as possible, in the greatest discomfort, and in the most humiliating circumstances. As one " old-stager " puts it with great exaggeration:

" An appeal for leave at Blackdown usually resulted in an affair akin to High Court proceedings.

" The Commanding Officer resembled the ' beak ' on these occasions. C.S.Majs. Stenner, Thompson, Steggell, and many others, served the ' assizes ' in some capacity. The Adjutant invariably acted as ' Prosecuting Counsel ' —being ready when called on to drag up any possible ' past ' of the applicant. The ' prosecution ' was very ably supported by that most suitable ' usher,' R.S.M. Lake. He spent most of the session bellowing ' Hat off! Quick March!' Left-right, left-right! Halt! Left Turn! Stand still!'

" After hearing the applicant patiently, the Commanding Officer would consider the matter, and if unable to accede to the request, would often explain why leave could not be granted, and in due course the assembled court would adjourn. Company Commanders (counsels for the defence) would sympathetically murmur comforting phrases like: ' Insufficient grounds,' and other distressing comments as their client passed from the ' court '—as all had before him—with the words, ' Application refused,' ringing in his ears. Within a very short space of time the applicant would probably find himself ' named ' for a draft to France, and later would be fully equipped and swinging along the road from Aldershot to Farnborough Station, and ultimately bundled into a railway carriage for a trip to sunny Southampton, thence shipped to the ' Continong.'

" Le Havre! Harfleur! Sergeants everywhere. The *Pimple!*"

The term " lead-swingers " might perhaps have been appropriately used to designate some of the officers, warrant-officers, and N.C.O.'s who formed the staffs at the base camps, but it was certainly not a fair description to apply to all. Most of them were men who earlier had seen much service in the front line—men like C.S.Maj. A. Yelf, of the *Sixth*, who adds the following note:

" The usual procedure for drafts was that after disembarkation, the troops, who were travelling with light equipment only, were formed up on the quayside under specially detailed officers, known as Reinforcement Conducting Officers, then marched to Harfleur, a suburb of Havre, where were situate the various Infantry Base Depôts (known in short as I.B.D.'s). For example, the 47th Division originally occupied No. 11 I.B.D., but when the members became too large to handle at No. 11 I.B.D., a change was made to No. 8 I.B.D., farther up the camp, but at both camps the general procedure was the same.

" The draft, on arrival in camp, was formed up in column of companies by regiments, according to their brigade, i.e., 140th, 141st, 142nd, as the case may be. Reinforcements to each brigade were handed over to the respective warrant-officer in charge; the roll was then called and checked over with the

Officer-in-Charge of Drafts. The men rested on the parade ground until the order came for medical inspection. This inspection usually took place in the camp cinema, all troops filing past the Medical Officer in single file, after having divested themselves of most of their clothing. After inspection by the Medical Officer, the troops were marched back to their place on the parade ground, and would wait there until instructions were received from the Camp Quartermaster that equipment was ready for issue.

" The system in use for the issue of kit was a particularly efficient one, in that 1,000 men could be issued with a complete trench equipment in the space of one hour. All equipment was laid out in separate piles, each pile containing one item of equipment under the charge of an N.C.O. The men then filed past and had to pick up one article from each pile, and return to their place on the parade ground, where they checked over all equipment to see that they had everything complete, including rifle, sword, pull-through, entrenching tool, etc.

" As soon as kit had been issued, and all checked, it was usually time for the midday meal (most reinforcements arriving in camp about 8 a.m.) when the respective detachments were marched under their own N.C.O.'s to the dining halls, where their rations were issued. After the meal, troops were allotted tents—sometimes sixteen or twenty-two men to a tent—according to numbers arriving. Parties were then detailed for the drawing of blankets from Quartermaster Stores in rolls of ten, these being issued two per man. As soon as tents had been allotted and blankets issued, the men set to fitting their equipment together ready for parade the following day.

" On the following day, all troops paraded about 8 or 8.30 a.m., and were addressed by the officer commanding the depôt (in the case of No. 11 and No. 8 I.B.D., the Commanding Officer being Colonel Moore, of the 20th London, with Capt. Marchant, of the 20th London, as his Adjutant, R.S.Maj. Spackman (Potman Bill) of the 17th London, as Camp Sgt.Maj., and R.Q.M.Sgt. Rapson, of the 19th London, as Camp Q.M.Sgt., and C.S.Maj. A. Yelf (C.L.R.). After the address by the officer, troops were marched up the hill to the Bull Ring, at such times that detachments, on arrival at the training ground, would be in numerical sequence. At the training ground they were handed to the staff there, who undertook their training.

" When drafts were passed out of the training camp, they were held in readiness for proceeding to the line, and on receipt of instructions for drafts to be dispatched, a further inspection was carried out by the Medical Officer, and if passed fit, troops were then ' stood by ' to await instructions as to which regiment they were to be posted. Many drafts were transferred from the regiment to which they belonged complete to other units, and on one particular occasion a big draft from the *Reserve* was transferred to a battalion of the K.R.R. Corps, for service near Nieuport, in Belgium.

" This question of transfer to other regiments was a very sore point with men newly out from England, because the first thing that had to be done was the collection of each man's cap badge and numerals. This the men begrudged very much, particularly so in such regiments as the 6th, 15th, and 21st Battalions, London Regt., especially when it was a question of being transferred, as happened on one occasion, to Irish battalions. Of course, efforts were made where possible to transfer men to regiments to which their own were affiliated. When troops were ready for departure to the front, they were paraded in full kit, marched down to the station at Le Havre and there entrained for their particular destinations, and there was much speculation as to where each destination would prove to be.

" Sometimes drafts arrived every four to seven days, and as soon as one batch of drafts was seen off to the front preparations were put in hand for receiving the next batch, when the whole procedure was gone through again. At times there were close on 10,000 men moving up to the training ground each morning; this can be realised when one remembers that there were from twelve to fourteen Infantry Base Depôts at Le Havre alone."*

*C. S. Maj. A. Yelf, D.C.M., C. de G.

Chapter 19

GERMANY'S BLACK DAY

When Ludendorff, at the end of April, realised that he had failed to separate the British and French armies, failed to drive the northern British divisions into the sea, failed to secure any of the Channel ports, failed indeed, decisively, to give the German people the one piece of news for which they waited so eagerly—a resounding victory over the English—he fell back on the plan which, had he adhered to strictly, might have ended badly for the Allies. In its essence, this plan provided for a series of powerful but limited assaults to be delivered in rapid succession against different parts of the British and French fronts with the object of confusing the Higher Commands of both armies, and completely disorganising supplies and the movement of troops. The conclusion to these operations was to be a last, final assault, with unlimited objectives, against the weakest front. In support of this plan it was argued by Ludendorff's military advisers that uncertainty as to the front to be attacked would lead both British and French Commands to hesitate before sending succour to each other, and that the frequent transference of divisions from one part of the line to another while the battle was in progress would, in a very short time, bring about chaotic conditions behind the British front, where already there was too little room for easy manœuvre.

Unquestionably this argument was valid. The Fifth Army's retirement was very largely due to the failure of the French to adhere to the arrangement whereby certain of their divisions should remain in Gough's new area as reserves until the British front had been reorganised, and this departure from the arrangement was due entirely to General Petain's obsession with the belief that the major German effort would be made against his front. If Ludendorff, having struck rapidly at the British and then at the French, and again at the British, and once more at the French, and finally between the two, he might quite well have succeeded in his first object of separation. As it was, the delivery of the first assault at the junction of the two armies had the almost immediate effect of making Sir Douglas Haig and the statesmen of both countries realise the necessity for unity of command on the Western front, and, in consequence, at Doullens, on March 26th, General Foch was charged with the responsibility of " co-ordinating the operations of the Allies on the whole Western front." His powers were more clearly defined on

April 3rd, and the title of Commander-in-Chief given him on the 24th of that month. By the end of April, then, there was virtually one army commander in France, and if friction between the two forces still continued, it could be said, merely, that the course of true love never did run smooth.

Since General Foch's appointment, the Germans had been hammering the British; now they were to fall on the French. On May 27th, after a devastating and quite unexpected bombardment, they attacked at the Chemin-des-Dames on a forty-mile front with such success that in places the line was penetrated on the very first day to a depth of thirteen miles, and by the 30th, they were within thirty miles of Paris, and once more upon the Marne. But the defence held, and Ludendorff's gain was but one more vulnerable salient bulging into the Allied line. Within ten days another assault was made upon the French, this time from the direction of Noyon, in the Oise area; but on this occasion it was beaten off with little loss of ground. There followed a lull in the operations, while Ludendorff prepared for his final and supreme effort before once again turning on the British to crush them. Every available German division was brought southwards to strike the knock-out blow against the French on either side of Rheims, and every available gun was dragged across the German front to paralyse resistance. The assault was timed to take place on July 15th, but the whole enemy time-table was known beforehand to the French, who had prepared such a defence in depth that no army could have penetrated it. To the east of Rheims the fight was broken off on the day on which it commenced, and to the west of it, a few days later. The Germans were beaten. Thrice they had failed before the British, thrice before the French; and the initiative passed finally to the Allies.

During these momentous battles towards the south, the British had not been idle, but on the contrary had taken every opportunity of improving their positions whenever the circumstances seemed to suggest that success would attend the effort. Aware, too, that ere long the Allies would return to the offensive, as much rest as possible was being given to every battalion in turn, and as much time as possible spent on training so that each might give a good account of itself when the day for its employment should arrive.

The *Sixth*, it will be remembered, was at Boutillerie during the second assault on Villers Bretonneux. When the attack against it was defeated, and the threat to Amiens removed, the 58th Division was taken out of the line, and on April 26th, the battalion was carried by bus to Bellancourt, a village more to the north, where for nine days it had an opportunity of recovering from the severe handling it had recently received. Then, on May 6th, it marched eastwards to the village of Mirvaux, lying about ten miles due west **Boutillerie**

Warloy from Albert, now in German hands. Its stay here was of very brief duration, for, three days afterwards, it moved closer to the line, and at Warloy, where it lived under canvas, became part of the III Corps Reserve, training, and providing working parties under the Royal Engineers engaged on strengthening the defences facing Albert. Here, the front line, after skirting Albert, ran in a southerly direction from the River Ancre to the River Somme, close to the junction of the two, with much of the high ground to the east and south of Morlancourt in enemy hands. The Somme country, with its rolling chalk hills, not unlike the downs of Kent, was well known to those of the *First* and *Second* who fought at High Wood, in 1916, and at Bullecourt, in 1917, and there were many of them who had come unscathed through the battles of those years who were still serving with the battalion. Old soldiers these; and the younger men who were now reaching the *Sixth* often owed their lives in subsequent actions to a ripe experience which in bitterness their elders had learned. The undulating hills with their treacherous valleys, the sunken roads inviting enfilade fire, the woods and copses hiding nests of machine-guns—all these were known to the veterans, and by them made known to the newest recruits.

The line of defence here as elsewhere along the British front was organised in depth by zones, having a forward-zone in which the companies would act as a kind of breakwater upon which the waves of an attacking infantry would spend their first force; behind it, on carefully selected ground, a battle-zone in which they could be checked; and a third, or reserve-zone, from which, if necessary, counter-attacks could be launched to repel the invading flood. It was the custom, naturally, for a battalion new to an area to serve consecutively in each zone, going first into reserve, then into the battle-zone, and finally into the forward-zone; and during the months of May, June, and July, the history of the battalion is mainly concerned with moves from one to the other, improving old and building new defences, and training when resting in some village close to the battle-area.

By May 15th, the battalion was occupying positions in the forward-zone
Millencourt east of Millencourt; by the 23rd, relieved by the 7th Battalion, it was in the
Henencourt support, or battle-zone, with two companies at Henencourt, and two companies in Melbourne Trench, about a mile east of the village; and by the 31st, relieved by the 11th Battalion, it was back in the Corps Reserve Camp at Warloy. These moves formed the typical sequence. Warloy, in the sheltered valley of the Hallue River, was the dwelling-place, but the high ground of Baizieux, two miles south of it, was the defensive position in which the battalion would have fought had the necessity arisen.

After the first few days of June, spent at Warloy, the battalion moved to Contay, but three miles to the west, and then, on the 10th of the month, to Fourdringroy, away to the west of Amiens, near Picquigny, on the Somme, where in billets it rested by night, and by day trained intensively for offensive action, being handled tactically by its officers, firing a musketry-course, and practising an attack. The Corps Commander had taken the salute as the battalion marched past him in column of route on leaving Contay, and now he was here to watch the training. Taken altogether, the signs were ominous. There was, however, no immediate cause for anxiety; and when the battalion, on the 17th, returned to the line, it was to do garrison duty and not to attack. On that day it relieved the 1st/18th Bn., London Regt., then the divisional reserve, in Lavieville, a mile and a half south of Millencourt, and on the next took over the extreme right sub-sector of the divisional front from the 15th Battalion in front of the village of Buire, where there was very little hostile activity. A few days later, upon relief, the battalion found itself back in Lavieville and Baizieux, when there was frequent manning of defence positions, not as a result of an enemy threat, but as a very necessary precaution. The truth was that the companies were quite far enough away from their battle-stations, and unless there was frequent practice in reaching them in record time, they might find themselves unready in an emergency.

Contay

Fourdringroy

Lavieville

Buire

Before the month of June was out the battalion was back in the line manning trenches a little to the left of those previously held, and here the enemy was more active, and casualties, though not heavy, were numerous. It enjoyed a brief respite during the middle of the month by holding the reserve positions at Lavieville and Baizieux for a few days, but by July 19th, was back in its old positions on the extreme right of the divisional front, covering Buire; and into these familiar trenches it welcomed, the following night, one company of the 2nd Bn., 132nd American Regiment, and showed them a thing or two, and did the same for two further companies, from the 2nd and 3rd Battalions of the same regiment, on succeeding nights. On the 23rd, this 3rd Bn., 132nd American Regiment, took over the front held by the *Sixth*, and the protracted relief will ever be remembered by those serving at the time. Colonel Benson had great difficulty in persuading all four American Company Commanders that their places were with their companies, and even more difficulty in convincing the officer commanding the American battalion that his troops wouldn't be of very much use without rations and Lewis-guns. He did everything to persuade them that a war was taking place in which presumably they were engaged, but gave up the attempt when the American drawled: "Waal, colonel, if my bo's can't fight without rations and Loois-guns, they'll give me wurms!" As may be supposed, the Americans eventually found their weapons, but as a precaution the Lewis-gun teams of the *Sixth* were not withdrawn from their positions until they had been properly relieved. This was not the last the battalion was to see of this American unit; after three days spent in support, it returned to the front line in relief of it, and the month was brought

Round Wood

to a close a couple of days later by the withdrawal of the *Sixth* to Round Wood,

Franvillers

near Franvillers, where in bivouacs and tents it made itself as comfortable as possible, and listened to the Transport Section nightly singing in unison

Contay

all the popular songs of the day. It should be remarked here that at Contay the *Sixth* (or certain members of it) had earlier introduced the American troops to another phase of active service. Eager to learn anything and everything pertaining to the war, the " Yanks " often visited the battalion, joining any group of men whose surreptitious behaviour seemed to suggest some new adventure. It was then they found themselves confronted with the complexities of " Crown and Anchor," " Housie-House," and " Banker," and not infrequently risked their " dimes, bucks, and dollars " in the luck of the game being played. Their greatest difficulty was to translate into English the many slang phrases used by the players, for, to the novice, such terms as " the mudhook," " Clickety-click," and " Legs eleven," are meaningless. But true comradeship finds a solution to such problems, and often the Americans were warmly welcomed by the " schools."

In Round Wood the battalion was acting as divisional reserve, which meant that if the enemy activity, which had been growing since the middle of July, should develop into an offensive, the *Sixth* would be amongst the first to be called upon to counter-attack, and by a queer coincidence, this virtually is what it did a few days later. On August 2nd, the battalion moved to Canaples, nearer the line, and on the 4th, nearer still, to La Houssaye, and the following day it relieved one of the battalions of the Northants Regiment

Sailly-le-Sec

in support position north of Sailly-le-Sec. The front line, here, ran down to the Somme and faced west, and the high ground upon which the British defences stood presented a serious obstacle to any further advance of the Germans to Amiens, the renewal of which was still contemplated as possible by Ludendorff, despite the fact that the French, in an attack on July 18th, had broken the German front at Soissons and compelled a retirement, placing the enemy there on the defensive. On August 6th, the Germans resumed the offensive east of Amiens, the battalion stood-to in its support positions, and awaited the almost inevitable orders to reinforce the front line. But no orders came, since the defence, organised in depth, held; and although the Germans advanced their front line a little, their gains were insignificant.

Lieut.-General Sir HEW D. FANSHAWE, K.C.B., K.C.M.G.,
G.O.C. 58th Division, 1916-1917.

Plate 42

Royal Air Force

Looking north-east towards Poelcappelle, the photograph shows, amongst others, the positions assaulted and captured on September 20th, 1917.

SPORTSMEN ALL!

Top Left: SGT. GEORGE WILLIAMS, RUNNER-UP, AMATEUR HEAVY-WEIGHT CHAMPIONSHIP OF GREAT BRITAIN (Killed at Loos)

Top Right: SGT. JIMMY BRITTEN, REPRESENTED GREAT BRITAIN AGAINST FRANCE (Sculling Championships).

Below: THE BOXING PLATOON AT BLACKDOWN, 1918.

Plate 44

C.S.Maj. STEGGALL. Sgt. "Chappy" HEYL. Sgt. WILSON. Rfm. GADSDON. Rfm. BROWNE.

C.S.Maj. WORRALL. Cpl. H. MILLARD. Sgt. PARKER. Sgt. LINES. Sgt. LOVELL.

Sgt. ZIEMAN. Sgt. SHARP. Sgt. HULLAND, M.M. Rfm. HEARD. L.-Cpl. ELLIS.

Sgt. MILLS. Sgt. LOVETT. R.S.Maj. (*Later* Lieut.) BAILEY, M.C., D.C.M. Sgt. WINGATE, M.M. C.S.Maj. SMALE.

Sgt. LARKWORTHY. Sgt. WINNUP. Sgt. WHITE. Sgt. LACEY. Sgt. WHITE.

Sgt. TATTERSALL. Sgt. DENNETT. Rfm. GAMBY. C.Q.M.Sgt. YELF. Cpl. S. DINMORE.

General Sir HUBERT (de la Poer) GOUGH, G.C.B., G.C.M.G., K.C.V.O.
G.O.C. Fifth Army.

None-the-less, the action was unwelcome, since it forestalled in this sector the great forward move by the Allied forces, which under Foch's direction was about to take place. In preparation for this advance, all ranks of the *Sixth* had been exercising themselves whenever an opportunity occurred, and during the last few days, when the projected offensive had become a certainty, thoughts had been concentrated on the positions known to be occupied by the enemy. By his attack on August 6th, he had altered the situation slightly in his favour, since the British could by no means in so short a time learn the exact positions he occupied. No effort had been spared to give the advancing infantry reliable information of the ground over which they would have to move (38,000 aeroplane photographs were supplied to them), but where the enemy had attacked, exact knowledge of the German forward defence was not available. *Sailly-le-Sec*

The attack of August 8th, in which the *Sixth* took part, deserves special notice not so much because of its magnitude (relative to other British offensives it was a small affair), but because its moral effect on the German High Command was profound, and because it contained the essential element of surprise which at long last, it seems, the British High Command had mastered. On a fourteen-mile front, north and south of the Somme, the British advanced in one day to a depth of from six to eight miles, and before the attack was broken off, had taken 21,000 prisoners and several hundreds of guns. This short, sharp action resulted in so complete a victory, and caused so much confusion behind the German lines, amounting almost to panic, that Ludendorff subsequently referred to it as Germany's black day, and from its date abandoned all his intentions to renew the German offensive, acting thereafter strictly on the defensive. To him the attack came as a complete surprise, and not without reason, for everything possible had been done on the British side to make it so. Elaborate precautions were taken to keep the action secret; the War Cabinet in London was ignorant of the Commander-in-Chief's intention; Divisional Commanders were not informed of it until July 31st, and the troops actually engaged not until two days before it. Painstakingly, hangars and casualty clearing stations were erected in Flanders to suggest to the enemy the intention of a British offensive in the north, and two Canadian battalions there manned the trenches to lend weight to the idea. Two thousand guns were brought into the line by night, and to crown all, no less than 456 tanks were assembled to be used, as their inventors had always contended they should be used, in mass. The usual preliminary bombardment was dispensed with, since by now it had been learnt that when large numbers of tanks were employed to crush wire and deal with strong points, no previous destruction of such obstacles to advancing infantry was necessary.

Some idea of the secrecy maintained can be gauged from the following, written shortly after the battle*: " The morning of Sunday, August 4th, 1918, the fourth anniversary of the outbreak of war, found us in billets in the village

Canaples of Canaples. We . . . were looking forward to a long-promised and frequently deferred rest and refit before going up again. The only points which vexed us the previous day were whether we were to stay there for three weeks or only a fortnight, and whether there was to be a church-parade. This latter point was disposed of eventually by an announcement in the negative, owing to it being impossible to unearth a *padre*. Everyone had, therefore, settled down on Saturday night to the prospect of an uninterrupted day of rest.

" This was not to be. At 9 a.m., as I was completing a leisurely toilet, a runner arrived from my Company Commander desiring my immediate presence. On arriving, he informed me that the battalion was under orders again to move that day to an unknown destination, and that I must report as soon as possible to the Battalion Orderly-room to take charge of an advance-party.

" After a hasty breakfast I duly arrived with my advance-party and was ordered to report to Brigade Headquarters at a neighbouring chateau. On arrival, I found similar parties from the 7th and 8th Battalions . . . . As there was to be a conference between the Brigadier and the Commanding Officers of the three battalions, at which the Divisional Commander was also expected, we were told to stand by, and this we did until 12.30 p.m., when we were dismissed, with the information that, as the brigade was proceeding by omnibus, no guides or advance-party would be required."

The narrative goes on to describe how the rest of the day was devoted to the collection of all surplus kit, the donning of battle-order dress, and the

Lahoussaye move at 10 p.m., with the subsequent drive through the night to Lahoussaye, and adds that: " the road was crammed with traffic . . . and our imagination was stirred by the sight of numbers of tanks making their way through the darkness in the direction of the enemy's line."

The companies slept in damaged barns until noon (August 5th) when dinners were served, and following a conference between the Commanding Officer and Company Commanders, all were told of the forthcoming attack, and maps and photographs were studied. At 10 p.m., the battalion paraded and companies moved off to the support positions they were to occupy. Rain

*By an officer of C Company.

had been falling, the roads were in a poor condition, mud was everywhere, and they did not reach their destinations until 4 a.m. on the 6th.

" . . . The last half-mile was the worst piece of all. The road led up a steep and narrow valley, deep in mud, and ended with a flight of steps, up which I had to pull each man in my platoon. We found our post was a trench, deep in mud and water, with no shelter at all. Whacked and exhausted, the men threw themselves down in the rain outside the trench and fell asleep at once . . . Other companies were more fortunate than we were, as they all had shelters of some kind, and two of them had deep, shell-proof dug-outs in which to rest."

It was as well that they had, for hardly had they reached their respective positions than desultory shelling commenced, to develop into a regular bombardment. The *Sixth* had arrived in time to catch the opening of the German offensive of August 6th, to which allusion has already been made, and although some casualties were suffered, they were fortunately not so severe as they would have been had the German attack been successful. Penetration of the British line occurred, indeed, where the 18th Division was holding the front, on the left of the *Sixth*, and attack and counter-attack went on in this sector for twenty-four hours and more, the British endeavouring to restore the position in time for the opening of their own offensive.

In contrast to the night, the whole of the following day (7th) remained bathed in sunshine, and to everyone's relief final orders were received regarding the attack to be delivered the next day; and at 10 p.m. the companies began to move towards their jumping-off positions.

The 58th Division was now part of the Fourth Army (General Rawlinson) to which the action had been entrusted. South of the River Somme stood the Australians and Canadians, north of it, the III Corps, with the 58th Division on the right, to advance along the river itself, and take Malard Wood, and the ground immediately to the north of it. The objective allotted to the *Sixth* was the wood itself, and the ground east of it, including a large quarry. No definite limit to the advance had been given, the new tactics being to advance until opposition compelled a halt. The 7th Battalion was to co-operate on the left, and the 8th Battalion, following behind both forward battalions, was to " mop-up " and reinforce the front line when objectives had been taken. Malard Wood, the farther edge of which lay about a couple of miles from the battalion's forming-up positions, was as its name implied, a collection of trees, shrubs, and undergrowth. Not every rectangle marked on the map as a wood could be so described, and in the Somme area, particularly, many had been reduced by shell-fire to skeletons of their former

Malard Wood

For extension eastwards see next page.

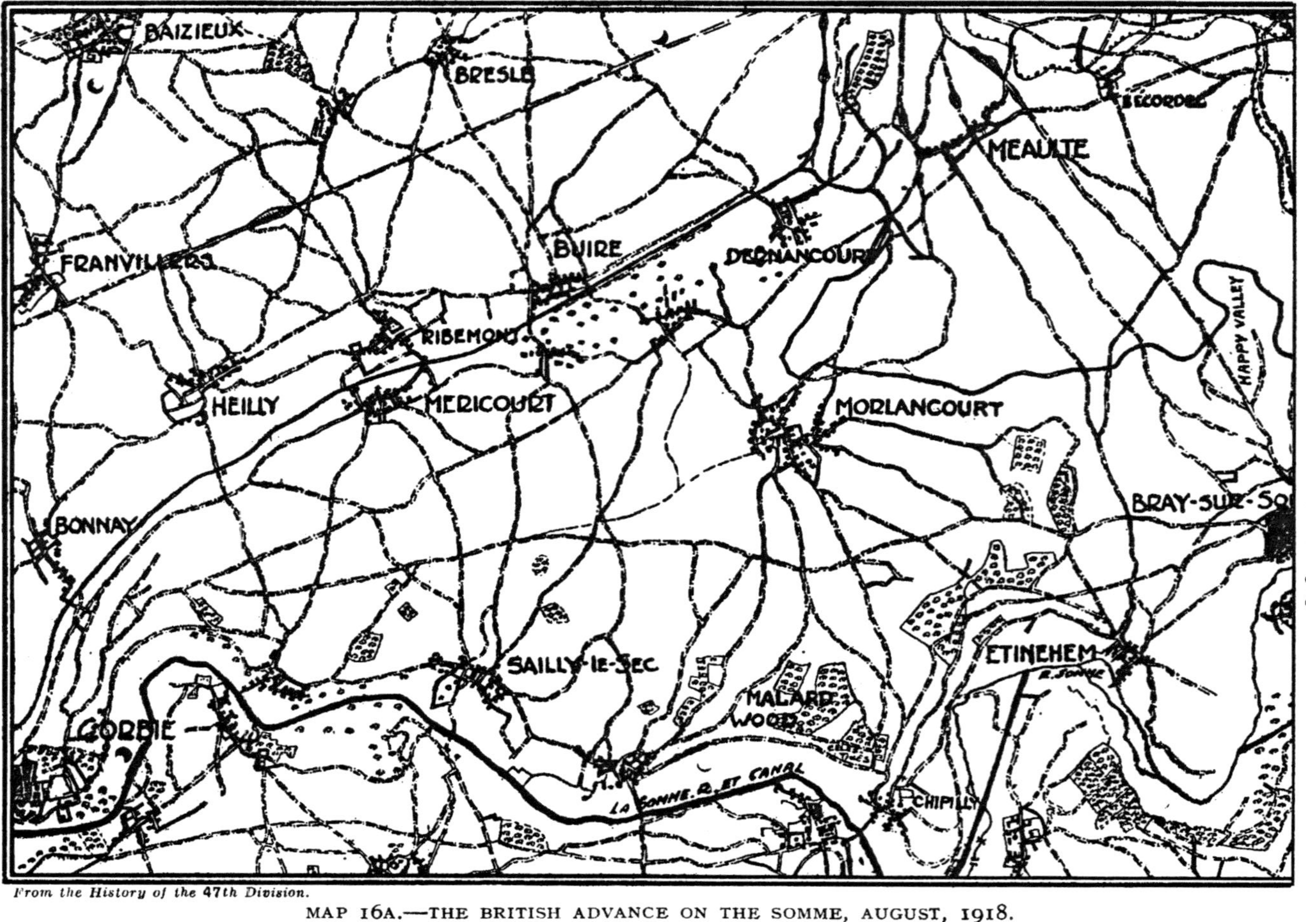

From the History of the 47th Division.

MAP 16A.—THE BRITISH ADVANCE ON THE SOMME, AUGUST, 1918.
Scale approximately 1½ inches to 1 mile.

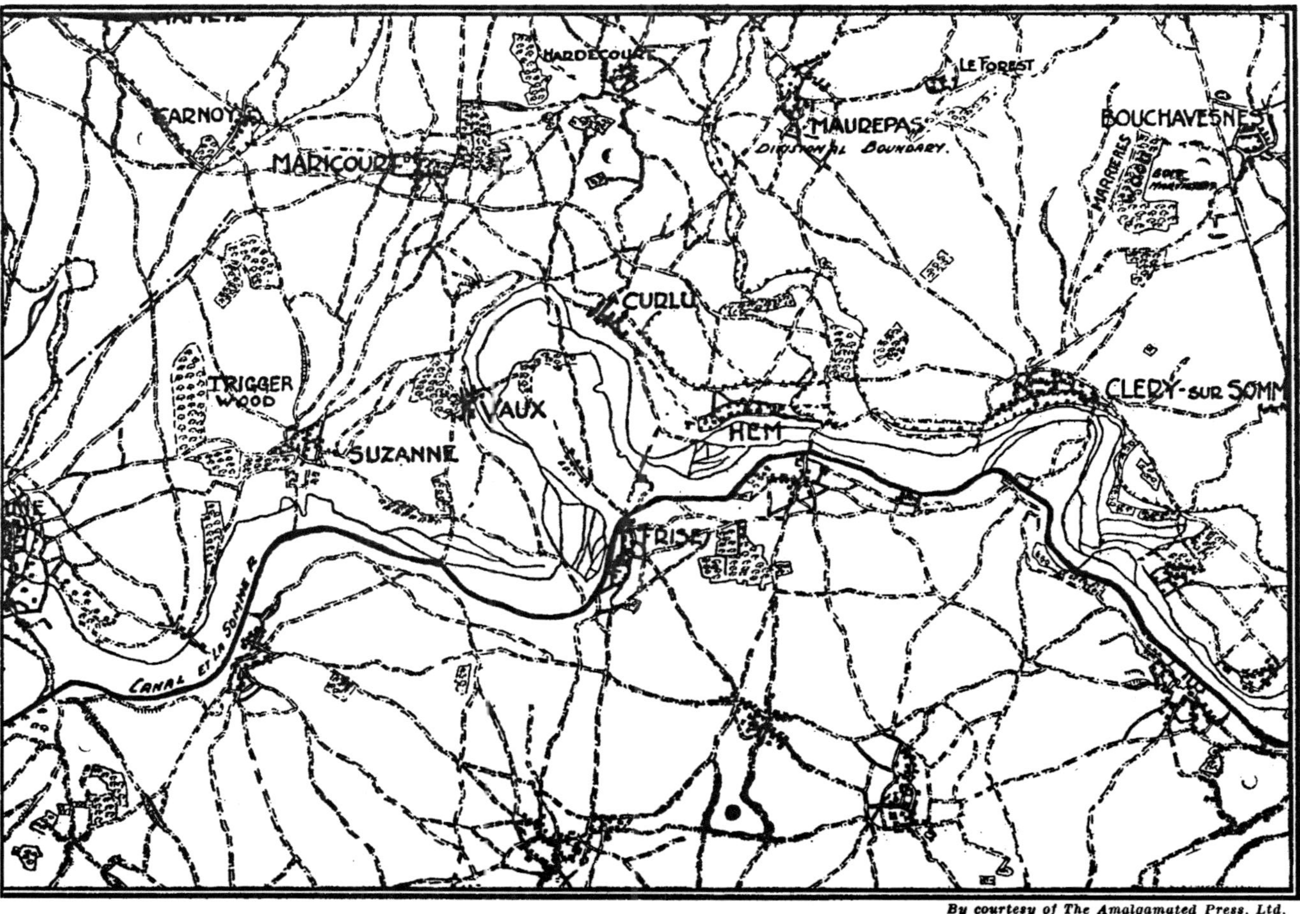

Extension eastwards of Map 16a.

By courtesy of The Amalgamated Press, Ltd.

MAP 16B.—THE BRITISH ADVANCE ON THE SOMME, AUGUST, 1918.

Scale approximately $1\frac{1}{4}$ inches to 1 mile.

Malard Wood

selves. But the battles of 1916 and 1917 had taken place farther to the east than that of 1918, and the countryside was far less disfigured, and the woods were still excellent cover for men and machine-guns. In size, Malard Wood, almost rectangular, measured about two thousand yards from north to south, and a thousand from east to west. There could be no question of making a frontal attack on it, and no tank could go through it; but at its southern end, reaching almost to the Somme, was a belt of grassland from two to three hundred yards wide, bounded on its north side by the wood and on its south by the river. To take Malard Wood, then, it was necessary for attacking troops to go north and south around it and unite beyond it, and such were the tactics employed by the *Sixth* in its assault. Two companies, A and B, were directed to work around its southern end, through the gap between the wood and the Somme, and two companies, C and D, were to work round its northern end. There were, of course, many obstacles, such as small copses, lying between the battalion's jumping-off positions and the wood, from which resistance might be encountered, but it was hoped and expected that tanks would subdue them.

"We had only just time to issue the rum ration after getting on the tapes," continues the narrative, "when our barrage came down with a thud on the Boche front line at 4.20 a.m. That was our signal to advance, and scrambling to our feet, we rushed forward with yells and shouts which were drowned in the deafening roar of the guns. I have never seen anything like it except in the most lurid and highly coloured pictures of the War. The barrage was beautiful, making a vivid red glow in front of us. I suppose there was counter-artillery and machine-gun work, as several were knocked out before we reached the enemy front line, but I personally never thought of it."

The barrage was beautiful or *picturesque*. The vivid red glow was due to natural causes frequently found in downland, for on this, as on many a summer morning, a thick mist lay upon everything and handicapped the attackers. Soon platoons were separated, and all sense of direction was lost, but the necessity for pressing on had been so instilled into all, that wherever groups of men met they joined forces and went forward until they met someone who knew his position, and pressed forward again.

"Except for the front line itself, the Hun seemed to have made very little in the way of organised defensive positions, beyond machine-guns posts, relying more on the ground itself . . . Ridges were strongly held, but on our approach were surrendered, the enemy either running away, or themselves surrendering. I found one tank, with which was one of our officers and a number of men of both 6th and 7th Battalions, and we helped them to clear out one or two enemy posts . . . It was broad daylight by now, but the mist was, if anything, thicker than ever, and it was impossible to make a straight line for my place, but from a knowledge of the ground obtained from maps, I knew that if I worked round the wood, keeping it on my right, I should eventually get where I wanted. So with five men I started off. We met and passed several other parties going in different directions and . . . at last we worked round to the east of the wood and there found a small party of the 7th and 8th Battalions . . . digging in. Passing them we pushed on to the quarry, which was the main landmark given to our company (C), and to our surprise we found no one there at all —friend or foe. Pushing on again, we came to a track junction which had been given to me as my platoon's objective, but no sign of our men could be seen anywhere."

Malard Wood

" It all felt weird and strange, the mist was thinning, and we could see farther, but not a man could we find . . . so we went on again, but quite soon we spotted in another wood a fairly large party of Boche with horses and field-guns. At the same time, another field-gun opened on our left, and machine-gun and rifle-fire began on our right . . . By this time we were certain that we were far ahead of all our comrades, and as we were only a small party, and from the direction of the fire had enemy on three sides, I decided that our best course was to combine with the party we had recently passed. So back we went until we found them, and there I had another consultation with the officer in charge of that party. While we were consulting, we were suddenly fired on from behind, and on looking back we saw a ridge lined with Huns firing from our rear. Seeing that we were surrounded, and having no desire to be captured or shot, we decided at once to attack and cut our way through. We rapidly extended, fired a few rounds, and then charged with the bayonet. The Boche did not wait. Some surrendered, and the rest made off in a north direction along the ridge. We went over the ridge, down the valley, and up the other side, and on our reaching the top, saw to our relief quite a number of our men coming towards us. They were a mixed crowd of all three battalions . . . and almost immediately afterwards a fairly large party from the 173rd Brigade turned up."

No battle is entirely without confusion, but the appearance of units of a sister brigade on top of men from all three battalions of the 174th Inf. Bde. suggests that on this occasion it was more than usual. The mist had, of

Malard Wood

course, made it difficult to keep direction, but there was another factor of prime importance which had led the advancing troops somewhat astray. From north to south the ground sloped until it reached the River Somme, to rise again on the other side, and across this slope all formations had to pass, and in the mist the tendency to veer to the right was impossible to correct. Instead, therefore, of being well to the left of the wood, the 7th Battalion had converged on its northern end, and the 173rd Brigade, destined to go through both 6th and 7th Battalions and take the farther ridge (from which the little party referred to above had returned), had likewise swung to the right. By now, however, the Commanding Officer of the 7th Battalion had arrived with his Second-in-Command, and no time was lost in sorting out the different units all congregated along the high ground north of the wood and putting it into a state of defence, and making arrangements for the 173rd Brigade to continue the advance. This they did at about 7.15 p.m., many hours behind schedule; and in co-operation with this move, those of the *Sixth* on the ridge moved into the wood and occupied its nearby edge.

Meanwhile, the advance on the right of the wood had been far more difficult. A Company, whose task it was to clear the gap at the southern end of the wood and advance to its farther edge, met with considerable opposition from a small quarry or sand-pit, not far from the river, and had made very little progress by the time B Company, in reserve, reached them. From then on, although intermittent, fighting was strenuous when it occurred, the Germans often resisting bravely. Four tanks from Sailly Laurette came to assist the advance, and opposition for the time being was overcome with their aid. Here a single incident went to show that these machines, although greatly improved, were not invincible even against infantry. One brave German left his trench armed with a bomb, and running at great speed towards a tank, placed a bomb beneath its caterpiller track and disabled it. This he did a second time with a similar result, but was shot on returning to his line. Individual exploits such as this were exceptional, tank-action generally causing demoralisation. No doubt the mist contributed to the Germans' sense of insecurity, and made them less ready to put up determined opposition. Many posts surrendered when they found the advancing companies upon them, and one incident alone indicates the extent of this demoralisation. Capt. Idris (B Company), finding it impossible to keep direction, took a compass-bearing from the map, and went ahead, compass in hand, to lead the way. Soon he was separated by the mist from his company, and on looking up found himself surrounded by Germans, all with their hands above their heads in the attitude of surrender. Whether through the mist they had seen the company approaching, it cannot be known, but on their arrival they were duly made prisoners and dispatched to the rear. *Malard Wood*

The original intention had been that B Company, with a company of the 10th London, on reaching A Company's objective, should pass it, and go on through a further part of Malard Wood, which lay corner-wise against its southern edge, and then assault a ridge running north from the village of Chipilly. But the advance had been delayed by the earlier action, and the scrub through which later they had had to pass slowed up movement. Consequently, by the time they were clear of it the day was considerably advanced, and numbers had been much reduced. An immediate attack was out of the question, and could not take place until reinforcements arrived and artillery support was arranged, both of which were highly necessary, since the ridge to be attacked was seen to be strongly held. Reports were sent back to this effect, and the company disposed tactically for defensive purposes. Incidentally, it is interesting to record that when Capt. Idris went back to explain the situation and to collect reinforcements, he found the 8th Battalion about two miles to the rear hastily digging-in, and on asking what they were doing, was told that they were preparing a front line! Heatedly he disabused their minds.

From the reports which Colonel Benson received, it was clear that the remnants of C and D Companies holding the forward edge of the northern half of the wood, were serving no useful purpose, since the 7th Battalion had the situation in that area well in hand. Arrangements were, therefore, made to withdraw them that night, and on the following morning (9th), they were sent to reinforce Capt. Idris and the various units he now had under his command farther to the south. With them went the officer whose narrative forms the basis of this account of the action. Let him continue his story:

"I tucked my men away into safe places and went off to find the officers . . . I found Idris and Nightingale tucked in a shallow trench. I told Idris all about my expedition, and we sent off a report to headquarters, and then about 3 p.m. I settled down to a meal of bully-beef and biscuits with the prospect of a snooze afterwards. I was about halfway through my meal when an officer came from headquarters with more orders. We were to organise our men into four platoons for another attack almost at once, and the Commanding Officer was coming up to give us full instructions himself.

" We had been hoping to be relieved the previous night, but as that had not come off, the worst we had anticipated was that we should have to hang on through the day until the relieving brigade came up. Everybody was absolutely fagged-out and sick of it . . . Still, it was no use growling, so we got our men together and went off to meet the C.O.

"When we met him it was ten minutes to four, and he told us we must kick-off at 4.15 p.m.! Pretty quick work! But as it had to be done, I think we were all relieved that it was to happen quickly, and there was to be no hanging about. It appeared that in the advance the day before, the Australians on our right (south of the River Somme) had made much greater progress than we had done, and there was a lump in the bend of the river still occupied by the enemy. We were to push off from a wood, called Les Celestines, a kind of south-eastern extension of Malard Wood, strike across a deep valley, up the other side, take the summit, and hold on until further orders.

Les Celestines

"We had very little time to sort out our men and explain the business, but we got it done somehow, moved off into the wood and got into position. There were four platoons, each about 40-50 strong. Leapman had the front platoon on the right, and I had the front platoon on the left. Nightingale had a third behind Leapman, and there was another, under C.S.Maj. Thorndyke, behind me . . . As soon as we were in position we kicked off, and then the fun began. The opposite hill was pretty strongly held, and there were heaps of well-placed machine-guns which got to work at once . . . Then I got hit in the leg and knocked down, and all I could do was to direct the men as well as possible from where I lay."

Chipilly

The attack on Chipilly Ridge had commenced. Co-operating on the right of the *Sixth* was the 10th Battalion, and with it a section of machine-guns and four tanks. Their task was to take the village of Chipilly, which lay in a hollow against the river. The ridge stood behind and to the north of the village. Its crest was about 300 feet above sea level, or, which was more to the point, 200 feet above the river, and the approach to it from the village meant an almost impossible climb. Because of this natural disadvantage for attacking troops, the *Sixth* were moving against their objective from the north-west. The operation was not as simple as it seemed, for there was a natural obstacle between the battalion's jumping-off position and its objective. Directly in the line of advance lay a valley, the descent to which was steep, with a stiff climb on the other side of the ridge, and it was not long before the advancing infantry were brought to a standstill. The machine-gun fire from the ridge was terrific, and the enemy's artillery was firing most effectively, and there was no possibility of making further progress. Appreciating the situation exactly, Capt. Idris realised that an entirely new attack would have to be launched if the position was to be gained, and accordingly he sent back all the men of the *Sixth* he could find to their jumping-off ground, leaving those of the 10th Battalion and other units which somehow or other in the confusion of battle had attached themselves to him, in the positions they had reached. There was cover for them and some natural protection. He then returned, himself, to the starting point to organise a second attack, and soon he found advancing through the wood large numbers of American infantry, whose confused knowledge of the progress of the battle and ignorance of what was expected of them, suggested he should use them for the purpose. Assuming command of them, he at once set to work explaining what had to be done . . . The American officers and men were only too glad that someone on the spot should tell them where to go and what to do, and in a very short while the Americans, and what was left of the *Sixth*, were formed into a long line awaiting his signal to start the advance. He gave it, and they moved forward. Nor did they stop. Down into the valley they went, and up the other side, on to the crest, the Germans in full flight. An aeroplane circling above the enemy positions had perhaps already given the order for the German retirement, but it was not less hurried on that account, for they left behind them men, machine-guns, and mortars.

Chipilly

Chipilly Ridge, which earlier that day had looked so formidable, had now changed hands and had passed into the mixed possession of British and Americans, the latter wholly out-numbering the former. To the Americans, therefore, obviously fell the responsibility of holding the newly-won ground. Consolidation commenced immediately under Capt. Idris's direction, and at 5 a.m. on the following morning the *Sixth* withdrew, leaving their comrades-in-arms in sole possession. It had been a most remarkable battle, and the battalion had acquitted itself well. Large numbers of prisoners had been taken, many machine-guns and mortars, one .77 field-gun, two 4.2 howitzers, and one bigger gun of a new pattern. Casualties had been heavy, and some losses which the battalion had sustained were irreparable. To everybody's profound grief the two popular commanders of A and C Companies, Capt. Anderson and Capt. Hill, had both been killed, and the total casualties, amounting to twelve officers and three hundred and eight other ranks, was a high price to pay; but this action, in contrast to some battles in which the battalion had fought, showed positive gain for the sacrifice so willingly given. The tide had turned. The Allied Commanders now saw the possibility of victory before the year was out, and what was more, the rank-and-file now felt themselves to be winning the war. Nor was this spirit of optimism confined to the fighting-men. It permeated everywhere and stimulated all to greater efforts. The Transport Section and Stores personnel worked as they had never worked before to keep pace with the advance. Both had remained *Sailly-le-Sec* at Lahoussaye when the battalion had moved to Sailly-le-Sec, and the cross-country journey to Malard Wood through valleys drenched in gas could not have been more difficult to make. To the many duties of the former was added yet another, that of acting as messengers, grooms and officers' chargers being so employed. It was a war of movement.*

OFFICERS, WARRANT OFFICERS and SECTION COMMANDERS at

MALARD WOOD—AUGUST 8th, 1918

OFFICER COMMANDING: COL. BENSON	SECOND-IN-COMMAND: MAJOR VENNING	ADJUTANT: LIEUT. BUBB
R.S.MAJ. BOSS		R.Q.M.SGT. SIMMONDS
A Co. CAPT. ANDERSON (killed)	C.S.MAJ. TEMPLAR	C.Q.M.SGT. WILLIAMS
B Co. CAPT. IDRIS	C.S.MAJ. THORNDYKE	C.Q.M.SGT. SIRED
C Co. CAPT. HILL (killed)	C.S.MAJ. MACLEAN-CANNON	C.Q.M.SGT. DAVIES
D Co. CAPT. KIDSON	C.S.MAJ. GRUNDY	SGT. DRURY

Quartermaster: CAPT. LOVETT
Transport: CAPT. BRASHER; SGT. PRICE; CPL. DORLING
Cooks: SGT. BUCKLAND
Stretcher-Bearers: SGT. WADE; CPL. BRETT
Signallers: SGT. SHARP; SGT. BURKE

*It will have been noted that this chapter is based largely on a personal narrative written just after the battle. The contributor desires to remain anonymous, but Capt. Idris writes: "If A. E. S. insists upon his name being omitted, an expression of appreciation should certainly be inserted and a reference made to his exceptional bravery and ability."

Chapter 20

"TOUT LE MONDE À LA BATAILLE"

"Everybody into battle!" General Foch, exponent of the principle of attack, was not going to let the enemy rest after the initial success of August 8th. Three days after the battle the whole German line as far south as the Oise started to go back. The enemy's successful advance in the spring had left the Germans with a front seventy miles longer than when earlier they had held the Hindenburg Line, and they were now determined to regain it as early as possible and so economise their forces. Equally, Foch determined they should do so as rapidly as possible, and with the maximum of loss; but when he and Haig met on August 15th to discuss the next moves, there was acute difference of opinion between them as to the tactics to be employed. The former wanted frontal attacks all along the line, and the latter, heavy thrusts against the Germans' weakest sectors; the British view prevailed, and later, when successful results followed these assaults, Foch was the first to give generous acknowledgment of the rightness of Haig's plans. First, the French, under Mangin, attacked south of the Oise, and then the British, under Byng, on August 21st, south of Arras; and both actions were successful, leaving French and British in possession of ground, prisoners, guns, and material of all kinds. The Germans, if not " on the run," were retiring not altogether according to plan.

Meanwhile, the *Sixth*, after the action on August 8th-9th, was withdrawn from Chipilly Ridge on the morning of the 10th, and after spending a day immediately behind it, in support of the American units left there in possession, was relieved by an Australian battalion and moved into trenches close to the positions from which the battalion had commenced the attack, there to remain for three days as reserves. But August 13th saw the unit back in the now familiar Round Wood, where refitting, reorganising, and training commenced immediately. Here, the Commander-in-Chief himself visited the battalion, watched the training, and personally complimented Colonel Benson on its recent fine performance.

Chipilly

Round Wood

The presence of any highly placed officer invariably gave rise to rumours of impending battles, and the occasion of this visit proved no exception to the general rule. None-the-less, veterans could scarcely credit the belief that the

Sixth was to be so soon engaged again in battle, particularly since so little time had been spent in reorganisation to absorb the drafts which were then reaching it, and they were convinced only on the 23rd, when the battle-surplus was made up and sent to Mirvaux, and when the battalion itself paraded and marched towards the front from which it had been but so recently withdrawn. The march was continued in the early morning of the following day, bringing the battalion into the former British front line. Now, there could be little doubt of it.

Morlancourt

Happy Valley

Trigger Wood

August 25th was spent in making a succession of moves, and it seemed as though no sooner had the battalion settled in one place than it was ordered to go forward again. As early as 2 a.m. the first move commenced, and in a couple of hours it reached a point about a mile east of Morlancourt. The march was resumed at 8.30 a.m., and again, in a couple of hours, it found itself in some German positions lying immediately before a deep depression incongruously named on the map as "Happy Valley," and moving once more, at 6 p.m., this time in artillery formation, it took up positions ostensibly to support the 7th Battalion, not far from a little copse known as Trigger Wood. The 8th Battalion was to act similarly on the left. According to plan, an assault was to be delivered that very evening; but the night was dark and wet and both battalions evidently had some difficulty in reaching their jumping-off positions on time, for when the *Sixth* reached theirs, no trace of the 8th Bn. was found. Major John Venning, an officer of the 1st Battalion, London Regiment, had earlier (July 21st) been posted to the *Sixth* as its Second-in-Command, and was now temporarily commanding the unit in Colonel Benson's absence, and after personally scouting the area and reporting their absence, learnt with considerable satisfaction that the attack had been postponed. But only until the morning: the assault was delivered at 4.35 a.m. by both 7th and 8th Battalions (the plan of action having been altered) and was highly successful, and at 6 a.m. the *Sixth* moved into a ravine close to Trigger Wood. About forty casualties had been sustained whilst the battalion was on the higher ground to the west, and all were glad to move into the comparative security of the valley. "We went forward in battle-formation," remarks a sergeant, "and although under heavy fire reached our position—guessing rightly that we should be in attack next day."*

The guess was a good one. That evening (26th) a conference of commanding officers was held, and plans for a continuation of the forward movement drawn up. Briefly, they comprised an assault by the 6th and 7th Battalions, on the left and right respectively, in a north-easterly direction,

*For maps, see pages 220-1.

towards high ground lying east of Maricourt, a little over a mile away. The slight northerly direction which the attack had to take was necessitated by a bend northwards in the River Somme, which prevented a direct easterly advance. To reach the final objective the battalion had first to cross a network of trenches, the capture and consolidation of which was a first objective.

With a unit of the 173rd Inf. Bde. on the left, and the 7th Battalion on the right, the *Sixth* went forward at 4.55 a.m., with A Company on the right and C Company on the left, with D and B Companies behind them. There was, however, this distinction between the fighting over the Somme battlefield of 1916 and 1918: whereas in the earlier year the attacking platoons advanced in waves, now, with a demoralised and retreating army in front of them, tactics were bolder, and the platoons went forward in lines of sections in file, ready to deploy and fight whenever the occasion arose.

The advance was covered as usual by a well-placed barrage, and progress was rapid. " There was very little enemy fire, as he was shelling well to the rear. In a very short time we came under machine-gun fire, but the ground favoured us, and very soon we were at grips with the enemy," wrote a sergeant of A Company, after the action. " On we went . . . things became more orderly as we approached Maricourt where a big enemy stand was expected. *Maricourt* This was met by sheer force of numbers, but after the village fell, a few machine-guns still fired on us from the houses. While disposing of one of these annoyances, we captured a German officer, who maintained a haughty attitude when I told him to get down to the prisoners-of-war cage. Speaking in good English and in a tone which implied that I was dirt beneath his feet, he demanded an escort of equal rank. I told him that if he didn't go there very quickly I would send him to a place where no escort was necessary. He went!"*

Reports from A and B Companies, reaching headquarters at 8 a.m., implied that the first objective had been captured; but there was evidently some doubt about this, for Captain Burt-Smith, himself reconnoitring the ground immediately in front, found trenches there unoccupied, and when Major Venning arrived on the scene shortly afterwards, he reported this information. To both it was clear that in the confusion of battle a trench running obliquely across the line of advance, known as South Street, had been incorrectly interpreted as the first objective, and that there was still some distance to go before it was reached. Thereupon, the advance was continued until the whole of the ground forming the first objective was in the battalion's hands.

*Sgt. Cowherd.

Maricourt

In the positions now occupied, the companies had some protection from the very heavy shell-fire which was almost at once directed against them. Trenches, not wholly demolished, such as Black Street and Market Street, afforded some cover, but not enough to prevent the infliction of a good many casualties. At 3 p.m., when Major Venning visited the battalion for a second time, he estimated the strength at about two hundred non-commissioned officers and men with only three officers, all junior in rank, who had not been either killed or wounded. The continuation of the advance had already been postponed on account of both heavy casualties and the stern defence of the enemy, but notwithstanding both considerations it was decided to renew the offensive at dawn on the following day. Reorganisation commenced immediately, platoons were amalgamated, and the plan of attack worked out and studied. Rations were hurriedly dispatched from the rear, and as early as possible served out to sections.

The advance during this day (27th), had brought the battalion close to the Maricourt-Clery road, which although taking a general south-easterly direction, ran due east for a distance of about a thousand yards from where the battalion had halted. The road was clearly discernible, despite the ravages of war, and it provided a good landmark by which the battalion might keep correct direction when continuing its advance in the morning. The battalion was therefore formed-up astride the road, with A and B Companies on the right, and C and D Companies on the left of it, B and D Companies being in support and forming the second line.

The advance commenced at dawn (28th) and was protected by a well-placed barrage. Enemy counter artillery-fire opened half an hour earlier in anticipation of an attack, but was not effective, and in a couple of hours the battalion's objectives were reached, not, however, without some opposition, principally from machine-guns. On the right, A Company over-ran a number of such posts and spent the remainder of the morning destroying them, during which many casualties were sustained and the battalion reduced considerably in strength. Indeed, when Major Venning reached the front line—a single trench into which all had crowded—he found a situation which might well have disconcerted a less resolute man; and since from now on the battle was under his personal direction, it is well to quote from the report he made immediately after it:

"At 7 a.m. I reached the front line and found only one officer left, Lieut. Willcocks, with Sec.-Lt. Dixon, of a machine-gun company, who had only two guns left. Lieut. Willcocks was severely wounded at about 8 a.m.,

L'ALOUETTE AND ARTHUR FRITH OF "THE GOODS," 58TH DIVISION.

"MURIEL" (RFM. BARRETT). THE LOND. COM. DEPOT CONCERT PARTY.

Cpl. JACOBS.

Sgt. DRAGE.

Lieut. HAMMOND.

Sgt. TILEY.

Cpl. E. HUBBARD.

Left to Right: Sgt. Wood, Sgt. Etherington, Sgt. Lloyd, Miss Ida Hubbard, Cpl. Nimmo, Cpl. Holmes, Cpl. Rogers, Lieut. Hammond, Sgt. Diggins, Cpl. Plumridge.

THE CONCERT PARTY OF THE "RESERVE" BATTALION, BLACKDOWN, 1918.

SYSTEMATIC DEVASTATION AT CHAUNY, 1918.

Legend

A TYPICAL SCENE ON THE SOMME IN 1918.

Plate 48

By courtesy of C.S.Maj. R. Stenner

ON THE HOME FRONT: THE DRILL HALL AT 57A, FARRINGDON ROAD AFTER AN AIR-RAID.

From left to right:
SGT. SWEET, CAPT. E. H. PYNE, CAPT. F. H. H. THOMAS, O.B.E., T.D.

BLACKDOWN—OCTOBER, 1918.

SERGEANTS' MESS, 6TH (RESERVE) BATTALION CITY OF LONDON RIFLES.

Each Row (reading left to right):

Sergts.—Hulland, M.M. Kaines Surl Venables Pite Wood Ixer Webber Lovell Thorne, M.M. Blogg Williams Haynes Mansbridge Fruin

Sergts.—Diggins Vandercamp Majer Saville, Mde. Mte. Hards Butler, D.C.M. Field Passmore Sheward Hines Worboys, M.M. Drage Willmott Hall, M.M. Gordon, D.C.M.

Sergts.—McNaughton Etherington Goode, M.M. Owers Florey Smith Harvey Boyd Brent West Lamont Florey Troughton Curry White

C.Q.M.Sgt. Yelf Sergts.—Swain Hurley Hume Wicks Turner Grice Mitchell Troughton Fox Addicott, M.M. Lush Solman, M.S.M. Burls C.S.M.I.M. Black

C.Q.M.Sgt. Godfrey Col.-Sgt. Barnes, D.C.M. Col.-Sgt. Greening C.S.Maj. Allen, D.C.M. C.S.Maj. Nash R.Q.M.Sgt. Percival, M.S.M. R.S.Maj. Lake R.S.Maj. Kemp R.Q.M.Sgt. Kent C.S.Maj. Smale C.S.Maj. Thompson C.S.M.I.M. Erwood C.S.Maj. Rakestrow C.Q.M.Sgt. Leat Sergt. Fuller

Col.-Sgt. BARNES, D.C.M.

C.S.Maj. THOMPSON.

Sgt. BLOGG.

C.Q.M.Sgt. G. SMITH.

Sgt. H. WEBBER.

C.S.Maj. CASTLEMAN,
C.Q.M.Sgt. HOWELL, C.Q.M.Sgt. YOUNGS,
C.S.Maj. BITTEN, C.Q.M.Sgt. WEEDON, C.S.Maj. ALLEN.

Sgt. BYRNE, Sgt. ELLIS, Sgt. PARKER,
C.S.Maj. THORNDYKE, C.Q.M.S. SIRED.

Sgt. FLOREY.

C.Q.M.Sgt. M. DAVIES.

Sgt. C. HAYWARD.

C.S.Maj. GODFREY.

C.S.Maj. SNOW.

C.S.Maj.
H. ALEXANDER. M.M.

R.S.Maj. H. KEMP.

Sgt. JOCK THOMSON.

C.Q.M.Sgt. WILLIAMS.

C.S.Maj.
McCLEAN CANNON.

Plate 51

MALARD WOOD.

This aerial photograph shows the actual positions of advance of the "Sixth" when they captured Malard Wood on Germany's "Black Day" of August 8th, 1918. The battalion advanced from Malard Wood to Epehy.

leaving me with no officer until 1 p.m., when Lieut. Trimm joined me with about thirty men. *Maricourt*

" I proceeded at once to organise the defence and to consider the possibility of reaching the ' line of exploration ' . . . and I got into touch with the 8th Battalion on the right and the 173rd Inf. Bde. on the left. During the morning I succeeded in driving out machine-guns—two or three —in front of my trench, and establishing a post of eight men in front. I considered this untenable, as the communication trench (to it) and the left flank were submitted to a very heavy machine-gun fire from the north, while the Bosche were bombing along the trench from the south. Also, I observed about two hundred enemy advancing in artillery formation from a crest (in front) and fired at them with Lewis-guns, scattering them. I therefore withdrew the post to the main line of defence. The sector was quiet during the remainder of the day, except for heavy and continuous shelling and machine-gun fire. It died away towards the evening, and ceased at 10 p.m.

"At 8 p.m. I was ordered to establish a strong-post under an officer as far forward as possible . . . the advance being co-ordinated with artillery, particulars of which would be forwarded to me. I received no details, but at 10.15 p.m. fire became very heavy, and I sent a party forward under Sec.-Lt. Woodhams, and the post was formed without opposition and with no sign of the enemy."*

There is a limit to human endurance, and the men who on two successive days had delivered two successful attacks were in need of a rest, and happily they were relieved by the 12th Battalion that very night (28th-29th) and moved into reserve positions north of Bray, where the Transport Section and " details " had previously assembled. But the rest here was of very short duration. On the evening of the 30th the battalion left its camp, marched to a point on the Maricourt-Clery road, south-west of the former village, embussed, and was carried eastwards as far as Hem Wood (a little north of the Somme village of that name), debussed, and marched north-west towards the battle-area which by now had moved eastwards. Here, in a valley close to Junction Wood, it rested in artillery formation, expecting any moment to receive the order to move eastwards as an advance-guard, close upon the heels of the retreating enemy. *Hem Wood*

The situation which had developed in this sector was similar to that elsewhere along the great Somme Salient. The Germans were retiring in very good order, sacrificing their rear-guards whenever necessary to check the

*Another forward post appears to have been established by A Company under Sgt. Cowherd, who at 8.30 p.m., led a small party along the Maurepas road for about six hundred yards. They captured a couple of prisoners.

British advance, and the bravery and discipline of their machine-gunners enabled them to withdraw according to plan. From time to time the plan had to be modified as some local British success forced a speedy evacuation of a particular area, and consequently the advancing troops never knew until operations commenced whether slight or stern opposition would be encountered, or whether last-minute changes in operation-orders would be issued. It was so on the night of the 30th. Until 10.30 p.m. that day, the *Sixth* was expecting to be employed on the morrow as a vanguard to the brigade, moving forward without opposition until the enemy's rear-guards should be met; but news from the 175th Inf. Bde., holding the front line, which on the previous day had been advanced about three and a half miles and now ran in a north and south direction flanking Marrieres Wood, indicated that opposition was likely to be severe. Thus, at this late hour a change in plan was made, and the 174th Inf. Bde. was ordered to attack the wood the following morning under cover of barrage, and consolidate on the ridge beyond it.

Marrieres Wood

Nothing perhaps so well illustrates the change that had come upon the general situation on the Western Front as this sudden variation in the orders for the advance. Whereas in 1916 before a battle every movement had been rehearsed, and every contingency provided for, now in 1918, an assault was calmly envisaged without any preliminary reconnaissance or previous training. It was the complete change in circumstances that rendered it possible to envisage success attending an operation which was to be conducted by troops newly arrived in a fresh area and knowing nothing of the ground in front of them; and it is one of the marvels of the Great War that despite the lack of thorough training the British Army in France was able to accommodate itself readily to the new conditions. The old "Contemptibles" of 1914 were by 1918 almost eliminated, and since then there had been little opportunity of training the Territorial units and those of the New Armies in the principles of open warfare; yet British officers and men adapted themselves readily enough to this new phase, and quickly learnt their lessons. Perhaps the *Sixth*, which had the advantage of the "Rifles" tradition established by the *First* in its pre-war training, and the *Second* during its sojourn in East Anglia and on Salisbury Plain, was better equipped than most battalions for this phase of the war, since it acquitted itself well in answering all calls made upon it. To its early training must be attributed, therefore, the relative ease with which the change-over, in this present instance, from one plan to another was conducted. It was taken as a matter of course by Major Venning, who recorded the battle thus:

" The battalion assembled with great difficulty, the night being dark and the country unknown, but it was in position by 4.30 a.m. in the usual formation. C Company was on the right under Sec.-Lt. Moore, and D Company on the left under Lieut. Ball. In the second line on the right was A Company, under Capt. S. T. Cooke, and on the left, B Company, under Sec.-Lt. Soulsby. There were only two other officers available to lead the battalion (who had joined the previous day) and three officers lent by the 7th Battalion. Only seven sergeants. Battn.: 344 O.R.s, including 53 at headquarters. No signs of the 8th Battalion, which should have been on our left, but the 7th Battalion assembled in our rear in support."* *Marrieres Wood*

The Australians were operating on the right immediately north of the Somme, and their advance was timed to commence at the same hour as that of the *Sixth*. Artillery support consisted of a heavy barrage opening for twenty minutes in front of the line held by the 175th Inf. Bde., and then advancing at the rate of one hundred yards every six minutes. The report continues:

" Zero 5.10. Barrage opened and line advanced in good order. Enemy opened heavy counter-barrage, but wood reached with little opposition, and enemy retired 300 yards east of the wood, and opened heavy machine-gun fire. From this point the Australians could be seen advancing along the ridge (from the south) while enemy machine-guns still fired on our men from Wary Alley Trench."

Wary Alley Trench was south of Marrieres Wood, and thus the Australians were advancing behind it. Its garrison forming a pocket, the enemy might have delayed the advance, but: " Capt. Cooke took charge of the situation and sent a party of twenty men, under C.S.Maj. Templar, southwards through the wood to attack this trench. The enemy for the most part surrendered, a few retiring north-east towards Bouchavesnes. Capt. Cooke was thus able to clear the plateau and advanced across the valley (between the wood and the ridge beyond it) with a mixed party of 6th and 8th Battalions, occupying a trench and getting into touch with the Australians on his right."

A little later a similar situation developed and again a party of the *Sixth* was sent to overcome opposition so that progress by the Australians might not be delayed, and again it was successful, and again the line advanced, so that

*But the 8th Battalion was soon to be in position, as Major Venning's narrative later shows.

by nightfall the battalion had covered a distance of many miles, and penetrated the enemy's defences to a depth of two thousand yards, and had established itself well beyond the high ground it had been ordered to take.

* * * * *

Old soldiers who had taken part in earlier battles in which the *Sixth* had been engaged could, when describing them afterwards, divide the actions into phases, the preparation, the assault, the consolidation, the enemy counter-attack, and the final relief. A battle was a battle; there were practice attacks, early reconnaissance of the front, perhaps a lecture, and certainly a conference in which the task of each section was discussed. Now, all was different. Everybody had indeed gone into battle. Orders came over-night, and you attacked in the morning. You made your way to the jumping-off position hoping all the time that supporting units would reach theirs before zero-hour. In front was the enemy, and if you kept direction during your advance, you would, with luck, reach your objective—usually large enough to be easily recognisable—a wood or a village. If you met with opposition, you fought; if it was severe you hastily concocted a plan and put it at once into execution. There was no standing still. At night you halted to continue, perhaps, the offensive the very next day. If you were relieved, it was to enable your unit to pull itself together in time for another attack.

Such was the life led by officers and men during the months of August and September. Already by the end of the first month the battalion had been engaged in four battles, and after each had been reorganised and re-equipped for the next; and now on the last day of August and the first of

Marrieres Wood

September, it was holding the ground east of Marrieres Wood, waiting to be relieved, and knowing that as soon as it was, there would be a brief rest, kit and arms would be overhauled, drafts would arrive, and platoons and companies would be reorganised, rations would be served out, and the march to the front begin again. September was like August. On the first day of the new month the 74th Division took over, and the *Sixth* moved back into bivouacs, a few miles behind the line, there to recover itself and to get ready for the next effort. On the 6th, as was to be expected, busses arrived to carry the battalion again to the front, and the battle-surplus to Maricourt. The

Nurlu

battalion debussed at Nurlu (nearly six miles north-east of Marrieres Wood) where the 21st Battalion (47th Division) was in reserve,* having captured the

*The 47th Division was operating on the left of the 58th, and not infrequently men of the *Sixth* encountered their former comrades then serving with that Division. Many met and spoke to Brig.-General Mildren.

village two days earlier, and marched to Guyencourt, another of the many Somme villages, lying in the same general direction of attack, from which the 7th and 8th Battalions were making a further effort to thrust the enemy from his temporary positions along a line which now ran southwards from Cambrai. Two days later the battalion took over the line established by the 7th Battalion in a sunken road south-west of the village of Epéhy, and held it until the 10th, when once again it launched itself against the enemy. The 3rd Battalion was in readiness behind the *Sixth* to continue the advance once the village was taken, but heavy machine-gun fire brought the companies to a standstill, and there was no alternative but to withdraw to the jumping-off positions, and with the aid of the supporting battalion, hold them as a front-line.

Epehy

Not every advance was met with passive resistance on the part of the Germans. On the 10th the effort was repulsed, and fresh British troops were brought forward to renew it, and these, comprising the 4th Battalion, Suffolk Regiment, arrived on the next day to relieve the *Sixth*, and to enable the latter to withdraw to Liermont and reorganise. But the time for resting and refitting was short-lived; the battalion moved back to Guyencourt on the 13th, and on the next day relieved the 12th Battalion in the sunken road south-west of Epéhy, to hold the line, however, only for a couple of days. Thereupon it went back to bivouacs in Ville Wood (where the honours conferred as a result of the successful actions on August 8th-10th were read in the routine orders of the IIIrd Corps), and on the 21st back again to Liermont. In these stirring days moves were rapid and unexpected, and it was not until the 25th, after one further spell of duty in the front line, that the *Sixth* was able to say good-bye to the devastated and devastating Somme area. On the previous day, the 2nd Battalion of the 105th American Regiment relieved the *Sixth* in the now familiar front line, and it moved back to Villers Faucon, from where it was carried in busses to Heilly. On the 26th a journey by rail brought the unit to Savy, in the Lens area, and billets were found in the Château de L'Haute. There was a church-parade on the 29th, and many must have given thanks for safe deliverance at the service—thanks heavy laden with remorse at the thought of the loss of so many gallant and glorious friends. It was sadness in the extreme to think that one's preservation often depended on the willing self-sacrifice of comrades whom one had known and loved, and it was humiliating to know from practical experience that it was Fate, and Fate alone, which often determined who should live and who should die. Yet by their deaths the dead had made demands upon the living. Not for nothing should they have sacrificed their lives. There was a set purpose

Liermont

Lens

behind this war, and not until Germany was defeated could there be a righteous peace; until then the *Sixth* would press on, conscious of its mission. What better conclusion to this episode could there be than Colonel Benson's narrative of events written during the middle of September, 1918?

Summary

" The battalion, after a long time in the trenches, was brought out of the line at the beginning of August, 1918. It was hoped that the time for a long deferred rest had come, and that three weeks of training and recreation was before us. This dream was soon shattered, for within forty-eight hours the battalion was brought up to the front line again. It was known to the Commanding Officer alone at this time that the battalion was to take part in an important operation which was kept most secret. The spirit of the officers and men was, as usual, excellent, but after a long period of trench warfare there was a great lack of experience in attack formations and offensive warfare generally. This, however, could not be helped, and practice was out of the question, as the battalion was put straight into appalling support-trenches, and not a word was permitted about the forthcoming operations. Thus we went into trenches under very adverse conditions, weather and otherwise, on August 5th. The trenches were in a dreadful state—full of water and mud, and there was not shelter or accommodation for half the men. The majority stood in these sloppy trenches in battle-order without coats or covering. To make matters worse, just as the relief was complete the Hun attacked the division on our left, and so we came in for very considerable shelling. The Bosches met with some success, and we had to stand by for immediate operations. On the afternoon of the 7th the Hun was counter-attacked and driven from the front line and support line, but still held the outpost line, from which no attempt was made to eject him . . . Although the battalion was not directly engaged, it got its full share of the shelling and all ranks had a very tiring time . . . The battalion moved up to the tape-line on the night of August 7th, and had a rough ride all the way; hostile artillery was very active, and it appeared that hostile counter-preparations were in progress. The battalion, although it had to traverse a spot of evil reputation near Sailly-le-Sec, named the " Mad-Acre " by the Australians, negotiated this death-trap and arrived on the tape-line practically unharmed. Although six hours was allowed to traverse three thousand yards and get on the tape-line, and every detail of assembly provided for, some companies only arrived a few minutes before zero. This was accounted for by elements of another brigade crossing them on their approach march. This is quoted as a lesson to young officers who frequently criticise the time they are kept on the tape before going over. It was a beautifully clear morning until 4 a.m. on August 8th, when a thick fog fell and blotted out all objects thirty yards away. Punctually at zero the barrage opened, and the battalion started off into the deep mist. Boches were soon encountered, and there was some fighting in their front line. All sense of direction was soon lost—it was like running about in a thick London fog—but there were plenty of Boches about, and wherever these showed they were chased, killed, or captured.

Summary

" As the battalion could not follow their lines of direction, they followed Boches instead, and did most excellent work. When the fog lifted it was found that companies, battalions, and even brigades were intermingled. The battalion was reorganised as well as could be at the time, and sent to finish off Malard Wood. This they did, and joined up with the 7th Bn., London Regt., and thus we gained our objectives for the day—an advance of more than three thousand yards in a difficult terrain. The 6th and 7th Battalions gained all their objectives, and took Malard Wood—no American troops had anything to do with it, although the papers said they took the wood—indeed, they did not appear on the scene for more than thirty hours afterwards. The battalion had done gloriously, and taken numbers of prisoners, machine-guns, and mortars, besides a field-gun of latest model.

" It is the reverse of the medal that one looks on always with sorrow. I refer to the good fellows that are lost. This day, besides several splendid men of the rank and file, two of the best fighting officers and finest leaders that the regiment has ever had, were killed. I refer to Capt. Anderson and Capt. Hill. The latter, although not actually a *Sixth* officer, had so long been associated with the regiment, that he was looked upon as an officer of the regiment.

" On the 9th the battalion again went on to take Chipilly Ridge. There was no barrage, but three tanks lent a hand. The advance was at first absolutely held up by very heavy machine-gun fire. American troops reinforced our battalion, and the 10th London came up on our right. Artillery support was asked for, and the battalion, merged with the Americans, succeeded in gaining their objective. They attacked from the west simultaneously with the 10th Battalion from the south. The latter battalion reached the summit of the ridge at practically the same time, but rather in advance of the 6th Bn. and the Americans. The position was held for a couple of days, and the battalion was taken out into support and made up to strength.

" It was not long idle, and went over the top again on August 27th and also the 28th, and again did splendidly . . . Although it was not the intention when writing this resumé to mention names, I am forced to name

Summary C.S.Maj. Thorndyke, who was simply magnificent on the 8th, 9th, 27th, and 28th, and also Lieut. Idris, whose leadership and courage on the 8th and 9th, and again in September, was beyond all praise. The casualties on the 27th and 28th were not heavy, although the loss of C.Q.M.Sgt. Martin and Sgt. McEloy is irreparable and greatly regretted—two fine soldiers of whom the regiment is justly proud.*

" The battalion again refitted and returned to the line, and was fighting practically the whole of the first twelve days in September. Of these actions I have at present no detailed news, except that Major Venning, who has been commanding the battalion since August 23rd was wounded . . . I had hoped that Major Venning would have been associated with the battalion until given the command of a battalion. The thanks of the regiment are due to him for all the excellent work he has done whilst with us. He is an excellent and very competent soldier, who worked for the interest of the regiment with all his great capabilities and without stint.

" Throughout the operations both officers and men showed that spirit and ready obedience which is expected of the regiment. No praise is too high for their fine fighting qualities and excellent work which resulted in the capture of positions, many prisoners, guns, mortars, and machine-guns innumerable. All ranks had striven to and succeeded in living up to and enhancing the fine traditions of the regiment—for which all thanks and praise are due to them."

BATTALION OFFICERS, WARRANT OFFICERS and SECTION COMMANDERS at

CHIPILLY RIDGE—AUGUST, 1918.

OFFICER COMMANDING :	SECOND-IN-COMMAND :	ACTING ADJUTANTS :
COL. BENSON	MAJOR VENNING	LIEUT. BUBB ; CAPT. COOKE
R.S.MAJ. BOSS		R.Q.M.SGT. SIMMONDS

A Co.	CAPT. JOHNSTON	C.S.MAJ. TEMPLAR	C.Q.M.SGT. WILLIAMS
B Co.	CAPT. IDRIS	C.S.MAJ. THORNDYKE	C.Q.M.SGT. SIRED
C Co.	CAPT. BURT-SMITH	C.S.MAJ. MACLEAN-CANNON	C.Q.M.SGT. DAVIES
D Co.	CAPT. KIDSON	C.S.MAJ. GRUNDY	SGT. DRURY

Quartermaster : CAPT. LOVETT.
Transport : CAPT. BRASHER ; SGT. PRICE ; CPL. DORLING
Cook : SGT. BUCKLAND
Stretcher-Bearers : SGT. WADE ; CPL. BRETT
Signallers : SGT. SHARP ; SGT. BURKE
Scouts and Snipers : LIEUT. FIELD ; SGT. WINNUP

*The total casualties from Aug. 8th to Sept. 11th amounted to 28 Officers and 638 Other Ranks.

Chapter 21

THE LAST POST

"The idea in Hadyn's mind when he composed the 'Last Post' was not that of a sad call at all. It seems to be that at first, but the high, ascending note upon which it ends is one of hope and expectancy, and is meant to lead on quite naturally to the 'Reveille,' with its message of a new and fuller life."*

Some such thought as this was actuating all, who, after the strenuous fighting of August and September, were now facing the retiring Germans in the neighbourhood of Lens. The sacrifices of the earlier years and particularly of the last two months, when victory for the Allied cause seemed to be within grasp, occasioned a note of sadness which was relieved only by the thought that soon the war would be over, and that those sacrifices would not have been in vain; that the "Last Post" which had sounded for so many would soon be followed by the "Reveille" of victory. *Lens*

There was good reason for this optimism: success was everywhere. On the very day when the *Sixth* was moving north (September 26th) from the Somme to Lens, French and American armies broke through the German lines between Rheims and the Meuse, and on the next day, the British First and Third Armies assaulted the German lines from Bullecourt to St. Quentin, successfully occupying the whole of the Bourlon Ridge, and on the 28th, the Belgians, supported by British and French, in one day swept across the Flanders battlefield of 1917 right up to Passchendaele; and to cap these three successful actions, the British Army, on the 29th, crossed the southern part of the Hindenburg Line and drove the Germans well beyond it. Everywhere Allied arms were successful, and soon the news trickled through to the effect that peace overtures were being made by the Germans. The last of these four blows had convinced Ludendorff that an immediate armistice was an imperative necessity, and he demanded that peace should be sought on the basis of President Wilson's Fourteen Points.

An historian has noted that whereas but one week was all that was necessary to see the world in arms, more than six were required to see peace restored. That is in the nature of things; it is easy to raise a fire, difficult

*Col. the Rev. A. E. Wilkinson, O.B.E., M.C., T.D.

to quench it. Meanwhile, and to avoid heavy casualties, the British troops in the north were ordered to adopt a role of peaceful penetration, occupying ground relinquished by the retreating enemy as and when the opportunity occurred, but avoiding, except when absolutely necessary, a pitched battle. Nevertheless, such tactics at times took a heavy toll of the advancing battalions, and certainly placed the greatest strain upon them, and especially their supply services. Not infrequently during the month of October was the *Sixth* called upon to make a ten-mile advance in a day, and take up outpost positions at the end of it.

Les Brebis

At the beginning of the month the battalion found itself in billets at Les Brebis—well known to those of the *First* who were still serving with the unit—and on the 2nd it moved into support positions north-west of Lens, the battle surplus going to the divisional reserve camp near Bois de Riaumont. The Germans were on the point of relinquishing Lens and were destroying as much of it as possible. The noise of explosions and number of fires that could be seen burning in the town were clear indications that they were soon to retire, but on the 4th, when the *Sixth* took over the line from the 8th Battalion, they still showed signs of resistence, and inflicted a few casualties. On the 8th the battalion moved back into reserve at Bois de Riaumont, and four days later took up positions in a new outpost line which had been formed in their absence west of the Canal de la Haute Deule, a wide waterway, typical of northern France and Belgium, which flowed north and east of Lens.* The Germans behind this obstacle were in a strong position, and if they were to be dislodged there would be no alternative but first to cross the water. How this might be done with the minimum loss of life was the question already being considered by the Divisional and Brigade Commanders, who hoped that the necessity for it might not arise, and that in a day or so the Germans would continue their retreat.

Bois de Riaumont

Canal de la Haute Deule

They did not. On the contrary the indications were that behind the canal, with banks lined with machine-guns, the enemy would make a determined stand. Reconnoitring patrols sent out by the *Sixth* quickly found the nature and strength of the defence, which if there was any doubt about it was dispelled when, one foggy night, an enemy patrol raided one of C Company's pickets, killed ten, wounded fourteen, and captured or killed eight non-commissioned officers and men. Nothing like such offensive action had been anticipated, and the picquet was taken unawares with disastrous consequences. The action impressed itself deeply upon all ranks. Indeed, perhaps more than any other incident it was the cause of the decision to try to drive the

*For map of Lens and surrounding country, see pages 56-7.

enemy back, and orders to cross the canal and form bridge-heads on the farther bank were given to the battalion on the 14th, and on the following day, to prepare for the effort, it was taken out of the line to billets at Courrieres. *Courrieres* Here, plans for the assault were drawn up, and the battalion returned to the line on the next day, taking up its former positions on the western bank of the canal, ready to attempt the crossing on the following morning.

Happily, the assault was not delivered; as if sensing that the *Sixth* was to come against them, the Germans withdrew during the night, and hastily made eastwards, with the battalion following as closely as possible. Once across the water the leading companies established themselves in some woods immediately beyond it, and at 3 p.m. the whole battalion moved forward to the village of Oignies, and there formed an outpost line. Next morning the *Oignies* advance was continued until the village of Mons-en-Pevele was reached, when the battalion became "Brigade support," the 8th Battalion having meanwhile passed through the *Sixth,* forming the outpost line facing the village of Bersee, *Bersee* a few miles in advance.

The *Sixth* was now traversing ground entirely untouched by the war, and passing through villages still occupied by their inhabitants. The Germans, in their retreat, whilst doing the maximum amount of damage that time would permit to roads and buildings, were sparing the villagers the last misery of seeing their homes destroyed and were even leaving notices on wooden boards informing the advancing British as to which villages were occupied by civilians. It was a death-bed repentance, perhaps, and perhaps also a desire themselves to escape from a harassing fire which the British artillery directed against them whenever a target was presented. Their present care for the unfortunate Belgians was by no means typical, and there was clear evidence from the behaviour of the people that such solicitation for their welfare was far from usual. Some men of A Company, billeted in a farmhouse, noted with disgust that when one of the company's officers called to inspect their quarters, the Belgian family crouched into the corner of the room, and could only with difficulty be persuaded that there was nothing to fear. It ought, also, to be noted here without dwelling upon the enemy's inhumanity (which may not have been general) that the eight non-commissioned officers and men captured in the raid on the 14th were found subsequently dead and stripped naked. Whether they were killed in the action, died of wounds received during it, or were deliberately done to death, is not known.

On October 19th, the battalion continued the march eastwards as the advance-guard of the brigade, going through the 8th Battalion, and met with no opposition until about 9 a.m., when, just after passing the crossroads a

La Coquerie mile and a half south-west of La Coquerie, C Company were fired on at close range by a machine-gun. A thick morning mist obscured all but the largest objects, and made conditions for an ambush almost perfect. Without waiting for the word of command the leading platoon deployed and opened fire in the direction from which the machine-gun was coming, and in a very short time the sounds of a vehicle rattling away over the pavé could be heard. Similar sounds had been heard on the right as soon as the machine-gun had commenced firing, and thus it was presumed that the enemy fire was no more than a delaying action to enable some light artillery section to withdraw. The advance was resumed, and no further opposition was encountered that day.

Nomain By the late afternoon, a line east and north-east of the village of Nomain was reached, and here the battalion rested the night, with standing patrols thrust out in front well before dawn to cover the renewal of the advance, on the next day to be led by the 3rd Battalion. Some of those fortunate enough to be allowed to sleep found agreeable quarters in a large farm surrounded by massive hay-sheds. The owner, a noted Belgian stock-breeder, offered every hospitality to the tired troops, and told them about his treasured animals, all of which had been confiscated by the Germans.

No account of these astonishing days would be complete without some reference to the extraordinary efforts made by the supply units, and particularly the Transport Section, Quartermaster's personnel, and cooks. With stores constantly being shifted forward, it was no mean task to keep the advancing companies supplied with food, ammunition, and clothing, and that it was done without any serious hitch speaks volumes for the devoted men engaged in the task. For them there was no rest. If the battalion halted at nightfall, they did not. On the contrary, it was then that often they knew the greatest exertion and had to make the greatest effort, and it was done, as usual, without complaint. For example, to delay the British advance, the Germans had erected on most of the roads leading from Lens a great number of massive concrete pillars, each two or three feet thick, arranging them in such a manner that no guns or limbers could pass until they had been demolished or until some way around them had been made. With a similar object they had sprung mines at road-junctions. To make up for lost time caused by these obstacles the Transport Section had to work for very long hours. There were others, too, who knew no rest. There were the clerks and staff at Battalion Headquarters, to whom the forward movement was a nightmare. Moving with the battalion by day, at night they would work upon the usual reports and returns for which the British Army was notorious, and perhaps after only an hour's sleep would be awakened at one or two o'clock in the morning to type or write out the operation-orders for the following day. Dispatch riders were constantly arriving to vary orders previously received, or to bring some urgent message that required immediate attention, and at once the Orderly-room, with Sgt. Brooks and his staff, would be a hive of industry. Then there were the signallers, who never for one moment left the companies without communication, who unwound and rewound wire by the mile to ensure that touch should not be lost with Headquarters, and that the weary legs of runners should be saved as much as possible. All these, by working twenty-three hours out of the twenty-four, alone enabled the companies to answer all calls made upon them in the hour of victory.*

The 173rd Inf. Bde., by passing through the outpost line of the *Sixth* on the morning of the 20th, with the 3rd Battalion leading, were now acting as the advance-guard, and thus the battalion were able to drop to the rear and rest for a few days in Nomain; but by the 27th it was on the move again, **Nomain** and that day marched a distance of only six miles, as the crow flies, but double that number by the route which it took through Aix, Rumegies, Howardries, and the beautiful forest of Rongy, to the place of that name. Here, in a village **Rongy** built on the slope of a hill, it remained for a few days, with Battalion Headquarters comfortably housed in a pleasant villa overlooking the dwellings which sheltered the companies lower down the hill. Rongy was practically intact when the battalion entered it, but only a day or two was required for it to begin to wear signs of the war. The Germans, forgetful of their exhortations to the British not to shell villages containing civilians, promptly sent high-explosives against Battalion Headquarters, and drenched the lower ground with gas. The owners of the villa in which headquarters had established itself, arrived soon after the occupation and were not a little annoyed to see soldiers in possession of it, but the shell-fire caused them to beat a hasty retreat. For the poor peasantry in the smaller houses at the foot of the hill there was no escape, and they stayed to watch the gradual demolition of the village, and when gassed, retired to cellars with their children to wait until the Germans should continue their easterly march. Meanwhile, the Medical Officer and his staff had much to do looking after them, and there must be many men and women living in that village to-day who date their lives from the time when as children they were tended and protected from gas by the Medical Section.

---

*For small-scale map showing the ground covered during the advance from Lens to Peruwelz, see page 248.

Rongy Beyond Rongy lay the village of Bleharies, just over the Franco-Belgian frontier, and skirting its eastern side was the Escaut River, the main waterway from Tournai to Valenciennes, which for some days provided the Germans with a natural fortification. The river, here deeply dredged and provided with steep banks and towing-paths, served as a canal and had a width of almost fifty yards. Fighting a rear-guard action with the now urgent necessity of delaying the British advance, the Germans lined the further bank with machine-guns and fired whenever targets presented themselves, thus showing their determination to hold the position as long as possible. To dislodge them from it seemed to be well-nigh impossible; and no one was more surprised than the Commanding Officer, when he received verbal orders from the Brigade Commander that the attempt was to be made by the *Sixth*. Colonel Benson remonstrated; the task would be beyond any troops unless there were weeks of artillery preparation and even then hazardous in the extreme. The only means of crossing the water would be by means of rafts, and the chances of their being launched and ferried across without the enemy garrison becoming aware of the movement were remote—so remote that he felt instinctively that the whole fantastic operation would be doomed to failure from the outset. He protested again and again and finally demanded written orders before he would comply with them.

They came, and preparations for the assault went forward. The *Sixth* had arrived in Rongy on October 27th, and before the end of the month, *Rumegies* companies were marching daily to the village of Rumegies, where there was a château with a moat. Here they could practice the forthcoming operation. Rafts capable of bearing four or five men were constructed out of tarpaulin sheets and brushwood, launched into the water, and propelled over it; and the most likely way of getting to the farther bank seemed to be for one or two good swimmers first to make the crossing and then to haul over the rafts, none of which proved to be stable. The greatest difficulty was found to lie in landing from them when the farther bank was reached, and what would happen in the dark hour before dawn with a vigilant enemy firing at any faintly discerned object moving on the water could only be conjectured.

In spite of the overwhelming objections the plan held, and the battalion *Bleharies* moved into Bleharies at 11 a.m. on November 8th ready to attempt the passage of the river on the following morning. But there was an anti-climax to the tragic act which had been staged: that very night the Germans retired, and before long men who but a few hours earlier had not dared to contemplate what their end might be were joking as they crossed a rickety bridge hastily constructed of tubs and planks, over which went men, horses, and transport of every description. At the best of times such a crossing would have been something of an adventure, and on this occasion the risk was intensified by the near presence of a battery of hostile field-guns which directed a steady fire against it. Happily, casualties were few, and it is interesting to note that the last two men of the *Sixth* to be wounded were Rfm. J. Farmer and Rfm. Pipe, both of whom were treated for wounds at the Aid Post in a brewery by the side of the river, and dispatched to the rear. The crossing of the Escaut had commenced at 4 p.m., and thus the battalion was able to make some progress in an easterly direction before night fell, when it took up positions in close support to the 2nd Battalion, with Headquarters at Cin. **Bleharies**

The action at the Escaut was the last for which the *Sixth* was to prepare; thereafter it met with no opposition. Advancing on the 9th, it covered a distance of about ten miles, halting at nightfall at Roucourt and Bitremont, with the Transport Section and " details " at Jerusalem, a tiny village to the west of Callenelle, remembered as much for its name as for some dead German soldiers lying in the roadway, and on the next day, after the 7th Battalion had passed through its outpost line, it marched eastwards to Beloeil, a market town of considerable size, and there spent the night. The entry into Beloeil was made memorable by the enthusiastic reception given to the battalion as it traversed the principal square, into which the whole town had crowded to cheer their deliverers. The inhabitants of every village through which the battalion had passed had shown in one way or another their joy in release from four years of servitude, and some of the scenes which it had witnessed were painful in the extreme. All able-bodied young men and women, so it was said, had been carried back by the retreating Germans to do work on their final defences, and only the old, the infirm, and the young remained to welcome the advancing platoons, which sometimes saw only a string of aged people weeping with emotion, and by them a group of undernourished, frightened children. But at Beloeil it was different; here the *Sixth* was welcomed vociferously, with the town band (whose instruments, it was said, had lain buried throughout the war) playing over and over again, and in the slowest possible time, the British national anthem. Here were flags of all the allied countries flying from the windows (one wondered from where the inhabitants got them) and here there was royal hospitality as soon as the companies were given their billeting areas, and dismissed. **Roucourt** **Jerusalem** **Beloeil**

Undoubtedly the War was drawing to a close, but how soon it would be over no one knew. There were rumours of revolts in the German Army, and during its march from Lens, the battalion had frequently passed groups of dead Germans who it was said had paid the penalty for disobedience. But

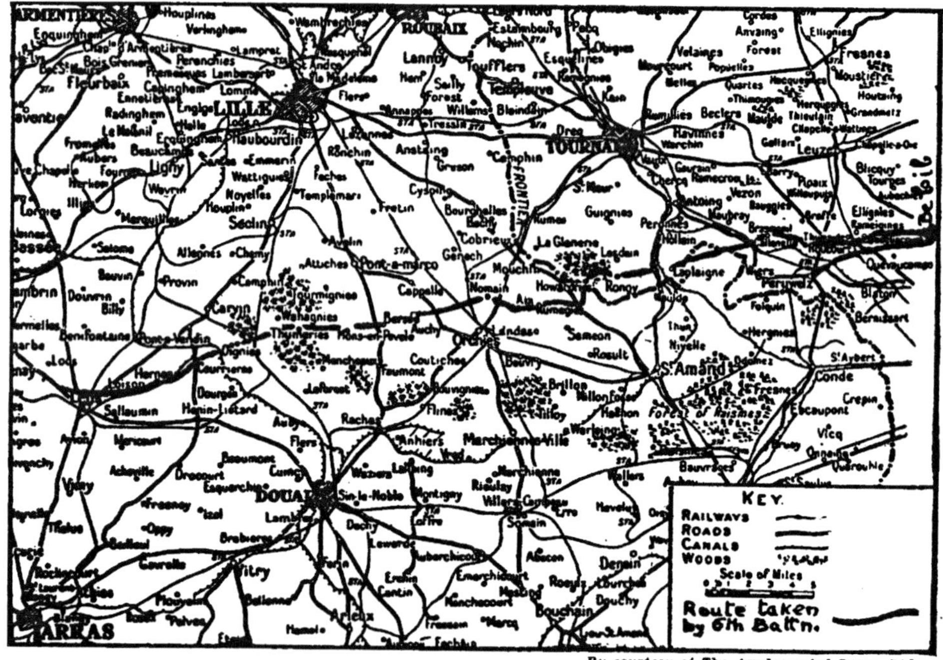

By courtesy of The Amalgamated Press, Ltd.

MAP 17.—FROM LENS TO PERUWELZ.

BATTALION OFFICERS, WARRANT OFFICERS and SECTION COMMANDERS at

THE FINAL ADVANCE

OFFICER COMMANDING :	SECOND-IN-COMMAND :	ADJUTANT :
COL. BENSON	MAJOR BOOTHBY	(1) CAPT. COOKE
R.S.MAJ. BOSS		(2) CAPT. GODFREY
		R.Q.M.SGT. SIMMONDS
A Co. CAPT. JOHNSTON	SGT. T. ABBOTT	C.Q.M.SGT. WILLIAMS
B Co. CAPT. IDRIS	C.S.MAJ. MONTIER	C.Q.M.SGT. SIRED
C Co. CAPT. BUBB	C.S.MAJ. MACLEAN-CANNON	C.Q.M.SGT. DAVIES
D Co. LIEUT. BALL	C.S.MAJ. GRUNDY	SGT. DRURY

Quartermaster : CAPT. LOVETT
Transport : CAPT. BRASHER ; SGT. PRICE ; CPL. DORLING.
Cook : SGT. BUCKLAND
Stretcher-Bearers : SGT. WADE ; CPL. BRETT
Signallers : SGT. SHARP ; SGT. BURKE
Scouts and Snipers : LIEUT. FIELD ; SGT. WINNUP

Top: THE "FIRST" TRANSPORT SECTION.
Middle: GROOMS MEDHURST, EMERY, M.S.M., AND DOUBLEDAY, SGT. ANDREWS AND CPL. DORLING, M.S.M.
Bottom: THE TRANSPORT SECTION IN GERMANY, 1919.

Plate 53

BELŒIL.—THE PALATIAL HOME OF THE PRINCE DE LIGNE WHERE THE BATTALION SPENT A NIGHT TWO DAYS PRIOR TO THE ANNOUNCEMENT OF THE ARMISTICE.

TOURNAI.—WHERE DURING THE ARMISTICE BRIG.-GEN. MILDREN HELD THE POST OF MILITARY GOVERNOR.

BASECLES.—A NEIGHBOURING VILLAGE OF PERUWELZ WHERE MANY MEMBERS OF THE BATTALION FOUND AMUSEMENT IN ITS DANCING SALON.

PERUWELZ.—THE MAIN SQUARE WHERE THE 174TH BRIGADE HELD A TORCHLIGHT PROCESSION TO CELEBRATE THE ARMISTICE.

HIS MAJESTY KING GEORGE V. ON HIS VISIT TO PERUWELZ DURING THE BATTALION'S STAY OF THREE MONTHS PRIOR TO ITS TRANSFER TO THE RHINE. BRIG.-GEN. MAXWELL CAN BE SEEN ON LEFT FOREGROUND OF PICTURE.

Plate 55

COLONEL R. BOOTHBY. T.D.
Commanding 1921-25.

COLONEL E. W. HUGHES, D.S.O., M.C., T.D. Commanding 1925-29.

MAJOR E. CLAY, M.B.E.,
Adjutant Reserve Bn.

MAJOR M. BULLER, M.C.
Adjutant 1926-29.

Plate 56

POST-WAR COOKS—SHOWING WEIR, WHITE, BAILEY AND CLIFTON, WHO SAW SERVICE WITH "FIRST" AND "SECOND" BATTALIONS.

"SECOND" BATTALION COOKS—SGT. C. BUCKLAND AND HIS MERRY MEN WHO "SERVED" SO WELL AT THE FRONT.

"RESERVE" BATTALION COOKS.

THE LAST GROUP OF OFFICERS OF THE "SIXTH" TAKEN ON FOREIGN SOIL. DECEMBER, 1918. (PERUWELZ).

It is interesting to note that Col. Benson (2nd/6th) has Major Boothby and Major Rose-Innes, two "1914" 1st/6th officers, on either side of him.

ONE OF THE PARADES IN THE DOM SQUARE, COLOGNE, IN WHICH THE BATTALION PARTICIPATED, 1919.

whatever truth there was in this, one thing was certain, that whenever the enemy had made a stand, there had been no sign of such disintegration. Thus, when on November 11th, the battalion paraded and moved out of Beloeil to continue the advance, it had no reason to suppose that that day would differ much from those that had immediately preceded it. The five companies were moving at intervals along the road to Grosage, the rank and file doubtless regretting bitterly that the stay in Beloeil was of such short duration, when about twenty minutes to eleven o'clock, Brig.-General A. Maxwell, commanding the brigade, rode up to the Adjutant and asked him where the Commanding Officer might be. The Adjutant replied that he did not know, but supposed him to be with the Headquarters Company. "Very well," said the Brigade Commander, "but I suppose you know the armistice commences at eleven hours?" And he added, as the officer looked at his watch: "Don't let there be any 'mafeking'!" *Grosage*

The Adjutant saluted, turned his horse in the direction of the leading company, rode towards it, and gave the news to the company commander in a voice loud enough to be heard at least by the leading files. The Company Commander nodded gloomily, a few enthusiasts raised a half-hearted cheer, and the company marched on. Soon, the Adjutant reached the second company, and again delivered the message, and was surprised to see the entire company halt and fall out on the roadside. It didn't occur to him that by now the time for the customary ten-minute halt had arrived, and for the moment he thought that this company had shown its feelings by immediately "downing-tools," and it was not until he came to the remaining companies, all fallen-out by the roadside, that he realised the meaning of the second company's extraordinary behaviour. For the British Army, the War finished not at 11 a.m., as is supposed, but at ten minutes to that hour.

* * * * *

"When this ruddy war is over,
Oh, how happy I shall be:
When this ruddy war is over,
No more soldiering for me."

One wondered how the *Sixth* would accustom itself to the idea of waiting, inactive, until orders to demobilise should be received. What an immense business that would be! The whole country was organised for war, and too much in the direction of demobilisation could not be done until it was certain

R

Grosage that Germany was beaten—beaten beyond recovery in a military sense. And when would that be known, and how long would one have to wait? The questions that posed themselves now that war had ceased were so immense that one's mind boggled at them. Very well, then: if there was to be a period of waiting it could be spent very pleasantly, provided agreeable billets could be found, and work and play made attractive. Fortunately, the problem had been foreseen, and the first steps to keep the Army happy and contented already taken. At Grosage, within twenty-four hours, came the first instructions to organise education classes to act as a diversion, and to re-equip men who might soon find themselves looking for work, and a few days later orders were received for the battalion to move to the much larger market-town of Peruwelz Peruwelz, which with the adjoining village of Bonsecours, was to house the brigade as well as the G.O.C. and the staff of the 58th Division.

The story of the battalion's stay in Peruwelz could well occupy a great deal of space, much of which would necessarily be devoted to the almost lavish hospitality shown to all ranks by the inhabitants, so warm was the welcome given. Most of the billets occupied were situated in or near the ***rue de la pont à là Faulx***, at one end of which, near the market-square, was the Battalion Orderly-room, housed by M. Marlier in one of his two shops. And halfway along the road, on its southern side, stood a large convent, into the schoolrooms of which went the whole of B and C Companies. And very comfortable they were, with bunks for beds, and additional blankets, and trestle tables from which to eat. A and D Companies were equally well provided; and to crown all, the company cooks excelled themselves in providing excellent meals. Perhaps the companies in the convent came off best in this respect, since Colonel Benson, ever resourceful, made a "deal" with the Mother Superior, whereby wheaten flour was drawn from the R.A.S.C. instead of a similar weight in bread, and from it loaves and sometimes rolls were made and baked by the nuns for the troops quartered on them. The Transport Section found accommodation in a factory in Vert Coron, a part of Peruwelz lying behind the convent, but most of its personnel were billeted in the homes of those employed in the factory.

A minimum of work was done. The mornings were devoted to education and training, as few guards as possible were mounted, and "fatigues" were infrequent. For the companies there was, however, the necessity once every four days of providing the fire-picquet, and this and the quarter-guard would parade with other units of the brigade in the square, there to be inspected by the Field-Officer-of-the-day, and after a simple ceremonial, marched off to the accompaniment of whichever battalion band happened to be on duty.

Occasionally, the routine was varied by a route-march or an inspection, and on Sunday there was usually church-parade. Work was over by dinner-time, and the afternoon was given to sport, and the evenings spent variously, as the following account suggests: **Peruwelz**

" The troops enjoyed an unheard-of type of soldiering. The whole brigade was in billets and the civilian population had never known such times. The 58th Divisional Concert Party, ' The Goods,' held nightly concerts, and at Christmas put on a show that would have given credit to anything running in London. On one night a torchlight procession was made by the whole brigade in the square, and it provided a magnificent spectacle. Afterwards, the whole place went mad, soldiers and civilians parading the streets and singing to mouth-organs and accordions the whole night through. Despite the rules and regulations, very few of the rank and file could be found in their billets before the early hours of the morning. Sure enough, the boys were making up for lost time!

" Many good jobs fell to the Transport Section. Well-to-do people of Peruwelz wanted to see relatives and friends living some miles away. The railway track had been blown up, and the station demolished by the departing Germans, and road transport was the only means of travel. Some drivers fell for such jobs as using a draft horse in an old carriage to take a farmer, his wife, and daughter to Lille; another made a journey to Charleroi, another to Tournai; and these three or four-day journeys were splendidly supported by the unstinted generosity of the travellers. The mess-cart was pressed into service to carry the Mother Superior (with an armed escort) to a neighbouring convent, and when on the appointed day for her return she failed to appear (the bad condition of the roads had caused considerable delay) there was a certain amount of alarm and despondency amongst the nuns, and Colonel Benson had to make two or three visits to reassure them that she hadn't been kidnapped by licentious soldiery.

" Football reigned supreme during the months of December and January, and there was much inter-unit sport. All teams played good football, and the final of the inter-battalion competition was played on the home ground between the *Sixth* and the 7th Battalion, the result of the game being a two-all draw. On Saturday, January 11th, the brigade boxing contests took place, and the spectators, including civilians, were treated to some good sport. The best fight of the evening was between Rfm. Jim Lumsden, of the *Sixth*, and the Bugle-Major of the 8th Battalion. The fight was full of thrills, and Jim finally knocked his opponent out.

Peruwelz

"The greatest day's sport came on January 23rd, when the *Sixth* organised a real, live race-meeting at Blaton. The judge was Brig.-Gen. Maxwell; Lieut. W. H. Brasher acted as Clerk-of-the-course; Sgt. Price as Clerk-of-the-scales (ammunition was used as weights for the riders); and the stewards were Colonel Benson, Major Boothby, Capt. Rose-Innes, and Capt. Johnston. Sgt.-Cook Charlie Buckland was the only recognised bookmaker on the course, who with his clerk, Sgt. Lacey, set up the Old Firm of 'Lacem & Bunkum.' There were many races, the five-furlong being won by Colonel Benson's *Molly*, rider, Bill Lister; and another over the same distance by 'Stiffy' Hilliard, on *Gelly*. The fourth race caused much amusement when all the entries proved to be heavy draft-horses, to trot four furlongs. It was won by Driver Emery, on his own *Tab*. So far the bookmaker had not done too badly, but he came to pieces in the open event when fifteen horses entered for the steeplechase. Somone had some inside information about a horse named *Longfellow*, ridden by a mounted military policeman, and several put their all on the outsider at twenty-to-one. It was an easy first, and the bookmaker didn't get away."

By the middle of February the terms upon which an armistice had been granted to Germany had been sufficiently fulfilled to warrant an immediate reduction in the number of men under arms in France. Until then only men in key industries had been released from service, but now orders were received to the effect that anyone who could show a letter from a former employer, promising immediate employment, might be demobilised, and the response to this offer was sufficiently great to keep the Battalion Orderly-room staff working as they had rarely worked before. For each man about seven different forms had to be completed, and the number of officers' signatures on them sometimes exceeded a dozen. On one memorable occasion the work of completing forms and signing them went on all night.

Demobilisation

The routine for those about to be demobilised was almost invariably the same. After a medical and kit inspection, the draft would assemble with all their military possessions and papers, to say nothing of a great many souvenirs; the Commanding Officer would wish them God-speed; and lorries would carry them to the nearest railhead, where they would entrain for the base, arriving at their destination in very much quicker time than had been taken in reaching the front. Then they would embark, and on arrival in England, would be dispatched as soon as possible to the various demobilisation stations. Here the drafts first of all would be ushered into a large shed resembling the big customs-rooms at the larger ports. On one side of a bench were men who checked all the military kit handed in; the first man would take the steel-helmet, the second the gas-mask, the third the entrenching-tool, and another the Webb-equipment, small kit, and so on, until by the time a man reached the end of the bench he would be wearing, in addition to his underclothes, only trousers, jacket, puttees, boots, and cap. The soldier (for he was still that) then passed into another shed, where he was offered a 30s. suit. This he could refuse, preferring his account to be credited with the amount (and most men chose the alternative) in which case he was free to walk away in the khaki that had served him for so many years, conscious of the fact that he was no longer under military discipline. At first, the new-found freedom seemed more than a little strange, and it was difficult to accustom oneself to the idea that now there was nobody to give one orders, and that the responsibility of the next step had to be born alone. Nor did the novelty wear off in a month or two; there are few who have served for any length of time in the army who do not feel on occasion that something is missing from their civilian lives, and sigh for the days when life was orderly and work regular. **Peruwelz**

It will be remembered that in January, 1918, when the two service battalions of the *Sixth* were amalgamated, many officers and men of the 1st/6th Bn. were drafted to the 1st/15th Bn. and the 1st/18th Bn., London Regt., both units forming part of the 47th Division; and although that division saw heavy fighting throughout the summer, by good fortune many of those then transferred were still alive when the armistice was signed on November 11th. They had lived through the anxious days of March and April and had resisted stubbornly all the German attacks upon them, retiring only when the situation on their flanks and particularly in the south rendered that course necessary. The 47th Division was on the extreme right of the Third Army and thus responsible for its right flank, and in the discharge of this heavy responsibility it gave renewed evidence of its fighting qualities and power of manœuvre. Its operations were over ground familiar to many then still serving in the Division who had fought on the Somme in 1916, and when the German offensive had spent itself, and the time had come for the counter-stroke in August, and the Division had replaced the losses it had sustained, it stood firmly on ground a little west of Albert, ready for retaliation. In the previous May the 47th Division came under the command of the III Corps which held also the 18th and 58th Divisions, and thus during the operations of August and September, two London Divisions were fighting shoulder to shoulder, and the 6th Bn. was often close enough to the 15th and 18th Bns. for friends to meet.*

*See page 215.

Before the end of September, 1918, the 47th Division moved north preparatory, it was believed, to relieving the 7th Division in Italy. Indeed, on the 27th it was concentrated in the neighbourhood of St. Pol, and was on the point of departure when orders were received for it to take part in what proved to be the final advance. The Germans were retreating rapidly, and General Mildren's 141st Infantry Brigade was hurried forward to get in touch with the enemy. On October 2nd the brigade advanced across the Aubers Ridge, overcoming such resistance as was offered by the German machine-gunners, and at the end of a fortnight was at the gates of Lille. The Army Commander's formal entry did not take place, however, until the 28th of the month, when leading the 47th Division into the town at ten o'clock in the morning, he performed the official act of liberation. "It was 'roses, roses all the way.' The tricolour was flying everywhere—with extemporised versions of the Union Jack and American and Belgian flags. Several hundred small flags adorned the rifles and equipment of our units, and flowers were on the guns. Brass bands played, and great crowds along the roads and at every window cheered and sang as the troops marched by."*

Soon the head of the procession reached the Grande Place and an exchange of flags took place between the Army Commander and the Mayor, who together then mounted a grandstand where the various commanders and a number of distinguished people, including the Secretary of State for War, Mr. Winston Churchill, were assembled to watch the 47th Division march past.

After a few days rest in Lille, the Division advanced to the west bank of the Scheldt, just north of Tournai, to relieve the 57th Division, and in these positions they remained for a week; but on November 8th, civilians crossed the river with the information that the Germans had withdrawn, and on the following day, after the river had been bridged, the advance continued. Two days later, while the 47th Division was in the neighbourhood of Tournai, the armistice was declared, and the 141st Infantry Brigade took over that town, Brig.-Gen. Mildren becoming its military governor. A fortnight later, however, the Division moved back and occupied villages lying to the west of Lille, and in them commenced its education classes, and made preparations for demobilisation, which began in earnest early in 1919, the *cadres* of the different units returning in May to England, where the artillery and infantry were demobilised respectively, at Shoreham and Felixstowe.

March, 1919, saw the *Sixth* still at Peruwelz, literally growing fat on the land. Nearly all were anxious for demobilisation, and because of this, and

*From the *History of the 47th Division.*

because they recognised the utter impossibility of dismissing the entire British Army, the utmost was made of all the many diversions provided. It ought to be recorded here that rumours reached the battalion of a military revolt at one of the bases, and also that one of the battalions of the brigade showed some unrest. But from officers and men of the *Sixth* there was never a regrettable act of any kind during this difficult month, and that alone speaks volumes for the spirit of mutual understanding and comradeship to which testimony has been paid on more than one occasion in these pages. The month was made memorable by a surprise visit of His Majesty King George V, who, accompanied by the Duke of Windsor, then H.R.H. the Prince of Wales, was at the time making a tour of the Belgian provinces to see his army now occupying territory in the liberation of which so much sacrifice had been made. Typically, he asked that there should be no ceremonial parade to welcome him, but that his London troops might see him as normally Londoners would, standing as a crowd at the side of the road as he passed them. The market-place was thronged for the occasion, and one wondered how it would be possible for his Majesty's motor-car to make its way through the press, and it was with feelings of surprise and delight that the troops learnt that it was not to make the attempt and that he was coming to them on foot.

Visit of H.M. King George V.

Stooping slightly, the King walked slowly through the crush, the narrowest of paths being kept open for him. He went directly to the Hotel-de-Ville, stayed there for a few minutes (while his son stood on the steps watching and enjoying the antics of an over-zealous gendarme) and then, continuing his walk, he crossed the square. Up to this time the crowd—for such it was—had remained quite silent, and then someone sent up a cheer, and the spell was broken; from two thousand throats came spontaneously a roar of applause which must have been heard a mile away. This was the third time during the war that the battalion had been privileged by a personal contact with the King, and it was deeply appreciative of his visit.

On the Rhine

Towards the end of the month the battalion learnt with pride that it had been selected as representative of the 58th Division to become part of the Allied Army of Occupation on the Rhine, and immediately all was activity. Officers, non-commissioned officers, and men were drafted to it from other units, and preparations made for the easterly march. For the remaining few days at Peruwelz the time was spent in overhauling kit and stores and in training the new arrivals (many of them old soldiers) in the intricacies of rifle-drill. Then, early in April, after many a fond farewell, the *Sixth* paraded for the last time in the square at Peruwelz, and received an ovation from the inhabitants as it marched away. Much could be told of the memorable journey across Belgium into Germany, and of the many pleasant months spent among a people who by their friendly behaviour could scarcely be thought of as former enemies; but every tale must have an end, and the fact that by now most of those who had enlisted in the *Sixth* were back in England, demands that most attention should be given to them. Suffice it to say, therefore, that the battalion remained in Germany until August, when, reduced to a *cadre*, it was brought back to England by Capt. Etheredge; and if there was nobody to welcome them on arrival, nor band to play them into the drill-hall, it must not be supposed that all interest in the battalion had been lost. If the truth were known, the probability is that the notification of its arrival came too late for a proper reception to be arranged. Be that as it may; here it is sufficient to remark that in a sense such a return was typical of the battalion's whole attitude towards life. The *Sixth* had a regard for itself; it came and went without fuss or flurry; it discharged the duties entrusted to it to the best of its ability, confident in the belief that if it failed, few other battalions could succeed; it expected neither praise nor blame; and it courted no publicity. Its ranks were made up of volunteers, joined together for a common purpose. The essence of the unwritten contract was that there should be sincere effort and willing co-operation; and if at times discipline was necessarily severe, never for one moment did it overshadow that mutual understanding and comradeship which ultimately was the basis of all its achievement.

Home With the return of the *cadre*, the battalion in its entirety was now in England. The War was truly over. The curtain had fallen on an heroic act; that it would rise again for the *Sixth* to play another in an atmosphere of peace was the confident hope of all.

EPILOGUE

Unlike many European countries, England immediately after the War presented a spectacle of almost unparalleled prosperity. The difficulties of settling demobilised soldiers in their old jobs or in new ones, envisaged as immense, proved in the event to be wholly false. There was a demand for labour everywhere. But the trading boom lasted little more than a year, and before long the country was facing the first of a series of slumps.

The reconstitution of the Territorial Force, soon to be known as the Territorial Army, must be considered in relation to this national set-back, for unless it is, the difficulty of recruitment cannot be understood. There were other factors militating against enlistment in any of the Armed Forces of the Crown. The country had been at war. Nothing was wanted to remind the citizen of it. Further, the era of world peace had been inaugurated, and henceforth the nations would settle their disputes amicably. Thus the *need* for enlistment was not felt.

At the time of the Armistice, the *Reserve* battalion was at Blackdown; but before long it moved to a camp at Mitchett, in Surrey, near the Ash ranges, where demobilisation commenced, recruits being sent to the depôt at Catterick. As soon as the battalion had been reduced to *cadre* strength, Colonel Whitehead, then in command, Captain Clay, the Adjutant, the four Company Commanders, with other officers and warrant-officers occupying key positions, came to the Headquarters at 57a, Farringdon Road, and as and when the various accounts were audited and found correct, they, too, were demobilised; and somewhere in its archives the battalion possesses a personal letter of congratulation from Earl Haig on the work done by the *Reserve*.

Meanwhile, the Government of the day had decided to reconstitute the Territorial Force, and before the summer of 1919 began, Brig.-Gen. Mildren had been offered and had accepted the position of Honorary Colonel of the 6th Bn., London Regt., Lt.-Col. R. C. Boothby, T.D., had been appointed to command the battalion, and Captain Clay, M.B.E., posted to it as its Adjutant. The battalion was to form part of the 2nd London Infantry Brigade (56th Division), its units being the 5th, 6th, 7th, and 8th Battalions, London Regiment. Brig.-Gen. A. Maxwell, who had last commanded the equivalent brigade in France, became its new commander.

To Capt. Clay, whose organising ability has already been commented upon in these pages, virtually fell the task of raising the new unit. With characteristic energy he set about inquiring of those who had served in the battalion whether they wished to continue their service, and soon had the names of many willing officers and men. A committee consisting of

Brig.-Gen. Maxwell, Lt.-Col. Boothby, and Col. Bates (5th Bn.), with Capt. Clay as secretary, selected the officers during 1920, and before the year was out the list was complete. Major E. W. Hughes rejoined the unit as its Second-in-Command, and the four Company Commanders appointed were Major M. J. Macdonald (A), Captain J. S. Macdonald (B), Capt. Cannon (C), and Capt. J. Thomson (D). Recruiting commenced in earnest in the autumn of 1920, and was continued into the spring of the following year; but progress was slow, and the figure of two hundred active members was scarcely reached when an event occurred which might well have been disastrous for the new Territorial Army.

One of the few trades which showed immediate signs of being adversely affected by the War from the point of view of employment, was that of coal-mining. Unemployment and short hours were a rule throughout nearly all the coalfields. The miners struck, demanding, amongst other things, the nationalisation of the mines, and the Government, regarding the industrial dispute as a threat to the political constitution of the country, decided to take measures to ensure their having a military force at their disposal should the threat take a militant form. The decision was therefore taken to raise a Defence Force, and to use the Territorial Army organisation as a basis upon which to build it. Recruiting opened in May, 1921, and many serving members of the battalion enlisted for a period of three months in the 6th. Bn. London Regt. (Defence Force). The three months were spent under canvas, first on Wormwood Scrubs, where tents were pitched in the biting cold of a late spring, and after a couple of weeks, in the more attractive Victoria Park. The battalion was not employed in any civil disturbance, and, indeed, rarely went beyond the park gates, except to fire the musketry course.

Service in the Defence Force drew to a close in July, 1921, when preparations for annual training, this year to be held at Dover, were begun. The Territorial Army's year commenced on November 1st, and as soon as the battalion reassembled after its customary break following camp, plans were laid for an intensification of winter activities, including the training of companies and specialist sections. The conditions governing the competitions for the various battalion challenge shields and cups were overhauled, the miniature rifle range put in order, and arrangements made for a rifle meeting to be held in the coming summer. Committees had been formed in the previous year to deal with such matters as battle honours, a proposed War Memorial, and the writing of the battalion's history.

With the spring and summer of 1922, training out-of-doors became regular. An Easter " camp " at Aldershot with the Argyll and Sutherland Highlanders was followed by musketry week-ends at Purfleet, the battalion rifle-meeting at which the various rifle and Lewis-gun competitions were decided, summer camp at Lyndhurst, and a series of week-end tactical schemes organised by companies for their officers and non-commissioned officers, which continued into the spring of 1923. Of all the work that was done in that year, perhaps the last mentioned, when parties of between twenty and twenty-five spent Saturdays and Sundays in such delightful surroundings as Loughton, working hard and playing hard, will be best remembered. Indoor activities were by no means confined to drill and weapon-training; there were, indeed, many social events, ranging from company sing-songs to gymnastic classes, not to mention the sergeants' dinners and dances, and the children's party, which, by their very nature, were confined, however, to the few.

Thus was spent the year of 1922, and succeeding years saw much the same activity, which increased rather than diminished. In April, 1923, Capt. M. L. Buller, M.C., of the K.R.R.C., was appointed as Adjutant to the battalion in the place of Capt. Clay,* whose tenure had come to an end; but the unit was not, fortunately, to lose the latter's services. There was no one serving who knew the battalion so intimately as he, and his retention as Quartermaster was a happy solution to a real difficulty. In the following year, Lt.-Col. Boothby resigned his command, and his place was taken by Lt.-Col. E. W. Hughes, D.S.O., M.C., for the last three years the Second-in-Command. Col. Hughes' war-time experience, both with the battalion and on the staff, was of inestimable value during a difficult period, and under him the battalion made steady progress towards real efficiency. But the question of increasing the strength of the unit was a burning one not only with the *Sixth* but with other units of the brigade. Indeed, except in the north of England, recruiting had come almost to a standstill, due, largely, it was thought, to the widespread belief following the inauguration of the Defence Force, that upon the Territorial Army organisation there could at any time be built a force to be used in an industrial dispute. It could hardly be expected when such views were widely voiced that recruiting would be brisk, and the reduction of the bounty from £5 to £1 15s. did not help matters.

Camps were held in 1924 at Felixstowe, and in 1925 and 1926 at Aldershot, the last being not so well attended as those previously held, perhaps partly on account of the facts to which allusion has already been made and partly to the General Strike of the previous May when the Territorial Army organisation was again used by the Government to uphold public order, this time to form a Civil Constabulary Reserve. Before this period is left, reference

*Later, Major Clay.

ought to be made to the ceremonial parades other than its own in which the battalion took part. Chief of these was on November 11th in each year, when contingents took part in the ceremonies at the Cenotaph in Whitehall and at the London Troops Memorial at the Royal Exchange. Sometimes, too, the battalion had a composite platoon marching in the Lord Mayor's Show, and always had its contingent lining the route at special events, such as the marriage of their present Majesties, and of H.R.H. Princess Mary to Lord Lascelles. A review in 1926 by H.M. King George V in Hyde Park of all London Territorial units provided a never-to-be-forgotten spectacle for all who witnessed it. The battalion's own ceremonial event was the annual church parade in September when divine service was attended, first at the church of St. Andrew, Holborn, and later at St. Bride's Church, Fleet Street. After the service the battalion would march to the London Troops Memorial, deposit a wreath at its foot, and on returning to the drill-hall place a second wreath before the Memorial: but in a sense this parade, at which past members of the battalion predominated, came to be identified with the Old Comrades' Association, and is referred to in that connection below. Yet another important annual event was the Distribution of Prizes when the Honorary Colonel presented shields, silver cups, and trophies to those teams and individuals successful in winning the various battalion competitions. On these occasions a dais erected in front of the Memorial would sparkle with dozens of massive silver prizes and their smaller replicas, while below it and to one side stood an oak tripod supporting the bell of the s.s. Marguerite, the ship that carried the *First* to France in 1915, saved from the scrap-heap by Major H. D. Myer, and presented by him to the battalion.

During the command of Lt.-Col. Hughes an official visit to the battlefields took place. The occasion was the unveiling of a memorial cross at High Wood to those of the 47th Division who fell fighting during that battle. Contingents were provided by all units of the Division, that from the *Sixth* including the Commanding Officer, the Second-in-Command, R.Q.M.Sgt. Percivall, C.Q.M.Sgt. Kent, and others. Present at the ceremony were General Gorringe, General Thwaites, and Brig.-Gen. Maxwell.

Capt. Buller's appointment as Adjutant came to an end in 1937, and his place was taken, first by Capt. P. G. Bower, and shortly afterwards by Capt. J. W. S. Maclure, both of the "60th Rifles." Capt Maclure, the elder son of Colonel Sir John Maclure, Bart., like Capt. Buller, had seen a good deal of active service, and like him was a most valuable addition to the battalion. The following year saw the appointment of Lt.-Col. M. J. Macdonald, M.C., as the Commanding Officer; and during his tenure of command a number of major and minor changes were introduced. First amongst these was the short-lived but none-the-less important alteration in the organisation of the infantry battalion which was to become a self-contained unit, with its light anti-tank guns, its mortars, its machine-guns, as well as its rifle-sections with their light automatics, and the change threw a good deal of strain both on Battalion Headquarters, Company Officers, and instructors, to say nothing of the rank and file who had to learn how to handle the new weapons. Annual training in 1927 was at Falmer, and in 1928 and 1929 at Shorncliffe and Aldershot respectively. The last year had seen the battalion with the Royal Engineers at Chatham learning the mysteries of Kapoc-bridging, and the success of the whole year's work left the impression that the battalion was at long last bearing the fruit, in the shape of increased numbers and efficiency, of the work of the devoted few who had served it continuously since the end of the War. In this regard mention should be made of two members of the *Sixth* who perhaps more than anyone typified the spirit of the battalion; R.Q.M.Sgt. T. W. Percivall, who had been with it continuously since 1895 doing active service both in South Africa and during the Great War, and C.Q.M.Sgt. F. G. Kent, whose enlistment dated from 1893 and who by 1929 had seen thirty-six years' continuous service. Both of these warrant-officers were awarded bars to their Long-Service Medals. Of lesser importance to be recorded was the commencement (1928) of the publication of a Quarterly Journal in which summaries of the first drafts of this *History* appeared. Little or nothing had been accomplished by the original committee, owing to lack of material, and the publication of a journal was the obvious way to start it. Moreover, the journal provided a link between past and serving members; and it ran for three years.

Throughout Lt.-Col. Macdonald's command sustained efforts were made, not without success, to increase the number of serving members. Realising the truth of the old adage that variety is the spice of life, much patient thought was given to making the work of the young soldier both interesting and stimulating, and this is exemplified by the pains taken to attract members to the voluntary Easter "camps." Kapoc-bridge building with the Royal Engineers has already been noted; but the previous year had seen the 6th and 7th Battalions as friendly enemies in battle at Bodiam. The *Sixth* was moved by water from London Bridge to Chatham, thence by R.A.S.C. vehicles to the battlefield; and after the affray was over, and lessons had been learnt, there were opportunities for enjoying the lavish hospitality extended by those over whose ground the battle had been fought. The Easter "camps" with the K.R.R.C. in 1927 at Winchester and with the Royal Marines in 1928 at

Eastney were remembered with equal enthusiasm by those who attended them. Taken together, these four novel attempts to arouse interest and aid recruiting typify the energetic thought given to the questions of training and strength in numbers.

Reference has already been made to the extra activities of the battalion in connection with both its work and play. To these in course of time were added the Divisional Rifle Meeting, usually held at Rainham or Purfleet, the *Daily Telegraph* field-firing competition at Pirbright, in which platoons drawn from all the battalions in the Division competed, and the Divisional Individual Boxing Championship.

In 1933 Major A. T. Cannon, T.D., who since Col. Macdonald's appointment had been Second-in-Command, was appointed as Commanding Officer. Lt.-Col. Cannon, as he became on appointment, had had a remarkable career in the *Sixth,* enlisting first as a boy in the band and serving in every rank, non-commissioned, warrant, and commissioned, which an infantry battalion could offer, and now he was to see the fulfilment of his dreams. Throughout his career he had set a splendid example of devotion to duty before, during, and after the War, and he deserved the reward he received for his long labours; and there was no one who was not proud to think that the *Sixth* was a unit in which a man might rise from the lowest to the highest rank. Col. Cannon's marked tenacity of purpose and his capacity of adapting himself to any altered circumstance enabled him to grapple successfully with the decision to convert the *Sixth* into a Searchlight Battalion of the Royal Engineers. The change officially took place in 1936, but it was not until the spring of 1938 that the battalion moved from its Headquarters in Farringdon Road to more commodious premises at Morden, in which neighbourhood it was understood the battalion would operate in the event of war. This change of both role and place necessitated a change of title, which was altered to "31st (C.L.R.) Anti-Aicraft Battalion, Royal Engineers."

No account of the post-war history of the *Sixth* would be complete without extensive reference to the Old Comrades' Association which through difficult days kept together more past members of a battalion than any unit in the Army, and made solid achievements in the direction of their welfare. Its re-formation after the war was largely due to Capt. F. H. H. Thomas, O.B.E., T.D., whose remarkable service in the battalion extended from the early 'nineties. The Association had for its objects that of fostering comradeship amongst its members, of arranging reunions and entertainments, and of assisting its members in need of help in any practical way that might suggest itself. In all three directions successive committees elected at Annual General

Meetings held in the March of each year surpassed previous efforts, and under the chairmanship of Mr. A. F. Papworth, the Association went from strength to strength and from activity to activity. Much of its membership was derived from the Amalgamated Press, Ltd., and the South Metropolitan Gas Company, by whom many past and serving members were employed and thus were almost daily in touch with one another, facilitating the Association's business.

The main events of the year, other than the reunions which in 1924 began to be held at regular monthy intervals, and the dances and smoking concerts held periodically, were the Annual Memorial Service, to which reference has already been made, and at which as many as six hundred would attend, the annual dinner, held in the drill-hall, and in more recent years the annual visit to the battlefields, or more correctly to the cemeteries in which lie buried those who made the supreme sacrifice during the War. This event and the memorial service in St. Bride's Church was intimately linked with the large oak and copper memorial recording the names of the fallen erected against the north wall of the drill-hall. Although originally entrusted to a small committee of serving officers, the Old Comrades' Association later played the major part in the raising of the necessary funds, by organising draws and issuing collecting cards for the purpose. Mr. F. W. Hagell, an Old Comrade, designed the memorial, and many Old Comrades were actually employed upon the engraving of the great copper plates bearing the names of the dead, under the direction of Mr. Vincent, whose son was amongst the names recorded. Disaster very nearly overcame the efforts of the combined committee when the fund's bankers closed their doors, but a sympathetic Government made up part of the loss, and an ever-generous patron, General Mildren, made handsome contributions, and thus enabled the work to go on, and it was unveiled on the 27th January, 1923, and dedicated by the Chaplain, the Rev. A. E. Wilkinson. But the Old Comrades' Association had always felt that something more than a material memorial was required if the memory of those who had made the supreme sacrifice was to be perpetuated, and the idea of endowing a bed in a London hospital, mooted by the original organisers of the fund, was enthusiastically taken up by the Association in the same year as the unveiling. Strenuously the committee worked to achieve this object, and had the satisfaction of seeing their labours well rewarded when, on Monday, 2nd November, 1931, the "Mildren" bed was dedicated in St. Bartholomew's Hospital.

The annual dinners in the drill-hall probably had their origin in a similar event organised by Mr. R. D. Ellis for past members of the battalion employed by the South Metropolitan Gas Company. The latter had been held without a break since the end of the War, and the demand for a larger gathering open to all Old Comrades made itself felt. The first of those organised by the committee in March, 1930, was attended by nearly 250, and in other ways was a conspicuous success. Subsequent dinners have seen double that number at table, and all have been marked by that cordiality and mutual understanding which alone is to be found among ex-service men.

The visit to the battlefields and War cemeteries grew out of a short tour organised by Old Comrades of A Company employed by the Amalgamated Press, Ltd., who undertook their first trip in October, 1929, since when it has become a regular feature of the year's programme, and most of the ground fought over by one or other of the two service battalions has been visited on several occasions. No brief description of these pilgrimages—for such they have become—is adequate to describe the deep significance these journeys hold for those going on them, or to convey their sense of gratitude to the committee for organising them, and it will not be attempted.

Names of individuals have been quoted sparingly in this narrative, but it would not be right in referring to these week-end tours without mentioning Messrs. F. S. Stapleton, R. G. Emery, G. R. Doubleday, and R. D. Ellis, all committeemen. The first, accepting the position of Honorary Secretary to the Association on Capt. Thomas' retirement in 1930, willingly sacrificed time, energy, and money on making his tenure of the office wholly successful. Amongst his many innovations was the monthly illustrated Newsletter distributed to every member of the Association, in which was recorded major activities and past and forthcoming events. With the inspiration of General Mildren, the organising ability of Mr. Stapleton, and the devoted work of the Chairman and Committee, the Association was on the firmest possible foundation when these last words were written.

In a special sense an old comrades' association enshrines the spirit of those who have gone before in a far more intimate fashion than can the military unit which gives it its birth, and the 6th Bn., London Regt. Old Comrades' Association is no exception to that rule. A battalion inherits the traditions set up by those who have served in its ranks. It hands them on to an ever-changing personnel. It jealously guards the honour gained for it by its predecessors, and it emulates their example and adopts their spirit. But the hallowed memories, the aches and the pains, the joys and sorrows, all these lie in the breasts of old comrades, locked there, yet linking them inseparably one to another.

So it is with the Old Comrades' Association of the *Sixth*.

OFFICERS IN 1925: MOST HAD BEEN IN ACTION WITH EITHER THE "FIRST" OR "SECOND" BATTALIONS.

THE SERGEANTS' MESS OF 1927 COULD TRULY BOAST OF OVERSEAS SERVICE.

THE MEMORIAL TO THOSE OF THE "SIXTH" WHO FELL IN THE WAR, 1914-1918, SURROUNDING THE MEMORIAL TO THOSE WHO DIED IN THE SOUTH AFRICAN WAR.

Plate 60

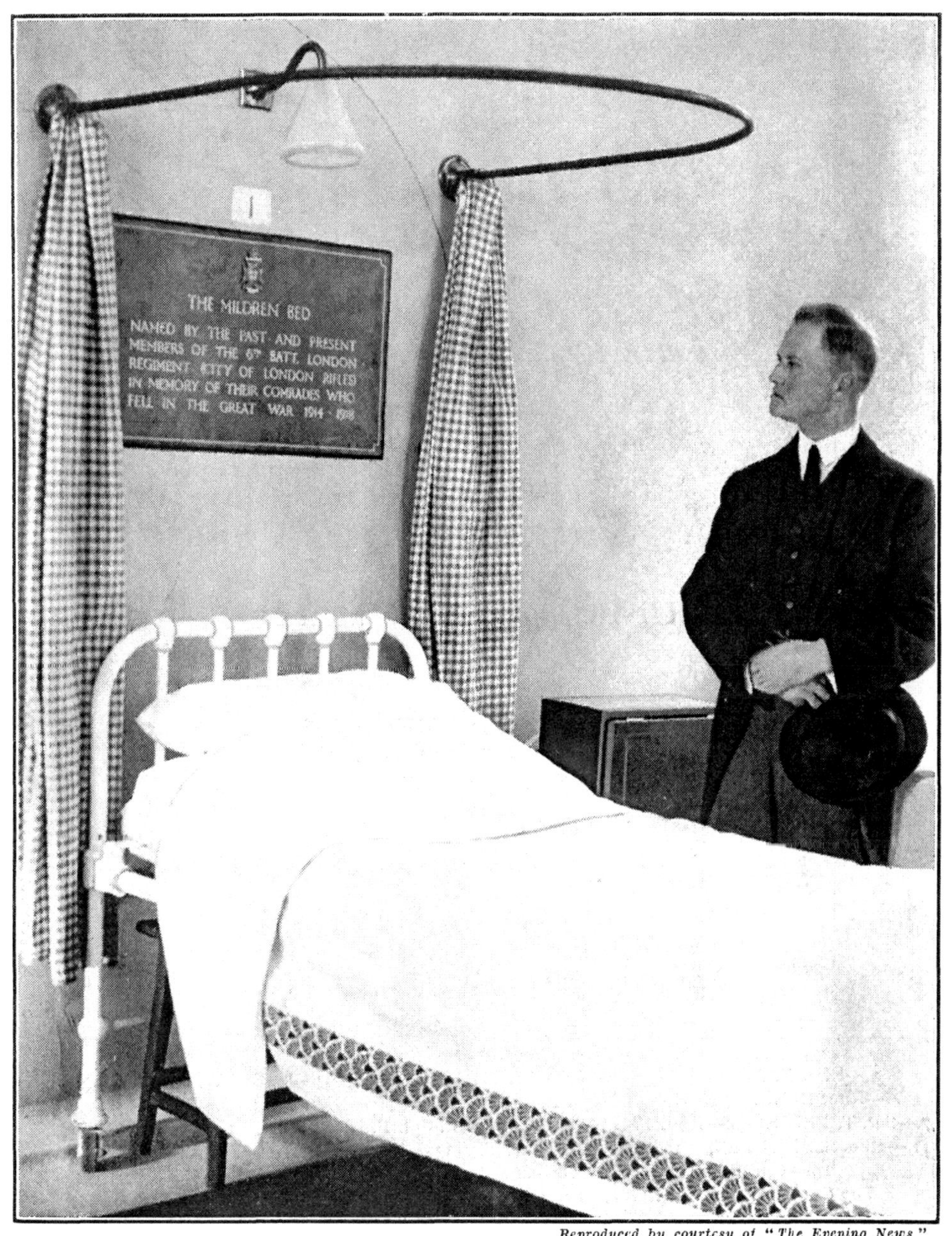

Reproduced by courtesy of "The Evening News"

THE "MILDREN" BED IN ST. BARTHOLOMEW'S HOSPITAL.

Plate 61

1.—Rfm. E. APPLETON, 2.—Rfm. W. THILTHORPE, 3.—L.-Cpl. W. TILLYER, 4.—Rfm. E. N. FRENCH, 5.—Cpl. E. LONSDALE, 6.—Rfm. F. CHALLONER, D.C.M., 7.—Sgt. T. PEILE, 8.—Rfm. F. HANCOCK, 9.—L.-Cpl. F. FREEMAN, 10.—Sgt. G. CRANN, 11.—Rfm. S. SKELTON, 12.—Rfm. H. BLOWS, 13.—Cpl. E. EMERY, 14.—Rfm. R. LYUS, 15.—Cpl. B. HORSMAN, 16.—Sgt. A. SNOW, 17.—Sig. G. JENNINGS.
Top Centre: Rfm. S. HART, *Left:* Rfm. BENNETT, *Right:* Rfm. HAMMOND.

In Memoriam

"They faced the foe as they drew near him in the strength of their own manhood; and when the shock of battle came, they chose rather to suffer the utmost than to win life by weakness . . . . So they gave their bodies to the commonwealth and received, each for his own memory, praise that will never die, and with it the grandest of all sepulchres, not that in which their mortal bones are laid, but a home in the minds of men."

PERICLES.

Ablett, John, Rfm.
Adie, Sidney, Rfm.
Adwinckle, Albert Frederick, Rfm.
Alderton, Thomas Albert Victor, Rfm.
Alexander, John Rees, Sec.-Lt.
Alexander, Thomas, Rfm.
Alexander, Leonard, Rfm.
Alford, Ernest Charles, Rfm.
Allden, William, Rfm.
Alldridge, Alfred John, Rfm.
Allen, Alfred John, Rfm.
Allen, Henry James Olaf, Cpl., D.C.M.
Allen, Henry Joseph, Rfm.
Allen, Henry Somerset, Sec.-Lt.
Allum, Alfred Edgar, Rfm.
Alvin, Sydney, L.-Cpl.
Amato, John, Rfm.
Ambrose, Albert Gerald, Rfm.
Ambrose, Bernard, Rfm.
Amos, Cecil Ernest, Rfm.
Anderson, David William, Capt., M.C.
Anderson, Thomas, Rfm.
Andrew-Marshall, Joseph, Lieut.
Andrews, John Lewis, Rfm.
Andrews, Reginald, Rfm.
Andrews, Charles John, Rfm.
Angus, George Edwin, Rfm.
Appleton, Edwin, Rfm.
Arnold, Percy John, Rfm.
Ashby, George William, Capt.
Ashby, Harry Ernest, Rfm.
Ashton, Sydney Arnold, Rfm.
Atkinson, Walter William, Rfm.
Auty, Louis Henry, Sgt.
Axon, Frederick William, Rfm.
Back, Frederick Percy, Rfm.
Baggett, Walter George, Rfm.
Baggs, Jack, Rfm.
Bailey, Charles, Rfm.
Bailey, Ernest Edgar, Rfm.
Bailey, Frederick John, L.-Cpl.
Bailey, Harry, Rfm.
Bailey, Thomas, Rfm.
Bain, Archibald James, Rfm.
Baker, Charles, Rfm.
Baker, Louis Harley, Rfm.
Baker, Walter, Rfm.
Baker, William Frederick Charles, Rfm.
Balding, Benjamin, Rfm.
Ball, Samuel George, Rfm.
Ballard, Sydney George, Rfm.
Balls, Ernest, Rfm.
Banting, Fred, Rfm.
Barber, alias Thornell, Ernest T., Sgt.
Barber, Robert William John, Rfm.
Barker, Frank William, Rfm.
Barker, John, Rfm
Barley, Harold Charles, L.-Cpl.
Barnes, Harry Colin, Rfm.
Barnes, Henry Charles, Rfm.
Barraclough, Harold Rider, Rfm.
Barrat, Frank Wilson, Rfm.
Barrett, Albert Victor George, Sgt.
Bartlett, Frederick Alfred, Rfm.
Barton, John, Cpl.
Bartram, Victor Henry, Rfm.
Bateman, Thomas Joseph, A.-Cpl.
Bates, Benjamin, Rfm.
Bates, George Percy, Rfm.
Baugh, Ernest, Rfm.
Baxter, Leonard James, Rfm.
Beagley, Albert Ernest, L.-Cpl.
Beard, Thomas Henry, Rfm.
Beauchamp, Frederick William, Rfm.
Beaumont, Sydney David, Rfm.
Beck, William, Rfm.
Beecher, Frank Alfred, Sec.-Lt.
Beeson, Stanley William, Rfm.
Bell, David William, Rfm.
Bell, Isaac, Rfm.
Bell, Thomas Walter, Rfm.
Bellamy, Ernest Walter, L.-Cpl.
Bence, Richard James, Cpl.
Bendle, William Richard, Rfm.
Bennett, Albert Henry, Rfm.
Bennett, Charles, Rfm.
Bennett, Frederick Charles, Rfm.
Bennett, Richard Henry, Rfm.

S

Bensley, Fasham Henry, L.-Cpl.
Berry, Reginald Laurence, Rfm.
Best, Thomas Edward, Rfm.
Bevan, Alfred, Rfm.
Bevan, Thomas George, Rfm.
Bibbing, William Charles, Rfm.
Bidgood, Reginald Edward, L.-Sgt.
Biffen, Frederick, Rfm.
Bilby, Victor Cassimir, Rfm.
Bindoff, Philip Edward, Rfm.
Binns, John Alfred, Rfm.
Bishop, George Frederick, Rfm.
Blackman, Charles Gordon, Rfm.
Blackmur, Robert John, Rfm.
Blake, Frederick George, Rfm.
Blakey, Ernest St. Clair, Rfm.
Blanchenay, William, Rfm.
Bland, Arthur James, Rfm.
Blanks, Frank Arthur, Rfm.
Bleeze, Ernest, Rfm.
Bliss, James Thomas, Rfm.
Blower, Arthur, Rfm.
Blows, Henry James, Rfm.
Board, Albert George, L.-Sgt.
Bodey, Ernest Ralph, Rfm.
Bond, Jack Herbert, Rfm.
Bond, Leonard Evelyn, Cpl., M.M.
Bond, Samuel Sidney, Rfm.
Booth, Arthur, Rfm.
Booth, Henry James, Rfm.
Booth, William Leslie, Capt.
Bottjer, Harold Thomas, L.-Cpl.
Boulton, Frank Edward, Rfm.
Bow, Frederick, Rfm.
Bowell, Alfred, Rfm.
Boyce, Frank John, Rfm.
Boyles, Tom, Rfm.
Brabbs, Anthony, Rfm.
Brabon, John, Rfm.
Bradford, John Frederick, Rfm.
Bradshaw, Ernest Stephen, Rfm.
Branton, Joseph, Rfm.
Bravery, Charles, Rfm.
Bray, John, Rfm.
Brazier, Alfred William, Rfm.
Brice, Horace Garnham, Rfm.
Brightly, Edward James, Rfm.
Brock, William John, Rfm.
Brooke, Thomas Wickham, Capt., M.C.
Brooks, John, Rfm.
Brown, Charles William, A.-Cpl.
Brown, George, Rfm.
Brown, Harvey, Rfm.
Brown, James, Rfm.
Brown, John George Joseph, Rfm.
Brown, Percy William, Rfm.
Brown, Thomas Henry Foster, L.-Cpl.
Brown, William, Rfm.
Brown, William, Rfm.
Browne, Neville Northey, Rfm.
Buckman, Lionel Sidney George, Rfm.
Bucknell, Albert, Rfm.
Budgen, William, Rfm.
Bullen, Albert Edward, Rfm.
Bull, Frederick John, Sec.-Lt.
Bullock, Frederick, Rfm., M.M.
Bullock, Frederick, Rfm.
Bundy, Cyril James Saunders, Rfm.
Bunn, Joseph, Rfm.
Bunting, Alfred Arthur, Rfm.
Burch, Frederick Thomas John, Rfm.
Burgess, Albert, Rfm.
Burgess, George Thomas, Rfm.
Burgess, John Thomas, Rfm.
Burgess, Ernest Malcolm, Rfm., M.M.
Burhenne, Ernest, Rfm.
Burr, Henry Sidney, Rfm.
Burt, Arthur Noel, Cpl.
Burtenshaw, Ernest Victor, Rfm.
Burton, Ezra, Rfm.
Burtt, Frederick James, Rfm.
Butcher, Walter, Rfm.
Butler, Arthur James Edgar, L.-Cpl.
Butler, Frederick Harold, Sec.-Lt.
Butt, Jack, Rfm.
Buxton, Philip, L.-Cpl.
Buzzacott, Albert, Rfm.
Byatt, James, Rfm.
Calloway, William, Rfm.
Campbell, Charles, Rfm.
Campbell, Harry, L.-Sgt.
Campbell, Stanley Fredk. John, Sec.-Lt.
Caplin, Frederick, Rfm.
Capon, Leonard Stanley, Rfm.
Carlick, Harris David, Rfm.
Carpenter, Edgar Stanley, A.-Cpl.
Carpenter, Arthur James, L.-Cpl.
Carpenter, Ernest, Rfm.
Carr, William, A.-C.S.Maj.
Carr, Arthur, Rfm.
Carr, William, Rfm.
Carter, Sydney James, Rfm.
Cartwright, George Frederick, Rfm.
Carver, George, L.-Cpl.
Cattle, Frederick Charles, Rfm.
Cave, Arthur, Rfm.
Cavilla, Frank Herbert, Rfm.
Challoner, Frederick, Cpl.

Chambers, William, Rfm.
Champness, Herbert, Rfm.
Chance, Henry, Rfm.
Channon, Harry, Rfm.
Chaplin, William George, Rfm.
Chapman, Charles, Rfm.
Chapman, Charles, Rfm.
Charlton, John, Cpl.
Chatfield, Benjamin, Rfm.
Chave, Stanley Lionel, L.-Cpl.
Childs, William Frederick, Rfm.
Claricoat, Arthur, Rfm.
Claridge, Alfred James Robert, Rfm.
Clark, Edgar Charles, Rfm.
Clark, George Destos, L.-Cpl.
Clark, John Robert, Rfm.
Clark, Sidney Thomas, Rfm.
Clark, William Arthur, Rfm.
Clark, William Michael, Rfm.
Clarke, Frederick James, Rfm.
Clarke, George, L.-Sgt.
Claydon, William Ernest, Rfm.
Cogger, Percy William, Rfm.
Coker, James, Rfm.
Colborn, Walter, Rfm.
Coleman, Frederick Charles, L.-Cpl.
Coleman, Gerald Cecil, Cpl., M.M.
Coley, William, Rfm.
Collar, Frederick George, Rfm.
Coller, Frank, Rfm.
Collett, John George, Rfm.
Collett, Reuben Kemp, Rfm.
Collins, Edward, Rfm.
Collins, Frederick William John, Rfm.
Collins, Robert Hayes, Major.
Collinson, F. G., Colonel, V.D.
Collyer, Lewis Wellington, L.-Sgt., M.M.
Coltman, Walter Joseph, Sec.-Lt.
Coldicott, H. E., Sec.-Lt.
Colvin, James William, Cpl.
Commins, Stanley Algernon, Rfm.
Cook, Frederick Samuel, Rfm.
Cook, Frederick Thomas, Rfm.
Cook, Harry James Thomas Fido, Rfm.
Cook, John Henry, Rfm.
Cook, Reginald John, L.-Cpl.
Cook, Robert William, Rfm.
Cook, Thomas, Rfm.
Cook, Wilson, Rfm.
Cooper, Albert Henry, Rfm.
Cooper, Alfred William, Rfm.
Cooper, Herbert, Rfm.
Cooper, Leonard, Rfm.
Coppard, Leonard Alfred Charles, Rfm.
Copping, Arthur Milton, Sec.-Lt., M.M.
Costella, James, Rfm.
Costin, Charles William, Rfm.
Cotter, Henry Thomas, Rfm.
Cottington, William Henry, Rfm.
Cotton, Harold, Rfm.
Cotton, Percy, Rfm.
Cotton, Montague Arthur Finch, Capt.
Couchman, Jesse Elijah, Rfm.
Couling, William Thomas, L.-Cpl.
Count, Edmund John William, Rfm.
Court, Alfred Charles, Rfm.
Courtney, Harold, Rfm.
Cousens, William, Rfm.
Cousins, Frank Squire, Rfm.
Coventry, Leonard George, Rfm.
Cox, Arthur, Rfm.
Cox, Frederick George, Rfm.
Crabb, George, Rfm.
Crane, William, Rfm.
Crann, George, Sgt.
Crawley, Ernest Victor, Rfm.
Crawley, Thomas Horace, Rfm.
Crews, Hubert Squires, Cpl., M.M.
Cridge, Ernest, Rfm.
Cripps, Charles Henry, Rfm.
Croager, Edwin Thomas, A.-Sgt.
Crook, Alfred, Rfm.
Croom, W. C., Sec.-Lt.
Cropper, William, Sec.-Lt.
Cross, Andrews James, Rfm.
Crouch, William George, Rfm.
Cue, Frederick Arthur, Rfm.
Cufley, Henry Thomas, Rfm.
Cullimore, Richard Theodore, Rfm.
Cumber, Robert, Rfm.
Cummings, Charles, Rfm.
Cummings, Joseph William, Rfm.
Cummins, George Henry, Rfm.
Cunningham, Edward Arthur, Rfm.
Curle, Charles William, L.-Cpl.
Cuss, Frank Shaw, L.-Sgt., D.C.M.
Cutmore, James, Rfm.
Cuttriss, William, Rfm.
Dale, Joseph, Cpl.
Dart, Walter Arthur, Rfm.
Darvell, John Albert, Rfm.
Davenport, Bromley, Rfm.
Davies, Arthur Ernest, Rfm.
Davis, William Henry, Rfm.
Dawdry, Henry Edgar, Rfm.
Deadman, Frederick, Rfm.
Dean, Frederick Thomas, Rfm.
Deeley, Benjamin, L.-Cpl.

Dell, Arthur, Rfm.
Dell, William, Rfm.
Denham, Douglas Harold, L.-Cpl.
Denison, Frederick John, Sgt.
Denney, Thomas, Drummer.
Dennis, Ronald Harry Hampson, Rfm.
De Vall, Harry William, Rfm.
Dice, William Harold, Cpl.
Dickson, Kenneth, Rfm.
Dietl, Joseph, Rfm.
Diggins, Charles William, C.S.Maj.
Dineen, George Ernest, Rfm.
Dinham, Frederick Walter, Rfm.
Dinham, Henry Alfred, Rfm.
Dinsdale, Herbert, Rfm.
Dipple, William John, Rfm.
Dockerill, William John, Rfm.
Dockree, Gilbert Arthur, Sec.-Lt.
Doddrell, William Thomas, Rfm.
Doherty, Harold Fitzgerald, Rfm.
Dommett, Stanley Alfred, Sgt.
Dorel, Maurice, Rfm.
Dowdeswell, Frederick James, Rfm.
Down-Deasey, Jeremiah, Rfm.
Dowry, Henry, A.-Cpl.
Dowsett, William David, L.-Sgt.
Dowst, William Charles Ernest, Rfm.
Drake, Edward George, Rfm.
Drew, Joseph, Rfm.
Ducker, Charles, Rfm.
Duckett, Albert Frederick, Rfm.
Duffy, Horace Stanley, Rfm.
Dulieu, Alfred, Rfm.
Dunn, Frederick Arthur, Rfm.
Dunn, William, Rfm.
Durst, John Maurice, L.-Cpl.
Dyer, Thomas R., Rfm.
Dyer, Wilfred, Rfm.
Edmonds, George Francis, Rfm.
Edney, James Edward, Rfm.
Edwardes, Eric Chilton, Rfm.
Edwards, Ernest Edwin, Rfm.
Edwards, Frederick, Rfm.
Edwards, Frederick Gilbert S., Rfm.
Edwards, Henry, L.-Sgt.
Edwards, Herbert Stanley Yates, Sgt.
Edwards, Walter, Sec.-Lt.
Edwards, William, Rfm.
Egan, Francis Michael, Rfm.
Ehrenberg, Joseph, Rfm.
Eldon, George William, Rfm.
Elliott, Cyril Charles, Rfm.
Ellwick, William Charles, Sgt.
Elstone, Frederick Harold, Rfm.
Emery, Ernest William, A.-Cpl.
Emery, Ernest Trevelyn, Rfm.
England, Albert, Rfm.
Enticknap, Albert Edward, Rfm.
Ersser, William Thomas, Rfm.
Evans, Alfred James, Rfm.
Evans, Charles Thomas, Rfm.
Evans, Thomas Hubert Davey, Sgt.
Everest, Basil Herbert, Rfm.
Eveson, William, Rfm.
Fair, Frank Joseph, Rfm.
Falck, Roydon Branfoot, Rfm.
Faraday, Ray, Lieut.
Farnes, William, Rfm.
Fennings, Frederick Ralph, Rfm.
Field, Arthur, Rfm.
Figgins, Henry Francis, Sec.-Lt.
Fincham, John Littler, Rfm.
Fisher, James, Rfm.
Fisher, Laurence Henry, Rfm.
Fitzgibbon, Francis William, Rfm.
Flaxman, William Henry, Rfm.
Fleming, Tom, Rfm.
Fodder, Frederick William Henry, Rfm.
Fogo, George Alfred James, Rfm.
Ford, Cyril John, Cpl.
Forrest, Sydney Harold, Rfm.
Forster, Harold Ker, Sec.-Lt.
Fosbury, Percy, Rfm.
Fossey, Frank Frederick, Rfm.
Foster, Charles Steven, L.-Cpl.
Foulser, Horace Edward, Rfm.
Foulsham, Thomas Henry, Rfm.
Fowler, Harold, Rfm.
Fowler, William Francis Godfrey, Rfm.
Fox, James John, Rfm.
Frampton, Reginald Frederick J., Rfm.
Francis, Leonard Henry, Rfm.
Francis, William, Rfm.
Francis, William Edward, L.-Cpl.
Franklin, George, Rfm.
Franklin, John George, Rfm.
Fraser, George, Rfm.
Freeman, Charles, Sgt.
Freeman, Frederick William J., L.-Cpl.
French, Edward Newton, Rfm.
French, Robert Douglas, Sec.-Lt.
French, Victor William, Rfm.
Fritchley, Joseph Bertram, Sec.-Lt.
Frith, Henry Lynes, Rfm.
Frost, Edward John, Rfm.
Fuller, Frederick George, Rfm.
Fuller, Herbert, Rfm.
Furlong, Walter James, Rfm.

IN MEMORIAM

Fussell, George, Rfm.
Gadsdon, Walter John, Sgt.
Gale, Charles Augustus, Rfm.
Galsworthy, James Douglas, Rfm.
Gardner, James Alfred, Rfm.
Gardner, Percy Alfred, Rfm.
Garnham, Stanley Victor, L.-Cpl.
Garrod, Arthur Edward, Rfm.
Garrod, Ronald Percival, Sec.-Lt.
Gatesman, James, Rfm.
Gayler, William Alexander, Rfm.
Gearing, James Thomas, Rfm.
George, Ashton Pearce, Rfm.
George, Edward James, Rfm.
German, George Frederick, Sgt.
Gianone, Constant, Rfm.
Gibson, John, Rfm.
Giddings, Frank, Rfm.
Gilbert, Charles William, Rfm.
Gilbert, George Edward, Rfm.
Giles, Lawrence Frederick, Rfm.
Giles, Walter Bernard Frank, Cpl., M.M.
Gilkes, Thomas, Rfm.
Gill, Albert, Rfm.
Gilson, Richard, L.-Cpl., M.M.
Glenister, Albert James, Rfm.
Godon, Ernest, L.-Cpl.
Godwin, George, Rfm.
Goldacre, George, Rfm.
Goldstone, Percy William Victor, Rfm.
Good, Hugh Arnold, Sgt.
Goode, Leslie Watson, Rfm.
Gooding, Robert Carrington, Rfm.
Gough, John Henry, Rfm.
Gowers, George Henry, L.-Cpl.
Graham, Ernest Walter, L.-Cpl.
Grant, Herbert Samuel, Rfm.
Grant, Waldemar Gillies, Cpl.
Gray, Philip Henry, Rfm.
Gray, Victor, Sgt.
Graysmark, John T., C.S.Maj., C. de G.
Green, Arthur, Rfm.
Gregory, John George, Sec.-Lt.
Gregory, Sydney Maurice, Sec.-Lt.
Greig, Oscar Otto Bertini, Rfm.
Griffen, George Herbert Albert, Rfm.
Griffin, James, Rfm.
Griffiths, Edward Bentley, Rfm.
Griffiths, Sidney, Rfm.
Griffiths, Thomas, Rfm.
Grigg, Charles Serl, Rfm.
Grimes, Alexander Thornton, Cpl.
Grimley, Ernest Frank Wyatt, Rfm.
Grosse, Alfred Albert, Rfm.
Grummitt, Walter Sidney, Rfm.
Guest, Herbert Alfred Charles, Rfm.
Gullock, George William, Rfm.
Gunning, Sidney George, Rfm.
Haacke, Ernest Charles, A.-Cpl., M.M.
Habgood, William Henry, Rfm.
Hadley, John, Rfm.
Haine, Edward, Rfm.
Hall, Charles Horace, Rfm.
Hall, Frederick George, A.-Sgt., M.M.
Hall, Frederick James, Rfm.
Hall, Harry, Rfm.
Hall, Herbert, Rfm.
Hall, John, Rfm.
Hall, Thomas, Rfm.
Hall, Samuel, Rfm.
Halls, Arthur, Rfm.
Halls, Benjamin, Rfm.
Halnon, Arthur Augustus, Rfm.
Hamilton, Frank, Rfm.
Hamilton, Samuel James, Rfm.
Hammond, Reginald Field, L.-Cpl.
Hancock, Frederick George, Rfm.
Hancock, James George, Rfm.
Hancock, Matthew James, Rfm.
Hardy, Norman Ewart, Rfm.
Harland, Henry John, Rfm.
Harley, Sidney, Rfm.
Harling, Richard, Rfm.
Harper, Bertie Samuel, Rfm.
Harrington, William, Rfm.
Harris, Arthur Gates, Rfm.
Harris, George Robert, Rfm.
Harris, George Robert, Rfm.
Harris, William Arthur, Rfm.
Harrison, Charles Henry, Rfm.
Hart, Harold George, Rfm.
Hart, Howard Victor, Lieut., M.C.
Hart, Sidney John, L.-Cpl.
Hartley, William John, Capt.
Harvey, Albert, Rfm.
Harvey, alias Harley, Charles, A.-Cpl.
Harvey, Ernest James, Rfm.
Harvey, Richard Thomas, Rfm.
Harvey, William Daniel, Rfm.
Hasker, Charles, Sgt.
Hassack, William, A.-Cpl., D.C.M.
Hate, Bertie, L.-Cpl.
Havis, Arthur Ernest, Rfm.
Hawes, David, Rfm.
Hawke, William Dryden, Cpl.
Hayes, Henry Arnold, L.-Cpl.
Hayes, John, Rfm.
Hayes, Michael, Rfm.

Haynes, George, Rfm.
Haysom, Harvey, Rfm.
Hayward, William Henry Charles, Rfm.
Hayworth, Charles Alfred, Rfm.
Hazeltine, Stephen, Rfm.
Head, William Charles, Cpl.
Hearne, John Henry, Rfm.
Heasman, Horace James, Rfm.
Heath, Henry Edward, Rfm.
Heath, Robert Harold, Rfm.
Heath, William John, Rfm.
Hebden, William, Rfm.
Hedderley, Arthur Leslie, Rfm.
Helliar, John, Rfm.
Hemings, Joseph, Rfm.
Hemstock, George Walter, Rfm.
Herbert, Charles, Rfm.
Hercock, Stanley, Rfm.
Herkes, Robert, Rfm.
Heslep, Sydney, Rfm.
Hewett, Thomas, Rfm.
Hewitt, Charles Aela, L.-Cpl.
Hewitt, Thomas Henry, Rfm.
Hewlett, William, Rfm.
Hewson, Stanley Barton, Sec.-Lt.
Heyl, Tobie John, L.-Sgt.
Higlett, Henry George, Rfm.
Hill, Austen Shelbourne, Sec.-Lt.
Hill, Edward Ernest, Rfm.
Hill, F., Capt. (Att.) D.C.M., C. de G.
Hill, Frederick Harry, Rfm.
Hill, William Henry, Rfm.
Hilton, Harry, Rfm.
Hinton, Arthur Frederick, Rfm.
Hirst, Alexander Edwin Richard, Rfm.
Hitch, William, Rfm.
Hitchcock, Ernest Henry, Rfm.
Hoare, Albert, Rfm.
Hockley, Horace John, Rfm.
Hodd, William, Rfm.
Hodge, Harry, Rfm.
Holder, Henry James, A.-Sgt.
Holdstock, William Percy, Rfm.
Hogan, Ernest, Rfm.
Hollis, Charles, Rfm.
Hollis, Walter Fredk., C.S.Maj., D.C.M.
Holt, Arthur James, Rfm.
Holton, Henry, Rfm.
Hooper, Frank Hastings, Rfm.
Horlock, William Henry, Rfm.
Hornsby, George Burlington, Rfm.
Horobin, David George, Rfm.
Horrod, Edwin, Rfm.
Horsman, Albert Ernest, L.-Cpl.
Horton, John Norman, L.-Cpl.
Hosier, Henry, Sgt.
Howard, Albert Hector, Rfm.
Howard, Frederick Frank, Rfm.
Howard, John Charles, L.-Cpl.
Howells, William, Rfm.
Hubback, Francis William, Sec.-Lt.
Hubbard, Gilbert Arthur, Rfm.
Hudgell, Francis Edward, Rfm.
Hudson, William Berks, Rfm.
Huggett, George Joseph, L.-Cpl.
Hughes, Enos George James, Rfm.
Hulbert, Frederick, L.-Cpl.
Hull, John Allingham, L.-Sgt.
Hull, Reginald Louis, L.-Cpl.
Hunt, Andrew, Rfm.
Hunt, Alfred Frederick, Rfm.
Hunt, Frederick Charles, Rfm.
Hunt, John Henry, Rfm.
Hunter, Henry Richard, Rfm.
Hunter, Samuel, Rfm.
Hurley, George Michael, Rfm.
Hurrell, James, Rfm.
Hussey, Charles Robert, Sgt.
Hutson, Arthur James Card, Rfm.
Hutton, Charles Alfred, Rfm.
Hyde, George Fielder, Rfm.
Inch, William Arthur, Rfm.
Ingott, Herbert John, Rfm.
Irving, Henry, Cpl.
Irwin, William Charles, Rfm.
Isaac, Ernest Charles, Rfm.
Izard, Henry George, Rfm.
Jackson, Albert Edward, Rfm.
Jackson, Ernest, Rfm.
Jackson, Frederick, Rfm.
Jackson, Harry, Rfm.
Jacobs, Frederick, Rfm.
Jacques, Herbert, Rfm.
Jakeman, William, Rfm.
James, Lewis, Rfm.
Jarritt, Frederick William, Rfm.
Jarvis, Walter Beddoe, Rfm.
Jasper, Ernest Albert, Rfm.
Jenkins, Charles, Rfm.
Jennings, Bertie, Rfm.
Jennings, Frank William, Rfm.
Jennings, George Thomas, L.-Cpl.
Jessel, George, A.-Cpl.
Jevans, Thomas John Victor, Rfm,
Johnson, Charles Edward, Rfm.
Johnson, George, Rfm.
Johnson, Sidney Rowland, Rfm.
Johnson, Leonard Charles, Rfm.

IN MEMORIAM

Jones, George Frederick, Rfm.
Jones, Sydney, C.S.Maj., M.C.
Jones, Frank Arthur, Rfm.
Jones, Frank Alexander, Sgt.
Jones, Frederick, Rfm.
Jones, Thomas Edward Painton, Capt.
Jones, William, Rfm.
Jones, William John, Rfm.
Joyce, Martin, Rfm.
Juler, Frederick, Rfm.
Jupp, William H., Sgt., Med. Militaire.
Keary, Sidney Reginald, Rfm.
Kearns, Theodore Benjamin, Rfm.
Keenor, Percy William, Rfm.
Keller, Francis Frederick, Lieut.
Kempton, John William, Rfm.
Kent, Charles Percival, Rfm.
Kenway, Reuben, Rfm.
Ker, Frederick Roxburghe, Sec.-Lt.
Kernot, William John, Rfm.
Kerridge, Charles Herbert, Cpl.
Kidby, Edward Alfred, Rfm.
Kidd, William Charles, Rfm.
King, George Edward, Rfm.
King, Leonard, Rfm.
Kingston, Frank Goodman, L.-Cpl.
Knight, Albert, Sgt.
Knight, Arthur Edwin, L.-Cpl.
Knight, George, Rfm.
Knight, Reuben, Rfm.
Koch, Douglas John, L.-Cpl.
Kunzie, Charles William, Rfm.
Kynaston, Sidney, L.-Cpl.
Laeuffer, Henri, Rfm.
Lambert, Allan, Rfm.
Lambert, Ernest Augustus, Rfm.
Lane, Ernest Edward, Rfm.
Langridge, William Charles, Rfm.
Langton, Edward Allen, Rfm.
Larby, Cedric, Rfm.
Lawrence, John Charles, Rfm.
Lawrence, Sidney Thomas, Rfm.
Lawrence, Edward, L.-Cpl.
Lawrence, Harold Roy, Sec.-Lt.
Lawrence, William, Rfm.
Layton, Edward George, Rfm.
Leader, Edwin Charles, L.-Cpl., M.M.
Leavitt, George, Rfm.
Leeds, William Charles, Rfm.
Lefevre, Mark James, Rfm.
Lemon, John, Rfm.
Levy, Harris, Rfm.
Levy, Phillip, Rfm.
Lewcock, William John, Rfm.
Lewis, Frederick John, Rfm.
Lewis, Gordon, L.-Sgt.
Lewis, John Gordon, Rfm.
Lewis, Leonard Arthur, Rfm.
Lewis, William Alfred, Rfm.
Linsell, Henry George, Rfm.
Lindsey, John Charles, Rfm
Lindsey, Robert Frederick, Rfm.
Lineham, Charles Patrick, L.-Cpl.
Ling, William George, Rfm.
Linley, Alfred, Rfm.
Lipsham, Percy, Rfm.
Little, Edwin Walter, Rfm.
Little, James, Rfm.
Livemore, James, Rfm.
Lloyd, Edward, Rfm.
Lloyd, George William, Rfm.
Lloyd, Percy, Rfm.
Lloyd, Thomas James, Cpl.
Lloyd, William, Rfm.
Long, Harry, Rfm.
Lonsdale, Edwin, Cpl.
Lovegrove, George, Rfm.
Lovell, Arthur Lawrence, Rfm.
Lowe, Alfred Ernest, Rfm.
Lowthian, Robert, Rfm. M.M.
Lucas, Sidney Edward, Rfm.
Lunn, George Ord, Rfm.
Lyus, Richard, Rfm.
Lywood, Henry John Joseph, Rfm.
Mace, Alfred James, L.-Cpl.
Macey, Walter Harold, Sgt.
Machin, Harry Richard, L.-Cpl.
Mackenzie, James, L.-Cpl.
Mackenzie, Osmond, Rfm.
McCarthy, George Joseph, Rfm.
McClatchie, Alexander, Rfm.
McGregor, Albert Edward, Rfm.
McKelvie, William, Cpl.
McLaughlin, Edmund Caldicoate, Lieut.
McLellan, Donald Thomas, L.-Sgt.
McLeod, John, Rfm.
Maitland-Addison, Roy C. A., Rfm.
Males, David, Rfm.
Males, William Henry, Rfm., M.M.
Malkin, Henry John, Cpl.
Mallett, Alfred John, Rfm.
Mallett, Henry James, Rfm.
Manley, William Arthur, Sgt.
Manning, Richard Alfred, Rfm.
Mansell, Alfred Joshua, Rfm.
Mansfield, Harry, Rfm.
Manwaring, Edward Joseph, Rfm.
Marks, Harry, Rfm.

Marritt, Frederick Charles, Sgt., M.M.
Marsh, Ernest Alfred, Rfm.
Marsh, Harold, Rfm.
Martin, Frederick Edward, Rfm.
Martin, Frederick John, Rfm.
Martin, John George, Rfm.
Martin, John Allan W., C.Q.M.Sgt.
Martin, John William, Rfm.
Martin, Thomas, Rfm.
Martin, William, L.-Cpl.
Marwood, Thomas, Rfm.
Massey, Charles, Rfm.
Masters, Clarence Walter, Rfm.
Matthews, Cecil, Rfm.
Matthews, Leslie Edward Fredk., Rfm.
Matthews, Sidney Thomas Terry, L.-Cpl.
May, Arthur, Rfm.
May, Harry, L.-Cpl.
Maynard, John Edwin, Major, M.C.
Meader, Reuben Frank, L.-Cpl.
Meadows, George, L.-Cpl.
Medlicott, Thomas George, Rfm.
Meech, Albert Victor C., Rfm.
Meinert, Frederick Arthur, Rfm.
Meredith, Richard Llewellyn, Rfm.
Merle, Arthur Ernest, Rfm.
Miller, Ernest Henry, Rfm.
Mills, Charles Thomas, Rfm.
Mills, John F., L.-Cpl., M.M. and Bar.
Mills, John Leonard, Rfm.
Mills, William Charles, A.-Cpl.
Millett, Arthur Joseph, Rfm.
Millward, George, Rfm.
Milton, John Frederick, L.-Cpl.
Mitchell, Alfred, Rfm.
Mitchell, Frank, Rfm.
Mitchell, James Edgar, Rfm.
Money, Edward John, Rfm.
Monk, Alfred, Rfm.
Monk, Henry, Rfm.
Monk, Mark, Rfm.
Montandon, Edward, Rfm.
Montier, Charles, Rfm.
Moore, Albert, Rfm.
Moore, Bert Frederick, Rfm.
Moore, Charles Harry, Rfm.
Moore, David Thomas, Rfm.
Moore, John Victor, Rfm.
Moore, James William Lewis, Rfm.
More, Charles John, Rfm.
Morey, Arthur William, Rfm.
Morgan, William George, Rfm.
Moriarty, Flurance William, Rfm.
Morley, Alfred William, Rfm.
Morris, William Thomas, Sgt.
Morss, Henry James, Rfm.
Moseley, Edward William, Rfm.
Mott, Clinton Leslie, Rfm.
Mulvey, Philip Godfrey, Rfm.
Mummery, Percy Charles, Rfm.
Muncey, Edward Herbert, L.-Cpl.
Munday, Ernest Alfred, Rfm.
Munns, John, Rfm.
Murphy, Charles William, C.S.Maj.
Murray, Patrick, Rfm.
Murray, William, Rfm.
Musk, Alfred, Rfm.
Myer, Ernest Alex, Major.
Nelson, Richard James, Rfm.
Newbury, Alvin Henry, Cpl.
Nicholls, Dutton, L.-Cpl.
Nicholls, Thomas, Rfm.
Nightingale, Ernest James, L.-Cpl.
Nightingale, George William, Rfm.
Nightingale, Sidney, Rfm.
Nilen, Francis, Rfm.
Nokes, Harry, Rfm.
Norris, Donald, L.-Cpl.
Norris, George Deane, Rfm.
Norris, Reginald, Rfm.
Northcott, Charles Henry, Sgt.
Northam, Frederick William, Rfm.
Northam, George Henry, Rfm.
Odam, Cecil Wilfred, Sec.-Lt.
Odell, Albert Thomas, Rfm.
O'Driscoll, Gerald Francis, Rfm.
O'Leary, Francis, Sgt.
Oliver, Dan Charlie, Rfm.
Oliver, William, Sgt.
Olver, John, Rfm., M.M.
Ordish, Henry Thomas, Capt., M.C.
Orpin, Edward, Rfm.
Orsborn, Frederick William, Rfm.
Ovenden, Edward Henry, L.-Cpl.
Overall, Henry, Rfm.
Owens, William George, Rfm.
Oxenham, Frederick James, Rfm.
Page, George, Rfm.
Page, Ralph, Rfm.
Pageot, Leon Auguste, Rfm.
Paine, Cecil George, Rfm.
Palmer, Augustus, Rfm.
Parkin, Harry Davis, Rfm.
Parks, Albert, Rfm.
Parsons, William Homer, Rfm.
Partington, Joseph, Rfm.
Partridge, Allan Samuel, Rfm.
Pask, Walter William, Rfm.

IN MEMORIAM

Paskell, William George, Rfm.
Patterson, George, Rfm.
Paulton, William, Rfm.
Paveley, Arthur Charles, Rfm.
Paxman, Edgar, Rfm.
Payne, Harold George, Rfm.
Payne, William John, L.-Cpl.
Payne, William, Rfm.
Pead, Frank Thomas, Rfm.
Pearce, Charles, Rfm.
Pearce, John Odell, Rfm.
Pearce, Thomas George, Rfm.
Pears, Thomas, Rfm.
Pearsall, Frank, Rfm.
Pearson, Alexander William T., Rfm.
Pearson, Bertie, Rfm., M.M.
Pedley, Joseph, A.-Cpl.
Peile, Thomas, Sgt.
Peisley, Charles Ashton, Cpl.
Perkins, Herbert Harold, Rfm.
Penny, Alfred John, Cpl.
Perry, Francis Stephen, Rfm.
Perry, Leslie Roy, Sec.-Lt.
Perry, Walter John, Rfm.
Petter, Lewis Norman, Sgt.
Phillips, Arthur, Rfm.
Phillips, Joseph Henry, Rfm.
Pickering, Edmund Charles, Sec.-Lt.
Pike, Henry, Cpl.
Pinder, Arthur, Rfm.
Piper, Ernest Frederick Arthur, Rfm.
Piper, Frederick Mostyn, L.-Cpl.
Piper, Malcolm, Cpl.
Playsted, Lionel Harry, L-Sgt.
Plummer, Alfred George, Rfm.
Plumridge, Walter Samuel, Rfm.
Pointing, William George, Rfm.
Pollard, Frederick James, Cpl.
Poore, William, Rfm.
Porter, Ralph, Rfm.
Postle, Arthur Franklin, Rfm.
Potter, George, Rfm.
Potter, Harold Robert Edgar, Cpl.
Powell, Albert Gabriel, Rfm.
Powell, Cecil Arnold, Cpl.
Powell, George William, Rfm.
Powlesland, John Northley J., Sec.-Lt.
Prentice, Ernest, Rfm.
Presswell, George Henry, L.-Cpl.
Prichard, John Edward, Rfm.
Pritchard, Edward.
Proctor, Thomas, Rfm.
Puleston, George Edmund Charles, Rfm.
Purdue, Albert Thomas, Rfm.
Quilter, Frederick Walter, Sec.-Lt.
Rainbird, Thomas, Rfm.
Raker, Charles Henry, Rfm.
Ram, Charles Henry, Rfm.
Rance, Charles Frederick, Rfm.
Rand, Albert, Rfm.
Randall, James, Rfm.
Randall, George William, Rfm,
Randell, Ernest William, Rfm.
Randell, George Thomas, Rfm.
Rangecroft, Stanley, Rfm.
Ransome, Alfred, Rfm.
Ratley, Alfred Robert, Rfm.
Rattee, Walter Edward, Sgt.
Rawlings, Joseph, Rfm.
Rawston, Frederick Bazel, Sgt.
Rayfield, Arthur, Rfm.
Rayment, Robert, Rfm.
Raymond, Frederick Arthur, Rfm.
Rayner, Harry Arthur, Rfm.
Reace, George Edward, Rfm.
Read, Harold Walter, Bglr.
Reed, Charles William, Rfm.
Reed, Herbert William, Rfm.
Reed, Richard George, L.-Sgt.
Reeves, Alfred Charles, Rfm.
Reid, James William, Rfm.
Reynolds, Edward Samuel, Sgt., M.M.
Reynolds, George, Rfm.
Rice, Frank, Rfm.
Rice, Frederick Joseph, Rfm.
Richards, Frederick Francis H., Rfm.
Richardson, William Charles, L.-Cpl.
Richmond, William James, Rfm.
Riley, Joseph Norman, Cpl.
King, William Edward, Rfm.
Robb, George Craig, Sgt.
Roberts, George, Rfm.
Roberts, Edward Daniel Augustus, Rfm.
Roberts, Field Marshal Earl, V.C., K.G., K.P., O.M., V.D.
Roberts, Percy William, L.-Cpl.
Robertson, Albert George, Rfm.
Robertson, George William M., Rfm.
Robinson, Frederick, Sgt.
Robson, Montague Charles, Rfm.
Roff, Alexander Victor, Rfm.
Rogers, Frank John, L.-Cpl.
Rogers, George William, Rfm.
Rome, Lewis, Rfm.
Ronayne, Owen, Rfm.
Roper, Horace Edward, Rfm.
Rose, Albert, Rfm.
Rose, Douglas John, Rfm.

Rose, John Barton, A.-Cpl.
Roots, Walter Joseph, Rfm.
Ross, Charles Frederick, Rfm.
Rowen, John George, Rfm.
Rowland, John, Rfm.
Rumble, Charles John, Rfm.
Rummery, Clark Stephen, Rfm.
Rumsey, Archibald, Rfm.
Ruse, Charles Ridgwell, Rfm.
Rush, Joseph, Rfm.
Russell, Henry Beaconsfield, Sgt.
Rutt, William, Rfm.
Sadler, James, Rfm.
Salter, Ernest William, Rfm.
Sanders, Francis Herbert, Rfm.
Sanford, Sidney Albert, Rfm,
Saving, Sydney Charles, Rfm.
Scanlan, William Jack, Sec.-Lt.
Scholl, Claude, Rfm.
Schooling, Frederick Ammon, Rfm.
Schwefel, Charles, Rfm.
Seabrook, Walter William, Rfm.
Sear, James William, Rfm.
Searle, Richard, Rfm.
Seymour, George, Cpl.
Sharpe, Harry, Rfm.
Shattock, Frederick Arthur, Rfm.
Sheen, Morgan, Rfm.
Shephard, Albert, Rfm.
Shephard, Alfred Edward, L.-Cpl.
Shepherd, Albert Harold, Rfm.
Sherwood, Ernest William, Rfm.
Shipman, Henry, Rfm.
Shippey, George Edward, Rfm.
Shipton, Joseph Preston, Rfm.
Shone, Charles, Rfm.
Shoobert, Leslie Charles, Rfm.
Short, Frederick Cyril, Sgt.
Shurley, Leicester Alfred, Rfm.
Shurrock, Frank, Sgt.
Simonds, Arthur, Rfm.
Simmonds, Edward George, Rfm.
Simmonds, Henry William, Rfm.
Simmons, George Henry, Rfm.
Simpson, John Henry Percy, Rfm.
Simpson, Alfred Howard Walter, Rfm.
Singer, Walter Frederick, Rfm.
Sink, Leonard, Rfm.
Sippett, Abraham, Rfm.
Skeggs, Benjamin, Rfm.
Skeggs, William Charles, Rfm.
Skeet, Henry David, Rfm.
Skelton, Sidney Herbert, Rfm.
Skinner, John William, Rfm.
Skinner, Horace Alfred, L.-Cpl.
Skiggs, George, Cpl.
Smale, William Richard, Rfm.
Smart, Edgar Herbert, Lieut.
Smart, Walter Richard, L.-Cpl.
Smith, Archibald Walter, L.-Cpl.
Smith, Charles Henry, Rfm.
Smith, Ernest Edward, L.-Cpl.
Smith, Frederick William Stephen, Cpl.
Smith, George James, Rfm.
Smith, Herbert James, Rfm.
Smith, John, Rfm.
Smith, Francis James, Rfm.
Smith, Sydney James, L.-Sgt.
Snell, Norman, Rfm.
Snelgrove, Henry John, Rfm.
Snow, Arthur, Sgt.
Snow, Samuel, Rfm.
Solerti, Albert, Rfm.
Solman, Horace Vicary, Rfm.
Solomons, Harry, Rfm.
Solomons, Henry, Rfm.
Soul, Frederick William, Rfm.
Soulsby, William Dobson, Sec.-Lt.
Southgate, Albert Edward, Rfm.
Spain, James, Rfm.
Sparling, Thomas William, Rfm., M.M.
Spencer, George, Rfm.
Spencer, George Charles, Rfm.
Spencer, Geoffrey Harold, Rfm.
Spink, Christopher John, Rfm.
Spink, Dennis Boucher, Sec.-Lt.
Spooner, James Mason, Rfm.
Spriggs, William, Rfm.
Springall, Herbert John, Rfm.
Springett, Charles John, Rfm.
Springett, William Edward, Rfm.
Spurge, Arthur, L.-Cpl.
Stanley, Edward George, Rfm.
Stapleton, Frank Herbert, Rfm.
Steele, George Watson, L.-Cpl.
Steer, Alfred George, L.-Cpl.
Steiner, Ernest, Rfm.
Stephens, David, Rfm.
Stevenson, Horace Fred, Rfm.
Steward, Morris, Rfm.
Stewart, James, Rfm.
Stewart, Archibald George, Rfm.
Smiles, Alfred John, Rfm.
Stoker, Charles James, L.-Cpl.
Stovold, Herbert Charles, Rfm.
Stovold, William Arthur, Rfm.
Stratford, Ernest George, Rfm.
Stratton, Archer, Rfm.

Stratton, William Gerald, Rfm.
Strohm, Charles David, Rfm.
Strong, Thomas Henry, Cpl.
Stubbings, Frederick, Rfm.
Sturgeon, Charles Robert, Rfm.
Sturtridge, Frank, Sgt.
Stiles, Percy Reginald, L.-Cpl.
Such, Anthony, Rfm.
Suckling, Alfred James, Rfm.
Sugg, George Gerald, Rfm.
Surtees, Horace, Rfm.
Sutton, Henry William, Rfm.
Sutton, Oswald, L.-Sgt.
Swift, Reginald George, Rfm.
Sykes, John, Rfm.
Syratt, Ernest Ambrose, Cpl.
Taffs, Arthur James, Rfm.
Talbot, Thomas, Rfm.
Talbott, Herbert Edward, Rfm.
Tame, George Arthur, Rfm.
Tappin, Robert, Rfm.
Tarran, James Stephen, Cpl.
Tasker, Herbert Edwin, Sec.-Lt.
Tate, Albert Percy Victor, Rfm.
Tattersall, Frank Alfred, Sgt.
Taylor, Arthur Leonard, L.-Cpl.
Taylor, David Jack, Sgt.
Taylor, John Amos, Sgt.
Taylor, Richard, Rfm.
Taylor, Sidney Frederick, Rfm.
Taylor, Thomas Henry.
Taylor, William, Rfm.
Taylor, William George, Rfm.
Taylor, William John, Rfm.
Teahen, James, Rfm.
Templar, Sidney George, Rfm.
Tenten, Augustus Henry, Rfm.
Terry, John Norman, Capt. (Temp.).
Thatcher, Harry Alfred, Rfm.
Theobald, James, Rfm.
Thilthorpe, Walter Franklin, Rfm.
Thomas, Arthur Samuel, Rfm.
Thomas, Geoffrey, Rfm.
Thomas, John Henry, Rfm.
Thompson, George Frederick, Rfm.
Thompson, Henry Peck, L.-Cpl., M.M.
Thompson, Horace, Rfm.
Thompson, Robert Charles, Rfm.
Thompson, William Henry, Rfm.
Thorndycraft, Edward Charles, Rfm.
Thorne, Leonard John, L.-Cpl.
Thornett, Charles, Sgt., M.M.
Thornton, Reginald Alfred, Rfm.
Thrussell, John Thomas, Rfm.
Thurland, Walter Thomas, Rfm.
Thurley, Harold James, Rfm.
Thurling, Henry John, Rfm.
Tickle, Gordon Philip, Sec.-Lt.
Till, Frederick George, Rfm.
Tilley, Edward Alfred, Rfm.
Tillyer, William John, L.-Cpl.
Titmuss, Walter Charles, Rfm.
Tolhurst, George, Rfm.
Tootill, William, Rfm., M.M.
Topley, William John, L.-Cpl.
Tortise, George Harold, Rfm.
Towers, Percy, Rfm.
Tredinnick, William Percy, Rfm.
Tuite, Patrick, Rfm.
Tunmer, William, Rfm.
Turner, Herbert, Rfm.
Turner, Herbert Francis, L.-Cpl.
Turner, Percy, Rfm.
Turner, William, Rfm.
Turner, Henry George, Rfm.
Turpin, Percy.
Twyford, Frank George, Rfm.
Twyman, William Herbert, L.-Cpl.
Tyack, William Henry, Rfm.
Tye, Albert Henry, Rfm.
Tyson, Albert Edward, Rfm.
Uffold, Frederick Charles, Rfm.
Valentine, Guy, Capt.
Vanstone, Bertram, Rfm.
Varenholz, Charles Louis, Rfm.
Varney, Albert Edward, Rfm.
Vater, Jesses, Rfm.
Verge, William George, Rfm.
Vernon, Thomas Henry, Rfm.
Vicary, Albert William, Rfm.
Vickers, Henry, L.-Cpl.
Villa, Cyril, L.-Cpl.
Villa, William, Rfm.
Vincent, Herbert William, Rfm.
Wade, Ernest James, L.-Cpl.
Waight, Albert George, L.-Cpl.
Waight, Sydney Joseph, Rfm.
Walden, George William, Rfm.
Wale, Sydney John, Sgt.
Walker, Ernest, Rfm.
Wall, Henry Arthur, Rfm.
Wallace, Robert, Rfm.
Wallington, Arthur, Rfm.
Walliss, Ernest Edward, Rfm.
Walsh, John, Rfm.
Walters, Frederick, Rfm.
Ward, Frederick Thomas, Rfm.
Ward, John Edward, L.-Cpl.

Ward, Herbert Arthur, Rfm.
Ward, Walter James, Cpl.
Warne, Henry Thomas, Rfm.
Warren, Alfred, Sgt.
Warren, Frank, Rfm.
Warren, Henry, Rfm.
Warren, Victor William, Rfm.
Wass, William John, L.-Cpl.
Waters, Harry Douglas, Rfm.
Watkins, George Edward, Rfm.
Watkins, William Edmund John, Rfm.
Watson, William Charles, L.-Cpl.
Watts, George Bowen, Sgt.
Watts, Leslie William, Rfm.
Watts, Stanley George, Sgt.
Webb, George Frederick, Rfm.
Webb, Harry, Rfm.
Webb, John Timms, Sec.-Lt.
Webb, Thomas Frederick, Capt.
Webber, Ernest, Rfm.
Webster, William Shaftesbury, Rfm.
Weeden, George Benjamin, Rfm.
Weeden, George, Rfm.
Weir, Alfred Robert Harris, Rfm.
Welch, Sidney, Rfm.
Wells, Bertram Thomas, Rfm.
Wells, Cecil, Rfm.
Wells, Federick Arthur, Rfm.
Wells, Frederick, Rfm.
Wells, Leonard Alphonso, Rfm.
Wells, William Martin, Rfm.
Welsh, Albert, Rfm.
West, Walter William, Rfm.
Weston, Albert, A.-Cpl.
Weston, William Sidney, Cpl.
Wharfe, Alfred Thomas, Cpl.
Wheeler, George Minns, L.-Cpl.
Wheeler, John William, Rfm.
White, Alfred, Rfm.
White, Cecil Reginald, Rfm.
White, Harry, Rfm.
White, Henry Thomas, Rfm.
White, Thomas George, Col.-Sgt.
White, William Ewart Cecil, Sec.-Lt.
Whitby, Frank, Rfm.
Whitehorn, Thomas Robert, Rfm.
Whitmill, George Charles, Cpl.
Whittlesey, William Robert, Rfm.
Wicker, George, Rfm.
Wickham, Edward, Rfm.
Wickington, George, Rfm.
Wickstead, John, L.-Cpl.
Wild, Albert, Rfm.
Wildsmith, Sec.-Lt.
Wilkin, Thomas, Sgt.
Willcox, Edward Alfred, Rfm.
Willett, Harry George, Rfm.
Williams, Albert, Rfm.
Williams, Cecil, Sgt.
Williams, Edward Charles, Rfm.
Williams, George Alfred, Sgt.
Williams, James Harold, Rfm.
Williams, William Henry, Rfm.
Williams, Sidney, Rfm.
Willis, Edward, Rfm.
Willis, John Richard, Rfm.
Willis, Sydney James, L.-Cpl.
Willoughby, Walter Valentine, Rfm.
Willson, Reginald Francis, Rfm.
Willson, Reginald, Rfm.
Wilsher, Harold, Sgt.
Wilson, Albert, Rfm.
Wilson, Ernest, Rfm.
Wilson, Frederick, Rfm.
Wilson, Leonard William, L.-Cpl.
Wilson, Tom Henry Brooks, Rfm.
Wiltshire, Huse Lindsay P., L.-Cpl.
Winney, Harold, Cpl.
Winslow, Benjamin Harmer, Sec.-Lt.
Winter, Alfred James, Rfm.
Winyard, Alfred, Rfm.
Wiskar, Joseph William, Capt.
Withers, Arthur Robert, Rfm.
Wolfe, John Lewis.
Wood, James Charles, Rfm.
Wood, Herbert, Rfm.
Woodall, Charles John, Rfm.
Woodroff, John, Rfm.
Woollams, William Arthur, Rfm.
Woolley, Ernest James, Rfm.
Woolley, Ernest William, Rfm.
Woolston, Thomas Ernest, L.-Cpl.
Wootton, Alfred James, Rfm.
Wootton, Harold Sidney, Rfm.
Worboys, John, Rfm.
Workham, Henry Herbert, Sgt.
Wotton, William Daniel, Rfm.
Wraith, Percy, Rfm.
Wren, Christopher Bray, Sec.-Lt.
Wright, Henry Thomas, Rfm.
Wright, Richard William, Rfm.
Wyman, Alfred Edward, Cpl., D.C.M.
Yeo, Harry Samuel, Sgt.
Young, Charles Henry, Rfm,
Young, Edward, Rfm.
Young, Harry, Rfm.
Young, Henry Archie, Rfm.
Young, Percival Augustus, Rfm.

INDEX

INDEX

Printed in the United Kingdom
by Lightning Source UK Ltd.
134610UK00001B/75/A